Two Wasted Years 1943

Eric Arthur Blair – better known as George Orwell – was born on 25 June 1903 in Bengal. He was educated at Eton and then served with the Indian Imperial Police in Burma. He lived in Paris for two years, and then returned to England where he worked as a private tutor, schoolteacher and bookshop assistant. He fought on the Republican side in the Spanish Civil War and was wounded in the throat. During the Second World War he served as Talks Producer for the Indian Service of the BBC and then joined *Tribune* as its literary editor. He died in London in January 1950.

Dr. Peter Davison is Professor of English and Media at De Montfort University, Leicester. He has written and edited fifteen books as well as the Facsimile Edition of the Manuscript of *Nineteen Eighty-Four* and the twenty volumes of Orwell's *Complete Works*. From 1992 to 1994 he was President of the Bibliographical Society, whose journal he edited for twelve years. From 1961 Ian Angus was Deputy Librarian and Keeper of the Orwell Archive at University College, London, and from 1975 Librarian of King's College, London. With Sonia Orwell he co-edited the *Collected Essays, Journalism and Letters of George Orwell* (4 vols., 1986). Since early retirement in 1982 he has divided his time equally between assisting in the editing of this edition and growing olives in Italy.

Sheila Davison was a teacher until she retired, for some time teaching the deaf. She checked and proofread all twenty volumes of the complete edition and assisted with the research and indexing.

Down and Out in Paris and London
Burmese Days
A Clergyman's Daughter
Keep the Aspidistra Flying
The Road to Wigan Pier
Homage to Catalonia
Coming Up for Air
Animal Farm
Nineteen Eighty-Four
A Kind of Compulsion (1903-36)
Facing Unpleasant Facts (1937-39)
A Patriot After All (1940-41)
All Propaganda is Lies (1941-42)
Keeping Our Little Corner Clean (1942-43)
Two Wasted Years (1943)
I Have Tried to Tell the Truth (1943-44)
I Belong to the Left (1945)
Smothered Under Journalism (1946)
It is What I Think (1947-48)
Our Job is to Make Life Worth Living (1949-50)

Also by Peter Davison

Books: *Songs of the British Music Hall: A Critical Study; Popular Appeal in English Drama to 1850; Contemporary Drama and the Popular Dramatic Tradition; Hamlet: Text and Performance; Henry V: Masterguide; Othello: The Critical Debate; Orwell: A Literary Life*

Editions: Anonymous: *The Fair Maid of the Exchange* (with Arthur Brown); Shakespeare: *Richard II*; Shakespeare: *The Merchant of Venice*; Shakespeare: *1 Henry IV*; Shakespeare: *2 Henry IV*; Shakespeare: *The First Quarto of King Richard III*; Marston: *The Dutch Courtesan; Facsimile of the Manuscript of Nineteen Eighty-Four; Sheridan: A Casebook; The Book Encompassed: Studies in Twentieth-Century Bibliography*

Series: *Theatrum Redivivum* 17 Volumes (with James Binns); *Literary Taste, Culture, and Mass Communication* 14 Volumes (with Edward Shils and Rolf Meyersohn)

Academic Journals: *ALTA: University of Birmingham Review*, 1966-70; *The Library: Transactions of the Bibliographical Society*, 1971-82

Publication of *The Complete Works of George Orwell* is a unique
bibliographic event as well as a major step in Orwell
scholarship. Meticulous textual research by
Dr Peter Davison has revealed that all the current editions
of Orwell have been mutilated to a greater or lesser extent.
This authoritative edition incorporates in Volumes 10-20
all Orwell's known essays, poems, plays, letters, journalism,
broadcasts, and diaries, and also letters by his wife, Eileen,
and members of his family. In addition there are very many of
the letters in newspapers and magazines of readers' reactions
to Orwell's articles and reviews. Where the hands of others
have intervened, Orwell's original intentions have been restored.

Two
Wasted Years
1943

GEORGE ORWELL

Edited by Peter Davison
Assisted by Ian Angus and Sheila Davison

SECKER & WARBURG

LONDON

Revised and updated edition published by Secker & Warburg 2001

2 4 6 8 10 9 7 5 3

First published in Great Britain in 1998 by
Secker & Warburg
Random House, 20 Vauxhall Bridge Road,
London SW1V 2SA

Random House Australia (Pty) Limited
20 Alfred Street, Milsons Point, Sydney,
New South Wales 2061, Australia

Random House New Zealand Limited
18 Poland Road, Glenfield,
Auckland 10, New Zealand

Random House South Africa (Pty) Limited
Endulini, 5A Jubilee Road, Parktown 2193, South Africa

The Random House Group Limited Reg. No. 954009
www.randomhouse.co.uk

A CIP catalogue record for this book
is available from the British Library

ISBN 9780 436 40409 2

Printed and bound in Great Britain by Clays Ltd, elcograf S.p.a

Penguin Random House is committed to a sustainable future for
our business, our readers and our planet. This book is made from
Forest Stewardship Council® certified paper.

CONTENTS

Titles may be modified and shortened
TBF = BBC Talks Booking Form; dates booked for broadcasts are given in numerals

Contents

Contents

Contents

Contents

Contents

INTRODUCTION to VOLUME XV

1 March to 26 November 1943: *Two Wasted Years*

On 14 March 1942, after six months at the BBC, Orwell wrote in his War-time Diary that the atmosphere at the BBC was 'something half way between a girls' school and a lunatic asylum, and all we are doing at present is useless, or slightly worse than useless. Our radio strategy is even more hopeless than our military strategy' (XIII, 229), and 1942 was a very bad year militarily for Britain. He continued working at the BBC under great pressure with his few colleagues for another twenty months, attempting to broadcast not only commentaries on the war as honest as he could make them, but offering his Indian and Far Eastern audiences education, culture, and intelligent features. To the last he was innovative. He had edited a series of broadcast talks for George Allen & Unwin and this was published on 18 November 1943, a few days before he left the Corporation's service, as *Talking to India: A Selection of English Language Broadcasts to India* (see *2359* for details and Orwell's introduction). An interesting feature, and typical of Orwell, was the inclusion of a talk by the Indian nationalist, Subhas Chandra Bose, broadcast from Berlin. The edition had sold out by 1945, nearly half the copies overseas.

Another innovation was a series of 'featurised stories,' a form that interested Orwell and which he tried to persuade the BBC (through Rayner Heppenstall) to develop after the war. Writing to Lydia Jackson in October 1943, asking her to featurise a Russian story, he described what was required (see *2305A* and *2317A*, Volume XX, Appendix 14, 312 and 313). Anatole France's *Crainquebille* was broadcast on 11 August 1943 (*2230*); 'The Fox' by Ignazio Silone on 9 September (*2270*); H. G. Wells's 'A Slip Under the Microscope', 6 October (*2297*); and the fairy tale (a genre in which he was greatly interested—so his description of *Animal Farm* on its title-page), Hans Andersen's *The Emperor's New Clothes*, 18 November 1943, just six days before his last day of service (*2361*). On 17 October his adaptation and commentary on *Macbeth* (Orwell's favourite play by Shakespeare) was broadcast, and he gave a talk on *Lady Windermere's Fan* on 21 November.

Orwell continued to produce more than one news commentary every week. His series of newsletters to India came to an end with No. 59 on 13 March 1943, but he was currently then also writing (and broadcasting) a newsletter for occupied Malaya, which he had started on 20 November 1942. That series ran until No. 40 on 2 July 1943. The following week he started a series for occupied Indonesia and the last of these that he wrote, No. 21, was broadcast two days after he left the BBC (*2373*). He also wrote twenty-eight or twenty-nine newsletters for translation into Tamil from 22 April 1943 (see *2024*), the last of these being broadcast the day after he finished working for the BBC. He was, therefore, working to the bitter end, however despondent he felt, and even though, as he wrote to Philip Rahv on 9 December 1943, these had been two wasted years (*2390*, XVI, 22).

But were these years so wasted? There was (as he as well realised) much waste of lives and years at this time and in comparison Orwell's time was relatively productive: he worked hard and seriously and gave the tasks before him all his imagination and energy. But in terms of what might have been possible, of opportunities not taken, it was a waste. Laurence Brander's report on Indian programmes of 11 January 1943, printed as Appendix 1 to this volume (*2374*) gives some measure of what might have been. Brander was one of Orwell's friends (he wrote one of the first studies of Orwell, *George Orwell*, 1954) and it is possible that, added to Orwell's own experience, his discussion with Orwell in the BBC canteen may have helped drive home how useless were the efforts of Bokhari's little staff. First and foremost, no one seems to have given thought to the very small number of radios in India. Whereas there was one radio to 5·36 people in the United Kingdom in 1939, there was only one for 3,875 people in India—and broadcasting had to be in several languages (see *892*; XIII, 90). Worse still were the kinds of people in charge. In *The Lion and the Unicorn* he had written bitterly that at the outbreak of war in 1939, 'All the old duds were back on the job . . . A generation of the unteachable is hanging upon us like a necklace of corpses' (*763*, XII, 413). On 29 April 1942 he wrote, after a visit to witness a debate in Parliament (probably in connexion with the BBC series he ran called 'The Debate Continues'), 'This is the twilight of Parliamentary democracy and these creatures are simply ghosts gibbering in some corner while the real events happen elsewhere' (*1130*, XIII, 291). One might respond that 'this was simply Orwell' (or *plus ça change* . . .) were it not that so far as those responsible for broadcasting to India (those above Bokhari and Orwell) were seen in much the same light by whoever wrote the notes for Sir Stafford Cripps in preparation for his Mission to India. Beresford Clark, Controller of Overseas Programmes, was described as never having made a programme, 'suave, indecisive, conscientious, unimaginative'; R. A. Rendall, Assistant Controller, 'not a programme man: is youngish, well-meaning, discouraged, tired out by routine; never been to India and knows nothing about it'; L. F. Rushbrook Williams, Director of Eastern Services, sailed with the wind; and Sir Malcolm Darling, Indian Editor (Hindustani), was 'Obstinate, unimaginative, limited and very patronising to Indians. A joke' (*847*, XIII, 20–21). Only Bokhari was given credit (for being an excellent speaker and writer); Orwell was not mentioned. It was against such an Establishment in public life and at the BBC that Orwell constantly fought and the BBC offered him an epitome of Britain (perhaps 'England' would be more just) at its most hopeless and depressing.

Against that background, though Orwell could not see it at the time, all was not wasted. Despite his fears, although evidence is in short supply (as it would be from occupied countries), his broadcasts *were* heard in Malaya and perhaps elsewhere (see *1669*). He did experience the kind of institution from the inside that he would develop horrifically in *Nineteen Eighty-Four*, and the

BBC produced one of Orwell's wry jokes for that novel in the source of Room 101: that was the Committee Room where Orwell obviously was thoroughly bored (see *870*). It was ironic that on his last day at the BBC he had to attend a committee meeting. It is hard to delineate possible future influences (and that is not the task of an editor) but one can certainly be suggested. Balraj Sahni (1913–1973), who with Damyanti (d. 1947) broadcast with Norman Marshall in the 'Let's Act it Ourselves' series, went on, as Dr Abha Sharma Rodrigues puts it, to occupy a 'special place in the history of Indian theatre and cinema' and he was more than once awarded the National Award for outstanding performance. He helped develop the Indian People's Theatre Association (which he mentions in a letter to Orwell commiserating with him on Eileen's death, 20 November 1945, *2799*, XVII, 390). This 'played a significant role in the social and cultural life of independent India. Linking itself closely with the lives of common people . . .'[1]

Orwell's fostering of performances of Indian, and specifically Sanskrit, plays was far in advance of its time. In January 1986 the Arts Theatre in London presented *The Little Clay Cart*, in ten-acts with eight players and two musicians. An enthusiastic review in *The Times* (11 January 1986) was headed 'Rich in eccentrics.' No one mentioned that Orwell had produced a more modest version *for India* forty-three years earlier (*1874*). The BBC was, indeed, fertile ground for the continuation of Orwell's interest in what would now be classed as post-colonial literature but in its 'pre-post-colonial' stage, with his encouragement of Indian drama and such writers as Ahmed Ali, Mulk Raj Anand, Prem Chand, and Cedric Dover.

It is tempting to see Orwell's courses and publications for Indian university students as a precursor to the idea of the open university, and his cultural programmes, especially 'Voice', as the seed from which the Third Programme sprang (and some of those who worked with Orwell, such as Rayner Heppenstall, would go on to work for the Third Programme when it opened up three years later; Heppenstall produced Orwell's adaptation of *Animal Farm* for that service). Whether or not direct links can be shown, what is certain is that Orwell was in advance of these grand projects and he was not wasting his time.

This volume is not exclusively devoted to Orwell at the BBC. There are a number of reviews, including the important 'Gandhi in Mayfair' (*2257*) with Lionel Fielden's response (*2258*), and the long article, 'The Detective Story', which appeared in the French journal, *Fontaine*, now published in English for the first time (*2357*). Appendix 2 contains Orwell's notes for 'The Quick & the Dead' and 'The Last Man in Europe', conjecturally dated September 1943 (see *2375*, *2376*, and *2377*).

1. Abha Sharma Rodrigues, 'George Orwell, the BBC and India: A Critical Study', Edinburgh University, Ph.D. thesis, 1994, pp. 176–7.

A full General Introduction will be found in the preliminaries to Volume X Reference should also be made to the Introductions to Volumes XIII and XIV

Two letters from this period were kindly sent by Michael C. D. Macdonald after the whole edition had been set and page-proofed. They are reproduced here with appropriate item numbers. They are indexed.

2098A. To Dwight Macdonald
    26 May 1943   Typewritten

10a Mortimer Crescent London NW 6

Dear Macdonald,

Many thanks for your letter (dated April 13 and arrived yesterday!) and cheque.[1] I enclose a list of 15 people who I should think would be possible subscribers to PR.[2] Some of them I know are acquainted with the paper, and some may possibly be subscribers, but not to my knowledge. I am circularising all of them, telling them you can accept foreign subscriptions, and offering to lend copies so that they can have a look at it. Forster was interested when I showed him a copy some time back, so I am pretty certain he would subscribe if you prodded him, also Myers and Rees.

I am glad the last letter was a success and I will send another as soon as possible. As you see by the above address I didn't get the job I was trying for (in North Africa) and am still at the BBC.[3] I enjoy very much doing these letters for PR, it is a tremendous relief every now and then to write what one really thinks about the current situation, and if I have occasionally shown signs of wanting to stop it is because I keep fearing that your readers will get tired of always hearing about affairs in England from the same person. My point of view isn't the only one and as you will have seen from the various letters from Alex Comfort etc. there are some pretty vigorous opponents of it.[4] But within my own framework I have tried to be truthful and I am very happy to go on with the arrangement so long as you are.

We have shortly coming out a book made up from the broadcasts sent out to India by my department.[5] I think some copies will be sent to the USA, and I will try to get a copy to PR. Of course all books of broadcasts are crashingly dull, but it might interest you to see some specimens of British propaganda to India.

I will send off my next letter probably in about a fortnight. In that case it should reach you before the end of July unless the mail service comes unstuck again.

All the best.

Geo. Orwell

1. Presumably for 'A Letter from England', 3 January 1943, for *Partisan Review*; 1797. See also 1796.
2. Orwell enclosed a list of names (with addresses). These comprised L. H. Myers, Tilecoats, Marlow, Bucks; Paul Willert, 14 Halsey Street, Chelsea, London SW; Fredric Warburg, 29 St Edmunds Court, St Edmunds Terrace, London NW8; E. M. Forster, West Hackhurst, Abinger Hammer, Near Dorking, Surrey; Mulk Raj Anand, 8 St George's Mews, Regents Park Road, London NW1; Reginald Reynolds, A.R.P. Billets. St Marks College, Kings Road, London SW10; Desmond Hawkins, Todds Farm, Saxtead, Framlingham, Suffolk; Herbert Read, Broom House, Seer Green, Beaconsfield, Bucks; John Atkins, Care of the "Tribune", 222 Strand, London WC; G. R. Strauss, M.P., House of Commons, London SW1; Dr. C. H. Waddington, Christ's College, Cambridge; Professor Lancelot Hogben, 33 High Street, Aberdeen, Scotland; Lt. Sir Richard Rees, R.N.V.R., The

Admiralty, Whitehall, London SW1; J. F. Horrabin, 16 Endsleigh Gardens, London NW4; V. S. Pritchett, Maiden Court, Great Shefford, Near Newbury, Berks. Against Hawkins's and Read's names someone has written 'no.'

3. No letter to Macdonald on this subject has been traced.

4. In his London Letter of 1 January 1942, *913*, Orwell had attacked Comfort and others. For responses, see *913, n. 4* and 'Pacifism and War: A Controversy', *1270*, in which Comfort took part.

5. *Talking to India*, published 18 November 1943; see *2359*.

2222A. To Dwight Macdonald
  6 August 1943   Typewritten

10a Mortimer Crescent, London, N. W. 6.

Dear Macdonald,

I sent you earlier a list of 15 people who I thought were possible subscribers to PR. I have since canvassed all of them and about eight said that they would like to take the paper in. However, there was no way of getting copies except through Horizon, who at present only have six copies to spare. I think you send them a dozen each month but they have some arrangement by which they send six copies to Zwemmer's (book shop), so we have at any rate got six new subscribers and it is clear that it would be possible to get a good many more if more copies were available. I don't know how things stand about sending magazines overseas. I suppose you have to get a licence to send a certain number and to show reason if you want to increase it, but whether the chief hold-up is this end or your end I don't know. If you want to go on with this and can see your way to exporting more copies I can send you some more lists of likely names and can canvass some of them myself. I have no doubt that you could put on an extra circulation of at least fifty in Britain, which I suppose is worth while from your point of view, and which is certainly very desirable in the general state of international black-out we are living in. I am afraid I am thoroughly vague about how these things are done. Connolly, when I questioned him, did not even know on what terms he was getting copies of PR from you, but seemed to have a vague idea that it was *not* in exchange for copies of Horizon. Eliot has just taken over some job which Professor Arthur Newell previously had, something to do with the exchange of books between Britain and the U.S.A., and we might be able to mobilize him to help with this. At present it is almost impossible to get any American magazines regularly in England, except rubbish like Time etc.

I hope all goes well with you.

Yours sincerely,
Geo. Orwell

ACKNOWLEDGEMENTS and PROVENANCES

specific to Volume XV

The editor wishes to express his gratitude to the following institutions and libraries, their trustees, curators, and staffs for their co-operation and valuable help, for making copies of Orwell material available, and for allowing it to be published: BBC Written Archives Centre, Caversham; Bodleian Library, University of Oxford; Penguin UK Archive, Bristol University Library; British Library, Department of Manuscripts (for the Orwell papers, Add. Mss 49384 and 73083); Lilly Library, Indiana University, Bloomington, Indiana; Royal Literary Fund; Harry Ransom Humanities Research Center, University of Texas at Austin; and the Library of University College London for material in the Orwell Archive and the J.B.S. Haldane papers.

Gratitude is expressed to George Allen & Unwin Ltd and to Penguin UK for having made available their material relating to Orwell.

Thanks are due to Michael C. D. Macdonald for making available two letters by Orwell to Dwight Macdonald. I am also deeply indebted to those whose Orwell letters are available because they donated them or presented copies of them to the Orwell Archive: the Hon David Astor (Editor of *The Observer*), John Atkins, Alex Comfort and S. Moos; also to William Phillips and Philip Rahv (Editors of *Partisan Review*).

I would like to thank the following publications for permission to reproduce material which first appeared in their pages: *The Listener* (by courtesy of the BBC and the Independent Television Association Ltd), *The Nation* (New York), *The New Statesman*, *The Observer*, *Partisan Review*, *The Spectator* and *Tribune*.

I would like to thank the following for granting me permission to use material whose copyright they own: George Allen & Unwin Ltd to quote from their correspondence with Orwell; Mulk Raj Anand to reprint a letter by him to *Tribune*; Alex Comfort to reprint his poem 'Letter to an American Visitor' by 'Obadiah Hornbooke'; Michael Kopp and Mary Kopp Wheeler and other members of the family to publish a letter by their father, Georges Kopp; Kenneth Muir to reprint a letter by him to *Tribune*; Eva Rhys to reprint a letter by Keidrych Rhys to *Tribune*; Darina Silone to publish Orwell's dramatisation of Ignazio Silone's 'The Fox'; The Estate of the late Roy Oliver Walker to quote from letters by Roy Walker; A. P. Watt Ltd on behalf of The Literary Executors of the Estate of H. G. Wells to publish Orwell's dramatisation of H. G. Wells's 'A Slip under the Microscope'; and the University of Sussex Library to reprint a letter by Leonard Woolf to *Tribune*.

I would like to thank the following for their help and giving valuable information: Mulk Raj Anand, the Hon David Astor, Honor Balfour,

Laurence Brander, Sir Roger Falk, Clive Fleay and Desmond Hawkins.

Thanks are due to Shirley E. Jones, Patrick Parrinder, Janet Percival and Ian Willison for their translations.

The editor and publishers have made every effort to trace copyright holders of the material published in this volume, but in some cases this has not proved possible. The publishers therefore wish to apologise to the authors or copyright holders of any material which has been reproduced without permission and due acknowledgement.

PROVENANCES

The major part of the documents and letters reproduced in this volume are in the BBC Written Archives Centre, Caversham and it should be taken that any document or letter that does not have its location indicated on the list below is at Caversham. Only documents and letters in other archives have their locations listed below. However, in cases where there are documents or letters at an item that are in different archives, this is indicated, even though one of the archives is the BBC Archive at Caversham, e.g. 1980 OA, BBC (the top copy of a letter is in the Orwell Archive and the carbon copy is at the BBC Archive at Caversham).

For simplicity's sake, the Orwell papers in the British Library, Department of Manuscripts (Add. Mss 49384 and 73083) are not indicated as such in the location list, but are regarded as being available for consultation in the form of copies in the Orwell Archive.

KEY TO LOCATIONS

A & U   George Allen & Unwin Ltd

BBC   BBC Written Archives Centre, Caversham

Bodleian Bodleian Library, University of Oxford

Bristol   Penguin UK Archive, Bristol University Library

Lilly   Lilly Library, Indiana University, Bloomington, Indiana

OA   Orwell Archive (and the J.B.S. Haldane papers), University College London Library

RLF   Royal Literary Fund

Texas   Harry Ransom Humanities Research Center, University of Texas at Austin

1942 Bristol	2013 Bristol	2183 OA
1949 Bristol	2026 OA	2185 OA
1973 A & U	2031 OA	2193 A & U
1980 OA, BBC	2034 OA	2201 OA
1983 A & U	2059 OA	2213 OA
1996 A & U	2078 RLF	2228 OA
1998 OA	2110 OA	2240 Bodleian
2008 OA	2145 A & U	2247 Texas

2255 OA   2331 OA, BBC   2368 A & U
2259 OA   2356 OA   2376 OA
2299 Lilly   2367 Bristol   2377 OA
2314 OA

Editorial Note

THE CONTENTS are, in the main, arranged in chronological order of Orwell's writing. Letters arising from his articles or reviews are usually grouped immediately after that item and Orwell's replies to those letters follow thereon. If there is a long delay between when it is known an article or essay was completed and its publication, it is printed at the date of completion. If items are printed much earlier in the chronological sequence than their date of publication, a cross-reference is given at the date of publication. All entries, whether written by Orwell or anyone else, including lengthy notes and cross-references, are given an item number. Because the printing of the edition has taken place over seven years, some letters came to light after the initial editing and the numbering of items had been completed. These items (or those that had in consequence to be repositioned) are given a letter after the number: e.g., *335A*. Some items included after printing and page-proofing had been completed are given in a final appendix to Volume XX and two (received by the editor in mid January 1997) in the Introduction to Volume XV. Numbers preceding item titles are in roman; when referred to in notes they are italicised.

The provenance of items is given in the preliminaries to each volume. Every item that requires explanation about its source or date, or about textual problems it may pose, is provided with such an explanation. Some articles and broadcasts exist in more than one version. The basis upon which they have been edited is explained and lists of variant readings provided. No Procrustean bed has been devised into which such items must be constrained; individual circumstances have been taken into account and editorial practice explained.

Although this is not what is called a 'diplomatic edition'—that is, one that represents the original precisely even in all its deformities to the point of reproducing a letter set upside down—the fundamental approach in presenting these texts has been to interfere with them as little as possible consistent with the removal of deformities and typographic errors. Orwell took great pains over the writing of his books: the facsimile edition of *Nineteen Eighty-Four*[1] shows that, but in order to meet the demands of broadcasting and publication schedules he often wrote fast and under great pressure. The speed with which he sometimes wrote meant that what he produced was not always what he would have wished to have published had he had time to revise. And, of course, as with any printing, errors can be introduced by those setting the type. It would be easy in places to surmise what Orwell would have done but I have only made changes where there would otherwise have been confusion. Obvious spelling mistakes, which could well be the compositor's or typist's (and the typist might be Orwell), have been corrected silently, but if there is any doubt, a footnote has drawn attention to the problem.

In brief, therefore, I have tried to present what Orwell wrote in his manuscripts and typescripts, not what I thought he should have written; and what he was represented as having written and not what I think should have been typed or printed on his behalf. This is not a 'warts and all' approach because gross errors are amended, significant changes noted, and textual complexities are discussed in preliminary notes. The aim is to bring Orwell, not the editor's version of Orwell, to the fore. Although textual issues are given due weight, an attempt has been made to produce an attractive, readable text.

The setting of this edition has been directly from xeroxes of original letters (if typed), typed copies of manuscript (prepared by one or other of the editors), surviving scripts for broadcasts, and xeroxes of essays, articles, and reviews as originally published (unless a headnote states otherwise). For *The Collected Essays, Journalism and Letters of George Orwell* a 1968 house style was adopted but for this edition, no attempt has been made to impose a late twentieth-century house style on the very different styles used by journals and editors of fifty to eighty years ago. Texts are therefore reproduced in the style given them in the journals from which they are reprinted. To 'correct' might well cause even more confusion as to what was and was not Orwell's: see below regarding paragraphing. Nevertheless, although it is not possible *to know*, one may sometimes hazard a guess at what underlies a printed text. Thus, I believe that most often when 'address' and 'aggression' are printed, Orwell typed or wrote 'adress' (especially until about the outbreak of World War II) and 'agression.' Although American spellings (such as 'Labor') have been retained in articles published in the United States, on very rare occasions, if I could be certain that a form of a word had been printed that Orwell would not have used—such as the American 'accommodations'—I have changed it to the form he would have used: 'accommodation'. Some variations, especially of proper names, have been accepted even if they look incongruous; so, 'Chiang Kai-Shek' as part of a book title but 'Chiang Kai-shek' throughout the text that follows.

Hyphenation presents tricky problems, especially when the first part of a word appears at the end of a line. Examples can be found in the originals of, for example, 'the middle-class,' 'the middle class', and 'the middleclass.' What should one do when a line ends with 'middle-'? Is it 'fore-deck' or 'foredeck'? If 'fore-' appears at the end of a line of the copy being reproduced, should the word be hyphenated or not? *OED* 1991 still hyphenates; Chambers in 1972 spelt it as one word. Where it would help (and it does not include every problem word), the ninth edition of F. Howard Collins, *Authors' & Printers' Dictionary*, Oxford University Press, 1946 (an edition appropriate to the mature Orwell) has been drawn upon. But Collins does not include fore-deck/foredeck. On a number of occasions Orwell's letters, or the text itself, is either obscure or wrong. In order to avoid the irritating repetition of *sic*, a small degree sign has been placed above the line at the doubtful point (°). It is hoped that this will be clear but inconspicuous. It is not usually repeated to mark a repetition of that characteristic in the same item. Orwell was sparing in his use of the question-mark in his letters; his practice has in the main been followed.

Paragraphing presents intractable problems. Orwell tended to write in long paragraphs. Indeed, it is possible to show from the use of many short paragraphs that News Review scripts so written are not by Orwell. The key example is News Review, 30, 11 July 1942 (*1267*), for which there is also external evidence that this is not by Orwell. This has twenty-one paragraphs as compared to eight in the script for the following week. It so happens that we know that Orwell was not at the BBC for two weeks before the 11 July nor on that day: he was on holiday, fishing at Callow End, Worcestershire (and on that day caught a single dace). But though paragraph length is helpful in such instances in identifying Orwell's work, that is not always so. It is of no use when considering his articles published in Paris in 1928–29 nor those he wrote for the *Manchester Evening News*. These tend to have extremely short paragraphs—sometimes paragraphs of only a line or two, splitting the sense illogically. A good example is the series of reviews published on 2 November 1944 (*2572*) where a two-line paragraph about Trollope's *The Small House at Allington* should clearly be part of the preceding four-line paragraph, both relating the books discussed to Barchester; see also *2463, n. 2* and *2608, n. 4*. There is no question but that this is the work of sub-editors. It would often be possible to make a reasonable stab at paragraphing more intelligently, but, as with verbal clarification, the result might be the more confusing as to what really was Orwell's work and what this editor's. It has been thought better to leave the house-styles as they are, even if it is plain that it is not Orwell's style, rather than pass off changes as if the edited concoction represented Orwell's work.

Usually it is fairly certain that titles of essays are Orwell's but it is not always possible to know whether titles of articles are his. Reviews were also frequently given titles. Orwell's own typescript for his review of Harold Laski's *Faith, Reason and Civilisation* (*2309*), which survived because rejected by the *Manchester Evening News*, has neither heading (other than the name of the author and title of the book being reviewed), nor sub-headings. That would seem to be his style. In nearly every case titles of reviews and groups of letters, and cross-heads inserted by sub-editors, have been cut out. Occasionally such a title is kept if it is an aid to clarity but it is never placed within quotation marks. Other than for his BBC broadcasts (where Orwell's authorship is clear unless stated otherwise), titles are placed within single quotation marks if it is fairly certain that they are Orwell's.

Telegrams and cables are printed in small capitals. Quite often articles and reviews have passages in capitals. These look unsightly and, in the main, they have been reduced to small capitals. The exceptions are where the typography makes a point, as in the sound of an explosion: BOOM! Orwell sometimes abbreviated words. He always wrote an ampersand for 'and' and there are various abbreviated forms for such words as 'about'. It is not always plain just what letters make up abbreviations (and this sometimes applies to his signatures) and these have regularly been spelt out with the exception of the ampersand for 'and'. This serves as a reminder that the original is handwritten. Orwell often shortened some words and abbreviations in his own way, e.g., Gov.t, Sup.ts (Superintendents), NB. and N.W (each with a single stop), and ie.; these forms have been retained. In order that the diaries should readily be apparent for what they are, they have been set in sloped roman (rather than italic, long passages of which can be tiring to the eye), with roman for textual variations. Square and half square brackets are used to differentiate sources for the diaries (see, for example, the headnote to War-Time Diary II, *1025*) and for what was written and actually broadcast (see, for example, Orwell's adaptation of Ignazio Silone's *The Fox*, *2270*). Particular usages are explained in headnotes to broadcasts etc., and before the first entries of diaries and notebooks.

Orwell usually dated his letters but there are exceptions and sometimes he (and Eileen) give only the day of the week. Where a date has to be guessed it is placed within square brackets and a justification for the dating is given. If Orwell simply signs a letter, the name he used is given without comment. If he signs over a typed version of his name, or initials a copy of a letter, what he signed or initialled is given over the typed version. There has been some slight regularisation of his initialling of letters. If he omitted the final stop after 'E. A. B', no stop is added (and, as here, editorial punctuation *follows* the final quotation mark instead of being inside it). Sometimes Orwell placed the stops midway up the letters: 'E·A·B'; this has been regularised to 'E. A. B'.

Wherever changes are made in a text that can be deemed to be even slightly significant the alteration is either placed within square brackets (for example, an obviously missing word) or the alteration is footnoted. Attention should be drawn to one particular category of change. Orwell had a remarkably good memory. He quoted not only poetry but prose from memory. Mulk Raj Anand has said that, at the BBC, Orwell could, and would, quote lengthy passages from the Book of Common Prayer.[2] As so often with people with this gift, the quotation is not always exact. If what Orwell argues depends precisely upon what he is quoting, the quotation is not corrected if it is inaccurate but a footnote gives the correct reading. If his argument does not depend upon the words actually quoted, the quotation is corrected and a footnote records that.

So far as possible, I have endeavoured to footnote everything that might puzzle a reader at the risk of annoying some readers by seeming to annotate too readily and too frequently what is known to them. I have, therefore, tried to identify all references to people, events, books, and institutions. However, I have not been so presumptuous as to attempt to rewrite the history of this century and, in the main, have relied upon a small number of easily accessible histories. Thus, for the Spanish Civil War I have referred in the main to *The Spanish Civil War* by Hugh Thomas; and for the Second World War, to Winston Churchill's and Liddell Hart's histories. The former has useful and conveniently available documents, and the latter was by a historian with whom Orwell corresponded. They were both his contemporaries and he reviewed the work of both men. These have been checked for factual information from more recent sources, one by Continental historians deliberately chosen as an aid to objectivity in an edition that will have world-wide circulation. It is assumed that readers with a particular interest in World War II will draw on their own knowledge and sources and the annotation is relatively light in providing such background information. Similarly, biographical details are, paradoxically, relatively modest for people as well known as T. S. Eliot and E. M. Forster, but far fuller for those who are significant to Orwell but less well known and about whom information is harder to track down, for example, George(s) Kopp, Joseph Czapski, and Victor Serge. It is tricky judging how often biographical and explicatory information should be reproduced. I have assumed most people will not want more than one volume at a time before them and so have repeated myself (often in shortened form with cross-references to fuller notes) more, perhaps, than is strictly necessary. Whilst I would claim that I have made every attempt not to mislead, it is important that historical and biographical information be checked if a detail is significant to a scholar's argument. History, as Orwell was quick to show, is not a matter of simple, indisputable fact. In annotating I have tried not to be contentious nor to direct the reader unfairly, but annotation cannot be wholly impartial.[3]

Each opening is dated. These dates, though drawn from the printed matter, are not necessarily those of the text reproduced on the page on which a date appears. The dates, known or calculated of letters, articles, broadcasts, diaries, etc., will correspond with the running-head date, but, for example, when correspondence (which may have run on for several weeks) springs from an article and follows directly on that article, the date of the article is continued *within square brackets*. Sometimes an item is printed out of chronological order (the reason for which is always given) and the running-head date will again be set within square brackets. Wherever practicable, the running-head date is that of the first item of the opening; if an opening has no date, the last date of a preceding opening is carried forward. Articles published in journals dated by month are considered for the purpose to be published on the first of the month. Inevitably some dates are more specific than is wholly justified, e.g., that for 'British Cookery' (*2954*). However, it is hoped that if readers always treat dates within square brackets with circumspection, the dates will give a clear indication of 'where they are' in Orwell's life.

Great efforts have been made to ensure the accuracy of these volumes. The three editors and Roberta Leighton (in New York) have read and re-read them a total of six times but it is obvious that errors will, as it used to be put so charmingly in the sixteenth century, have 'escaped in the printing.' I offer one plea for understanding. Much of the copy-preparation and proof-reading has been of type set during and after the war when newsprint was in short supply and mere literary articles would be set in microscopic-sized type. Many of the BBC scripts were blown up from microfilm and extremely difficult to puzzle out. When one proof-reads against xeroxes of dim printing on creased paper, the possibilities for error are increased and the eyes so run with tears that vision is impaired. We hope we have corrected most errors, but we know we shall not have caught them all.

P.D.

A slightly fuller version of this note is printed in the preliminaries to Volume X.

1. *George Orwell, Nineteen Eighty-Four: The Facsimile of the Extant Manuscript*, edited by Peter Davison, London, New York, and Weston, Mass., 1984.
2. Information from W. J. West, 22 July 1994.
3. The problems of presenting acceptable history even for the professional historian are well outlined by Norman Davies in *Europe: A History*, Oxford University Press, Oxford and New York, 1996, 2–7. I am obviously attempting nothing so grand, yet even 'simple' historical explication is not always quite so simple.

REFERENCES

References to Orwell's books are to the editions in Vols I to IX of the *Complete Works* (edited P. Davison, published by Secker & Warburg, 1986–87). The pagination is almost always identical with that in the Penguin Twentieth-Century Classics edition, 1989–90. The volumes are numbered in chronological order and references are by volume number (in roman), page, and, if necessary (after a diagonal) line, so: II.37/5 means line five of page 37 of *Burmese Days*. Secker editions have Textual Notes and apparatus. Penguin editions have A Note on the Text; these are not identical with the Secker Textual Notes and Penguin editions do not list variants. There is a 32-page introduction to the Secker *Down and Out in Paris and London*. Items in Volumes X to XX are numbered individually; they (and their notes) are referred to by italicised numerals, e.g. *2736* and *2736 n. 3*.

REFERENCE WORKS: These are the principal reference works frequently consulted:

The Oxford English Dictionary, second edition (Compact Version, Oxford 1991): (*OED*).

The Dictionary of National Biography (Oxford 1885–1900, with supplements and *The Twentieth-Century*, 1901–): (*DNB*).

Dictionary of American Biography (New York, 1946, with supplements).

Dictionnaire biographique du mouvement ouvrier français, publié sous la direction de Jean Maitron, 4ᵉ ptie 1914–1939: De la Première à la Seconde Guerre mondiale (t. 16–43, Paris, Les Éditions Ouvrières, 1981–93).

Who's Who; Who Was Who; Who's Who in the Theatre; Who Was Who in Literature 1906–1934 (2 vols., Detroit, 1979); *Who Was Who Among English and European Authors 1931–1949* (3 vols., Detroit 1978); *Contemporary Authors* and its *Cumulative Index* (Detroit, 1993); *Who's Who In Filmland*, edited and compiled by Langford Reed and Hetty Spiers (1928); Roy Busby, *British Music Hall: An Illustrated Who's Who from 1850 to the Present Day* (London and New Hampshire, USA, 1976).

The Feminist Companion to Literature in English, edited by Virginia Blain, Patricia Clements, and Isobel Grundy, Batsford 1990.

The New Cambridge Bibliography of English Literature, edited by George Watson and Ian Willison, 4 vols., Cambridge, 1974–79.

Martin Seymour-Smith, *Guide to Modern World Literature*, 3rd revised edition, Macmillan 1985.

The War Papers, co-ordinating editor, Richard Widdows, 75 Parts, Marshall Cavendish, 1976–78.

The following are referred to by abbreviations:

CEJL: *The Collected Essays, Journalism and Letters of George Orwell*, ed. Sonia Orwell and Ian Angus, 4 volumes, Secker & Warburg 1968; Penguin Books, 1970; references are by volume and page number of the more conveniently available Penguin edition.

Crick: Bernard Crick, *George Orwell: A Life*, 1980; 3rd edition, Penguin Books, Harmondsworth, 1992 edition. References are to the 1992 edition.

Eric & Us: Jacintha Buddicom, *Eric and Us: A Remembrance of George Orwell*, Leslie Frewin, 1974.

Lewis: Peter Lewis, *George Orwell: The Road to 1984*, Heinemann, 1981.

Liddell Hart: B. H. Liddell Hart, *History of the Second World War*, Cassell, 1970; 8th Printing, Pan, 1983.

Orwell Remembered: Audrey Coppard and Bernard Crick, eds., *Orwell Remembered*, Ariel Books, BBC, 1984.

Remembering Orwell: Stephen Wadhams, *Remembering Orwell*, Penguin Books Canada, Markham, Ontario; Penguin Books, Harmondsworth, 1984.

Shelden: Michael Shelden, *Orwell: The Authorised Biography*, Heinemann, London; Harper Collins, New York; 1991. The American pagination differs from that of the English edition; both are given in references, the English first.

Stansky and Abrahams I: Peter Stansky and William Abrahams, *The Unknown Orwell*, Constable 1972; edition referred to here, Granada, St Albans, 1981.

Stansky and Abrahams II: Peter Stansky and William Abrahams, *The Transformation*, Constable 1979; edition referred to here, Granada, St Albans, 1981.

Thomas: Hugh Thomas, *The Spanish Civil War*, 3rd edition; Hamish Hamilton and Penguin Books, Harmondsworth, 1977.

Thompson: John Thompson, *Orwell's London*, Fourth Estate 1984.

West: *Broadcasts*: W. J. West, *Orwell: The War Broadcasts*, Duckworth/BBC 1985.

West: *Commentaries*: W. J. West, *Orwell: The War Commentaries*, Duckworth/BBC, 1985.

Willison: I. R. Willison, 'George Orwell: Some Materials for a Bibliography,' Librarianship Diploma Thesis, University College London, 1953. A copy is held by the Orwell Archive, UCL.

2194 Days of War: *2194 Days of War*, compiled by Cesare Salmaggi and Alfredo Pallavisini, translated by Hugh Young, Arnoldo Mondadori, Milan 1977; rev. edn Galley Press, Leicester 1988.

A Bibliography of works, books, memoirs and essays found helpful in preparing Volumes X to XX of *The Complete Works of George Orwell* will be found in the preliminaries to Volume X.

CHRONOLOGY

THE BBC YEARS

In the main, Orwell's publications, except books, are not listed

25 June 1903 Eric Arthur Blair born in Motihari, Bengal, India.

---

18 Aug 1941–24 Nov 1943 Talks Assistant, later Talks Producer, in the Indian section of the BBC's Eastern Service.

21 November 1941 First of over 200 newsletters written by Orwell for broadcast to India, Malaysia, and Indonesia, in English; and translated for broadcast in Gujarati, Marathi, Bengali, and Tamil.

8 March 1942 First contribution to *The Observer*.

15 May 1942 *Victory or Vested Interest?* published by George Routledge & Sons, containing Orwell's lecture, 'Culture and Democracy'.

Summer 1942 Moves to Maida Vale, London.

11 August 1942 'Voice 1,' first of six literary 'magazines' devised by Orwell for broadcast to India.

19 March 1943 His mother, Ida Blair, dies.

24 August 1943 'I am definitely leaving it [the BBC] probably in about three months' (letter to Rayner Heppenstall).

18 Nov 1943 *Talking to India* published by Allen & Unwin, edited and with an Introduction by Orwell.

23 Nov 1943 Leaves BBC and joins *Tribune* as Literary Editor. Leaves Home Guard on medical grounds.

Nov 1943–Feb 1944 Writes *Animal Farm*.

---

21 January 1950 Orwell dies of pulmonary tuberculosis, aged 46.

THE COMPLETE WORKS OF
GEORGE ORWELL · FIFTEEN

TWO WASTED YEARS

1916. Jack London: 'Landmarks in American Literature,' 5

Recorded 1 March 1943; broadcast 5 March 1943

This talk exists in two different versions. The version reproduced is that printed with Orwell's authority in 1946 (BBC Pamphlet No 3, Oxford University Press, Bombay). This more or less follows the text as broadcast; there are slight differences to take account of the difference in media, but as originally written the talk was too long for the time available. Even the cut version was slightly too long—14½ minutes at rehearsal—and additional cuts on the final page were necessary to get the time as broadcast down to 14' 8". The passages cut from the original version (so noted) or changed in the script as broadcast are given in the notes. Minor, consequential, changes are not noted. The surviving timings are given in italic within square brackets. A second typescript in the BBC Archive appears to be a fair copy of the broadcast as amended by Orwell; it does not offer new readings. The earlier typescript carries the two triangular stamps showing that Rushbrook Williams passed the script for Security and Policy.

There is an introduction to Orwell's talk. It has the appearance of being written hastily and amended in a hand other than Orwell's, and slightly by Orwell. Had Orwell written the introduction, he would hardly have failed to mention *Burmese Days* in the initial version when speaking to Indian students. The introduction was censored by Anthony Weymouth on 5 March, the date of the broadcast.

We are approaching the end of our survey of American literature, and as we get nearer our own time the landmarks are more difficult to distinguish. Who are the great American writers of the past fifty years? It is not an easy question to answer, especially if we exclude a novelist like Henry James, who lived most of his time in Europe and actually became a British citizen. But there are certain American writers whose names have gone round the world, and who therefore, apart from all questions of greatness, do possess a representative value. Such a writer is Jack London, whose books have been read by the million in all parts of the world, especially in Germany and Russia. Today, therefore George Orwell is going to talk to you about the significance of Jack London. There is no need for me to introduce George Orwell—he is the Talks Producer[1] in this programme and his voice is more familiar to you than mine. But apart from producing[2] these broadcasts, he is, as you probably know, the author of *The Road to Wigan Pier, Burmese Days,*[3] and several critical studies which show fine penetration and an independent judgment.

Today, therefore George Orwell is going to talk to you[4] about the significance of Jack London.[5]

Jack London, like Edgar Allan Poe, is one of those writers who have a bigger reputation outside the English-speaking world than inside it—but indeed, more so than Poe, who is at any rate taken seriously in England and America, whereas most people, if they remember Jack London at all, think of him as a writer of adventure stories not far removed from penny dreadfuls.

Now, I myself don't share the rather low opinion of Jack London which is held in this country and America, and I can claim to be in good company, for another admirer of Jack London's work was no less a person than Lenin, the central figure of the Russian Revolution. After Lenin's death his widow, Nadeshda Krupskaya, wrote a short biography of him, at the end of which she describes how she used to read stories to Lenin when he was paralysed and slowly dying. On the last day of all, she says, she began to read him Dickens's *Christmas Carol*, but she could see that he didn't like it; what she calls Dickens's 'bourgeois sentimentality' was too much for him. So she changed over to Jack London's story 'Love of Life', and that was almost the last thing that Lenin ever heard. Krupskaya adds that it is a very good story. It *is* a good story, but here[6] I want only to point to this rather queer conjunction between a writer of thrillers—stories about Pacific islands and the goldfields of the Klondike, and also about burglars, prizefighters and wild animals—and the greatest revolutionary of modern times. I don't know with certainty what [2'] first interested Lenin in Jack London's work, but I should expect that it was London's political or quasi-political writings. For London was among other things an ardent socialist and probably one of the first American writers to pay any attention to Karl Marx. His reputation in continental Europe is largely founded on that, and in particular on a rather remarkable book of political prophecy, *The Iron Heel*.[7] It is a curious fact that London's political writings have almost escaped attention in his own country and Britain. Ten or fifteen years ago, when *The Iron Heel* was widely read and admired in France and Germany, it was out of print and almost unobtainable in Britain, and even now, though an English edition of it exists, few people have heard of it.

This has several reasons, and one of them is that Jack London was an extremely prolific writer. He was one of those writers who make a point of producing a fixed amount every day—a thousand words in his case—and in his short life (he was born in 1876 and died in 1916) he produced an immense number of books, of very different types. If you examine Jack London's work as a whole, you find that there are three distinct strains in it, which don't at first sight appear to have any connexion with one another. The first is a rather silly one about which I don't want to say much, and that[8] is a worship of animals. This produced his best-known books, *White Fang* and *The Call of the Wild*. [3¾'] Sentimentality about animals is something almost peculiar to the English-speaking peoples, and it[9] isn't altogether an admirable trait. Many[10] thoughtful people in Britain and America are ashamed of it, and Jack London's short stories would probably[11] have received more critical attention if he hadn't also written *White Fang* and *The Call of the Wild*. The[12] next strain to notice in Jack London is his love of brutality and physical violence and, in general, what is known as 'adventure'. He is a sort of American version of Kipling, essentially an active, non-contemplative writer. By choice he wrote[13] about such people as goldminers, sea-captains, trappers and cowboys, and he wrote his best work [4½'] of all about tramps, burglars, prizefighters and the other riff- raff of great American cities. To this side of him belongs that story I've already mentioned, 'Love of Life', and I shall have more to say about it, because it produced nearly all of his work that is still worth reading. But on top of this there is also that other strain, his interest in sociology and in economic theory, which led him in *The Iron Heel* to make a very remarkable prophecy of the rise of Fascism.

Well, now let me return to 'Love of Life' and the other short stories which are Jack London's greatest achievement. He is essentially a short-story writer, and though he did produce one interesting novel, *The Valley of the Moon*, his especial gift is his power of describing isolated, brutal incidents. I use the word 'brutal' advisedly. The impression one brings away from Jack London's best and most characteristic stories is an impression of terrible cruelty. Not that Jack London himself was a cruel man or enjoyed the thought of pain—on the contrary he was even too much of a humanitarian, as his animal stories show—but his vision of life is a cruel one. He[14] sees the world as a place of suffering, a place of struggle against a blind, cruel destiny. That is why he likes writing about the frozen polar regions, where Nature is an enemy against which man has to fight for his life. The story[15] 'Love of Life' describes an incident which is typical of Jack London's peculiar vision. A gold-prospector who has missed the trail somewhere in the frozen wastes of Canada is struggling desperately towards the sea, slowly dying of starvation but kept going simply by the force of his will. A wolf, also dying [6½'] of hunger and disease, is creeping after the man, hoping that sooner or later he will grow weak enough for it to attack him. They go on and on, day after day, till when they come within sight of the sea each is crawling on his belly, too weak to stand up. But the man's will is the stronger, and the story[16] ends not by the wolf eating the man but the man eating the wolf. That is a typical Jack London incident, except that it has in some sense a happy ending. And if you analyse the subject-matter of any of his best stories you find the same kind of picture. The best story he ever wrote is called 'Just Meat'. It describes two burglars who have just got away with a big haul of jewellery. As soon as they get home with the swag it occurs to each of them that if he killed the other he would have the whole lot. As it happens they each poison one another at the same meal, and with the same poison—strychnine. They have a little mustard which might save one or other of them if used as an emetic; and the story ends with the two men writhing in agonies on the floor and feebly struggling with one another for the last cup of mustard. Another very good story describes the execution of a Chinese convict in one of the French islands in the Pacific. He is to be executed for a murder committed in the prison. It happens that the prison governor, by a slip of the pen, has written down the wrong name, and consequently it is the wrong prisoner who is taken out of his cell. His guards do not discover this till they have got him to the place of execution, which is twenty miles from the prison. The guards are uncertain what to do, but it hardly seems worth the trouble of going all the way back, so they solve the question by guillotining the wrong man. [8½'] I[17] could give further instances, but all I am anxious to establish is that Jack London's most characteristic work always deals with cruelty and disaster: Nature and Destiny are inherently evil things against which man has to struggle with nothing to back him up except his own courage and strength.

Now it is against this background that Jack London's political and sociological writings have to be seen. As I have said, Jack London's reputation in Europe depends on *The Iron Heel*, in which—in the year 1910 or thereabouts—he foretold the rise of fascism. It's no use pretending that *The Iron Heel* is a good book, as a book. It's a very poor book, much below Jack London's average, and the developments it foretells aren't even particularly close to what has actually happened in Europe. But Jack London did foresee one thing which socialists[18] of nearly all schools had astonishingly failed to foresee, and that was that when the working-class movements took on formidable dimensions and looked like dominating the world, the capitalist class *would hit back*. They wouldn't simply lie down and let themselves be expropriated, as so many socialists had imagined. Karl Marx, indeed, had never suggested that the change-over from Capitalism to Socialism would happen without a struggle, but he did proclaim that this change was *inevitable*, which his followers, in most cases, took as meaning that it would be *automatic*. Till Hitler was firmly in the saddle it was generally [10¼'] taken for granted that Capitalism could not defend itself, because of what are generally called its internal contradictions.

Most[19] socialists not only did not foresee the rise of fascism but did not even grasp that Hitler was dangerous till he had been about two years in power. Now Jack London would not have made[20] this mistake. In his book he describes the growth of powerful working-class movements, and then the boss class organizing itself, hitting back, winning the victory and proceeding to set up an atrocious despotism, with the institution of actual slavery, which lasts for hundreds of years. Who now will dare to say that something like this hasn't happened over great areas of the world, and may not continue to happen unless the Axis is defeated? There is more in *The Iron Heel* than this. In particular there is Jack London's perception that hedonistic societies cannot endure, a perception which isn't common among what are called progressive thinkers. Outside Soviet Russia left-wing thought has generally been hedonistic, and the weaknesses of the Socialist Movement spring partly from this. But Jack London's main achievement was to foresee, some twenty years before the event, that the menaced capitalist class would counter-attack and not quietly die because the writers of Marxist textbooks told it to die.[21]

Why could a mere story-teller like Jack London foresee this when so many learned sociologists could not? I think I have answered that question in what I said just now about the subject-matter of Jack London's stories. He could foresee the rise of fascism, and the cruel struggles which would have to be gone through, because of the streak of brutality which he had in himself. If you like to exaggerate a little, you might say that he could understand fascism because he had a fascist strain himself. Unlike the ordinary run of Marxist thinkers, who had neatly worked it out on paper that the capitalist class was bound to die of its own contradictions, he knew that the capitalist class was tough and would hit back; he knew that because he himself was tough. That is why the subject-matter of Jack London's stories is relevant to his political theories. The best of them deal with prison, the prize-ring, the sea and the frozen wastes of Canada—that is, with situations where toughness is everything. That is an unusual background for a socialist writer. Socialist thought has suffered greatly from having grown up almost entirely in urban industrialized societies and leaving some of the more primitive sides of human nature out of account.[22] It was Jack London's understanding of the primitive that made him a better prophet than many better-informed and more logical thinkers.

I haven't time to speak at length about Jack London's other political and sociological writings, some of which are better, as books, than *The Iron Heel*. I will only shortly mention *The Road*, his reminiscences of the time when he was a tramp in America, one of the best books of its kind ever written, and *The People of the Abyss*, which deals with the London slums—its facts are out of date now, but various later books[23] of the same kind were inspired by it. There is also *The Jacket*, which is a book of stories but contains at the beginning a remarkable description of life in an American prison. But it is as a story-writer that Jack London best deserves to be remembered, and if you can get hold of a copy I earnestly beg you to read the collection of short stories published under the title *When God Laughs*. The best of Jack London is there, and from some half-dozen of those stories you can get an adequate idea of this gifted writer who has been, in a way, so popular and influential but has never in my opinion had the literary reputation that was due to him. [14½']

1. Producer] Director
2. producing] directing
3. *Burmese Days*] *Homage to Catalonia*
4. you] us
5. This announcement is preceded in the typescript by an alternative cue-line: 'Here is George Orwell. . . .' Either may have been used, but the alteration of 'us' to 'you' in the second one suggests that the first and shorter cue-line was not used.
6. story, but here] story, and you will hear a passage from it read presently by Herbert Read. Here *in broadcast*
7. Reviewed by Orwell in *Tribune*, 12 July 1940; see *655*.
8. a rather silly one about which I don't want to say much, and that] something which seems almost too silly to mention, but which has its importance and is the best-known side of his work in the English-speaking countries. This
9. This produced . . . English-speaking peoples, and it] Jack London wrote quite a number of those books which I believe are almost peculiar to the English-speaking civilization, in which the hero is an animal—usually a dog—an animal which thinks and talks and is credited with the feelings of a human being. The best known are "White Fang" and "The Call of the Wild", though there are a number of others. Naturally these books, each of which is a sort of biography of a dog, usually a sledge-dog in the wilds of Alaska, make first-rate children's books, but they have been much read by grown-up people as well, and their existence has done something towards securing Jack London a big public and at the same time towards

damaging his reputation as a serious writer. This animal cult which is so common in the English-speaking countries—the tendency to be sentimental about animals and to pity their sufferings more than those of human beings *in uncut script*

10. trait. Many] trait and many *in uncut script*
11. it, and Jack London's short stories would probably] it. Jack London's short stories and books like "The Road" and "The People of the Abyss", would, *in uncut script*
12. *Wild*. The] Wild". But it is important to note that Jack London did have this boyish, animal-worshipping side to him, co-existing with two other strains which are very different. The *in uncut script*
13. writer. By choice he wrote] writer. In so far as one can father this kind of thing on to any one writer, one might say that Jack London was the originator of the American cult of the "he-man", the cult of violence and masculinity which you get in a vulgarised form in every American magazine and which reappears in a more sophisticated form in writers like Hemingway. By choice Jack London wrote *in uncut script*
14. He] Like the great French novelist, Emile Zola, he *in uncut script*
15. story] short story *in uncut script*
16. the story] it
17. man. I] man. Another, rather touching, story called "A Piece of Steak" describes an old superannuated prizefighter, who has been weakened by underfeeding, fighting a hopeless battle against a man much younger than himself. I *in uncut script*
18. The script, here and elsewhere, has an initial capital 'S.'
19. contradictions. // Most] contradictions. Even Lenin wrote off as impossible the idea that the whole capitalist class might organise itself into a vast corporation, sinking its differences in order to fight against the working class—which in fact is what has happened in Germany. Most *in uncut script, with no paragraph break*
20. would not have made] did not make
21. die because the writers of Marxist textbooks told it to die] die of something called "historic necessity"
22. human nature out of account] human nature—for instance the hunting instinct—out of account *in uncut script*
23. Presumably a reference to Orwell's indebtedness in writing *Down and Out in Paris and London*.

1917. To Norman Collins, Empire Talks Manager

1 March 1943   Original: typewritten and annotated   EB/WMB

APPROACHING EMINENT SPEAKERS

We propose approaching Lord Woolton[1] for an interview on the subject of FOOD RATIONING AND CONTROL, to be broadcast both in English and in Hindustani. The Hindustani version will merely be a reporter's account of the interview with Lord Woolton but in the English version we hope to include a recording of 2/3 minutes of Lord Woolton's own voice, if he will consent to it then.

The English broadcast would go out on Saturday, March 6th, at 1115–1130 GMT.

[Signed] Eric Blair
(Eric Blair)

P.S. [handwritten] Lord Woolton probably will not be interviewed personally but the Min. of Food will hand out his stuff & he is willing to do the 3-minute b'cast.

E.A.B

1. Frederick James Marquis (1889–1976; Baron, 1939; Viscount, 1953; Earl, 1956), a department-store executive, became a household name as Lord Woolton when Minister of Food, 1940–43. Later he was a member of the War Cabinet and Minister of Reconstruction, 1943–45; Lord President of the Council, 1945, 1951–52; Chancellor of the Duchy of Lancaster (with a seat in the Cabinet), 1952–55. As Minister of Food, he won praise and respect for his efficiency and fairness, and for making the unpalatable palatable.

1918. To H. D. Graves-Law

1 March 1943   07/ES/EB

Dear Mr. Graves-Law
I am sorry not to have replied earlier to your letter of February 17th but I have been rather busy. The passage you objected to has been completely excised from Mr. Ardaschir's script.[1] I will see to it that he does not use your name as an authority.

Your sincerely
[Initialled] EAB
Eric Blair
Talks Producer
Indian Section

1. See letter to Graves-Law, 16 February 1943, *1888, n. 2.*

1919. BBC Talks Booking Form, 1.3.43

Bahadur Singh: 'In the Public Eye,' 11; broadcast 3.3.43; fee £3.3s + 13s 2d fare. Signed: M Blackburn for I.P.O.

1920. BBC Talks Booking Form, 1.3.43

Catherine Lacey: 'Women Generally Speaking'; producer Eric Blair; broadcast 10.3.43; fee £8.8s + repeat fees. Signed: S.F.A. for Programme Contracts Department.

1921. BBC Talks Booking Form, 1.3.43

Lester Powell: talk on the Indian Red Cross; broadcast 11.3.43; fee £10.10s. Signed: M Blackburn for I.P.O.

1922. Talk to Oxford University English Club

2 March 1943

The Oxford Magazine for 25 February 1943 announced that George Orwell would speak to the Oxford University English Club at 8.15 P.M. on 2 March 1943. No further details have been traced.

1923. To R. R. Desai

3 March 1943   07/ES/EB

Dear Desai

The Indian Government have cabled asking us to do something in Gujerati° about the Beveridge report so we shall have to use your Gujerati° period on Monday next for this. They evidently want to have the whole story, i.e. what the scheme proposes and also the history of the Parliamentary Debate. I need not tell you that the censorship would not allow through any comment, i.e. any comment on our part which amounted to a criticism of the Government for watering the Beveridge scheme down. On the other hand, the debate on the subject with the arguments brought forward for and against the report could be given, objectively. I should suggest simply setting out the provisions of the report, not going into too much detail, but emphasizing the more important clauses, especially family allowances, then mention the debate and then explain how much of the report the Government actually proposes to adopt. You can say, with safety, that whatever else goes out, family allowances on some scale or another are certain to be adopted. And it would be worth adding that this itself is an important advance and likely to raise the British birth-rate. However, they evidently want an objective report on the Beveridge scheme rather than a propaganda statement. You can use the whole of your period on Beveridge or use about ten minutes and reserve about three minutes for the headline news of the week, just as you wish. I hope you will let us have your script in good time. We have already cabled our people in India that we're going to deal with Beveridge this week.

Yours
Eric Blair
Talks Producer
Indian Section.

P.S. If I could have this particular script on Saturday I shall be much obliged.

1924. BBC Talks Booking Form, 3.3.43

Herbert Read: 'Landmarks in American Literature,' 5; '5 min. reading of extract from one of Jack London's books, following the recorded talk by George Orwell on this author. George Orwell is Staff (Eric Blair)'; broadcast 5.3.43; fee £5.5s.

Signed: M Blackburn for I.P.O. Remarks: 'Mr. Read will read the extract only
— it has been chosen by Mr. Blair.'

1925. BBC Talks Booking Form, 3.3.43

J. Chinna Durai: ex-gratia payment, 'see attached PRIVATE AND CONFIDENTIAL
correspondence on this subject. Return the correspondence to E.S.D. Room
314, after you have seen it'; fee £10.10s; 'no contract.' Signed: M Blackburn.[1]

1. This form was marked as from the Indian Programme Organiser's Office but was initiated by
   Rushbrook Williams. He wrote to Durai on 2 March telling him that the Contracts
   Department would be getting in touch with him following his agreement to accept ten
   guineas in settlement of his claim (and see *1889*). On the carbon of this letter, Williams
   instructed Bokhari's secretary, Mary Blackburn, to make the appropriate arrangements with
   the Contracts Department. The form has typed at its head, 'THIS IS URGENT.'

1926. To L. F. Rushbrook Williams

4 March 1943   Original; typewritten and annotated   MB/EB

We are hoping that Lord Woolton will consent to record a short three to
five-minute talk (in English) on Saturday, 6th March, and we have therefore
booked Studio 2 at Oxford Street for this purpose from 10.00 a.m. to 10.45
a.m. BST., as this was the time mentioned to Princess Indira when she met
the Public Relations Officer at the Ministry of Food the other day.[1]

Princess Indira will then build a Food Talk around Lord Woolton's
recording and on her visit to the Ministry of Food, for broadcast to India on
Saturday, 6th March, from 1115–1130 GMT.

[Signed] Eric Blair

[Handwritten] I have now had a talk with Robert Westerby[2] who tells me
that Lord Woolton hopes to record his b'cast on his way to the office on
Saturday, & therefore might be here any time after 10 am. I will try
tomorrow to get a more accurate time, but I suppose we should expect him as
from 10 am onwards.

Eric Blair   4.3.43

1. This meant that the regular Newsletter to India could not be broadcast on 6 March.
2. Public Relations Officer, Ministry of Food.

1927. To Norman Collins

4 March 1943   Original; EB/WMB

APPROACHING EMINENT SPEAKERS

With reference to the proposed approach to Bernard Shaw. We want him to do talk No. 4 in our series GREAT DRAMATISTS which will happen every other week starting in Week 11. These programmes, which might be extended beyond the initial six, if they appear successful, will in each case be made up as follows:—

Ten minutes talk on the chosen dramatist by an acknowledged expert, ten minutes from one of his plays acted by the B.B.C. Repertory and about 8 minutes music. It would obviously be a great scoop to get Bernard Shaw for IBSEN as he is the only survivor of the small group of critics who first introduced IBSEN to the British public. His chances of making undesirable remarks are not very great in a programme of this type in which he will be tied down pretty closely to a given subject of a mainly literary nature. In any case it should be possible to record his talk a good time before the broadcast which would be in Week 17.[1]

[Signed] Eric Blair
(Eric Blair)

1. On 5 March 1943, Collins sent a memorandum to G. F. Barnes, Director of Talks, Home Service, saying that Orwell was considering approaching Shaw and requesting clearance. The memorandum is annotated: 'we have nothing out to G.B.S.'; 'ETM's secretary informed on telephone 9/3   JW'; and 'GBS. has turned down Close-Up: "Getting past that sort of thing".' Weymouth was asked about a John Burns Obit.' Collins wrote to Shaw on 23 March asking him to speak on Ibsen in Orwell's series, but the letter was not sent. It is annotated 'Mr Foot [the Director General] doesn't think the occasion warrants writing to Mr Shaw.' That marks the end of this attempt to have Shaw speak in an Eastern Service Programme.

1928. New Marathi General Assistant

On 4th March 1943, Mrs. M. I. Hunt, one of two assistants in the Headquarters and Liaison Department of the Overseas Services Division, wrote to the Overseas Services Establishment Officer outlining the case for the appointment of a new Marathi assistant and suggesting that Venu Chitale be given this responsibility. Her memorandum continued:

'In addition, however, to the expansion in the Green Network a daily quarter-hour in the Red between 15.15 and 15.30 has been added and will be the responsibility of Mr. Blair, with Miss Chitale's assistance. Thus, she will have a full time post immediately and as she has to devote herself more to Marathi in the future so she will drop her English programmes with Mr. Blair. In fact from now on she will not have time to work at all on Hindustani programmes and this will have to be handed over as soon as possible to one of the candidates brought over from India by Mr. Bokhari.

'E.S.D. has very definite reasons for wanting Miss Chitale to remain on the Staff now that he knows the Sahni's° are leaving. After their departure for India the only Hindu representative will be Mr. Bakaya, and as E.S.D. points out it is important to keep the balance between Hindus and Muslims. He also explains that there is great value in keeping an Indian woman on the Staff. Permission is, therefore, asked for the creation of the new Marathi post before the 28th March and the transfer to it of Miss Chitale, subject, of course, to her good report at the end of the month. Her present post (OS.1031) will thus be left vacant for Mr. Pant who is the Hindu candidate suggested by Mr. Bokhari for the appointment in connection with Hindustani programmes.'

On 18 March 1943, Sir Guy Williams, Overseas Establishment Officer, wrote to the Secretary, Establishment Control, recommending the appointment of such an assistant with a view to establishing a daily Marathi service. He concluded:

'Until the daily Marathi service is available the Assistant will be employed as follows:
- (a) Working up the Marathi in preparation for the expanded schedule
- (b) The principal work in connection with an additional 15 minute period in the Red Network
- (c) Maintaining the Hindu Balance in the main Hindustani programme output.'

1929. To Bonamy Dobrée

4 March 1943   07/ES/EB

Dear Dobrée

Thank you for your letter of March 1st.

I am sorry you cannot do the talk for us[1] but perhaps you will be able to do another talk in the same series later on.

The suggestion you make[2] about the talks for the Home Service sounds promising but of course I have nothing to do with the Home Service. The person I would write to is Mr. Salmon, Home Talks Department.

Yours sincerely
[Initialled] E.A.B
George Orwell
Talks Producer
Indian Section

1. Dobrée could not get away because of his Senior Training Corps duties at camp.
2. For a talk on 'The Progress of Philosophic Thought.'

1930. To T. S. Eliot

4 March 1943   07/ES/EB

Dear Eliot

Thanks for your letter. I was very sorry to hear you were ill and as soon as I heard this from your Secretary I abandoned the idea of your doing the first talk, which would have given you very little notice.

I wonder whether you would, by any chance, care to do the second in the series, which is two weeks later, that is to say, on Thursday, April 1st, at the same time. This talk is on DRYDEN, the play being the INDIAN EMPRESS,[1] and the plan of the programme would be the same as I gave you. You might let me know whether you could do this, as otherwise I must approach someone else. I am hoping to get George Sampson[2] to do the one on MARLOWE

I quite agree about the stuff in the LISTENER and I will try and get this regulated for the future. In theory the BBC. holds the copyright of all broadcast material for 28 days after transmission but I have no doubt we could come to an agreement with them.

Yours sincerely
[Initialled] E.A.B
George Orwell
Talks Producer
Indian Section

1. Orwell confused *The Indian Emperor* and *The Indian Queen*; see his letter to Eliot, 15 March 1943, *1953*. Dryden was sole author of the former (1655) but collaborated with Sir Robert Howard on the latter (1664).
2. George Sampson (1873–1950), author, editor, and reviewer, was an inspector of London County Council schools. A biographical note in the BBC pamphlet *Books and Authors*, 1946, described him as 'the author of *The Concise Cambridge History of English Literature*, and of many other works of literary criticism. He has also edited the works of Coleridge, Berkeley, George Herbert and many other writers, ancient and modern. He is a member of the Departmental Committee on the Teaching of English in England.'

1931. BBC Talks Booking Form, 4.3.43

Tom Driberg, MP:[1] 'The Debate Continues,' 'The Work of the Army Bureau of Current Affairs (ABCA)'; 6-minute talk; broadcast 8.3.43; fee £5.5s. Signed: M Blackburn for I.P.O. Against his address at the *Daily Express* is the note, 'Envelope should be marked PRIVATE & CONFIDENTIAL.'

1. Tom Driberg (1905–1976), journalist, lecturer, broadcaster, was on the editorial staff of the *Daily Express*, 1928–43 (gossip columnist 'William Hickey' from 1930); war correspondent, 1939–45 and Korean war; Independent M.P., 1942 and Labour M.P., 1945. It has been claimed that he was for many years an agent of both MI5 and the KGB. Among books written by him was *Guy Burgess: A Portrait with Background* (1956). He flaunted his homosexuality and, at a time when this was illegal, he escaped some close brushes with the law. See Francis Wheen, *Tom Driberg: His Life and Indiscretions* (1990).

1932. News Commentary in English for Malaya, 23
5 March 1943

This was written and read by George Orwell. No script has been traced.

1933. To A. Morley, India Office

5 March 1943   ES/EB

Dear Mr. Morley

I enclose a copy of the script which Lord Woolton is proposing to record for the Indian Section tomorrow, Saturday, 6th March at 10.30 a.m. BST. Would you kindly look at this script and let me know that it meets with your approval for broadcast in English to India.

We intend to transmit the recording made by Lord Woolton on Saturday the 6th March at 1115–1130 GMT (within this programme period). It will be incorporated into a talk to be broadcast by Princess Indira of Kapurthala.

Yours very truly,
[Signed] Eric Blair
Eric Blair
Talks Producer

1934. To Talks Booking Manager

5 March 1943   Original   MB/EB

RECORDING OF SHORT TALK BY LORD WOOLTON, Minister of Food

We have just received written notification from the Public Relations Officer of the M. of F. saying that Lord Woolton has kindly consented to do a short recorded talk for broadcast in the Eastern Service (Red Network) on Saturday, 6th March, within the period 1115–1130 GMT. Lord Woolton will record this talk at 200 O.S. in Studio 2. on Saturday, 6th March (tomorrow) at 10.30 a.m. BST.

Would you kindly arrange for the usual and suitable acknowledgement to be made to Lord Woolton for his kindness.[1]

[Signed] Eric Blair

1. This memorandum is annotated 'No fee letter not exclusive.' This implies that Lord Woolton took no fee but, as a letter to his secretary from the Programme Contracts Director of 8 March indicates, the BBC was anxious to retain broadcasting, recording, and translation rights for twenty-eight days after the broadcast and publication rights within the UK for the same period and elsewhere for six months after the broadcast.

1935. To L. F. Rushbrook Williams

5 March 1943   Original   MB/EB

RECORDED TALK BY LORD WOOLTON

We have now been informed definitely to expect Lord Woolton at 200 Oxford Street at 10.30 a.m. BST on Saturday, 6th March, when he will record a short talk. Studio OS.2 has been booked for this recording.

Princess Indira is preparing a script around this recording by Lord Woolton and based on her visit to the Ministry of Food. Her live talk and the recording made by Lord Woolton will be broadcast in the Eastern Service (Red Network) on Saturday, 6th March, from 1115–1130 GMT, in place of the usual News Review.

We are trying to find out if Lord Woolton will consent to be photographed with Princess Indira and a member of the Indian Section staff in the Studio after the recording is completed.

[Signed] Eric Blair

1936. To Philip Unwin

5 March 1943   07/ES/EB/WMB

On 4 March 1943, the publishers George Allen & Unwin wrote to Orwell at the BBC sending details of a new book by Mark Benney[1] on his work in an aircraft factory, *Over to Bombers*, to be published on 16 March. Orwell was asked if he would 'care to have a personal copy of it with a view to making some reference to it publicly.'

Dear Mr. Unwin
I fancy that Benney's book is of the kind that E. M. Forster would like to publicise in his monthly Book talk to India, so if you will send me a copy I will see that it is brought to his notice.

Yours sincerely
[Signed] Geo. Orwell
George Orwell
Talks Producer
Indian Section

1. Mark Benney (Henry Ernest Degras, 1910–) achieved immediate recognition for *Low Company: Describing the Evolution of a Burglar* (1936), written in prison. His *Over to Bombers* was a fictional account of the transformation of a luxury-car factory to the manufacture of airplanes. After the war he migrated to the United States and taught social science. Orwell reviewed his *The Big Wheel*, in *Tribune*, 23 August 1940 (see 676), and his *Charity Main* in *The Observer*, 10 March 1946; see 2925.

1937. Newsletter to India Replaced

6 March 1943

No newsletter was broadcast to India on 6 March 1943. PasB for 6 March notes, 'Special Talk on Food Situation by Princess Indira of Kapurthala, 8' 45", including 3-min rec; talk by Lord Woolton, rec DOX 11944, rec 6.3.43, 4' 13".' See Orwell's memorandum to Rushbrook Williams, 4 March 1943, *1926*.

1938. To the Editor, *The Times Literary Supplement*
6 March 1943

Orwell reviewed *The Development of William Butler Yeats* by V. K. Narayana Menon in *Horizon*, January 1943; see *1791*. His review was discussed by Charles Morgan in his column 'Menander's Mirror,' in *The Times Literary Supplement*, 20 February 1943. Orwell responded on 6 March 1943. His letter is printed in the sequence following his review; see *1791*.

1939. To K. K. Ardaschir
8 March 1943   07/ES/EB/WMB

Dear Mr. Ardaschir
This is just to remind you about your broadcast on Friday, March 12th, at 12.45 (British Summer Time). Will you please be here about 11.45 for rehearsal.

Mr. Blair has asked me to return the attached script to you, as he regrets he is unable to make use of it.

> Yours sincerely
> [Initialled] W B
> (For Eric Blair)
> Talks Producer
> Indian Section

1940. To Lester Powell
8 March 1943   07/ES/EB/WMB

Dear Lester
Thank you very much for your script. I am sending you back a copy and you will notice there are one or two minor alterations.

Would you please be here at about 11.30 on Thursday morning for a rehearsal.

> Yours sincerely
> [Initialled] G. O.
> George Orwell
> Talks Producer
> Indian Section

1941. To Arthur Wynn, Music Bookings Manager

8 March 1943   Original   EB/WMB

Contract for Dr Narayana Menon

Referring to our memo. of the 24th February, will you kindly arrange a contract and payment for Dr. Menon for planning and choosing a 15 minute programme of gramophone records.[1] This will be broadcast on Thursday, March 25th, at 1130–1145 GMT, in the Eastern Service (Red Network).

Dr. Menon's address is 176 Sussex Gardens, W.2.

[Signed] Eric Blair

P.S. This is a fortnightly programme and we will send you another memo. for the next programme, as you mentioned that it would be better to issue the contracts for each broadcast.

1. This series is to be distinguished from that of six eight-minute programmes starting on 18 March 1943, for which Menon was paid £2.2s per broadcast; see *1961*. The proposed fee for this fifteen-minute series was £3.3s; see *1966*.

1942. [To Penguin Books][1]

8 March 1943   Typewritten; original   EEF/SGO

10a Mortimer Crescent
London   NW 6

Dear Sir,

With reference to your letter dated 5.3.43. I am not absolutely certain without looking up my contracts how I stand about the rights in my books, but I am *almost* certain that if the publisher has issued no cheap edition two years after publication, the rights revert to me. I can verify this, but in any case neither of my publishers is likely to make trouble about the republication of books which appeared some time ago. The books of mine which might be worth reprinting are (I give date of publication with each):—

"Burmese Days" (1934–1935).
"Homage to Catalonia" (1938)
"Coming Up for Air" (1939)
"Inside the Whale" (1940).

I should say "Burmese Days" was much the most hopeful. It was first published by Harper's in the USA, then a year later in a slightly bowdlerised edition by Gollancz. The English edition sold 3000 to 4000, the American about 1000.[2] I think it deserves reprinting, and it has a certain topicality owing to the campaign in Burma. Gollancz's stock of it has come to an end and it is totally out of print, but I possess a copy of the American edition. "Inside the Whale" is also totally out of print, the stocks of it having been blitzed, but I have a proof copy. It didn't sell much but got a certain notoriety owing to parts of it being reprinted in magazines. "Homage to Catalonia" I think ought [to] be reprinted some time, but I don't know whether the present is quite the moment. It is about the Spanish civil war, and people probably don't want that dragged up now. On the other hand if Spain comes into the war I suppose it would be for a while possible to sell anything which seemed informative about Spanish internal affairs, if one could get it through the press in time.

I shall be happy to give you any further information you want.

Yours faithfully
[Signed] George Orwell

1. This letter, written on BBC letterhead, has no addressee. It can be assumed it is to Penguin Books from that of 11 March 1943; see *1949*.
2. In the light of Orwell's later bitterness over the way Gollancz had 'garbled' *Burmese Days* (see *CW*, II, Textual Note, 310), his comment that it was 'slightly bowdlerised' is surprising. In his letter to Leonard Moore on 22 February 1935 (see *238*), he had said that Gollancz required 'a few trifling alterations.' The U.S. edition sold better than Orwell remembered. It was, in fact, reprinted. The first printing, I-1, was of 2,000 copies, published 25 October 1934. A second impression, marked K-1, was probably issued on 11 December 1934, but the number of copies is not known; 976 copies were remaindered. It seems unlikely that a second printing of only 1,000 copies would have been made if all were to be remaindered, so the second printing may have been 1,500 or 2,000 copies, which would give total sales of the U.S. edition of some 2,500 to 3,000 copies. The Penguin edition was published in May 1944.

1943. BBC Talks Booking Form, 8.3.43

Princess Indira of Kapurthala: 'The Debate Continues'; one form is for Mondays, 8, 15, and 22.2.43 and 1.3.43; another for 15, 22, and 29.3.43; 'Usual fee' was typed on each, then crossed out by Miss Blackburn, who wrote: '£10–10–0. Suggest this is checked with P[rogramme] C[ontracts] D[epartment],' and '12 gns' (£12.12s). [From the entries made by the Talks Booking Manager, Princess Indira was paid £12.12s for 8 March and £10.10s for the others.] Forms signed: M Blackburn for I.P.O.

1944. BBC Talks Booking Form, 8.3.43

Bahadur Singh: 'In the Public Eye,' 12 (last), M. Maisky;[1] broadcast 10.3.43; fee £6.6s + 13s 2d fare. Signed: M Blackburn for I.P.O.

1. Ivan Maisky (1884–1975), Soviet Ambassador to Britain, 1932–43, and Assistant People's Commissar for Foreign Affairs, 1943–46, had negotiated and signed the Non-Aggression Treaty with Finland, 1932, and other pacts. Among his publications were *Before the Storm* (1944), *Spain (1808–1917)* (1957), *Reminiscences of a Soviet Ambassador in Britain* (1960), and *Spanish Notebooks* (1962).

1945. To B. H. Alexander, Copyright Department

10 March 1943   EB/WMB

<u>BBC extracts from original memoranda</u>

Contract for Mr. Narayana Menon—INDIAN PLAY

Mr. Narayana Menon was responsible for making a radio version of INDIAN PLAY (No. 3) THE VISION OF VASAVADATTA (from the Sanscrit). This was broadcast on Tuesday, March 9th at 1145–1200 GMT, in the Eastern Service (Red Network). Mr. Menon used the English translation of this play by A. C. Woolner (Oxford University Press 1930), but he did adapt it freely and suitably into a radio drama of 13½ minutes duration. Will you please therefore issue a contract for him for this work. His address is 176 Sussex Gardens, W.2.

This also applies to the INDIAN PLAY (No. 2) MROCCHAKATIKA—THE LITTLE CLAY CART which was also freely adapted for radio by Mr. Menon. Duration 13½ minutes. In this case he used Professor Ryder's translation of the Sanscrit play. THE LITTLE CLAY CART was broadcast on Tuesday, February 9th, at 1145–1200 GMT in the Eastern Service (Red Network).

Sgd. W. BEDWELL for Eric Blair

Miss Alexander replied on 22 March:

With reference to your memo of the 10th March, I have now obtained from the Oxford University Press retrospective authority for the use of A. C. Woolner's translation of the play "The Vision of Vasavadatta".

I should like to emphasise once again that it is essential that I should be notified in advance of the use of copyright material in this way. On the last occasion when the Indian Service used one of their translations, the O.U.P. took strong exception to our failure to obtain permission in advance and I had every expectation that they would take an even stronger line on this occasion. Fortunately, permission has been forthcoming with nothing more than a mild protest, but we really cannot afford to run the risk of antagonising publishers in this way, and I shall be very glad if in future you will be sure to notify me in advance when you are making either direct or indirect use of published material.

Sgd. H. A.

1946. To the Sirdar Ikbal Ali Shah

10 March 1943   07/ES/EB/WMB

Dear Sirdar

Thanks for your letter dated March 8th. I wonder whether you would like to do a talk on THE KORAN on Friday, March 26th. Some time ago we did a series of talks which had some success in India, called BOOKS THAT CHANGED THE

WORLD. These talks dealt with European books, from about Seventeen Hundred onwards, which could be considered to have had a direct effect on history. We now want to follow them up with a series on Oriental books, particularly religious books. You will see, therefore, that I would want your talk to be not so much a scholarly thesis on the KORAN as a talk on its social and political influence through the expansion of Islam.

This would be of 13½ minutes duration that is to say, about 1600 words, and would be delivered at 12.45 to 1 pm. (British Summer Time). I should like, if possible, to have the script in a week beforehand.

If you want any further guidance I am at your disposal any time you care to ring me up.

Yours sincerely
[Signed] Eric Blair
Talks Producer
Indian Section

1947. To J. B. Clark, Controller, Overseas Services
11 March 1943

ORIGINS OF LITERARY TALKS REPRINTED IN *THE LISTENER*

On 26 February 1943, L. F. Rushbrook Williams, Eastern Service Director, asked Sir Richard Maconachie, Controller, if Eastern Service talks reprinted in *The Listener* might be attributed to Eastern Service rather than 'the generic term of Overseas Services.' Maconachie asked R. Rendall, Assistant Controller, who thought such requests 'should be routed through "divisional" channels,' and that only articles that would strike a reader as 'odd' should be so designated—and such articles were seldom reprinted. Rushbrook Williams then explained that articles on English literature intended for Indian listeners did have a different character than they would if they were addressed to English audiences.

On 9 March, Clark gave his opinion: 'With reference to E.S.D.'s memo of 26/2 and subsequent minutes attached, I don't think on balance there is any strong reason for attributing these talks to the Eastern Service instead of to Overseas Services unless in the Editor's opinion the former would have real value from the point of view of readers. Unless, therefore, the Editor wishes to make the change I think the past practice should continue—at least for the present.'

Rushbrook Williams forwarded this to Orwell, with the annotation 'We haven't got any change out of them here!' Orwell added 'Noted' and his initials, and sent a fully-argued case for such ascriptions to Clark through Rushbrook Williams on 11 March 1943:

I have been in communication with the Editor of The Listener about the designation of Service printed at the end of contributions. He referred me to you.

The position is that various speakers in the Indian Section of the Eastern Service are beginning to complain about their talks being reprinted without any indication that this talk was specially directed to India. Previously, 'Indian Service' used to be printed at the end of any such contribution, but in recent months, this has been changed to 'Overseas', making no differentiation between our stuff and that of the African and North American Services. The Editor tells me that this cannot be changed without your authorisation.

Our speakers complain, I think justly, that when they do a talk for India they do not do it in the same manner as they would to, for instance, America because, especially in literary talks, the same degree of knowledge cannot be assumed in the Indian listener. The trouble came to a head over a talk by T. S. Eliot on "Edgar Allen° Poe". Eliot could not, of course, necessarily assume that the average Indian student would even have heard of Poe. He therefore had to go on record in The Listener as putting out some very elementary remarks about Poe which the reader would quite likely imagine to have been directed at America. He now tells me that if his contributions continue to be printed without indication of the audience they are addressed to, he may have to stop broadcasting. This would be a serious loss to our own and other Services, and a much more serious loss would be E. M. Forster, who is also beginning to complain on the same score. I should be very much obliged if it were thought possible to revert to the old practice of indicating the Service at the end of a reprinted talk. Failing this, it might be possible to arrange that these speakers' talks shall not be printed without their consent, but this would involve drawing up a kind of Contract which so far as I know, is quite unprecedented.

[Signed] Eric Blair 11.3.43

Rushbrook Williams sent the following comment on Orwell's memorandum to Clark and to Rendall: 'In view of C.(O.S.)'s decision conveyed to me in his memorandum of 9th March, the circumstances—now for the first time fully set forth in Mr. Eric Blair's memorandum which I annexe—seem a little awkward. I suggest it is hardly worth while getting on the wrong side of people like T. S. Eliot and E. M. Forster on a small point like this. If their objection is as strong as Mr. Blair believes, and if C.(O.S.) still decides that it is impossible to make the exact ascription which they desire, the only way out that I can see is to ask the Editor of "The Listener" not to reprint their talks.'

Rendall thought it not unreasonable to agree to the original proposal but 'it's a pity we had not the full facts at the start.' Clark wrote to the Controller of the Home Service, 'I fear we have been misled owing to non-statement of the case which gave rise to the first request. I offer my apology for the oversight.' He thought that, though there was a point made by Eliot and Forster, 'it is slightly exaggerated in Blair's minute.' He then outlined a proposal which evidently the Controller of the Home Service and the Editor of *The Listener* found acceptable, for it was set out in the following memorandum from Clark to Rendall and Rushbrook Williams on 20 March 1943:

'With reference to Blair's memo of March 11th, the Editor of the Listener has agreed when necessary to ascribe the special talks mentioned to "Eastern Services" provided that we on our side make it clear in *each* case what is required. The onus is therefore on us to keep the thing straight and I should be glad if accordingly you would arrange for the Listener copies of literary talks given by T. S. Eliot, E. M. Forster and others in precisely similar cases to be endorsed "to be acknowledged to Eastern Services if published". As I have indicated in earlier minutes, I am anxious that this endorsement should not automatically go on all

Eastern Service talks scripts, but only on those for which Blair made a special case in his memo of March 11th. It is unfortunate that some effort was wasted in the earlier stages of this business owing to an incomplete statement of the request being put forward in the first instance.'

Rushbrook Williams sent this on to Orwell with the annotation, 'You will now be able to console Eliot and Forster! I shd like you to assume responsibility for seeing that C(OS)'s distinction at A is carefully observed.' 'A' was marked against the passage 'I am anxious . . . memo of March 11th.' Orwell returned the memorandum annotated 'I will see to this' and initialled.

1948. To T. S. Eliot

11 March 1943   07/ES/EB

Dear Eliot

Following on our telephone conversation—here are the particulars about the talk on DRYDEN, just in case you haven't seen the other letter.

This talk is the second in a series called GREAT DRAMATISTS and each programme will deal with one dramatist, with special reference to one of his plays. The play chosen for Dryden is "The Indian Empress".[1] The programme consists of a ten-minutes' talk, a scene from the chosen play, acted by the BBC Repertory and taking about ten minutes, and about eight minutes of music. The layout is like this:

1. There is about a couple of minutes of music, and then—cutting into this—a few lines from the acted scene, which will have been recorded beforehand, as a sort of trailer. The speaker then
2. gives his talk.
3. After this, the recorded scene is acted right through, and then there is more music.

You will see therefore that the speaker's opening words should have some reference to the fragment of the scene which has just been heard. If you start off—"Those lines you have just heard come from John Dryden's play 'The Indian Empress' "—or words to that effect, that would be the kind of thing. If you liked you might also refer to the forthcoming scene at the end of your talk.

A ten-minutes' talk means about 1200 words. This is to be broadcast on April 1st at 12.30 p.m., so if you were here on that day at a quarter-to-twelve it would be all right. Of course you can record beforehand if that date is not convenient. I should like to have the script in by March 25th if possible. In case you would like to know, the other people taking part in the series are: George Sampson, Sherard Vines,[2] James Stephenson[3] and I hope Bernard Shaw.

Yours sincerely,
Eric Blair
Talks Producer.

1. Orwell meant *The Indian Emperor*.

2. Walter Sherard Vines (1890–), Professor of English, University of Tokyo, 1923–28; Professor of English Literature, University College, Hull, 1928–52; and author of a number of academic books, among them *The Course of English Classicism* (1929) (see Orwell's review, *The New Adelphi*, June–August 1930, *97*), and *A Hundred Years of English Literature* (1950).
3. Presumably James Stephens; see *1901, n. 1.*

1949. To Penguin Books

11 March 1943   Typewritten, original   EEF/SGO

10a Mortimer Crescent
London   NW 6

Dear Sir,
I will procure copies of the four books named and send them to you.[1] I hope it will be possible for me to get them back, at any rate those that you are not publishing, as in two cases this is literally the the only copy in existence, so far as I know.

[Signed] Geo. Orwell[2]
Yours truly

1. *Burmese Days, Homage to Catalonia, Coming Up for Air, Inside the Whale.*
2. Orwell signed his name above 'Yours truly.'

1950. News Commentary in English for Malaya, 24

12 March 1943

This was written and read by George Orwell. No script has been traced.

1951. BBC Talks Booking Form, 12.3.43

Dr. E. D. Edwards: 'Women Generally Speaking,' Everyday Chinese Heroes; 13-minute talk; broadcast 31.3.43; fee £9.9s. Signed: M Blackburn for I.P.O. Remarks: 'Please mark envelope "PRIVATE & CONFIDENTIAL." '

1952. Weekly News Review, 59

13 March 1943

The text of this Newsletter is taken from the typescript used for the broadcast, which carries stamps indicating it was passed for Policy and Security. It is marked in Orwell's hand, 'As b'cast   13½'   EAB,' and was read by Orwell. There are a few amendments, some in his hand. Attached to the typescript is a written version—not in Orwell's hand—of the addition to the first paragraph (see *n. 1*), the position of which is not clear. It may have been written out for use in the broadcast or for the typist who later prepared a fair copy of the script. Its word order has been followed here.

At the beginning and end, Orwell speaks of bringing these weekly commentaries to an end. This has misled some to imagine that he was delivering a last message because he was being excluded from participation in direct propaganda of this kind. Thus, West: *Commentaries* has this footnote: 'Orwell's delivery of a "final message" shows his realisation that, whatever else he might do for the BBC, direct propaganda was not going to be part of it (219, n. 385).' This is a false conclusion. Orwell is speaking only of the end of *this* series of news commentaries for India. He continued to prepare scripts for translation into the vernacular, starting a news series for Tamil listeners on 22 April 1943, which was still running when he left the BBC seven months later; continuing the series he himself transmitted to Malaya until 2 July 1943; and, when he finished the series to Malaya, broadcasting commentaries he had written to Indonesia until he left the BBC. From this commentary it is plain that Orwell expected 'the Anglo-American attack on Europe' to begin early enough in 1943 'to finish the war this year' (paragraph 4). This is even more optimistic than the statement in his Letter to *Partisan Review*, 3 January 1943 (*1797*) where he said it was 'now widely expected that Germany would be defeated 'some time in 1943 and 1944.' The possible stalemate described at the end of paragraph five looks forward to that of *Nineteen Eighty-Four*.

As this is the last News Commentary that I shall do in this series I would like to end up with a general review of the World situation rather than a survey of the week's news. As a matter of fact there has not been a great deal that is new to comment on this week. The big events of the week have been the Russian capture of Vyasma° on the central Front, the German counter-attacks against Kharkov on the Southern Front, —from this morning's news it is evident that Kharkov is in danger—the Germans claim to be already in the City,[1] and the unsuccessful German attack in the southern part of Tunisia, but the situation has not fundamentally changed. Even the Red Army's re-capture of Vyasma, important though it is, could be foreseen, as probable when Rzhev fell. So, let me use my time, this week, in trying to give a comprehensive picture of the whole war and trying to predict in very general outlines what is likely to happen.

If you look at the war, as a whole, there are six factors which really count, four of them military, and two political. Of course, they're not separable from one another, but one can see the situation more clearly by listing them separately. The first factor is the failure of the Germans to carry out their full plans in Russia. The second factor is the coming Anglo-American attack on Continental Europe. The third factor is the war of the German U-boats against the United Nations lines of supply. The fourth factor is the Japanese offensive in the Far East and its slowing down for reasons which we are not yet quite sure about. The fifth factor is the failure of the Nazi New Order in Europe, and the sixth is the attempt of the Japanese in the Far East to set up a New Order designed to benefit only themselves, like that of the Germans in Europe.

The first of these factors,° is the most important, because Germany is the main enemy and the Japanese cannot really continue to fight alone if Germany goes out—they might manage to prolong the war for several years. If you look at the map of Russia, you can see that however much territory they've over-run, the Germans have totally failed in what was probably their most urgent war aim and are likely to fail in their secondary one. Their primary war aim was to captue the oil-fields of the Caucasus. It was for this reason that the Germans decided to attack Soviet Russia, probably as far back as the winter of 1940. Since Britain had failed to collapse, like France, they saw they were in for a long war, and it was absolutely necessary for them to have bigger supplies of oil than they could get from European sources and from synthetic production. Secondly, they had to have food, which meant that they had to have the fertile lands of the Ukraine. Europe is capable, or nearly capable, of feeding itself, but not if a large proportion of its man-power is making weapons of war for the German army instead of producing food. In peace-time, Europe could import food from the Americas, but with Britain blockading Germany at sea, the Ukraine was an absolute necessity for the German war machine. As everybody knows, the Germans have failed to get to the Caucasus, but they still hold the greater part of Ukrainia.° It is probably a mistake in spite of the defeats they have had in the last few months to imagine that they will give this up without fighting. They would probably regard the Dneiper river and a line containing the whole of Poland and the Baltic States, as the last Frontier, to which they could afford to retreat. Probably they will try to stand on the defensive on this line and muster their forces to meet the Allied attack from the west, but this strategy puts them in a dilemma. If they give up the Ukraine, they have not the food resources to carry on the war indefinitely. If they hold on to it, they're defending an immensely long[2] Frontier, inevitably tying up a bigger army than they can afford to use. We don't really know what the German casualties have been in the two Russian winters, but certainly they have been large and the total mobilisation orders in Germany, together with endless attempts to make the European populations work harder, shows that the German man power position is becoming serious. Broadly, one can say, that by provoking both Britain and Soviet Russia, and the United States, against them, the Germans have made sure that they cannot win and can only hope, at best, for a stalemate. We may expect them, therefore, during this year to make violent political offensives aimed at sowing dissension among the United Nations. They will try to play on American fear of Bolshevism, Russian suspicion of Western capitalism, and Anglo-American jealousy, and they probably calculate that they have better chances along those lines than on purely military action.

The second and third factors, the Anglo-American attack on Europe, and the submarine war, cannot be considered separately. Much the best chance the Germans have of staving off an attack from the West is to sink so many ships that the United Nations, not only cannot transport a big force oversea, but what is more important, keep it supplied. When one realises that one infantry soldier needs about seven tons of supplies, one realises what an attack against Europe means in terms of shipping. Even if the Germans could not stave off an attack from the West altogether they might keep the United Nations embarrassed until the attack started too late to finish the war this year. In that case, the stalemate the Germans are probably hoping for, will become more likely of attainment. The campaign in Tunisia really has the same object, that is, to keep a big Allied Army tied up in Africa, and prevent it crossing the sea to Europe. I don't care to predict too much about the results of these German delaying tactics because there're two things we don't yet know. First of all, naturally, we don't know what is the Allied plan of attack. Secondly, we don't know the real facts about the shipping situation because the Governments of the United Nations, probably justifiably, don't publish figures of shipping losses, but we do know certain facts from which inferences can be[3] drawn, and on the whole, they're hopeful. The first is that the United Nations succeeded in transporting a large army to Africa, evidently to the surprise of the Germans, and are transporting an American Army which grows every day across the Atlantic to Britain. The second is that the food situation, which is probably an index of the shipping situation, has not deteriorated in Britain during the past two years. The third is the enormous expansion of the American shipbuilding industry, and the fourth the growing improvement in the methods—surface ships, aeroplanes and bombing of bases, —of dealing with the submarine. The U-boats have been the Germans' strongest card hitherto, but there is no strong reason for thinking that they will be able to slow down Allied preparations indefinitely.

We don't know enough[4] about Japanese strategy to be certain whether they've been seriously crippled by the blows they've had in the past eight months, or whether they've slowed down their campaigns according to some definite plan. All we do know is that a year ago they over-ran very rapidly the countries bordering the south-west Pacific and since then have made no progress but on the contrary have lost some valuable bases and an enormous amount of war material. Japan's weakest spot, like that of Britain, is shipping. They have certainly lost an immense quantity, both war ships and merchant ships, at a time when they need ships more and more in order to keep their island possessions running. Moreover, they've nothing like the power of replacement of the highly industrialised states. It is safe to say that the United States can build more ships in a month than Japan can in a year. And in aeroplane construction the margin is even greater. It seems likely, therefore, that if the Japanese did not go on to attack India and Australia, as everyone expected, it was not because they did not want to but because they could not. On the other hand, we ought not to assume that they will collapse quickly when Germany is finished with. The Japanese cannot afford to retreat from the mainland of Asia any more than the Germans can afford to give up Eastern Europe. If they did so, their industrial and military power would decline rapidly. We may expect, therefore, that the Japanese will defend every inch of what they have got and in the past few months they have shown how obstinately they can fight. But probably Japanese grand strategy, like that of Germany, is now aiming at a stalemate. They perhaps calculate that if they can consolidate their position[5] where they are, the United Nations will be too war weary to go on fighting when Germany is defeated, and might be

27

willing to make terms on the basis of everyone keeping what he has got. Of course, the real object of this would be to renew the war at the first favourable[6] opportunity and we ought to be on our guard against Japanese peace-talk, no less than against German.

As to the political factors, there is no need to talk any longer about the failure of the Nazi New Order in Europe. By this time, it stinks in the nose of the whole world. But it is important to realise that Japanese aims and methods are essentially similar, and that the Japanese New Order or, as they call it, the Greater East Asia Co-Prosperity Sphere, will have the same appearance when the necessary time-lag has elapsed. The Japanese are plundering the lands under their control and it does not make very much difference if in one place they plunder by naked violence and in another by means of a faked paper money which will not buy anything. They must plunder Asia, even if they did not wish to do so, because they cannot afford to do otherwise. They must have the food and raw materials of the occupied countries and they cannot give anything of corresponding value in return. In order to pay for the goods they seize, they would have to turn their factories over to producing cheap consumption goods, which would be impossible without slowing down their war industries. The same essential situation exists in Europe, but less crudely because the countries over-run by the Germans are more industrialised. It is as certain as anything can well be that within a fairly short time, the Malays, Burmese and other peoples now under Japanese rule will find out all about their so-called protectors and realise that these people who were making such golden promises a year ago are simply a hoard of locusts eating their countries naked. But[7] just how soon that will happen is a more[8] difficult question and I do not intend to be able to answer it exactly. At present, comparatively little news comes to us from Japanese occupied territory, but we have one great and unimpeachable source of evidence and that is, China. The war in China began five years[9] before it began in the rest of Asia and there are innumerable eye witness accounts of the way the Japanese have behaved. By almost universal agreement it is a regime of naked robbery with all the horrors of massacre, torture and rape on top of that. The same will happen, or has already happened, to all the lands unfortunate enough to fall under Japanese rule. Perhaps the best answer to the propaganda which the Japanese put out to India and other places is simply the three words LOOK AT CHINA. And since I am now bringing these weekly Commentaries to an end[10] I believe those three words LOOK AT CHINA are the best final message I can deliver to India.

1. —from this morning's news . . . in the City,] *handwritten interlinear addition. The position of this insertion is not marked, but the passage* 'on the central front . . . the southern part of Tunisia' *has been written out and attached to the original typescript (see headnote).*
2. long] strong; *handwritten substitution*
3. can be] have been; *handwritten substitution*
4. There is a handwritten note in the margin: '4th factor.'
5. The last word of this page has only 'po'; 'position' has been written below it.
6. favourable] available; *handwritten substitution*
7. But] *handwritten insertion*
8. more] *handwritten insertion*

9. The typescript has 'nearly five years' but 'nearly' is crossed through.
10. Only the series of commentaries to India was being concluded; see headnote.

1953. To T. S. Eliot

15 March 1943   07/ES/EB/WMB

Dear Eliot

I suppose you've had my wire,[1] I am sorry I made the mistake of calling the play you are to talk on THE INDIAN EMPRESS. It should have been THE INDIAN EMPEROR.[2] As I believe there is another one called THE INDIAN QUEEN it would have been rather a puzzle to know just which play was intended.

Although THE INDIAN EMPEROR refers to the Mexican Indians I wonder whether you could tie your talk on to India by just mentioning even if only in one sentence that Dryden wrote a play about Aurungzib,[3] or however it is spelt. We shall expect your script round about the 25th.

Yours sincerely
[Initialled] E.A.B
George Orwell
Talks Producer
Indian Section

1. Not traced.
2. See *1930, n. 1*.
3. *Aureng-Zebe* (1676) was Dryden's last play in rhyme; like the two others mentioned, it was in the heroic mode.

1954. Note to Norman Collins

c. 16 March 1943

On 9 March 1943, Ursula Eason, of BBC Northern Ireland, asked Collins whether it was possible to make available a copy of a script by E. M. Forster in which he had reviewed *Landslide* by Stephen Gilbert.[1] His mother had tried unsuccessfully to hear the broadcast. Collins sent the memorandum to Orwell, asking if the broadcast could be traced in the African Service and 'Is there anything we can do to heal this mother's heart.' Orwell replied by annotating the same memorandum.

Mr Collins.
I find E. M. Forster *did* mention this book. I am sending a copy of what he said to N. I. Programme Director.

Eric Blair.

1. Stephen Gilbert (1912–), born in Northern Ireland, was a newspaper reporter, 1931–33, a seed merchant, 1933–39, then served in the army, 1939–41. He was also the author of *Bombardier*

(1943), *Monkeyface* (1948), *The Burnaby Experiment* (1952), and *Ratman's Notebooks* (1968), later published as *Willard* and filmed in 1971.

1955. On Orwell's behalf to E. M. Forster

16 March 1943   07/ES/EB/WMB

Dear Mr. Forster

Mr. Orwell has asked me to write and ask you what you feel like talking about this month, for your broadcast on the 31st March—SOME BOOKS.

 Perhaps you could let us have some idea of the books you will speak about and we will try and get them for you.

Yours sincerely
[Signed] W Bedwell
(For George Orwell)
Talks Producer
Indian Section

1956. BBC Talks Booking Form, 16.3.43

Oliver Bell: 'Women Generally Speaking'; 13½-minute talk, 'Films of the Month,' with an introduction by Lady Grigg; broadcast 24.3.43; fee £9.9s. Signed: M Blackburn for I.P.O.

1957. BBC Talks Booking Form, 16.3.43

T. S. Eliot: 'Calling All Students,' 'Great Dramatists,' 2; 'Mr. Eliot will give a talk on John Dryden with special reference to "Indian Emperor" (Dryden's play)'; broadcast 1.4.43; fee £10.10s. Signed: M Blackburn for I.P.O. Remarks: 'Mr. Eliot is writing the script and giving a live talk of approximately 10 mins. duration in this broadcast.'

1958. BBC Talks Booking Form, 16.3.43

Dr. N. Gangulee and Shridhar Telkar, jointly: three scripts for series 'In Your Kitchen,' called 'The Health of a Nation'; 13½ minutes; Mrs. K. C. Roy will take part in the discussion; broadcast 17, 24, and 31.3.43; fees £6.6s for each broadcast for Gangulee and Telkar; £3.3s for Mrs Roy. Signed: M Blackburn for I.P.O. [Separate forms were produced for each participant. Annotations show that Mrs Roy's contract was cancelled, as were Gangulee's second and third appearances and Telkar's final appearance. See memorandum to Miss Boughen, *1975*.]

1959. BBC Talks Booking Form, 16.3.43

Sirdar Ikbal Ali Shah: 'Books That Changed the World,' 1, 'The Koran'; 13½-minute talk; broadcast 26.3.43; fee £12.12s + fare 13s 2d. Signed: M Blackburn for I.P.O.

1960. To Norman Collins

17 March 1943   Handwritten

On 9 March 1943, Mary Blackburn wrote to B. H. Alexander, of the Copyright Department, asking that payment be made to G. A. Broomfield for a script he had written in English for the Hindustani series, 'Shuroo Shuroo Men.' This was translated and read by a member of the staff for transmission on 11 March. Miss Alexander, having arranged payment of £8.8s, drew Norman Collins's attention to what was evidently a new speaker, on 16 March. On the 17th, Collins asked Orwell 'what Broomfield was like as a broadcaster.' Orwell replied on the same day:

Mr Collins.
Mr Broomfield did not actually b'cast for us but wrote a script which was translated into Hindustani. I believe he once b'cast in "In Town Tonight"[1] but I don't know anything abt his capabilities (have not met him).

Eric Blair   17.3.43

1. This was a long-running talk-show featuring personalities 'in London Town,' often fashionable visitors, which was broadcast in the United Kingdom from before the outbreak of war.

1961. To Arthur Wynn, Music Bookings Manager

[17 March 1943?][1]   Original   EB/WMB

INTERLUDE

Commencing Thursday, March 18th, we are starting six new talks in the series CALLING ALL STUDENTS, entitled GREAT DRAMATISTS. In these programmes there will be an interlude of recorded music (approximately 8 minutes) which will be chosen and presented by Dr. Narayana Menon. Dr. Menon is chosing appropriate music to the broadcast, which will appeal to Indian listeners, and this will entail some thought and care on Dr. Menon's part. The dates of these broadcasts are Thursdays, March 18th, 1st, 15th, 29th April, 13th and 27th May. (They are fortnightly talks).

We shall be glad, therefore, if you will issue a contract for Mr. Narayana Menon, 176 Sussex Gardens, London, W.2. for these six broadcasts.

[Signed] M Blackburn
(For Eric Blair)

1. This has been dated in relation to Wynn's letter to Menon of 18 March booking the six eight-minute programmes at £2.2s each. In alternate weeks with these eight-minute programmes, starting on 25 March 1943, Menon gave fifteen-minute programmes; see *1905* and *1941*.

1962. Extract from Minutes of Eastern Service Meeting

17 March 1943

Calling All Students   Mr. Blair reported permission obtained to approach G. B. Shaw for fourth edition, and explained presentation technique.

1963. To James Stephens

18 March 1943   07/ES/EB/WMB

Dear Mr. Stephens

Thank you for your letter of the 27th February.[1]

We are looking forward to receiving your script and would like to have it about May 15th, not later.

We shall be acting a bit from the HOUR GLASS, and a few lines from this will be trailed immediately before your talk, so could you start off—"Those lines you have just heard came from W. B. Yeats' play the HOUR GLASS"—or words to that effect.

The broadcast will take place at 200 Oxford Street.

Yours sincerely
[Initialled] E.A.B
George Orwell
Talks Producer
Indian Section

1. It was actually dated 26th February.

1964. Review of *Letters on India* by Mulk Raj Anand

Tribune 19 March 1943

Dear Mulk,—I write this review in the form of a letter since your book is itself written in the form of letters answering somebody else's letters, and has provoked yet another letter from Mr. Leonard Woolf,[1] a rather angry one this time, which is printed as a foreword.

On strictly political grounds I can't whack up any serious disagreement with you. I could point to statements in which you have probably been unfair to Britain, but it doesn't seem to me that you misrepresent the essential relationship between your country and mine. For a hundred and fifty years we have been exploiting you, and for at least thirty years we have been artificially holding back your development. I should never think of disputing that. I prefer to start with the policy that we do agree upon, and then point to some of the difficulties that lie in its way—difficulties which it seems to me no one has yet faced up to. You and I both know that there can be no real solution of the Indian problem which does not also benefit Britain. Either we all live in a decent world, or nobody does. It is so obvious, is it not, that the British worker as well as the Indian peasant stands to gain by the ending of capitalist exploitation, and that Indian independence is a lost cause if the Fascist nations are allowed to dominate the world. Quite manifestly the battle against Amery and the battle against Hitler are the same. But if this is obvious, why do so few people grasp it? Well, here are some of the things that stand in the way, and since this must be a short letter I will simply tabulate them instead of trying to weave them into one picture:—

Nationalism.—"Enlightened" people everywhere refuse to take this seriously. Because of this refusal the huge European Fascist movement grew up under their noses, not merely unfeared but almost unnoticed. You know as well as I do, though you don't emphasise, the element of mere nationalism, even colour-hatred, that enters into the Indian independence movements. Most Indians who are politically conscious hate Britain so much that they have ceased to bother about the consequences of an Axis victory. Here in London young Indians have assured me that Japan is "civilising" China and has no ill intentions towards India. An Indian friend in Delhi, himself a Communist or ex-Communist, writes to me that the Indian masses are "whole-heartedly for Germany against Russia"; he describes the newsboys shouting in Urdu, "Germany smashes Russia at the first battle," etc., etc.; and you know how hard colour-prejudice dies in this country also. A *News Chronicle* despatch from North Africa informs me that the British soldiers' nickname for an Arab village is a "woggery"—that is, a place inhabited by Wogs, i.e. golliwogs, the most offensive of all the English nicknames for coloured people: this in 1943, when we are fighting a war which is said to be and actually *is* for Democracy against Fascism. Don't let's underrate the danger of this kind of thing.

Differential standard of living.—You put your finger on the difficulty when you said that for a century or two Britain had been almost "a middle-class country." One mightn't think it when one looks round the back streets of Sheffield, but the average British income is to the Indian as twelve to one. How can one get anti-Fascist and anti-capitalist solidarity in such circumstances? The normal Socialist arguments fall on deaf ears when they are addressed to India, because Indians refuse to believe that any class-struggle exists in Europe. In their eyes the underpaid, downtrodden English worker is himself an exploiter. And so long as Socialism teaches people to think in terms of material benefit, how would the British worker himself behave if told that he had to choose between keeping India in bondage and lowering his own wages?

Sentimentalism of the Left.—Why did your book annoy Mr. Leonard Woolf so much when the views it uttered were less "extreme" than those that the *New Statesman* utters every week? At bottom, no doubt, because it gave him the impression that Indian nationalism is a force actually *hostile* to Britain and not merely a pleasant little game of blimp-baiting. You will have noticed that the causes favoured by the English Left in the past have, as often as not, ended by turning into some form of Fascism. Look back the necessary years or decades, and you find 'enlightened" British opinion supporting Japan as against Russia and China, the Boers and Sinn Feiners as against Britain, and the Germans as against the Poles and French. In each case the left wing orthodoxy of the moment was accepted without any attempt to think out its full implications, because of the false world-view which assumes that all "enlightened" people think more or less alike. At this moment nearly every English left winger is pro-Jew as regards Palestine and pro-Congress as regards India. How many of them even know that many, if not most, Congress Indians are violently anti-Jew? And how pained and surprised the Left was when that well-known anti-Fascist Subhas Chandra Bose began broadcasting from Berlin! You see, Mr. Woolf was annoyed by your book because he had expected you to be anti-British in *his* way, whereas *your* way involved a condemnation of Mr. Woolf himself. You were right, of course, we are all nearer to the blimp than we are to the Indian peasant, but don't expect people to like being told so. Opinions sentimentally held are always liable to be suddenly reversed. I know more than one intellectual who has started out with a burning zeal to "free India" and ending up by feeling that there is a lot to be said for General Dyer. One shouldn't underrate the danger of that either.

Well, I could go on, but I haven't space. There at least are three of the difficulties that lie in the way of a juster and saner relationship between Britain and India. What arises from this? Only that one must work to make people realise that long-term and short-term interests don't necessarily coincide. The Englishman must see that his domination in India is indefensible; the Indian must see that to side with the Fascists for the sake of revenge against Britain would do him no good. It is largely a question of letting each know that the other's viewpoint exists. That brings me back to what I have often said before, that the best bridge between Europe and Asia, better than trade or battleships or aeroplanes, is the English language; and I hope that you and Ahmed Ali and the others will continue to write in it, even if it sometimes leads you to be called a "babu" (as you were recently) at one end of the map and a renegade at the other.

Yours ever
GEORGE ORWELL

On 2 April, Leonard Woolf took up Orwell's reference to his 'rather angry letter,' and that was followed on 9 April by a rejoinder from Mulk Raj Anand. The letters, respectively, read:

Mr. Orwell in a letter which reviews Mr. Anand's *Letters from India°* in a recent issue, states that the book
"has provoked yet another letter from Mr. Leonard Woolf, a rather angry letter this time, which is printed as a foreword."

The statement completely misrepresents, no doubt unintentionally, both the facts and my attitude towards the book. So far from the book "provoking" me to write "a rather angry" letter, I was asked by Mr. Anand himself and the publishers of the book to write a foreword, and it was Mr. Anand himself who suggested to me that I should write it in the form of a letter. I dislike writing forewords and I dislike writing public letters; and the only thing which "provoked" me to do so in this case was that I thought that Mr. Anand's book should be published and that I understood that if I did what I was asked to do I should be helping to get it published.

Mr. Orwell says that the book annoyed me because it gave me "the impression that Indian nationalism is a force *hostile* to Britain." The book did not annoy me and I do not think that there is the slightest anger in what I wrote. I wrote:

"We are both Socialists, and therefore I agree with all the 'socialist interpretation' of the history of India which you give in your book. Like you, I have for years been in favour of the British Government giving India independence, and I have made much the same criticism of the 1935 Act as you do. I hate imperialism for the harm it does both to the imperialist and the subject peoples."

I said that I disagreed with Mr. Anand on probably not more than 20 per cent. of his statements and arguments. The most important point on which I disagree is his and Congress's attitude to the Muslim minority, and I pointed out that by pretending that the Muslim problem does not exist "you are playing into the hands of the British imperialists." Does this really justify Mr. Orwell in implying that after starting out "with a burning zeal to 'free India,'" I have ended "up by feeling that there is a lot to be said for General Dyer"?

Leonard Woolf

In his answer to Mr. Orwell's review of *Letters on India*. Mr. Leonard Woolf misrepresents the facts which led him to write an introductory letter to my book. I at no time asked him to write a foreword on my account. Actually, the Advisory Council of the Labour Book Service asked Mr. Woolf whether he could write a note amplifying his reader's report (with which they were more or less in agreement) to enable them to publish my book in their series. I did see Mr. Woolf to explain to him the nature of my argument and my differences with him on certain vital points. And when he wrote a letter (the form was certainly suggested by me) with a great deal of which I disagreed, I insisted on an answer to it being included in the Labour Book Service edition. Also, I refused to allow his letter to be published in the ordinary edition of my book.

Mulk Raj Anand

1. Leonard Woolf (1880–1969), author, editor, and publisher, served in the Ceylon Civil Service, 1904–11, and one of his novels was based on his time in Ceylon. He and his wife, Virginia, daughter of Sir Leslie Stephen, founded the Hogarth Press in 1917, which published early works by, among others, E. M. Forster and T. S. Eliot. He was literary editor of *The*

Nation, 1923–30, and joint editor of *Political Quarterly*, 1931–59. Among his political and social books were *Socialism and Co-operation* (1921), *Imperialism and Civilization* (1928), and *After the Deluge: A Study of Communal Psychology* (2 vols., 1931, 1939). He also wrote five volumes of autobiography (1960–69), and published them and the diaries of his time in Ceylon.

1965. News Commentary in English for Malaya, 25

19 March 1943

This was written by George Orwell; read by John Morris.[1]. No script has been traced.

1. John Morris (1895–1980; CBE, 1957) served in the army, 1915–34, and was a member of the 1922 and 1936 expeditions to Mt. Everest; Professor of English Literature, Keio University, and lecturer at Imperial and Bunrika Universities, Tokyo, from 1938, and concurrently adviser on the English language to Japan's Department of Foreign Affairs. He was head of the BBC Far Eastern Service, 1943–52 (replacing Rushbrook Williams), and Controller for the BBC Third Programme, 1952–58. At the time he read this Newsletter he was not yet ESD and worked in a room adjacent to Orwell's. His memoir of Orwell, 'Some Are More Equal Than Others,' appeared in *Penguin New Writing*, 40, September 1950; reprinted in *Orwell Remembered*, 171–76, as 'That Curiously Crucified Expression.' A note to the entry for 14 December 1952 in Stephen Spender's *Journals 1939–1983* (edited by John Goldsmith, 1985) describes Morris as 'A not very daring promoter of the cause of culture, cruelly teased by his friend, E. M. Forster, who referred to him as "the pudding".'

1966. To Arthur Wynn, Music Bookings Manager

22 March 1943   EB/WMB

Contract for Dr Narayana Menon

With further reference to our memo. of the 24th February, also ours of the 8th March, would you please revise the contract for Dr. Narayana Menon, for the 15 minute programme of gramophone records he is planning and choosing for Thursdays (fortnightly) from March 25th onwards. This programme will be broadcast at 1130 to 1145 GMT in the Eastern Service (Red Network).

This will be a Feature Programme, involving careful planning and choosing of music, and also the writing of such commentary as the programme demands. We are not asking Dr. Menon to present it himself, as we want to have someone with a better English accent, but otherwise, he will be doing all the work of the programme and we feel that he[1] might receive a higher fee than that offered, which, I believe, is only £3.3.0.

[Signed] Eric Blair
(Eric Blair)

1. Typed as 'we.'

1967. To P. Chatterjee

23 March 1943   Handwritten draft and typed versions
07/ES/EB/WMB

Dear Mr. Chatterjee

Many thanks for your letter—we are arranging for the renewal of your contract.[1] So far as I am able to judge from the English translation, I think your News Commentaries are very good and just the kind of thing that is wanted. The one or two reactions we have had from India state that your commentaries are an improvement on the preceding ones. In the case of getting any reactions yourself, e.g. of airmail letters from friends, please let me know, as any information we can obtain about our audience is of value to us.

Yours sincerely
[Signed] Eric Blair
Eric Blair
Talks Producer
Indian Section

1. On 22 March, Chatterjee wrote to Orwell to say that C. R. Tonkin, Far East Editor, after seeing four of the seven Newsletters he had done in Bengali did not think too badly of them. Orwell wrote out the reply reproduced above in draft on the verso of Chatterjee's letter. Assuming Chatterjee included 20 March in these seven, this would suggest that Orwell had written only two Newsletters after 16 January 1943—he was ill 20 January to 11 February. The two he wrote were probably those for 20 and 27 February 1943.

1968. To Quintin Hogg

24 March 1943   07/ES/EB/ED

Dear Captain Quintin Hogg,[1]

We understand from Princess Indira of Kapurthala that you have consented to broadcast, in our Eastern Service directed to India on Monday, 5th April, a talk of approximately 6 minutes' duration on the work of Indian troops in the Libyan campaign.

The broadcast will be at 1.15 p.m. DBST and we should be glad if you would come to 200 Oxford Street at 12.45 p.m., so that we may run through and time your talk before you go on the air.

We shall also be glad if you will let us have your script by Thursday, 1st April, at the latest. We are instructing our Contracts Department to get in touch with you.

Yours sincerely,
[Initialled] E.A.B
(Eric Blair)
Talks Producer

1. Quintin Hogg (see 512, n. 3) was at this time a Conservative M.P. serving in the army.

1969. BBC Talks Booking Form, 24.3.43

Capt. The Hon Quintin Hogg, M.P.: 'Work of Indian Troops in the Libyan Campaign'; approx. 6 minutes within 'The Debate Continues'; broadcast 5.4.43; fee £5.5s. Signed: M Blackburn for I.P.O.

1970. To G. V. Desani

25 March 1943   07/ES/EB/WMB

Dear Mr. Desani

Following on our telephone conversation I will explain just the sort of talk we want.[1] These books° are intended to discuss the chief books of Oriental sacred literature, giving some sort of idea of their doctrines and showing the influence they have had upon human history. The first talk will be on THE KORAN and there will be others on THE BIBLE, THE UPANISHADS, THE ANALECTS OF CONFUCIUS, and others.

I want you to talk on BHAGAVAT GITA. As you are talking about a Hindoo° book to an Indian audience, I have no doubt you can assume a good deal of knowledge of doctrine and should concentrate rather on putting the whole thing in an historical framework, and showing its effect on the Indian way of life and characteristic civilisation.

These talks are of 13½ minutes duration, which probably means 1500 words.

I told you the wrong date: your talk will be delivered on Friday, the 9th April, at 1.45 pm. (DOUBLE BRITISH SUMMER TIME).[2] I shall hope to receive your script not later than Tuesday, April 6th.

Yours sincerely
[Initialled] E.A.B
Eric Blair
Talks Producer
Indian Section

1. Desani had written to Orwell in an undated letter (but before 14 April 1943) suggesting that a Buddhist classic be included in this series. He offered to give such a talk. On the recto of this letter Orwell wrote: 'Ansd. 14.4.43,' but that letter has not been traced.
2. For Double British Summer Time see *1096, n. 2*.

1971. To Paul Potts

25 March 1943   07/ES/EB/WMB

Paul Potts[1] had written an undated letter to Orwell asking, 'Could you let me give a talk on the B.B.C. say on the Indians in Canada not red ones.° Or on Canadian opinion on India. . . .' At the top of this letter Orwell wrote in pencil, 'Answd. 25.3.43. File':

Dear Paul Potts
Thanks for your letter. I cannot actually broadcast a talk at this moment because my schedule is full up, but I would like very much to have a talk by you to put by until I get a blank period. The one on the Indian community in Canada would do very well. We cannot have one on Canadian Opinion about India, because it would never get past[2] the censorship.

What I would like is a 13½ minute talk, which means approximately 1500 words. As it is not certain when it will be broadcast you should not put anything into it that would date.

Ring me up about any other points you want cleared up or else just send the script along at a time convenient to you and we will arrange a recording. I suppose I hardly need tell you that you need to watch your step in what you say. If you want to ring me up my 'phone number is EUSTON 3400 Ext. 208.

Yours sincerely
[Signed] Geo. Orwell
George Orwell
Talks Producer
Indian Section.

1. Paul Potts (1911–1990), a Canadian poet, was to become one of Orwell's friends and visited him at Barnhill, Jura. The chapter 'Don Quixote on a Bicycle' in Potts's *Dante Called You Beatrice* (1960), partially reprinted in *Orwell Remembered*, 248–60, describes Orwell affectionately. Potts says, 'The happiest years of my life were those during which I was a friend of his' (79). His *A Poet's Testament* was published in 1940.
2. past] passed, *in carbon*

1972. News Commentary in English for Malaya, 26

26 March 1943

This was written and read by George Orwell. No script has been traced.

1973. To Philip Unwin

26 March 1943   Original   07/ES/EB/WMB

On 24 March 1943, Orwell called at the offices of George Allen & Unwin to discuss the publication of a selection of broadcasts to India under the title *Talking to India*. On the 25th the publishers sent him a formal agreement embodying the terms discussed the previous day, and they asked him to let them have '100 to 150 words' describing the book for use 'as the basis of our announcements of the book.'

Dear Mr. Unwin
I return herewith the contract, duly signed. I have struck out Clause 16. The reason is that I am referred to throughout the contract as "the author", and I am not certain that this clause, as drafted, would not bind me to send you the

next book I might write myself. I know that your firm have first refusal on books of broadcasts but I assumed that the striking out of this clause will not affect that general agreement.

I have sent out a circular letter to all the authors concerned and will see to it that written consent to publication is obtained from each of them. There may be difficulty in getting in touch with two of the contributors but both will presumably have literary executors of some kind. I will let you know when all the agreements are in. Meanwhile, I presume that it would be quite safe to go ahead with printing.

If possible, it would be nice if we could have more than the usual six free copies as a lot of the contributors will probably expect to be given one.[1]

Yours sincerely
[Signed] Geo. Orwell
George Orwell

1. From annotations made at Allen & Unwin's, it seems that although there were '20 in all' contributing to the book, twelve copies were to be allowed, assuming that not all the contributors would want one. On 30 March, Allen & Unwin wrote to Orwell accepting the deletion of Clause 16, prompting Orwell to send them the 'blurb' (see *1983*), and saying, 'In these days of acute paper shortage, when it is almost certain that a book of this type will sell right out, we have to watch our free list carefully.' However, if every contributor did 'clamour for a copy,' they would provide them.

1974. To the Editor, *The Times Literary Supplement*

27 March 1943

Following the discussion in *The Times Literary Supplement* arising from Orwell's review of V. K. Narayana Menon's *The Development of William Butler Yeats*, Orwell wrote a second, and final, letter to the *TLS* on 27 March 1943. This is reprinted after the review; see *1791*.

1975. To E. W. D. Boughen, Talks Booking

27 March 1943   Original   EB/WMB

Cancellation of Booking Slips

Confirming telephone conversation this morning, will you please cancel the booking slip for the 31st March 1943 only, for the series IN YOUR KITCHEN, which is usually broadcast at 1115–1130 GMT on Wednesdays, in the Eastern Service (Red Network); for the following:—

Mrs. K. C. Roy, Dr. Gangulee and Shridhar Telkar.[1]

Every fourth Wednesday, in this period, E. M. Forster broadcasts a talk SOME BOOKS, and we had overlooked, when we made out these booking slips, that Mr. Forster's broadcast was on the 31st March.[2] We much regret any inconvenience caused to you.

[Signed] W Bedwell
(For Eric Blair)

1. See *1958* for Booking Form.
2. See *1893* for Booking Form.

1976. BBC Talks Booking Form, 27.3.43

G. V. Desani: 'Books That Changed the World,' 'Bhagavat Gita'; broadcast 9.4.43; fee £10.10s. Signed: M Blackburn for I.P.O.

1977. BBC Talks Booking Form, 27.3.43

Dr. N. Gangulee, Mrs. K. C. Roy, and Shridhar Telkar: 'In Your Kitchen'; broadcast 7, 14, and 21.4.43 for Gangulee and Telkar, with Mrs Roy on 7 and 21.4.43; cancelling booking for 31 March for all three; fees £8.8s for Gangulee and Telkar for each broadcast,[1] £3.3s for Mrs Roy for each. Signed: M Blackburn for I.P.O. [Miss Blackburn added to Gangulee's form]: '*NB*: 28th Apr: There's *no* B'cast of Your Kitchen. E. M. Forster instead.'

1. On 29 March 1943, Miss E. W. D. Boughen, writing on behalf of the Programme Contracts Director, told Telkar that although it was not possible to pay each speaker in a thirteen-minute discussion programme the same fee that a single speaker would receive broadcasting alone for that time, it was proposed to raise his rate for 'In Your Kitchen' to eight guineas, so he would not 'feel that we are paying you inadequately for your valuable services.'

1978. BBC Talks Booking Form, 27.3.43

Lady Grigg: 'Women Generally Speaking'; broadcast 7, 14, 21, and 28.4.43; fee £8.8s each broadcast. Signed: M Blackburn for I.P.O.

1979. BBC Talks Booking Form, 27.3.43

Shridhar Telkar: 'Behind the Headlines'; broadcast 1, 8, 15, 22, and 29.4.43; fee £9.9s each talk. Signed: M Blackburn for I.P.O.

1980. To Reginald Reynolds

29 March 1943   Top and carbon copies   07/ES/EB/WMB

Dear Reg.

Thanks for your letter of the 27th. I am glad it is O.K. about the contribution to the book.[1] Re your query. I signed that letter "Orwell" because it was a circular letter and some of the contributors only knew me as that.

I would like, very much, to have a talk on the Russian discovery of Alaska. Russia is always news, more or less. But I would like to have this talk to keep in what is called "The Ice-box" to be broadcast at any odd moment when something or other falls through. So could you do it so that nothing is tied down to a particular date, e.g. don't say "last week there was a paragraph in the paper which said", etc., etc. Although we might keep the talk for months before using it you will get paid when it is recorded.

I would like, very much, also to have something about Elizabethan literature, but I can't have it yet because of changes in our programme. During the summer months they are shoving us on to a time of day which means that our broadcasts will reach India at half-past four in the afternoon. It is no use broadcasting literary stuff at that hour but I shall be going back to our old programmes in September and perhaps we can fix something then. Let me have the talk on Alaska whenever convenient to you. 13½ minutes, which means about 1500 words. Perhaps you could mention in the talk that the United States acquired Alaska from Russia by the peaceful method of buying it. I think that is good propaganda.

I have just heard from Cedric Dover, who is in the Army, apparently in Nottinghamshire. He doesn't seem to be enjoying it but then who does.[2]

Yours
[Signed] Eric Blair
Eric Blair
(Talks Producer)
Indian Section

1. *Talking to India*; see Orwell's letter to Philip Unwin, 26 March 1943, *1973*.
2. In a lettercard dated 26 March 1943, Cedric Dover had told Orwell that he had been suddenly called up and was serving in the Royal Army Ordnance Corps as a private. He was ill, work had piled up, and, since he had only his army pay, he had 'defaulted' on his debt to Orwell, despite cutting down even on smoking. He asked if there were any possibility of more talks. It seems extremely unlikely that Orwell failed to reply, but no response has been traced.

1981. BBC Talks Booking Form, 29.3.43

Princess Indira of Kapurthala: 'The Debate Continues'; broadcast 5, 12, 19, and 26.4.43; fee £10.10s. Signed: Miss M Blackburn for I.P.O. Remarks: Usual fee [in Blackburn's hand] '£10–10–0. check with P.C.D.'

1982. BBC Talks Booking Form, 29.3.43

Miss Indira Roy: 'Indian Play,' 4, 'The Post Office'; broadcast 6.4.43; fee £3.3s. Signed: M Blackburn for I.P.O. Remarks: 'Rehearsal from 7.45–9.45 p.m. on 5.4.43 and from 10.30 a.m. BST on 6.4.43.'

1983. To Philip Unwin

31 March 1943   Original   07/ES/EB/WMB

Dear Mr. Unwin

Many thanks for your letter of the 30th March and the contract.

I have now got agreements from all but about two of the authors in TALKING TO INDIA, and no doubt the remaining ones will write in before long. I will try and keep the demand for free copies down, and I should say twelve would easily cover it, but of course it is important that all the oriental speakers should have a copy.

I am not certain what you want for the blurb. Did you want me to write this? I did once write a blurb but I am not good at it. Meanwhile, I enclose some publicity notes about some of th[e] speakers.[1]

Yours sincerely
[Signed] Geo. Orwell
George Orwell
(Talks Producer)
Indian Section

1. On the verso of this letter are some notes, presumably written in the offices of Allen & Unwin, outlining points to be made in publicity for *Talking to India*: '1. Competes with German radio   2. More freedom of speech to India than in other b/casts.' Also noted: '*Some* copies must go to India & U.S.A. George Orwell would act as editor.' In another hand, 'File. J. C. Thornton, B.B.C.'

1984. Draft for postcard to Reginald Reynolds

[31 March 1943?]   Handwritten

Reg. Reynolds.

Thanks for your postcard. I hope you can let me have the first script by the 1st week in June. As to the other talk, I'll get Cedric Dover to let me see your script; I hope to be able to have some talks along those lines at a later date, but of course it's impossible at this moment.[1]

E.A.B

1. The first talk is, perhaps, that on Alaska mentioned in Orwell's letter of 29 March 1943; see *1980*. The other talk would then be on Elizabethan literature.

1985. To R. R. Desai

[31 March 1943?]¹   07/ES/EB/WMB

Dear Desai
Thanks for your letter. I have been in touch with the Studio Booking people and found that it is quite impossible to book a studio at 5 pm. on Monday. It is the worst possible time of day. I could get you a studio after 6 or later, or probably in the morning, provided I have a day or two's notice. I am sorry Miss Chitale° started off by telling you that 5 on Monday was a possible time, but she is quite right in saying that they have nothing vacant at that time. I could, however, get you a listening room at that time, if you don't mind holding your rehearsal in somewhat cramped circumstances. I understand the difficulty is that Mrs. Kanna cannot come here later than 6. If you will let me know it would be quite easy for me to reserve a small listening room on the third floor for you at 5 on Monday.

Yours sincerely
[Initialled] EAB
Eric Blair
(Talks Producer)
Indian Section

1. This letter is not dated. The Monday probably refers (from the position in the file) to 5 April 1943, when Desai was to broadcast Gujarati Newsletter, 58. This letter could also be dated 1 April 1943.

1986. To Osbert Sitwell

1 April 1943   07/ES/EB/WMB

Dear Mr. Sitwell
I wonder whether you would like to do a ten-minute talk on OSCAR WILDE for the Indian Service of the B.B.C. I had better explain about the series of which this talk will be part.

We have a series of half-hour programmes called GREAT DRAMATISTS. Each programme consists of a ten-minutes talk on the dramatist in question, with special reference to one of his plays; a scene or extract from the play acted by the B.B.C. Repertory, and some music. The play of Wilde's which we should like you to tackle is THE IMPORTANCE OF BEING ERNEST,¹ but of course your talk should also give some sort of account of Wilde's work as a whole. The way we introduce these programmes is to record the scene which is acted and start the programme by trailing a few lines from the scene. The speaker's talk follows immediately after this, without any announcement. So your talk should start off—"Those lines you've just heard come from Oscar Wilde's play, THE IMPORTANCE OF BEING ERNEST", or words to that effect.

I hope very much you will undertake this talk. I may mention that the other playrights dealt with in the series are MARLOWE, DRYDEN, SHERIDAN, IBSEN and YEATS. The date of the Wilde talk will be Thursday, May 13th, and the time, 1.30 pm. If this date is not convenient to you we can easily record beforehand. Could you let me know whether you will do this.[2]

Yours sincerely
[Initialled] E.A.B
George Orwell
(Talks Producer)
Indian Section

1. The name of the character in Wilde's play is Ernest, but the spelling in the title should be 'Earnest.'
2. Sitwell replied from Renishaw Hall, near Sheffield, on 4 April, declining because he was too busy. He had a play to do for the BBC and was not only behind with that but had a thousand tasks weighing him down. He told Orwell to ask him again later on. See Orwell's letter to him of 13 April 1943, *2006*.

1987. 'Not Enough Money: A Sketch of George Gissing'

Tribune, 2 April 1943

All books worth reading "date," and George Gissing, perhaps the best novelist England has produced, is tied more tightly than most writers to a particular place and time. His world is the grey world of London in the 'eighties, with its gas lamps flickering in the everlasting fog, its dingy overcoats and high-crowned bowler hats, its Sunday gloom tempered by drunkenness, its unbearable "furnished apartments," and, above all, its desperate struggle against poverty by a middle class which was poor chiefly because it had remained "respectable." It is hard to think of Gissing without thinking of a hansom cab. But he did much more than preserve an atmosphere which, after all, is also preserved in the early *Sherlock Holmes* stories, and it is as a novelist that he will be remembered, even more than as an interpreter of the middle-class view of life.

When I suggest that Gissing is the best novelist we have produced I am not speaking frivolously. It is obvious that Dickens, Fielding and a dozen others are superior to him in natural talent, but Gissing is a "pure" novelist, a thing that few gifted English writers have been. Not only is he genuinely interested in character and in telling a story, but he has the great advantage of feeling no temptation to burlesque. It is a weakness of nearly all the characteristic English novelists, from Smollett to Joyce, that they want to be "like life" and at the same time want to get a laugh as often as possible. Very few English novels exist throughout on the same plane of probability. Gissing solves this problem without apparent difficulty, and it may be that his native pessimism was a help to him. For though he certainly did not lack humour, he did lack high spirits, the instinct to play the fool which made Dickens, for instance, as unable to pass a joke as some people are to pass a pub. And it is a fact that *The Odd Women*, to name only one, is more "like life" than the novels of bigger but less scrupulous writers.

At this date Gissing's best-known book is probably *The Private Papers of*

Henry Ryecroft, written towards the end of his life when his worst struggles with poverty were over. But his real masterpieces are three novels, *The Odd Women*, *Demos* and *New Grub Street*, and his book on Dickens. In an article of this length I cannot even summarise the plots of the novels, but their central theme can be stated in three words—"not enough money." Gissing is the chronicler of poverty, not working-class poverty (he despises and perhaps hates the working class) but the cruel, grinding, "respectable" poverty of underfed clerks, downtrodden governesses and bankrupt tradesmen. He believed, perhaps not wrongly, that poverty causes more suffering in the middle class than in the working class. *The Odd Women*, his most perfect and also his most depressing novel, describes the fate of middle-class spinsters flung on to the world with neither money nor vocational training. *New Grub Street* records the horrors of free-lance journalism, even worse then than now. In *Demos* the money theme enters in a somewhat different way. The book is a story of the moral and intellectual corruption of a working-class Socialist who inherits a fortune. Writing as he was in the 'eighties, Gissing shows great prescience, and also a rather surprising knowledge of the inner workings of the Socialist movement. But the usual shabby-genteel motif is present in the person of the heroine, pushed into a hateful marriage by impoverished middle-class parents. Some of the social conditions Gissing describes have passed away, but the general atmosphere of his books is still horribly intelligible, so much so that I have sometimes thought that no professional writer should read *New Grub Street* and no spinster *The Odd Women*.

What is interesting is that with all his depth of understanding Gissing has no revolutionary tendency. He is frankly anti-Socialist and anti-democratic. Understanding better than almost anyone the horror of a money-ruled society, he has little wish to change it, because he does not believe that the change would make any real difference. The only worth-while objective, as he sees it, is to make a purely personal escape from the misery of poverty and then proceed to live a civilised, aesthetically decent life. He is not a snob, he does not wish for luxury or great wealth, he sees the spuriousness of the aristocracy and he despises beyond all other types the go-getting, self-made business man; but he does long for an untroubled, studious life, the kind of life that cannot be lived on less than about £400 a year. As for the working class, he regards them as savages, and says so with great frankness. However wrong he may have been in his outlook, one cannot say of him that he spoke in ignorance, for he himself came of very poor parents, and circumstances forced him to live much of his life among the poorest of the working class. His reactions are worth studying, even at this date. Here was a humane, intelligent man, of scholarly tastes, forced into intimacy with the London poor, and his conclusion was simply this: these people are savages who must on no account be allowed political power. In a more excusable form it is the ordinary reaction of the lower-middle-class man who is near enough to the working class to be afraid of them. Above all, Gissing grasped that the middle classes suffer more from economic insecurity than the working class, and are more ready to take action against it. To ignore that fact has been one of the major blunders of the Left, and from this sensitive novelist who loved Greek tragedies, hated politics and began writing long before Hitler was born, one can learn something about the origins of Fascism.

1988. News Commentary in English for Malaya, 27

2 April 1943

This was written and read by George Orwell. No script has been traced.

1989. Comment on Robert Duval's 'Whitehall's Road to Mandalay' and Correspondence on Nationalism

Tribune, 2 April 1943

Robert Duval expressed apprehension in this article about the British government's attitude towards Burma, at that time occupied by the Japanese. His article began:

"Of course we shall reconquer Burma," said General Alexander after his epic retreat over the Assam border. "It is part of the British Empire."

The General's statement was obviously made *ad hoc*; from the standpoint of diplomatic delicatesse, it suffered from its soldierly over-bluntness, Whitehall has spoken with more subtlety; a reconquered Burma, Amery has indicated, would resume her course towards Dominion status at the point where the Japanese invasion intervened. But despite such blandishments, it is becoming increasingly apparent that General Alexander's crude assertion represents the real pith of British policy.

The article concluded:

The situation boils down to this: that with the invasion of Burma an imminent possibility, Whitehall can think of no more convincing theme for its propaganda than that of Burman criminality and Burman ineptitude and incapacity for self-government. If we continue in this vein, we can look forward to a rousing welcome from the Burmese people! One is almost inclined to believe the Tokyo report that British parachutists dropped in Burma were wiped out by the local inhabitants—*armed by the Japanese*.

The Burmese people *can* be won over to the side of the Allies. But it is impossible to appeal to the Burmese people by promising them a return to the *status quo ante*. Sir Paw Tun, the Burmese Premier, has at various times appealed for the application of the Atlantic Charter to Burma, for the extension of the Cripps offer to Burma, for a categorical pledge of Dominion status after the war. Sir Paw Tun, it must be pointed out, is an ardent supporter of the British. Dominion status does not represent a maximum condition; it represents an irreducible minimum. Without such a promise, we may still succeed in winning Burma back. But we shall have to do it without—and perhaps against—the Burmese people.

Orwell was asked by the editors of *Tribune* to comment on Duval's article:

As background to Mr. Duval's article I suggest the following considerations:—

Burma is a small, backward agricultural country, and to talk about making it independent is nonsense in the sense that it will never be independent. There is no more reason for turning Asia into a patchwork of comic opera states than there is with Europe, and the sole question that arises here is whether it is good propaganda to offer the Burmese an independence which many of them probably want, but which in practice they will not have. The implication of Mr. Duval's article is that we *must* offer the Burmese independence because the Japanese have succeeded in making their own offers convincing. Granted that this is so , there are several other factors to be taken into consideration:

(*a*) If the Burmese are to be independent how are they to defend themselves; who is going to arm them; are we to promise them the Burmese flag and a British army of occupation on the Japanese model?

(*b*) What about Congress opinion in India, which is probably hostile to Burmese independence?

(*c*) What about China?

To sum up, I suggest that even from the short-term propaganda point of view it is dangerous to transfer European slogans and habits of thought to Asiatic countries where, for example, there are no trade unions and the name of Marx has barely been heard.

Two letters on this issue appeared in *Tribune* for 16 April, from 'A Burmese Observer' and E. A. Richards, C.C., the latter being particularly concerned with Orwell's comment:

When I read George Orwell's "footnote" to Robert Duval's "Whitehall° Road to Mandalay," I began to wonder whether I had stumbled on the *Daily Telegraph* instead of *Tribune*. Surely Orwell's new cheap brand of Imperialism, as displayed in that note, is not the authentic policy of *Tribune*? But if not, why ask him to contribute it without any disavowal of what it contains?

Mr. Orwell is entitled to his own opinion; but surely he should make it clear that he is speaking only for himself—at any rate I hope he is. Mr. Amery[1] would be delighted with his article. Every one of his arguments against Burmese self-government, if valid, would be equally clinching against self-government for India. If Burma is backward so is India, in many ways. If Britain is to be the sole judge of what is good for the Burmans (and I cannot see any other meaning to Orwell's views), then the same thing applies to India. In effect, he says virtually that we must not give the Burmese freedom because they are not Socialists. Come to that, is Britain Socialist?

Orwell's suggestion that it is "dangerous to transfer European slogans and habits of thought" to countries like Burma is an echo (whether or not intended as such) of what the Tories are always saying. They say that Democracy is such a tender plant that it would not stand planting in India. Does Orwell think that the British Raj, under Amery's care, is going to develop the trade unionism and Socialism whose absence in Burma he makes the excuse for the retention of empire?

When Orwell says that it is not desirable for Burma to have absolute independence, I agree. It is not desirable for *any* country to have absolute independence! But it is evident by his sneering reference to "comic-opera" States that it is only small countries, in his view, who ought to be denied separate existence. Are Norway, Denmark, Holland, Belgium, Switzerland, Czecho-Slovakia, Jugo-Slavia, Greece, Poland "comic-opera" States? Let me tell George Orwell that if Britain had shown a quarter of the democracy and statesmanship of Czecho-Slovakia under Masaryk and Benes, we should not have been in the mess we are. I suppose Orwell would like to go back to pre-1914, the Balance of Power, with a big German-Austro-Hungarian Empire, the state of things which produced the first World War!

Duval's article doubtless contains some exaggeration, but it is, at any rate, in line with international Socialist policy. Orwell's isn't.

Orwell replied in the next issue of *Tribune*, 23 April 1943:

I am interested to learn that it is "in line with international Socialist policy" to encourage petty nationalism all over the place. If Burma is to be "independent," what about Lithuania or Luxembourg? And how about Welsh nationalism and the separatist movement which probably exists in Cornwall? The absurdity of this kind of thing is apparent enough when applied to Europe, and its absurdity has also been demonstrated in the Far East. Siam, owing to a series of accidents, had remained "independent"; as soon as it was attacked it collapsed without a single day's fighting, and would have done the same any time these fifty years if faced with a similar threat. The plain fact is that small nationalities *cannot* be independent, because they cannot defend themselves. Look at the history of the last few years in Europe! Except for Poland, Greece and Finland, no small nation has fought for its independence for as long as a week. It is quite true that several of the small European States lost their freedom because we ourselves let them down. But that simply clinches what I have said: if they could only be independent under the protection of a great Power their independence was a sham.

The angry tone of Mr. Richards's letter seems to derive partly from his thinking that I want to retain Burma under the British flag. It seems that I am "against Burmese self-government," and profess a "new cheap brand of imperialism." Where did I say anything of this kind? I should be most interested if he could produce the passage. What I did say is that it is impossible for a country like Burma to be fully independent, with its own private army, tariff barriers, etc., and that we had no right to promise anything of the kind. Since then I have been approached by several Socialists who have told me that what I say about Burma is objectively true, but should not be put in print because we have got to compete with Japanese propaganda. I stick to it, however, that it does not pay to tell lies, even in propaganda. Concretely, what would be the result of promising Burma complete independence and trying to win over the extremer Burmese nationalists, including the priesthood? If we lose the war and the Japanese retain Burma, what we say will have made no difference. If we win the war and the Japanese are driven out, we are left with an unrealisable policy on our hands, a policy extremely distasteful to both India and China. Would it not be better, in our propaganda, to try to make the Burmese nationalists see what the modern world is like, and what part their country is capable of playing in it? I can well imagine that the Burmese believe the Japanese promises *now*, but will they still be believing them in 1944 or 1945?

"Burmese Observer" asks what policy I would advocate for Burma, and what I would say in our propaganda if I were directing it. He himself makes the very modest demand that Burma should be offered Dominion status within the Empire. If the Burmese want that, let them have it, but I myself would go further. If I could redraw the map I would place the whole mainland of south-east Asia, together with Formosa, under the guidance of China, while leaving the islands under an Anglo-American-Dutch condominium. I would advocate that Burma should retain its trade links with Britain and India, and should borrow such British experts (civil engineers, etc.) as it needed, but that the British should not remain in Burma in the capacity of rulers; and I would tell the Burmese now that the best future for their country lay in co-operating in a general Asiatic federation of which China and India would be the leaders. That may be less attractive than "independence" but it has the advantage of being realisable. I am sure "Burmese Observer" understands that, even if Mr. Richards doesn't.

Robert Duval responded on 30 April 1943:

The viewpoint put forward by Mr. Orwell in his footnote to my article on Burma is one which merits more serious consideration than some of my left wing friends apparently think. At the time of the October Revolution, a dispute along similar lines developed between Rosa Luxembourg[2] and Lenin. Luxembourg held that it was Socialism's task to transcend national boundaries, to achieve larger integrations, rather than to parcel up the Russian State according to the parochial aspirations of the various national minorities. On these grounds, she opposed Lenin's slogan of "National Self-Determination." On certain points time has proved that Rosa Luxembourg was right and Lenin wrong; but there are few things more certain than that the revolution would have suffered an early collapse had it not been for the national policy of the Bolshevik Party.

Mr. Orwell's error is essentially that of Rosa Luxembourg. His analysis is mechanical and over-objective. Objectively it is true that a backward peasant country cannot hope to be independent in the modern world—complete independence, for that matter, has become a thing of the past even for the major Powers. From this ultimate truth, Mr. Orwell draws the conclusion that it is wrong to promise independence to Burma after the war. But a cold statement of objective fact is not enough. Politics is a science which, more than anything else, involves an understanding of the mass mind and the mass heart. And of all the emotions which govern communal conduct, that of nationalism is still the most universal and the most deep-rooted. (Witness the heroic resistance of the Greeks—despite the hated Metaxas[3] regime.) Abstract justice does not enter into the question: there is nothing more human, more elemental, than for a subject people to hate its foreign governors.

I find it difficult to comprehend Mr. Orwell when he stresses the paucity of the Burmese intelligentsia, and the ignorance and indifference of the Burmese masses. The difference between pre-revolutionary Russia and Burma to-day is only a matter of degree—and the Russian Revolution demonstrated how much can be accomplished by a politically conscious handful, who are capable of interpreting the inarticulate aspirations of the masses. (The outsider frequently makes the mistake of identifying inarticulateness with indifference.) On one point Mr. Orwell seems to misunderstand me. I do not advocate Burmese independence in order to compete with Jap propaganda—as a half-penny catchphrase with which to enlist the support of the Burmese people. I believe in Burmese independence because I believe that there can be no such thing as compulsory collaboration; that national independence is a pre-condition of international collaboration; that it must be the right of every nation, from the largest to the smallest, to say when and on what terms they will adhere to a European or an Asiatic or a World Federation of Autonomous States. Mr. Orwell and myself have, I believe, the same ultimate ideal. It is in the political method of achieving this ideal that we differ.

Orwell's dismissive comments on Welsh nationalism and Cornish separatism were taken up by Keidrych Rhys[4] on 7 May, and by John Legonna on 21 May (not reproduced here). Legonna took Rhys to task for his 'flippant attitude' towards Cornwall. Rhys wrote:

Is George Orwell merely being provocative when he talks of "comic-opera" States, "petty nationalism" and "the absurdity" of giving small nations their freedom? I respect Orwell as a writer; but what is his line now? Some time ago he told me that intellectuals had underrated the depth of national feeling everywhere. Apparently he has now changed his views. Yet I would have thought that his experience of Catalonia would still be a constant reminder to him of the dangerous power of the centralised State.

Now he would seem to commit progressives to a line of policy which would be against devolution and decentralisation after the war. To drag in

Wales was a very unhappy analogy, for Wales happens to be an historic *national entity*. Even Fabians like G. D. H. Cole would approve of Wales being a separate administrative unit. And Ministers, such as R. A. Butler,[5] at least, would probably go nearly as far. Tom Wintringham and Common Wealth already advocate that Wales should have Home Rule and a Parliament of her own.

Then Orwell confuses the aims of Welsh nationalism, which stands for the attainment of Dominion status for Wales and the protection of the cultural and economic life of the Welsh nation, an old historic entity with a language of its own which still flourishes, with a Cornish movement that doesn't yet exist—except, perhaps, in the adventurous mind of A. L. Rowse,[6] that dab hand at *realpolitik*.

What are members of the small nations fighting for, then? The war has made the Welsh realise that they are a nation with a country, a people, a culture, and a tradition different from England's to fight for. At long last even two or three Welsh Socialist M.P.s are beginning to put up a gallant fight for Wales! No longer are Welshmen content to pander to English nationalism, English tastes and English interests and vilely let their own land down. Injustices and grievances abound in Wales at the present moment. Very few of the younger generation of Socialists here have much time for the existing political parties which have all seriously neglected Wales and Welsh problems. There is even talk of a new Welsh party. Yet no Socialist party organisation, except Common Wealth, treats Wales as a nation and us as Welshmen. If Orwell and his fellow progressives would read some Welsh history they might even prevail on Aneuran Bevan to see the light.

Orwell wrote again, for the last time, on 14 May 1943:

It is rather difficult to conduct a controversy when your opponents refuse to answer your questions. On the subject of the independence of small nationalities, I posed two quite plain questions: (*a*) If a small weak country is to be independent, how is it going to defend itself? and (*b*) if it is right to encourage small agglomerations of peoples to set up as independent states, with private armies, etc., where is the process to stop? I got no answer to either, and I must be forgiven for thinking that no satisfactory answer exists.

Mr. Keidrych Rhys, however, also charges me with being "against devolution and decentralisation," and in general, with not wanting small nationalities to be autonomous. He seems to think that because I realise that small states can't stand on their own feet in the age of the bombing plane, I therefore want to stamp out all local culture and turn all the minor racial groups into "natives" governed from Whitehall. But so far from wanting to see less local autonomy in the world, I want to see more of it! Not only would I be happy to see Wales a separate administrative unit, but I would like to see a great deal more decentralisation in England itself. But Mr. Rhys should realise that small units can only enjoy autonomy while they accept the protection of larger units. Small states can be free provided they don't try to be big states. In a world of power politics and intolerant nationalism, if that is the kind of world you want, there are only five or at most six countries capable of holding their own, and each of those would, of necessity, be quite ruthless in crushing any minor national group that got in its way. That is happening all over the world at this moment. On the other hand, let it once be recognised that complete independence is impossible, that being a "nation" doesn't necessarily give you the right to set up tariff barriers, stage "frontier incidents" and generally annoy your neighbours, and the small units can be as free to choose their own institutions as the big ones. Let us stick to Wales, as Mr. Rhys instances that. Wales enjoys a certain amount of cultural autonomy, and could, without hurting anybody, enjoy a good deal more, precisely because there is no real Welsh separatist movement. But suppose there was such a movement, suppose the Welsh hated us as much as the Czechs presumably hate the Germans, and were constantly in touch with our enemies in Europe and doing their best to facilitate an invasion of Britain—does he suppose that in that case we should tolerate Welsh autonomy? In self-defence we could not. We should have to do our best to crush every trace of Welsh nationalism, including the Welsh language. As to "injustices and grievances," those are not necessarily cured by securing national autonomy. There were quite a few injustices and grievances in Poland, Rumania, etc. Foreign oppression is not the only kind of oppression in the world.

The correspondence ran on into August. John Rowland, a Cornishman, wrote on 4 June that, though Cornwall was an interesting part of Britain with its own peculiarities, 'to suggest that it has any sort of national culture of its own is to land in the morass of the Celtic bards and all that sort of nonsense, with musical comedy uniforms and ceremonies, which are the laughing-stock of all forward-looking people.' Decentralisation would lead to the Balkanisation of the British Isles. He concluded by arguing that 'the death of the Welsh language would be an exceedingly good thing for literature in general, since it would force the talented writers of Wales to devote themselves to writing in a language which is understood by more than a handful of people.' On 28 May, John Jennings of Swansea said he would feel greater sympathy towards 'movements such as the Welsh Nationalist Party' if they displayed greater realism about the implications of nationalism. Would Wales be better off under Welsh capitalism than English? Fewer, not more, frontiers were essential. On 11 June 1943, F. W. Evans of Neath wrote to support Orwell:

As a Welshman I support the views expressed by George Orwell in your issue of 14th May.

The demand for national autonomy must always be examined not only on the case presented, but also on the *realpolitik* of the group who make it.

A reactionary caucus in power locally may be requiring a free hand to deal with local progressive elements.

Indian Nationalism means quite different things to Gandhi than it does to Palme Dutt,[7] and the results, in the working out of the policies of one, as opposed to the other, would have quite different results to India.

In the same way Welsh Nationalism, as visualised by the local minister and by, say, Dan Griffiths, would be absolutely different. It may well be that the former would require it in order the more successfully to deal with the latter, and to ensure that the chapel should continue to have the monopoly in catering for the social and cultural life of Wales.

Wales is fortunate in possessing a very large number of men of culture and genius, many of whom prefer to try and fertilise the life of the local community than undertake the trek to London for fame, but up to now their influence has been pretty effectively "neutralised."

What Wales requires as much as anything is the help of cultured and progressive Welshmen all over the world in supporting their counterparts in Wales itself. These people have had to leave Wales in order to gain recognition in the fields in which they happen to excel, and then direct their criticism at Wales for its backwardness, instead of helping to remove the cause of this backwardness.

The last two letters to be published appeared on 30 July and 27 August. Despite a relatively large amount of space given to the subject by *Tribune*, 'Welsh Subscriber' wrote noting that the correspondence had been allowed to tail off. The writer asked where *Tribune* stood on this matter and whether it was in touch with Welsh public opinion. Was *Tribune* aware of the many resolutions passed asking for a Secretary of State for Wales? Finally, John Legonna, of Llanrhystyd, wrote again, obliged, he said, by the 'meagre and pitifully unenlightening correspondence . . . upon the "Welsh Question"' to conclude that either readers of *Tribune* were not aware of the rapidly strengthening demand for Welsh and Scottish political autonomy, or simply not interested in the question. In his opinion, unless Great Britain found itself governed by 'Fascist-minded and Fascist-actioned rulers ruthlessly enforcing their whims and devices,' Wales, and very probably Scotland, 'will contract out of the present ignoble sterilising status of utter servility to Westminster. . . .'

1. L. S. Amery (1873–1955), Conservative politician and journalist; Secretary of State for India and Burma, 1940–45.
2. Rosa Luxemburg (or Luxembourg; 1870–1919) was a leader, with Karl Liebknecht, of the Spartacists, a revolutionary splinter group which broke away from the German Social Democratic movement in 1917, demanding the violent overthrow of the German government in order to end the war and bring about a socialist society based on its beliefs. The Spartacists founded the Communist Party of Germany in December 1918. The following month they instigated a series of mass demonstrations, in the course of which Luxemburg and Liebknecht were arrested and shot.
3. For Ioannis Metaxas, dictator of Greece, 1936–41; see *773, n. 2.*
4. Keidrych Rhys (1914–1987), a poet, journalist, broadcaster prominent in Welsh national affairs, directed the Druid Press from 1945, was editor of *Wales*, and contributed to *Horizon*, *The Listener*, *Penguin New Writing*, and *The Times Literary Supplement*. He served in the Royal Artillery for three years during World War II. Orwell included him in the sixth group of Modern Poets, 'Apocalyptics, etc.,' in a series of broadcasts he was about to arrange. See Orwell's letter to Mulk Raj Anand, 20 October 1942 (*1592*), regarding a radio interview with Rhys.
5. R. A. Butler (see *644, n. 8*) was Minister of Education, 1941–45. His policies tended towards the left of the Conservative Party, and his name was linked with that of Hugh Gaitskell, leader of the Labour Party, as 'Butskillism,' to suggest a moderate, centre approach in politics.
6. Alfred Leslie Rowse (1903–), historian and author whose works include collections of poems and stories of Cornwall and of and by the Cornish.

7. Rajan Palme Dutt (1896–1974), author, journalist, Vice-Chairman of the Communist Party;
   editor of *Labour Monthly* from 1921 and of the *Daily Worker* 1936–38. Orwell had several of his
   pamphlets in his collection. See also *519, n. 45*.

1990. To Noel Sircar

2 April 1943   Handwritten draft and typed versions
07/ES/EB/WMB

Dear Sircar
Thanks for yours.[1] I haven't anything to offer you at present, because our
time is shortly being altered to a time of day at which our stuff will reach India
about 4.30 pm. This means cutting out a good many of the talks and
concentrating on music. But we shall be going back to the old arrangement
about September. Meanwhile, there may be odds and ends about which I
could let you know later.

Yours sincerely,
[Initialled] E.A.B
Eric Blair
Talks Producer
Indian Section.

1. Noel Sircar had written to Orwell on 31 March 1943 asking if there was any work he could
   do—'scripts or the like.' He was 'not keen on the "Personality of the Week" series, for the
   reasons I explained to your secretary.' Orwell wrote out his reply on the verso of Sircar's
   letter. In the draft, 'may' in the last sentence is underlined.

1991. To Arthur Wynn, Music Bookings Manager

2 April 1943   Original   EB/WMB

Contract for Dr. Narayana Menon

Will you kindly arrange a contract and payment for Dr. Narayana Menon
for planning and choosing the 15-minute programme of gramaphone°
records, which will be broadcast on Thursday next, the 8th April, at 1130–
1145 GMT, in the Eastern Service (Red Network).

    Dr. Menon's address is 176 Sussex Gardens, W.2. and the programme is
a Feature Programme.

    Please refer to our memo. of the 22nd March on this subject.

[Signed] W Bedwell
(For Eric Blair)

1992. BBC Talks Booking Form, 2.4.43

E. M. Forster: 'Some Books,' usual monthly series; 13½-minute talk; broadcast 28.4.43; fee £21. Signed: M Blackburn for I.P.O.

1993. To Reginald Reynolds

[5 April 1943?]   Handwritten draft for postcard

Answer: (post card)

Dear Reg.,[1]
Thanks for the script[2]—just the kind of thing we wanted. I'll get it censored etc. & then we'll arrange a recording. I'll see that a copy goes to the Home Service.

E.A.B

1. 'Dear Reg.' is crossed through.
2. Probably 'The Second Discovery of America.'

1994. To E. M. Forster

5 April 1943   07/ES/EB/WMB

Dear Forster
Thanks for your letter. I am going to go through all the scripts of yours which we have and pick out the ones which I think would make a suitable pamphlet. You can then have a look at them. I can guarantee that they will not be messed about in any propagandist manner as they have already passed the censorship and that is all that is required. You could make any alterations of a literary kind that you felt they needed. However, I don't want to press you into this against your will. Perhaps we could talk it over? Would you like to have lunch with me on Friday, the 9th? Owing to summer time I shan't be free for lunch until 2 o'clock, but I could make it 2 o'clock sharp at the ARISTON, where we had lunch before, if you could manage it.
    Perhaps you could let me know?

Yours
[Initialled] E.A.B
George Orwell
(Talks Producer)
Indian Section

1995. To Benjamin Musgrave

5 April 1943   07/ES/EB/MB[1]

Private and Confidential

Dear Sir

Please forgive me for not having answered your letter of April 1st earlier.[2]

Mr. K. K. Ardaschir has done a great number of broadcasts for us on North Africa and the Middle East. He has travelled widely and evidently has considerable knowledge of the countries bordering the Mediterranean. I am not competent to give an opinion on him as a public speaker, as I have only heard him broadcast. Simply as a broadcaster, he is not in the first-class owing to a tendency to talk too fast. This might not matter on the platform, however. He is a ready writer and can always produce a competent and convincing-sounding script at short notice. Although he is not of English parentage, he has no foreign accent. I should say the audiences that would suit him best would be fairly well-informed middle-class or upper-middle-class audiences.

Yours faithfully,
[Initialled] E.A.B
Eric Blair
(Talks Producer)
Indian Section

1. 'MB' is not an error for 'WMB.' The letter was presumably typed by Mary Blackburn, not by Winifred Bedwell. The layout of the letter is not in the latter's style.
2. Ardaschir had written to Orwell in February 1943 asking if he would act as a referee for him. He said his other referee was Sir Gerald Woods Wollaston, Garter King of Arms, who had known him for many years. Musgrave worked in the Public Meetings section of the Ministry of Information.

1996. To Philip Unwin

5 April 1943   Original   07/ES/EB/WMB

Dear Mr. Unwin

Many thanks for your letter[1] and the specimen "blurb", which I return.

I have altered one word.[2] As to the photographs; it may well be better to do as you suggest and not include photos of people who don't feature in those particular broadcasts. In that case we should stick to just one for the jacket and the one of Tambimuttu and Hsiao Chien° might be best, unless it is possible to make up some sort of composite picture from several photographs put together? I have now got acceptance from all of our authors.

Yours sincerely
[Signed] Geo. Orwell
George Orwell
(Talks Producer)
Indian Section

1. In a letter of 2 April 1943, Philip Unwin proposed to go ahead and set the type for *Talking to India* (see *2359*). He sent a rough draft of a possible 'blurb' and asked if all the photographs Orwell had sent were to be used; some were of people whose talks were not being included.
2. Winifred Bedwell originally typed 'your word,' but 'your' was changed by Orwell to 'one.' Two carbon copies of the blurb survive. One is unaltered; the other has three changes. In 'A distinguished gathering of authors have collected for this book . . .,' 'have collected for' has been changed to 'is represented in'; in the first paragraph, 'intended' has been crossed out; and at the end of the blurb, 'represents' has been changed to 'is.' In a letter of 6 April from Allen & Unwin, the verbal change was said to be 'very desirable.' It is not clear which 'one word' Orwell altered. Allen & Unwin also indicated a preference for the illustration of Tambimuttu and Hsiao Ch'ien to a composite of several photographs.

1997. To E. M. Forster
6 April 1943   07/ES/EB/MB

Dear Forster

I am sorry to ask such a thing, but I wonder if you would be kind enough to re-fund the cost of the book you lost—"Arthur Ponsonby" by Henry Ponsonby. It was 12/6d. Apparently The Times Book Club hold us responsible and expect us to pay the price of the new copy.

Yours
[Initialled] E. A. B
George Orwell
(Talks Producer)

1998. To J. B. S. Haldane
7 April 1943   Original   07/ES/EB/MB

Dear Professor Haldane

I wonder if you would like to do a talk for us in a forthcoming series to India. I should want the script not later than the middle of May.

We nowadays do series of talks which are designed, after being broadcast, to be printed as pamphlets in India. Usually there are *six* talks in a series, making a pamphlet of about 10,000 words. In most cases these talks are literary, but I want for the next one, to have a series of Scientific ones. The subjects are: Malnutrition, Soil Erosion, Plant or Animal Breeding, Malaria, House-flies and Drinking Water. This sounds a very heterogeneous collection, but each touches on problems important to India, and if put together, they should make a readable popular pamphlet. I wonder whether you would like to do the one on "Plant or Animal Breeding". You could concentrate on Plants or Animals, whichever you prefer, but I suppose that in a talk of *thirteen-and-a-half* minutes—that is about 1500 words, it would be better to stick to one or the other. The main thing we want emphasised is the great differences that can be made in Agricultural production by breeding only from good strains.

Could you let me know as soon as possible whether you will undertake this. I will let you know later the exact date of the broadcast, which would be early in June. Of course, you can always record if the date is inconvenient, but my main concern is to have the scripts in early, so that I can send them to India to be printed. I should be much obliged if you could also suggest somebody able to talk about House-flies.[1]

Yours sincerely,
[Signed] Geo. Orwell
George Orwell
(Talks Producer)
Indian Section

1. This letter is reproduced from the top copy in the Haldane Papers, University College London. It is on the regular BBC, Broadcasting House, London, W.1. paper, but the telephone number has been changed to 'Euston 3400, Ext 208.' The letter is annotated, '12.30 pm. *Yes.* House-flies try Prof Buxton F.R.S., London School of Hygiene. He could do it himself (he has tropical experience) or recommend someone.' A carbon copy survives in the BBC Written Archive.

1999. To J. F. Horrabin

7 April 1943   07/ES/EB/MB

Dear Horrabin

I wonder if you would like to do us another talk, about the same length as you did before. I should be wanting the script not later than the middle of May.

We now do series of Talks which are designed to be printed in India in pamphlet form: in general, *six* talks—about 10,000 words, make one pamphlet. I am now sketching out a Scientific Series and the subjects of the six talks are to be: Malnutrition, Soil Erosion, Genetics, Malaria, House-flies and Water. This sounds rather heterogeneous, but they all touch on problems important to India. Do you think you could do us a talk on "Soil Erosion and Soil Deterioration"—its causes and prevention. The main thing that I think wants rubbing in to India is the disastrous effect of cutting down all the trees. There should be good illustrations for this in what has happened round[1] the Mediterranean.

Could you let me know as soon as possible whether you will do this? I will let you know later the exact date of the talk, which will be sometime early in June. If that actual day is inconvenient to you, we can always record beforehand, but I am chiefly concerned to get the scripts in in good time, so that I can send them to India to be printed.

Yours —
[Signed] Geo. Orwell
George Orwell
(Talks Producer)
Indian Section.

1. 'round' was an alteration in Orwell's hand from the typed 'as regards.'

2000. To Lord Winterton

7 April 1943   07/ES/EB

Dear Lord Winterton,
I understand from Princess Indira that you have kindly agreed to broadcast a short talk, of about ten minutes' duration, in our Eastern Service directed to India, 1.15–1.30 p.m. on Monday, 3rd May, 1943.

I should be glad if you could let us have a copy of your script not later than Friday, 30th April, and at the same time perhaps you will let us know at what time we may expect you at *200 Oxford Street* on the 3rd May, to rehearse your script before transmission.

Yours sincerely,
[Initialled] E.A.B
(Eric Blair)
Talks Producer

2001. BBC Talks Booking Form, 7.4.43

Lord Winterton: 'A talk of approx. 10 minutes on "Agriculture" within the "Debate Continues" period'; broadcast 3.5.43; fee £8.8s. Signed: M Blackburn for I.P.O.

2002. News Commentary in English for Malaya, 28

9 April 1943

This was written and read by George Orwell. No script has been traced.

2003. To Lord Winterton

9 April 1943   07/ES/EB/WMB

Dear Lord Winterton
Many thanks for your letter dated April 8th. A ten minutes talk would probably be 12 or 1300 words. It does not matter if you do rather more because we have no other speaker on that day and Princess Indira will merely be introducing you.

It will be quite all right for you to rehearse your India talk on the same day as your talk for the Home Service. As soon as I hear from Guy Burgess[1] I will fix it up.

> Yours sincerely
> [Initialled] E.A.B
> Eric Blair
> (Talks Producer)
> Indian Section

1. Guy Burgess was then a talks producer in the Home Service; see *1134*.

2004. To Sir John Russell

12 April 1943   07/ES/EB

Dear Sir John

I wonder if you would like to do another talk for the Indian Section of the B.B.C.[1] I should be wanting the script not later than the middle of May.

We now do series of talks which are designed to be printed in India in pamphlet form—in general, *six* talks—about ten-thousand words—make one pamphlet. I am now sketching out a popular scientific series and the subjects are to be:— Malnutrition, Soil Erosion, Genetics, Malaria, House-flies and Water. This sounds rather heterogeneous, but they all touch on problems important to India. I wonder whether you could do us the talk on "*Soil Erosion and Soil Deterioration*"—its causes and prevention. I won't presume to dictate to you what line you should take because I know very well that you are one of the leading authorities on this subject, and also know all about agricultural problems in India. I think, however, that your talk should contain mention of Soil Erosion in other parts of the world, such as the Middle West of America and round the Mediterranean. These talks are 13½ minutes, probably meaning about 1600 words. As they are designed to be printed, it does not matter if they are in rather more formal style than the average talk.

Could you let me know as soon as possible whether you will do this. I will let you know later the exact date of the broadcast of this talk, which will be sometime early in June. If the actual day is inconvenient to you, we can always record beforehand.

> Yours sincerely,
> [Signed] E. Blair
> Eric Blair
> (Talks Producer)
> Indian Section

1. Over the weekend of Saturday and Sunday, 10 and 11 April 1943, Eastern Service transmissions were split into a Programme Division and a News Division.

2005. To K. K. Ardaschir

13 April 1943   07/ES/EB

Dear Ardaschir

Thanks for your letters of April 5th and April 11th.

I think we could use the talk about the Turkish University on May 6th, which would mean I should want the script about the beginning of May (not later as I have to get it censored). The usual length please—i.e. 1500–1600 words.

Yours sincerely
[Signed] Eric Blair
Eric Blair
(Talks Producer)
Indian Section

2006. To Desmond Hawkins, John Lehmann, Herbert Read, Osbert Sitwell, and L. A. G. Strong

13 April 1943   07/ES/EB/WMB

The letter to Hawkins, with its accompanying schedule, is given in full; alternative third paragraphs to the other speakers are given in note 1. Slightly different schedules must have been sent to the other speakers (see paragraph to Lehmann which indicates authors bracketed differently from this schedule), and Read is not included in this schedule. For David Cecil, see letters to him of 23 and 27 April 1943, *2035* and *2042*.

Dear Hawkins

I wonder whether you would like to do another talk for the Indian Section during June. I should want the script by the middle of May. I will explain about the series of which this is part.

From time to time, we do a series of talks which are afterwards printed in India as pamphlets, six talks making one pamphlet. This particular series is to deal with English poetry, since 1900, the title to be MODERN ENGLISH VERSE, or something of that kind. As there are to be six talks we have to divide it up into six periods, somewhat arbitrarily you may feel, but it would be difficult to do it in any other way. I enclose a copy of the schedule I have drawn up.

I would like you to deal with the sixth and last talk covering new departures since the Auden school. There seem to be several trends here and I am not certain that I know my way about them, but I have put Dylan Thomas, Rayner Heppenstall and George Barker[1] in brackets, because they seem to fall chronologically between this school and the previous one.

With each period there is a list of "Poets to be mentioned". This does not mean that you have to mention all those in the body of your talk, and, on the other hand, you can bring in any other poets of the period you choose to mention. I append these names merely because, when the pamphlet is printed, we shall print at the end of each talk, a list of the best known poets of the period.

I hope very much that you will undertake this. Can you please let me know, as soon as possible, whether you would like to do so? These talks are 13½ minutes, which means 15 or 1600 words. I will let you know the exact date later, and if it is inconvenient, we can easily record the talks beforehand. But, in any case, I must have the script by the middle of May, so that I can despatch all six to India simultaneously.

Yours sincerely
[Initialled] E.A.B
George Orwell
(Talks Producer)
Indian Section

Modern Poets

School	Speaker	Poets to be mentioned
Background	Desmond McCarthy	Hardy, Housman, Yeats, Belloc, W. S. Blunt, Bridges, Doughty, Trench, Francis Thompson, Kipling, Watson, Sturge Moore.
Georgians	L. A. G. Strong	W. H. Davies, Blunden, R. E. Flecker, W. J. Turner, Robert Nichols, Harold Monro, Squire, Shanks, Drinkwater, Binyon, Masefield, de la Mare.
The war		Wilfred Owen, Sassoon, Herbert Read, Julian Grenfell, Charlotte Mew, Brooke, Rosenberg, Robert Graves.
[Eliot], etc.	David Cecil	Eliot, Lawrence, Joyce, Pound, Yeats, Edith Sitwell, Aldous Huxley, Ruth Pitter, Laura Riding.
Auden, etc.	John Lehmann	Auden, Spender, Day Lewis, MacNeice, William Empson, Roy Campbell, William Plomer, J. A. Tessimond.
Apocalyptics, etc.	Desmond Hawkins	J. F. Hendry, Henry Treece, Roy Fuller, Keidrich Rhys, Alex Comfort, Nicholas Moore, G. S. Fraser, Francis Scarfe, (Dylan Thomas, Rayner Heppenstall) George Barker, Terence Tiller, Alan Rook, Gascoyne.

Paragraph 3 for John Lehmann:[2]

I would like you to deal with the fifth talk on what one might call the political poets. I have put Empson, Campbell and Plomer in brackets because we are bound to stick to a chronological arrangement in these talks and these three obviously don't belong, in a political sense, with the others.

Paragraph 3 for Herbert Read:

I would like you to deal with the fourth talk, which roughly covers the return of English verse from nature-worship, etc., to earlier traditions and contact with European culture.

> Read replied on 18 April declining Orwell's request. Though 'always anxious to help you in your good work,' he was too busy organising the Design Research Unit and felt unhappy writing about his contemporaries. He suggested Sitwell and proposed that a poet of the current war should talk about World War I poetry; he reminded Orwell that Alan Rook was available.

Paragraph 3 for Osbert Sitwell:[3]

I would like you to deal with the third talk on the poets of the war. This is perhaps an especially arbitrary division, as those who wrote what is called "War Poetry" were mostly writing beforehand. But I think the war itself was a dividing line and had its effect on the development of English verse, though those who learned most from the war did not usually survive it.

> Paragraph 3 for L. A. G. Strong (although for this letter, paragraphs 2, 3, and 4 are run into one):

I would like you to deal with the second talk, on Georgian poetry.

1. Barker was typed here and in the schedule as Barber. The schedule has three more errors (as well as missing initials). The following corrections have been made: Pitter (for Ritter); G. S. Fraser (for J. S. Frazer); Alan Rook (for Allan Rook). The name 'Doughty' caused problems, being given as 'Dougherty' and with a 'G' at one time for the initial letter. Of the names given, only four are not represented in the *New Cambridge Bibliography of English Literature, IV, 1900–1950*: Rhys, Scarfe, Heppenstall, and Rook.
2. John Lehmann (see *312, n. 1* and *506, n. 6*) was particularly important at this time as editor of *New Writing*, a literary magazine committed to anti-Fascism and in the pages of which Orwell's essays 'Shooting an Elephant,' 'Marrakech,' and 'My Country Right or Left' (in *Folios of New Writing*) appeared.
3. Although Sitwell, in declining to give a talk on *The Importance of Being Earnest* when replying to Orwell's request of 1 April (see *1986*) had said he was willing to do something later on, this was a gap of only nine days since Sitwell's refusal. Orwell seems to have forgotten his earlier request, for he goes over much the same ground. Sitwell replied on 18 April, again declining. Orwell's request was much welcomed, but his heart, he wrote, had 'gone wrong' and he was inundated with work.

2007. To R. U. Hingorani

13 April 1943   07/ES/EB/EB/WMB°

Dear Dr. Hingorani
As I said in our telephone conversation yesterday, I am returning the synopsis[1] which you kindly sent us. I am sorry to have delayed so long but as I explained I had hoped that we might have been able to fit in another talk by you and held the matter up until I could make certain of this. I am afraid we shall not be able to arrange anything for the present because, owing to schedule changes, I have very little blank space to dispose of for some months to come, but thank you for the suggestions.

Yours sincerely
[Signed] Eric Blair
Eric Blair
(Talks Producer)
Indian Section

1. Hingorani had sent Orwell four scripts on 18 March 1942: 'Youth and Beauty,' 'Indian Food,' 'Habits,' and 'Happiness.' He offered to broadcast any that appealed to Orwell. Presumably 'synopsis' should be 'synopses'; Hingorani wrote of 'four scripts' in his letter of the 18th, and because this is annotated, in Orwell's hand, 'Ansd. 13.4.43 File,' these must be the talks referred to.

2008. To Michael Meyer

13 April 1943   Handwritten

Broadcasting House

Dear Mr Meyer,[1]
Many thanks for your letter. I could meet you for lunch on Monday the 19th, but I can't get away from here before 1.30 because the time of my programme has altered with double Summer Time. Do you think we could meet about 10 to 2, preferably somewhere fairly near here?

Your sincerely
Geo. Orwell

1. Michael Meyer (1921–2000), author and translator (most notably of Ibsen and Strindberg), wrote what he described as a 'timid letter' to Orwell at the BBC and received this reply. They lunched and became good friends. Meyer describes Orwell in *Remembering Orwell*, 132–37.

2009. Extract from Minutes of Eastern Service Meeting

14 April 1943

GUJERATI°

Mr. Blair reported proposal, there being no gramophone disc of suggested signature tune, to record a choral version. As an experiment and subject [to] her consent, agreed to try Princess Indira as Gujerati° Newsletter announcer.

2010. To P. A. Buxton

15 April 1943   07/ES/EB/WMB

Dear Professor Buxton[1]

I wonder whether you would care to do a talk for the Indian Section of the B.B.C. on the subject of house-flies. You were recommended to me by Mr. A. D. Imms, as the foremost authority on this subject, and as being especially suited to do the talk because of having first-hand knowledge of this problem in Eastern countries. I would therefore like it very much if you would undertake the talk, and I will explain about the series of which it is to be part.

From time to time, we do a series of talks which, after being broadcast, are printed in India, in pamphlet form, six talks making one pamphlet. These talks are usually literary, but for our next lot I want to do a popular scientific series on the following subjects—Malnutrition, Soil erosion, Genetics, Malaria, House-flies, and Drinking Water. Though rather heterogeneous, these subjects are all important to India, and should make a readable pamphlet. The talks are of 13½ minutes, which usually means about 1600 words. Since they are intended to be printed it does not matter if they are written in a rather more formal style than the average broadcast.

If you are willing to do this talk I would like to have the script by the middle of May. The actual date of the broadcast would be some time in June and I could give you exact particulars later. In the event of the date being inconvenient to you, there would be no trouble in recording the talk beforehand. Perhaps you would be kind enough to let me know whether you can undertake this.

Yours sincerely
[Not signed or initialled]
Eric Blair
(Talks Producer)
Indian Section

1. Patrick Alfred Buxton (1892–1955), Professor of Entomology, University of London. Among his publications were *Animal Life in Deserts* (1923) and *The Louse* (1939).

2011. To John Lehmann

15 April 1943   07/ES/EB/WMB

Dear Lehmann

Many thanks for your letter. I am glad you will do the talk. Perhaps you could come round and have tea one day here and we could settle the outstanding points. Any day of the week, except Thursdays or Saturdays, would suit me.[1]

The classification of poets to be printed after each talk isn't hard and fast, and I only made it out in order to give speakers a general idea. In any case, as soon as I had made it out, I found that there were a lot I had forgotten. As to the ones you queried; I have put them into those classifications because it is difficult to avoid doing this on a chronological basis, but we can fix all that when we talk it over. I have no wish to dictate what speakers shall say, but I do want to avoid overlapping.

As to what you will be paid, I have no power over that, and am not supposed to know anything about it, but I should imagine that you will be paid £8.8.0. for a talk of about 1500 words. I think I told you that we proposed broadcasting one poem in each talk, where possible, spoken by the writer himself. You might think over what poem, from your period, you would like to broadcast, and I will see whether we have a recording of it.

Can you ring me up, and let me know when you're coming. My telephone number is Euston 3400, Extension 208.

Yours sincerely
[Signed] Geo. O.
George Orwell
(Talks Producer)
Indian Section

1. On 31 December 1942, Orwell wrote, 'Tuesdays is supposed to be my day off' (1788).

2012. News Commentary in English for Malaya, 29

16 April 1943

This was written and read by George Orwell. No script has been traced.[1]

1. Gentry's diary (see 1669) for this week shows he had access to news from the BBC. On 10 April he records a statement 'in House of Commons that Axis Southern Army [in Tunisia] expected to collapse within a few days'—an item that would hardly be so presented by any other broadcasting authority. On 14 April he gave his source as the BBC when writing of the drive on Tunis: 'This town is expected to offer stiff resistance, the BBC announcing that the troops there are tough.' Tunis was taken on 7 May, though some fighting continued for a day or two.

2013. To Penguin Books, Ltd
16 April 1943

10a Mortimer Crescent
N.W.6

Dear Sir

Many thanks for your letter of April 14th. I have not formally fixed things up with Gollancz about reprinting, but I do know that according to my contract I am allowed to issue a cheap edition two years after publication, if Gollancz himself has not done so. It was on these terms that you did another book of mine in the Penguins.

As to Harpers, they are not likely to raise any objection, as they allowed Gollancz to issue an English edition only a year after the book was published in New York.[1] I think, in any case, my contract with them is on the same terms as the one I have with Gollancz. I will make absolutely certain about this from my Agent, who keeps my contracts for me, but I think you can assume there will be no trouble. Just in case that Harpers did raise any objection, we could use the English edition but I would much prefer the American one, as the other was somewhat mutilated.

Yours truly
[Signed] Geo. Orwell
George Orwell

1. *Burmese Days* was published by Penguin Books in May 1944. The letter was typed on BBC letterhead. Penguin Books had published *Down and Out in Paris and London* in December 1940.

2014. To Sir John Russell
16 April 1943   Handwritten draft and typed versions[1]
07/ES/EB/WMB

Dear Sir John

Many thanks for your letter of the 15th April.

I think it would be just early enough if you could be ready to let us have the script by, say, May 25th, or, at any rate, *before* the end of May. You could either record it then or deliver it on the day of the broadcast, as you preferred. I would much rather have you do this talk than anyone else, if it can be arranged.

Yours very truly
[Signed] Eric Blair
Eric Blair
(Talks Producer)
Indian Section

1. Apart from the salutation, the draft lacks commas. Orwell first wrote 'Yours sincerely' but changed that to 'Yours very truly.' The typed version adds 'the' before '15th April.' At the head of the draft Orwell has written 'Reply:' indicating that it was not an aid to dictation but a

text written out for Winifred Bedwell to type. Presumably she added the punctuation. Paradoxically, where Orwell *did* have a comma (after 'Dear Sir John,') she did not, as was her customary style.

2015. To Arthur Wynn, Music Bookings Manager

16 April 1943   Original[1]

Contract for Mr° Narayana Menon

As usual, will you kindly arrange a contract and payment for Dr. Narayana Menon, for planning and choosing his 15 minutes programme of gramophone records, which will be broadcast on Thursday next, the 22nd April, at 1130–1145 GMT, in the Eastern Service, Red Network.

Dr. Menon's address is 176 Sussex Gardens, W.2. and the programme, as usual, is a Feature Programme.

[Signed] W Bedwell
(For Eric Blair)

1. There is no reference (EB/WMB would be expected), and Winifred Bedwell signed this memorandum, so it is almost certain that she initiated it. See also memorandum of 30 April 1943, *2050*.

2016. BBC Talks Booking Form, 16.4.43

Reginald Reynolds: The Second Discovery of America; recorded 21.4.43; broadcast 22.4.43; fee £10.10s.[1] Signed: M Blackburn for I.P.O.

1. On 18 April, Reynolds sent Orwell a postcard to say he had mumps and would be unable to make the recording. The booking form is marked 'Cancelled'; also, the fee is changed to £7.7s, presumably in the light of Orwell's memorandum of 19 April. Orwell annotated Reynolds's letter, 'Send R. R. a p.c. to tell him we shall have to have the b'cast read. EAB'; see memorandum to Miss Boughen, 19 April 1943, *2020*.

2017. Review of *The Development of William Butler Yeats* by V. K. Narayana Menon

Time and Tide, 17 April 1943

Two books on Yeats have appeared almost simultaneously, a more or less "official" biography and this one of Mr Menon's, which is only biographical to the extent of recognizing that an artist's work is conditioned by his circumstances. Like most "pure" poets Yeats had an uneventful life and it is perhaps more important to understand his family background than to know the history of his own quiet career. He was one of the founders of the Abbey Theatre and he was mixed up to some small extent in Irish politics—he even had a brief disillusioning interlude as a Senator—but the real events of his life were internal, and his almost continuous development as a poet was in its way just as dramatic as the most vivid life of "action".

As a poet Yeats had three main phases which were perhaps less separate than is generally supposed. In the first place, as a young man, he was influenced by the pre-Raphaelites and the literary lions of the 'nineties, and it was no doubt in that period that he adopted the "art for art's sake" attitude which he was to preserve more consistently than any of his contemporaries. Then there was his "Celtic twilight" phase, by which he is still probably best remembered; and the astonishing final phase in which he produced his best work, in language far simpler than he had ever achieved before, when he was more than sixty years of age. But there is a connecting thread that runs through all these seemingly separate periods, and that is Yeats's hatred of the modern world—hatred not only of industrial ugliness but still more of the democratic, rationalistic outlook which has ruled Western society since the Renaissance. He hated the concept of human equality, and said so with an outspokenness which is very rare in our time. Mr Menon quotes extensively from a book which was only privately printed, *A Vision*, in which Yeats set forth the philosophic system underlying his work. Stripped of a great deal of nonsense about phases of the moon, reincarnation, disembodied spirits and what-not (how literally Yeats believed in all this is uncertain), the system seems to reduce to belief in a cyclical universe in which human history repeats itself over and over again and can consequently be foretold if one knows how to interpret the signs. It is difficult not to feel that Yeats embraced this belief primarily because it did away with the concept of progress and promised an early end to the vulgar, scientific, equalitarian epoch which he hated. Civilization would soon be entering upon an authoritarian period—so he professed to believe, and, since he wished it, perhaps did believe. Inevitably he was sympathetic towards Fascism, at least the Italian version of it, and was influenced by Ezra Pound and various Italian thinkers. With positive exultation he looked forward to the coming destruction of democracy and even the justly famous lines:

> *The best lack all conviction while the worst*
> *Are full of passionate intensity*

in which the rise of the Nazis seems to be foretold, do not imply disapproval if one reads as a whole the poem (*The Second Coming*) in which they occur. What Yeats's attitude would have been if he had lived to see the present phase of the struggle between Democracy and Fascism we cannot tell. The greatest peculiarity of Fascism is its power to appeal to quite different types of men for incompatible reasons. To Yeats, offshoot of an impoverished family with aristocratic pretensions, it probably appealed because it appeared as an extreme version of conservatism. But he might have seen through this error if he had lived longer, and in any case, with his distaste for politics, he would not have been likely to follow the example of his old friend, Ezra Pound.

As Mr Menon rightly says, Yeats's acceptance of Fascism is a "disquieting symptom", but it in no way detracts from the interest of his literary development. There can have been few poets who have shown such a lifelong power of growth. On the other hand his mystical beliefs, with their sinister implications and their tinge of charlatanism, were not simply an eccentricity to be disregarded. They are integral to his work, and, as Mr Menon shows, many of his best passages are hardly intelligible unless one knows something about the yogey-bogey on which they are founded.

> *Where got I that truth?*
> *Out of a medium's mouth,*
> *Out of nothing it came,*
> *Out of the forest loam,*
> *Out of the dark night where lay*
> *The crowns of Nineveh.*[1]

It may seem strange to us that a poet of very high order can not only believe in spiritualism and magic but even found his work to some extent on that belief; but it is worth remembering in this connection that there have been other great writers (Edgar Allan Poe, for instance) whose outlook on life was not far removed from insanity. Perhaps, for a writer, common sense matters less than sincerity, and even sincerity, in the ordinary moral and intellectual sense, less than something that might be called artistic integrity. Yeats may have held some absurd or undesirable beliefs, and he may have laid claim to a mystic wisdom that he did not possess, but he would never in any circumstances have committed what he would have regarded as an aesthetic sin. To curry favour with the big public or to be satisfied with inferior work would have been quite impossible to him. His life was devoted to poetry with a completeness that has been very rare among the English-speaking peoples, and the results justified it. In spite of some patches of absurdity it is an impressive story, and Mr Menon retells it with great delicacy and acuteness.[2]

1. From the Introduction to the play *The Resurrection*; see also *The Variorum Edition of the Poems of W. B. Yeats*, edited by Peter Allt and Russell K. Alspach (New York, 1957), Fragment II, 'The Tower,' 439.
2. Also reviewed by Orwell, in *Horizon*, January 1943; see *1791*.

2018. BBC Talks Booking Form, 17.4.43

James Stephens: 'Calling All Students,' 'Great Dramatists,' 6: W. B. Yeats, with special reference to *The Hour Glass*;[1] broadcast 27.5.43; fee £10.10s + travel voucher. Signed: M Blackburn for I.P.O.

1. This talk was particularly well received. Frederick Laws (1911–), then radio critic of the *News Chronicle*, having read the printed version in *The Listener* for 17 June 1943, asked in his column why the programme had not been scheduled for the Home Service. This led to a memorandum from the Controller of the Home Service, Sir Richard Maconachie, to George Barnes, Director of Talks (printed in West: *Broadcasts*, 259), in which he said they should be prepared to answer this question were it raised internally.

2019. To V. B. Wigglesworth

19 April 1943   07/ES/EB/WMB

Dear Dr. Wigglesworth[1]

Many thanks for your letter of April 16th.[2] I wonder if you could be kind enough to do° suggest someone else, who would be able to do a talk for us on "House-flies". I am anxious to get all these talks done, as early as possible, and don't care to take the risk of waiting until Professor Buxton gets back. I should be very much obliged for any suggestions.

Yours truly
[Initialled] E.A.B
Eric Blair
(Talks Producer)
Indian Section

1. Vincent Brian Wigglesworth (1899–1994; Kt., 1964) was Director of the Agricultural Research Council Unit of Insect Physiology, 1943–67, and Reader in Entomology, University of London, 1936–44; Professor of Biology, University of Cambridge, 1952–66. His many publications include *Insect Physiology* (1934); *The Principles of Insect Physiology* (1939), both many times reprinted; and *Insects and Human Affairs* (1951).
2. Dr. Wigglesworth had replied to Orwell's letter to Professor Buxton of 15 April (see *2010*) on the following day. He was dealing with Buxton's correspondence while the Professor was in the United States for two or three weeks.

2020. On Orwell's behalf to E. W. D. Boughen

19 April 1943   Original   EB/WMB

REGINALD REYNOLDS — THE SECOND DISCOVERY OF AMERICA

With reference to our booking slip of the 16th—please note that Mr. Reginald Reynolds, is now unable to come and record his talk, as above, as he has gone down with mumps. His script will, however, be read by someone else (one of the announcers) in the period 1145–1200 GMT on the 22nd, in the EASTERN SERVICE (Red Network) as scheduled, so will you please see that he receives his fee for the script.

[Signed] W Bedwell
(For Eric Blair)

2021. To E. M. Forster

20 April 1943   07/ES/EB/WMB

Dear Forster

Herewith the book OVER TO BOMBERS by Mark Benney.[1] Do you mind sending it back when it is finished with?

Your broadcast is next week, the 28th, at 1.15 to 1.30 pm (DBST).

Yours
[Initialled] G.O.
George Orwell
(Talks Producer)
Indian Section

1. Benney's book had evidently been sent to Forster shortly after Orwell wrote to Philip Unwin on 5 March 1943; see *1936*. Forster must have returned it, for he sent Orwell a postcard (printed in West: *Broadcasts*, 252) asking for the book to be sent back to him because Orwell was unable to supply 'more Orientalia.'

2022. To Raymond Mortimer

20 April 1943   07/ES/EB

Dear Mortimer[1]
I am so glad to hear that you are willing to do the talk on OSCAR WILDE.[2] I had better explain about the programme of which this talk is to be part.

We have a series called GREAT DRAMATISTS. Each programme consists of a ten minutes talk on the dramatist in question, with particular reference to one of his plays, a short extract from that play acted by the B.B.C. Repertory, and some music. The other dramatists dealt with in this series are MARLOWE, DRYDEN, SHERIDAN, IBSEN, and YEATS. The play of Oscar Wilde's which we shall be acting is THE IMPORTANCE OF BEING ERNEST,° and I would like it if you could make your talk bear specially on that while giving some idea of Wilde's work as a whole. We always start the programme by trailing a few lines from the bit we're acting, after which the speaker does his stuff. So your talk should start "Those lines you've just heard come from THE IMPORTANCE OF BEING ERNEST"—or words to that effect.

The programme will be broadcast on Thursday the 13th May, at 1.30 p.m. If that time is not convenient we could easily record your talk beforehand. A ten minutes talk usually means about one thousand words. I would like it if I could have your script not later than the 5th May.

As to the fees; I have no power over this, and am not supposed to know *anything* about it, but I should say that for a ten minutes talk you would get about £8.8.0.

Yours sincerely
[Initialled] E.A.B
George Orwell
(Talks Producer)
Indian Section

1. For Raymond Mortimer, literary editor of *The New Statesman & Nation*, see *301, n. 3*. He was the author of *Channel Packet* (1942), *Manet's Bar aux Folies-Bergère* (1944), *Duncan Grant* (1944), and *Trying Anything Once* (1976).
2. This topic was offered to Osbert Sitwell on 1 April 1943. He was too busy to participate; see *1986, n. 1*. 'Ernest' in the title should be spelt 'Earnest'

2023. BBC Talks Booking Form, 20.4.43

Oliver Bell: 'Women Generally Speaking,' Films of the Month; a 13½ minute talk, given live; introduction by Lady Grigg; broadcast 28.4.43; fee £10.10s. Signed: M Blackburn for I.P.O.

2024. Tamil Newsletter, 1

22 April 1943

The Tamil Newsletter (or News Commentary, as it is sometimes described) came under the aegis of Rowan Davies. It was translated and read by J. D. S. Paul, who travelled to London from Cambridge for this purpose. From 22 April, Orwell wrote the English version, and his participation is numbered from one in the series here, although Tamil Newsletters had been broadcast for many months before Orwell's involvement. For Orwell's Newsletters in this series, the switch censor (who cut off transmission if anything unauthorised was broadcast) was the Reverend Gordon Matthews.

Orwell was always referred to in the Programmes as Broadcast as 'Eric Blair' in connection with these Newsletters, never as 'Orwell' (unlike, for example, the Newsletters in English for Malaya and Indonesia). PasBs always described these broadcasts as either 'Newsletter in Tamil' or 'Tamil Newsletter,' except for the programme of 13 May 1943, described as 'News in Tamil.'

Orwell wrote the English version until he left the BBC; his final script was transmitted on 25 November 1943, two days after he had completed his service. A clue to possible differences in the scripts for Tamil and Indonesian (English) Newsletters is provided by the fact that Orwell wrote the Newsletter for Indonesia on 3 September, the day he went on holiday, for John Morris to read on his behalf, whereas M. Phatak was commissioned to write the Tamil Newsletter for the preceding day. Morris also wrote the scripts for the following two Wednesdays.

Orwell wrote twenty-nine, or possibly twenty-eight, English versions of this series; there are no PasB details for 18 November 1943, but it is unlikely that a script was not written for that week.

No scripts have survived for either the English or Tamil versions of these Newsletters.

2025. To Desmond Hawkins

22 April 1943   07/ES/EB

Dear Hawkins

Thanks for yours. I am glad you will do the talk. As I said before, you don't have to mention the poets I listed, and you can bring in any others you like, provided they're not chronologically wrong. I forgot about Gascoyne, but he certainly belongs in that lot. The list which I made out is only there because in the pamphlet we intend to put a comprehensive list of poets of the period at the end of each talk. The next thing to fix is which poem of the period you think should be broadcast in the body of your talk. Of course, it is an advantage to have the poet broadcast it himself, which should be possible with these younger ones. We have got a very nice poem by Henry Treece, but we have broadcast it once already. How about getting Alex Comfort to do something? If he has a good voice something of his might be suitable. It should be not more than 30 lines, I should say. Or what about Alan Rook? You might let me know about this. I would like the poem to be fitted in somewhere in the middle of your talk, so that you can say—"Now here is an example of what I mean" or words to that effect.

Yours
[Initialled] E.A.B
George Orwell[1]

1. This letter runs to near the foot of the page, and there was no space to type Orwell's BBC position (nor, as quite often, the typist's reference). This is not elsewhere noted.

2026. To J. Elizabeth Jermyn

22 April 1943   Original 07/ES/EB/WMB

Dear Miss Jermyn[1]

Very many thanks for your letter of April 20th. I am so glad Professor Haldane will do the talk. We can arrange the recording at any time convenient to him if we are given two or three days notice, but I would like to have the script by the middle of May.

We approached Professor Buxton,[2] but he is out of England. However, Dr. Wigglesworth is doing the talk for us. I would be much obliged if Professor Haldane could suggest someone to do us a talk on "Drinking-water," which is to be another in the same series. I haven't yet been able to find a speaker for this subject.

Yours sincerely
[Signed] Geo. Orwell
George Orwell
(Talks Producer)
Indian Section

1. Miss Jermyn was J. B. S. Haldane's secretary. The original of this letter is in the Haldane Papers, University College London.
2. Professor Buxton had been suggested by Haldane as someone who could speak with authority on house-flies. See *1998, n. 1.*

2027. To Alan Rook

22 April 1943   07/ES/EB/WMB

Dear Mr. Rook[1]

Herbert Read told me that you are out of the Army now and might be willing to do a talk on the air for us. I wonder whether you would like to do a short talk in the series we are arranging for India, giving an account of English poetry from 1900 onwards.° The others who are taking part are Desmond Hawkins, John Lehmann, L. A. G. Strong, probably Desmond McCarthy, and one other. If you're willing, I will send particulars of what we want, but I would be glad if you could let me know, fairly soon, whether you are likely to be able to do the talk, as we have to get the whole series into order.[2]

Yours sincerely
[Signed] Geo. Orwell
George Orwell
(Talks Producer)
Indian Section

1. Major William Alan Rook (1909–), poet and critic, wrote *Songs from a Cherry Tree* (1938), *Soldiers, This Solitude* (1942), *These are my Comrades* (1943), *We who are Fortunate* (1945), *Not as a Refuge* (on the writing of poetry) (1948). He served in the army, 1939–44.
2. Rook replied on 23 April saying he would be delighted to give a short talk provided Orwell was satisfied as to his competence to do so.

2028. To V. B. Wigglesworth

22 April 1943   07/ES/EB/WMB

Dear Dr. Wigglesworth

Very many thanks for your letter of April 21st.[1] I should be delighted if you will do the talk. It should be a talk of about 13½ minutes, which means fifteen or sixteen hundred words. While being informative, it should not be too technical in language. But as these talks are designed to be reprinted afterwards, it does not matter if the style of writing is rather more literary than is usual in a broadcast.

I shall look forward to seeing your script about the middle of May.

Yours sincerely
[Signed] Eric Blair
Eric Blair
(Talks Producer)
Indian Section

1. Wigglesworth had replied to Orwell's letter of 19 April (see *2019*) on the 21st, saying he would be pleased to give the talk himself. He supplied a script very quickly, and on 27 April, Terry G. M. de L. Gompertz, a talks producer in the General Overseas Service, wrote apologising for the lack of an acknowledgement, explaining that she had been away and there was 'a muddle in my office.' However, she said that 'the script was in every way what I wanted.' The letter was initialled by 'DBG,' her secretary.

2029. BBC Talks Booking Form, 22.4.43

K. K. Ardaschir: 'The Turkish University inaugurated in 1933'; a '13½ mins. talk, which he will write and broadcast'; broadcast 6.5.43; fee £10.10s. Signed: M Blackburn for I.P.O.

2030. BBC Talks Booking Form, 22.4.43

Naomi Royde-Smith: 'Women Generally Speaking'; three 13½-minute talks under the general title 'Rationed Freedom': 'Food,' 'Dress,' and 'Mobility'; broadcast 19.5.43, 16.6.43, 21.7.43; fee £15.15s each talk + fare and subsistence. Signed: M Blackburn for I.P.O. Remarks: 'N. Royde-Smith has broadcast in W.G.S.[1] before and should receive a similar fee, not less. She sh'd receive a rlwy. voucher and subsistence allowance for the nights previous to her broadcasts.'

1. 'Women Generally Speaking,' see *1852*.

2031. To Tom Driberg

c. 22 April 1943

On 20 April 1943, Tom Driberg wrote to Orwell and sent him a pamphlet. This may have related to Driberg's interest in the Army Bureau of Current Affairs. He asked for the return of the pamphlet. It is unlikely that Orwell failed to respond, but no letter has been traced.

2032. News Commentary in English for Malaya, 30

23 April 1943

This was written and read by George Orwell.[1] Script has not been traced.

1. See, however, next item, about Orwell's absence on leave.

2033. Orwell's Leave

23–26 April 1943

Orwell's staff file shows that he took three days' leave from Friday, 23 April, to Tuesday, 26 April 1943. Nevertheless, he is still credited in the PasB with writing and reading News Commentary for Malaya, 30, on the 23rd.

2034. To Sir Richard Acland

c. 23 April 1943

On 22 April 1943, Sir Richard Acland, a leader of the Common Wealth Party, sent Orwell a copy of a speech he was to make at Manchester. He asked whether any of the points he made in it might be adapted for his broadcast to India, which Orwell was arranging for 17 May 1943. No reply from Orwell has been found. On that day, George Strauss, M.P., broadcast in the series 'The Debate Continues.' Orwell makes a detailed reference to 'the growth of Common Wealth, Sir Richard Acland's party' in his London Letter to *Partisan Review*, c. 23 May 1943; see *2096*.

2035. To Lord David Cecil

23 April 1943   07/ES/EB/WMB

Dear Lord David

Many thanks for your letter.[1] I wonder whether you would like to do a talk for the Indian Section of the B.B.C. This is one of a series of six talks on contemporary English poetry. As the talks have to fit in to a schedule, and afterwards be re-printed in the form of a pamphlet, I can't give you absolutely a free hand as to which poets you should talk about, but I could offer you the choice of two or three different schools.

The other speakers taking part in the series are L. A. G. Strong, John Lehmann, Desmond Hawkins, and probably Desmond McCarthy and Alan Rook. It would be a question of doing the script by some time in June and delivering the talk in July. Could you let me know whether you are interested and if so, I will send you fuller particulars.

Yours sincerely
[Initialled] E. A. B
George Orwell
(Talks Producer)
Indian Section

1. Cecil wrote an undated letter from New College, Oxford, on 22 April. It concluded, privately, and very amicably, their disagreement in *The Times Literary Supplement* over poetic language following Orwell's review in *Horizon*, January 1943, of V. K. Narayana Menon's *The Development of William Butler Yeats*; see *1791*.

2036. To E. D. Edwards

23 April 1943   07/ES/EB

Dear Professor Edwards[1]

Following up our telephone conversation I will tell you about the talk we want you to do for us. We have a series called BOOKS THAT CHANGED THE

WORLD, dealing with the sacred books of Asia. (This follows on an earlier series dealing with European books which have been specially influential).

As the title implies, these talks are not intended so much to discuss the doctrines of the various oriental religions as to show their historical influence. Of course, they have to give some account of the doctrines as well, and I think in dealing with an Indian audience you ought to assume that your hearers will not know very much about Confucius's teachings, less than they would know about Christianity, for example. These talks are of 13½ minutes, that is, 15 or 1600 words, and I should be much obliged if I could have this script in about a week's time. The actual broadcast is on Friday, May 7th, at 1.45 to 2 pm. If that is inconvenient for you, we could easily arrange a recording beforehand.

Yours sincerely
[Initialled] E.A.B
Eric Blair

1. 'Dr. Edwards (Miss)' (on talks booking form, for 23.4.43; see *2040*) submitted her script to Orwell on 3 May 1943 in draft, asking if there was anything he would like altered. She proposed sending the final draft the following day or the day after. She had found it difficult, she said, to get both the teaching of Confucius and the historical aspect of Confucianism into so short a script.

2037. To Malcolm Darling

23 April 1943   07/ES/EB/WMB

Dr. Gangulee, who had contributed to Orwell's 'In Your Kitchen' series, had written to Orwell on 21 April with some ideas for broadcasts. Orwell sent Gangulee's letter to Sir Malcolm Darling with this note on the verso, and, with it, the carbon copy of his letter to Gangulee (see *2038*).

Sir Malcolm Darling
I cannot book any English talks at present, but possibly some of Dr Gangulee's ideas have a bearing on the forthcoming Round Table discussions,[1] & he might be a conceivable speaker in one of the programmes? He has a rather soft voice, but is amenable to rehearsal.

[Signed] Eric Blair   23.4.43

1. The Minutes of the Eastern Service fortnightly meetings record, from 28 October 1942, proposals for a fifteen- or twenty-minute programme to be called 'Round Table Discussion.' Approval was sought for the programme from the Government of India, and on 11 November 1942, it was decided that Sir Malcolm Darling and Laurence Brander would draft a telegram to that government 'embodying the main points of the report, requesting comment on the type of subjects suggested, explaining difficulties due to the dearth of distinguished Indians in this country, and stressing the advisability of including other than British experts in the discussions.' It was hoped to interest the next Viceroy in the project. It was not until 9 July 1943 that the first discussion was recorded (Minute 108). The speakers were Wickham Stead, as chairman, Lord Hailey, Sir Ramaswamy Mudaliar, and Quintin Hogg. The producer was Anthony Weymouth. Six discussions were broadcast, and on 22 December 1943 (after Orwell had left the BBC) it was reported that the Government of India had been asked whether the

first series justified arranging a second. The protracted and delicate discussions surrounding this series, which attempted to deal with serious issues, is indicative of the sensitivity of Anglo-Indian relations at the time, in which atmosphere Orwell and his colleagues had to operate every day of the week.

2038. To N. Gangulee

23 April 1943   07/ES/EB/WMB

Dear Dr. Gangulee

Many thanks for your letter of April 21st. I cannot arrange any more talks at present because our schedule is full up, but I think some of your ideas might be of interest to Sir Malcolm Darling, and I am passing your letter on to him.[1] I am sorry I cannot be more helpful at present.

> Yours sincerely
> [Signed] Eric Blair
> Eric Blair
> (Talks Producer)
> Indian Section

1. Darling, in his turn, annotated Orwell's letter to Gangulee, 'Of no "interest" to me'. Is it to you?' and sent it on 7 July to Z. A. Bokhari, Indian Programme Organiser, who returned from his visit to India on 17 May 1943. Bokhari then added his annotation: 'Passed to Mr. Blair.' . . .

2039. To Alan Rook

23 April 1943   07/ES/EB/WMB

Dear Mr. Rook

I was very glad to get your telegram[1] agreeing to do the talk for us. I will explain about the series of which this is to be part.

From time to time we do series of talks which, after being broadcast, are printed in India in pamphlet form. This particular lot are to deal with English poetry since 1900. I enclose a list of the proposed headings of the talks. For this purpose, we have to divide English verse of this century into six periods, which is somewhat arbitrary, but it is difficult to see how to do it otherwise. Herbert Read suggested that you might like to do the one on the poets of the last war. This might be a good idea because I think there is much to be said for people not talking about their contemporaries. Opposite each heading there is a list of poets of the period. This doesn't mean that you have to mention all of these and, on the other hand, you can bring in any others you like, but I merely put this list because when we print the pamphlet we shall add a list of representative poets of the period at the end of each talk. If you don't want to do the one on the war poets you might like to do the one on Eliot and his associates, but, let me know which you prefer. You will, of course, be able to say exactly what you like except that I shall have to avoid overlapping between the different speakers.

These are talks of 15 to 1600 words. They will go out some time in July, which means that I would like to have your script by the middle of June. In each talk we shall have one poem of the period broadcast in a different voice, where possible, the writer's own voice. Can you pick something you think suitable of 20 or 30 lines and work it into your talk so that it acts more or less as an illustration. If the date of broadcast turns out to be inconvenient, we can arrange to record beforehand.

Yours sincerely
[Initialled] E.A.B
George Orwell
(Talks Producer)
Indian Section

1. Major Rook followed up his telegram in response to Orwell's letter of 22 April with a letter dated 23 April expressing his pleasure at being asked to broadcast.

2040. BBC Talks Booking Form, 23.4.43

Dr. Edwards (Miss): 'Books That Changed the World,' 4; The Analects of Confucius; broadcast 7.5.43; fee £10.10s. Signed: M Blackburn for I.P.O.

2041. To K. K. Ardaschir

27 April 1943   Handwritten draft and typed versions[1]
07/ES/EB/WMB

Dear Ardaschir

Thanks for a very good script. I have sent it along to be censored and trust there will be no trouble. The date of the talk is May 6th, at 1.45 pm.—can you be here about 1 o'clock for rehearsal?

As to the other talks. I think I could use one on the PANAMA CANAL, for my ice-box. The only thing is you say the subject-matter is "rather sordid" and I don't want to tread on too many toes. Perhaps you could tell me about this when we meet.

Yours sincerely
[Signed] Eric Blair
Eric Blair
(Talks Producer)
Indian Section

1. The draft and the typed version are verbally identical except that the draft omits 'the' before 'talk' in the third sentence. There are slight styling changes. Ardaschir acknowledged this letter on 30 April, and this was annotated by Orwell: '*Miss Bedwell*   NB that Mr Ardaschir wants his carbon copy back (also of the Turkish talk).'

2042. To Lord David Cecil

27 April 1943   07/ES/EB/WMB

Dear Lord David

Many thanks for your letter. I am glad you are ready to do the talk and I will explain about the series of which it is to be part.

From time to time, we do a series of talks aimed at the Indian University Students, which are published in India in pamphlet form, at the same time as they're broadcast.[1] This particular series, which will go out in July, is on English poetry since 1900. For the purpose of the series I have had to divide the last forty-three years into six periods, which is somewhat arbitrary but seems to be the only workable arrangement. I enclose herewith a copy of the schedule I have worked out.[2] As you say, you would like to talk largely about De la Mare, perhaps you would like to do the first period. I had put De la Mare in among the Georgians, but I think he would go equally well in the first lot. The list of poets against each division does not mean that you have to mention all of those and, on the other hand, you can bring in any others that you want to. I merely put the list because when we issue the pamphlet we shall print the names of the representative poets of the period at the end of each talk.

We shall probably include one poem, broadcast in a different voice, in each of these talks. You might perhaps care to pick the poem, something of about 20 or 30 lines, for your talk.

These talks are of 13½ minutes, which means 15 or 1600 words. As to fees—I have no jurisdiction over this but I should say you would get £8.8.0. and travelling expenses. I would like to have the script by the middle of June, because we want to send them all out together to be printed. If you want to see me about this, I am always in my office, except Saturdays. My telephone number of° Euston 3400, Extension 208.

Yours sincerely
[Initialled] E. A. B
George Orwell
(Talks Producer)
Indian Section

1. It was earlier said that publication would take place after the talks had been broadcast (*2006* and *2039*). Publication of the series 'Books and Authors' and 'Landmarks in American Literature' was over three years after the broadcasts, and these were the only two of Orwell's 'university' series to be published in pamphlet form in India; see *3101*.
2. The same schedule sent to Desmond Hawkins on 13 April 1943 (see *2006*) was enclosed with this letter.

2043. To Alan Rook

[27 April 1943?]   Handwritten draft for postcard

This note (for Winifred Bedwell?) is written at the foot of a letter from Alan Rook dated 'Easter Monday.' That, in 1943, fell on 26 April, and Orwell probably replied on the following day. Rook had asked for L. A. G. Strong's address in order to get in touch with him to ensure he did not overlap with what Strong said.

P.C.

I'll try & get you a copy of Strong's talk when done. I should think he would be fairly early with it. I have tried to avoid overlap as best I can, but at need we can make last-minute adjustments.

G.O.

2044. To Sir John Russell

[27 April 1943?]   Handwritten draft for postcard

Sir John Russell's letter suggesting a date for the delivery of his script of his talk is date-stamped 24 April 1943. That means it was received on that Saturday, and although Orwell might have replied then, he is more likely to have written on the Tuesday after the Bank Holiday.

P.C.

Thank you very much. It will do if we can have the script on "Soil Erosion & Soil Deterioration" by the date you name.

E. A. B

2045. S. J. de Lotbinière to Leslie Stokes on 'Great Dramatists' Series

27 April 1943

The Director of Empire Services, S. J. de Lotbinière, wrote this memorandum to Leslie Stokes, Empire Programme Planner, (see 845, n. 5) requesting production assistance for Orwell's 'Great Dramatists' series, part of 'Calling All Students.'

I've discussed "Great Dramatists" with Blair. He'd be very glad to have a producer to handle the casting and production of the dramatic illustrations in this series. He would, however, wish to control the choice of dramatist and play and the text both of the introductory talk and of the dramatic illustration—since he is in touch with the needs of the Indian students listening at the other end.

  Would you arrange for a producer to help Blair with the series—

Thursday's edition being the last to be produced under independent management.

The series runs fortnightly.

2046. Extracts from Minutes of Eastern Service Meeting

28 April 1943

Mr Brander reported latest rebroadcasting return [by All India Radio] showed an increase from 30 to 39 minutes in the daily average, mainly on "Calling All Students".

REBROADCASTING

E.S.D. reported that as it is not always possible to give items at times convenient for direct rebroadcasting by AIR, and following a request from them, Mr. Blair was exploring the intrinsic cost of clearing, from the BBC standpoint, the right of AIR to record, for rebroadcasting, definite items excluding dramatic performances: if cost not excessive, possibilities of assisting AIR in this way to be explored.

2047. Newsletter in Tamil, 2

29 April 1943

The English version was written by Eric Blair; translated and read by J. D. S. Paul. The switch censor[1] was the Reverend G. Matthews. No script has been traced.

1. Matthews appears to have been the regular switch censor for Tamil Newsletters; Sir Richard Winstedt, for Malay. The regular translator and reader was J. D. S. Paul; see *2024*.

2048. News Commentary in English for Malaya, 31

30 April 1943

This was written and read by George Orwell. No script has been traced.

2049. Review of *Voices in the Darkness* by Tangye Lean

Tribune, 30 April 1943

Anyone who has had to do propaganda to "friendly" countries must envy the European Service of the B.B.C. They are playing on such an easy wicket! People living under a foreign occupation are necessarily hungry for news, and by making it a penal offence to listen in to Allied broadcasts the Germans have ensured that those broadcasts will be accepted as true. There, however, the advantage of the B.B.C.'s European Service ends. If heard it will be believed, except perhaps in Germany itself, but the difficulty is to be heard at all, and still more, to know what to say. With these difficulties Mr. Tangye Lean's interesting book is largely concerned.

First of all there are the physical and mechanical obstacles. It is never very easy to pick up a foreign station unless one has a fairly good radio set, and every hostile broadcast labours under the enormous disadvantage that its time and wavelength cannot be advertised in the Press. Even in England, where there is no sort of ban on listening, few people have even heard of the German "freedom" stations such as the New British and the Workers' Challenge. There is also jamming, and above all there is the Gestapo. All over Europe countless people have been imprisoned or sent to concentration camps, and some have been executed, merely for listening to the B.B.C. In countries where surveillance is strict it is only safe to listen on earphones, which may not be available, and in any case the number of workable radio sets is probably declining for want of spare parts. These physical difficulties themselves lead on to the big and only partly soluble question of what it is safe to say. If your probable audience have got to risk their necks to hear you at all, and have also got to listen, for instance, at midnight in some draughty barn, or with earphones under the bedclothes, is it worth while to attempt propaganda, or must you assume that nothing except "hard" news is worth broadcasting? Or again, does it pay to do definitely inflammatory propaganda among people whom you are unable to help in a military sense? Or again, is it better from a propaganda point of view to tell the truth or to spread confusing rumours and promise everything to everybody? When it is a case of addressing the enemy and not the conquered populations, the basic question is always whether to cajole or to threaten. Both the British and the German radios have havered between the two policies. So far as truthfulness of news goes the B.B.C. would compare favourably with any non-neutral radio. On the other doubtful points its policy is usually a compromise, sometimes a compromise that makes the worst of both worlds, but there is little question that the stuff which is broadcast to Europe is on a higher intellectual level than what is broadcast to any other part of the world. The B.B.C. now broadcasts in over 30 European languages, and nearly 50 languages in all—a complex job, when one remembers that so far as Britain is concerned the whole business of foreign radio propaganda has had to be improvised since 1938.

Probably the most useful section of Mr. Tangye Lean's book is a careful analysis of the radio campaign the Germans did during the Battle of France. They seem to have mixed truth and falsehood with extraordinary skill, giving strictly accurate news of military events but, at the same time, spreading wild rumours calculated to cause panic. The French radio hardly seems to have told the truth at any moment of the battle, and much of the time it simply gave no news at all. During the period of the phoney war the French had countered the German propaganda chiefly by means of jamming, a bad method, because it either does not work or, if it does work, gives the impression that something is being concealed. During the same period the Germans had sapped the morale of the French Army by clever radio programmes which gave the bored troops some light entertainment and, at the same time, stirred up Anglo-French jealousy and cashed in on the demagogic appeal of the Russo-German pact. When the French transmitter stations fell into their hands the Germans were ready with programmes of propaganda and music which they had prepared long beforehand—a detail of organisation which every invading army ought to keep in mind.

The Battle of France went so well for the Germans in a military sense that one may be inclined, when reading Mr. Tangye Lean's account, to overrate the part that radio played in their victory. A question Mr. Tangye Lean glances at but does not discuss at length is whether propaganda can ever achieve anything on its own, or whether it merely speeds up processes that are happening already. Probably the latter is the case, partly because the radio itself has had the unexpected effect of making war a more truthful business than it used to be. Except in a country like Japan, insulated by its remoteness and by the fact that the people have no shortwave sets, it is very difficult to conceal bad news, and if one is being reasonably truthful at home, it is difficult to tell very big lies to the enemy. Now and again a well-timed lie (examples are the Russian troops who passed through England in 1914, and the German Government's order to destroy all dogs in June, 1940) may produce a great effect, but in general propaganda cannot fight against the facts, though it can colour and distort them. It evidently does not pay, for any length of time, to say one thing and do another; the failure of the German New Order, not to take examples nearer home, has demonstrated this.

It would be a good thing if more books like Mr. Tangye Lean's describing the B.B.C. and other organs of propaganda from the inside, were available to the general public. Even well-informed people, when they attack the B.B.C. or the M.O.I., usually demand the impossible while ignoring the really serious faults of British propaganda. Two recent debates in Parliament on this subject brought out the fact that not a single member seemed to know what does or does not happen in the B.B.C. This book should help towards a better understanding, though about half a dozen others along roughly the same lines are needed.

2050. On Orwell's behalf to Arthur Wynn, Music Bookings Manager

30 April 1943   Original

Contract for Mr° Narayana Menon

As usual, will you kindly arrange a contract and payment for Dr. Narayana Menon, for planning and choosing his 15 minutes programme of gramophone records, which will be broadcast on Thursday next, the 6th May, at 1130–1145 GMT, in the Eastern Service, Red Network.

Dr. Menon's address is 176 Sussex Gardens, W.2. and the programme, as usual, is a Feature Programme.

[Signed] W Bedwell
(For Eric Blair)

2051. BBC Talks Booking Forms, 30.4.43

Three, for Dr. N. Gangulee, Mrs. K. C. Roy, and Shridhar Telkar: 'In Your Kitchen,' 6, 7, and 8 (Mrs Roy engaged for 6 and 8 only); broadcast 5, 12, and 19.5.43; fees £8.8s each for each broadcast for Gangulee and Telkar; £3.3s for Mrs Roy. Signed: M Blackburn for I.P.O.

2052. BBC Talks Booking Form, 30.4.43

Princess Indira of Kapurthala: 'The Debate Continues'; broadcast 3, 10, 17, 24, and 31.5.43; fee £10.10s for each. Signed: M Blackburn for I.P.O.

2053. BBC Talks Booking Form, 1.5.43

Miss Leela° Erulkar: reading of Indian play 'The Jasmine Garland,' an adaptation of the Sanskrit play attributed to Dinnaga; recorded 3.5.43; to be kept as an emergency 'Ice-box' play to be used when needed, fee £4.4s. Signed: M Blackburn for I.P.O.

2054. BBC Talks Booking Form, 1.5.43

E. M. Forster: 'Some Books'; usual monthly talk, 13½ minutes; broadcast 26.5.43; fee £21. Signed: M Blackburn for I.P.O.

2055. BBC Talks Booking Form, 1.5.43

Lady Grigg: 'Women Generally Speaking'; broadcast 5, 12, 19, and 26.5.43; fee £8.8s for each broadcast. Signed: M Blackburn for I.P.O.

2056. BBC Talks Booking Form, 1.5.43

Raymond Mortimer: 'Calling All Students,' 'Great Dramatists,' 5; 'ten-minute talk on Oscar Wilde with spec. reference to *The Importance of Being Ernest*°'; broadcast 13.5.43; fee £8.8s. Signed: M Blackburn for I.P.O.

2057. BBC Talks Booking Form, 1.5.43

Shridhar Telkar: 'Behind the Headlines'; broadcast 6, 13, 20, and 27.5.43; fee £9.9s each talk. Signed: M Blackburn for I.P.O.

2058. To the Secretaries, Students' Unions, University of Cambridge, University of Edinburgh, London School of Economics, University of Oxford

3 May 1943   07/ES/EB/WMB   Reproduced from copy to
University of Cambridge Union

Dear Sir

I am writing to you on the advice of Mr. R. R. Desai, who frequently broadcasts for us. He tells me that the facilities which Indians have in this country for broadcasting messages to their families in India are not so well known as we could wish. You could, perhaps, help me by publicising one or two facts. I am writing at the same time to various other places where Indians resident in this country are to be found.

Previously, there was a rule that Indians here could only broadcast a message once in three months. This rule was made when a comparatively large number of Indians were living in this country. There are now much fewer and any one individual is now able to broadcast a message as often as once a month. This seems not to be generally known and we are very anxious that it should come to the notice of anyone interested in broadcasting messages.

Perhaps I should also state briefly the general regulations laid down for these messages. They should be about a minute in length, in one of the Indian languages, or in English, and should be of a strictly personal nature. We like to receive beforehand a copy of the message in the language in which it is to be broadcast, with an English translation. The messages are recorded and broadcast a few days later. For security reasons we cannot state in advance the exact date on which any message will be broadcast. A fee of one guinea, to cover all expenses, is paid to anyone broadcasting a message.

I should be greatly obliged if you could display these facts in any way convenient to you, for example, by displaying this letter on a notice-board or something of that description. It is in the interests, both of the B.B.C. and of the Indian community in London, that the facilities for broadcasting messages should be better known.

Yours truly
[Initialled] E. A. B
George Orwell
(Talks Producer)
Indian Section

2059. To J. Elizabeth Jermyn

5 May 1943   07/ES/EB/WMB

Dear Miss Jermyn

Many thanks for the suggestion about the London School of Hygiene. As to the fee, for Professor Haldane's talk, I have no jurisdiction over this, and am supposed not to know anything about it, but I do not fancy he would get less than ten guineas plus a small royalty from the profits of the pamphlet, if any.[1]

Yours sincerely
[Initialled] E. A. B[2]
George Orwell
(Talks Producer)
Indian Section

1. On 17 May 1943, Miss Jermyn wrote to tell Orwell that Haldane would not be able to broadcast. Because he was still not provided with the two assistants promised him, he was very tired and was cutting down on outside work. He suggested Dr. C. D. Darlington (with whom Orwell had already corresponded) and Dr. John Hammond, but he said he did not know how good they would be as broadcasters. Orwell annotated this letter: 'Answered 15.5.43   Written to Lauwerys / Darlington 15.5.43.'
2. The original of this letter is in the Haldane Papers, University College London. Although he initialled the copy E.A.B, he signed the original 'Geo. Orwell.'

2060. To the Director, London School of Hygiene & Tropical Medicine[1]

5 May 1943   07/ES/EB/WMB

Dear Sir

On the advice of Professor J. B. S. Haldane, I am writing to ask whether you can suggest somebody who would be able and willing to do a short talk for the Indian Section of the B.B.C. on the subject of drinking-water. This is for a series of talks which are afterwards to be printed in India in pamphlet form. They are to be broadcast in June, but I should want the script in about a fortnight's time, as I want to get them all together, so as to despatch them to India. I should be very much obliged if you could give me a suggestion as early as possible, and I will then send any proposed speaker fuller particulars.

Yours truly
[Initialled] E. A. B
Eric Blair
(Talks Producer)
Indian Section

1. The Director was Brigadier G. S. Parkinson (1880–1953; CBE). He also acted as Assistant Director of Hygiene, Eastern Command, 1939–45.

2061. Tamil Newsletter, 3

6 May 1943

The English version was written by Eric Blair. No script has been traced.

2062. BBC Talks Booking Form, 6.5.43

K. K. Ardaschir: The Panama Canal; '13½ mins. talk which he has written and will record. It will be kept as an emergency ice-box talk to be used when needed'; recorded 11.5.43; fee £10.10s. Signed: M Blackburn for I.P.O. The form has a sticker attached: 'VERY URGENT.'[1]

1. Ardaschir sent Orwell a lettercard dated 6 May 1943, which Orwell annotated: 'Miss Bedwell—Please see that Mr A gets his contract Tuesday   EAB.'

2063. BBC Talks Booking Form, 6.5.43

Rt Hon Arthur Greenwood, MP:[1] 'The Debate Continues'; 7 to 8 minutes on 'The Function of an Opposition'; broadcast: 10.5.43; fee £8.8s. Signed: M Blackburn for I.P.O.

1. Arthur Greenwood (1880–1954), M.P., 1922–31, 1932–54, was unanimously elected deputy to Clement Attlee, leader of the Labour Party in 1935. He famously urged Chamberlain on 2 September 1939 to 'speak for England.' He was a member of the War Cabinet, May 1940–February 1942, and when Labour gained power in 1945, he was appointed Lord Privy Seal. He left the Cabinet in 1947, due to frail health.

2064. BBC Talks Booking Form, 6.5.43

Catherine Lacey: 'Women Generally Speaking'; producer: Eric Blair; broadcast 12.5.43; fee £8.8s + repeat fees. Signed for S.F.A., Programme Contracts Department (Drama).

2065. BBC Talks Booking Form, 6.5.43

Miss D. Nanavati: 'In Your Kitchen,' 7; live discussion with Dr. Gangulee and Shridhar Telkar; broadcast 12.5.43; fee £3.3s. Signed: M Blackburn for I.P.O.

2066. News Commentary in English for Malaya, 32

7 May 1943

This was written and read by George Orwell. No script has been traced.

2067. To F. W. Mackenzie

7 May 1943   07/ES/EB/WMB

Dear Sir[1]

I am writing to you on the advice of the London School of Hygiene, who tell me that you might be willing to do a talk for the Indian Section of the B.B.C. I will tell you about the series of which this talk would be part.

From time to time, we do series of talks which are aimed at the Indian University students and are printed in India in pamphlet form, after being broadcast. This particular series is a popular scientific one on subjects of interest and importance to the Indian public. There are six talks, the subjects being—

> Malnutrition,
> Genetics,
> Soil erosion,
> Malaria,
> House-flies, and
> Drinking water.

It is the last that we hope you will undertake. These talks are of 13½ minutes, which usually means 15 or 1600 words. As they are to be printed afterwards it does not matter if they are written in a somewhat more formal style than the ordinary broadcasts. They are, of course, intended to be both informative and entertaining. With your knowledge of India you will know how much knowledge to assume in your hearers.

These talks will be going out during June and July but I should want the script in about a fortnight from now because I want to get them all together so as to despatch copies to India. I cannot say, with certainty, what you would be paid for the talk but I should say, probably, £10.10.0. plus a small royalty later on from the sale of the pamphlet. The latter, however, would, at best, only be a very small sum.

Could you be kind enough to let me know, as early as possible, whether you are willing to undertake this.

Yours truly
[Initialled] E. A. B
Eric Blair
(Talks Producer)
Indian Section

1. Lt. Col. F. W. Mackenzie was Director of Laboratories, [London] Metropolitan Water Board.

2068. To L. A. G. Strong

7 May 1943   07/ES/EB/WMB

Dear Mr. Strong

Many thanks for the talk, which is just what we wanted. There's no hurry about the broadcast as these are only going out in July. I'll let you know the exact date later.

Thanks for taking so much pains to keep within the framework I set.

Yours sincerely
[Initialled] E. A. B
George Orwell
(Talks Producer)
Indian Section

2069. To V. B. Wigglesworth

7 May 1943   Handwritten draft and typed versions
07/ES/EB/WMB

Dear Dr. Wigglesworth

Very many thanks for an excellent script. It is just what we wanted. The talk will be going out about the beginning of July. I will let you know the exact date later. Should it prove inconvenient to you we can easily arrange a recording beforehand.

I suppose you don't object to your talk being printed as part of a pamphlet in India? In theory[1] you will get a royalty on the pamphlet but at best this would be a small sum. I cannot say with certainty what you will get for the talk itself, but I should say in the neighbourhood of ten guineas.

Yours sincerely
[Initialled] E. A. B
Eric Blair
(Talks Producer)
Indian Section

1. Wigglesworth sent in his script on house-flies on 5 May. Orwell wrote out this reply on its verso. Winifred Bedwell could not read his writing at the word 'theory' and queried it.

2070. 'Three Years of Home Guard: Unique Symbol of Stability'

The Observer, 9 May 1943

It is close on three years since the eager amateurs of the L.D.V. doctored shotgun cartridges with candle-grease and practised grenade-throwing with lumps of concrete, and the value of the Home Guard as a fighting force can now be fairly accurately estimated.

Although it has never fought, its achievement has not been negligible. In the early days the Germans, to judge by their broadcasts, took the Home Guard more seriously than it took itself, and it must at all times have been part of the reason for their failure to invade Britain. If it were even five per cent. of the reason it would not have done so badly for a part-time and unpaid army.

The Home Guard has passed through three fairly well-defined phases. The first was frankly chaotic, not only because in the summer of 1940 the Home Guard had few weapons and no uniforms, but because it was enormously larger than anyone had expected.

An appeal over the radio, probably intended to produce fifty thousand volunteers, produced a million within a few weeks, and the new force had to organise itself almost unhelped. Since opinions differed about the probable form of a German invasion, it organised itself in innumerable different ways.

By the middle of 1941 the Home Guard was a coherent and standardised force, seriously interested in street-fighting and camouflage, and reasonably well armed with rifles and machine-guns. By 1942 it had Sten guns and sub-artillery as well, and was beginning to take over some of the anti-aircraft defences. This third phase, in which the Home Guard is definitely integrated with both the regular Army and Civil Defence, has its own problems, some not easily soluble.

During the past year it has been assumed that if the Continent is invaded the Home Guard will partly replace the Regular forces in these islands, and the result has been the tendency to train it for mobile warfare. This has been made easier by the fall in the average age of the Home Guard. But in some ways the results have not been happy. With a part-time and frequently-changing personnel, it is doubtful wisdom to imitate the training of Regular soldiers, and, in any case, the Home Guard could not be made fully mobile even if transport existed for it.

Most of its members are also workers, and even in the case of invasion the economic life would have to be carried on in any area where fighting was not actually happening.

If Britain is ever invaded the Home Guard will in practice fight only in its own areas and in smallish units. The steady tightening of discipline and the increasing contact with the Regular Army have been enormous advantages; but as a strategic plan it would probably have been better to stick to the original idea of purely local defence, and thus make use of the only advantage the amateur soldier has over the professional—that is, intimate knowledge of the ground he is fighting on.

But though the Home Guard has come to look and to be much more like an army than it was, its early days have left their mark on it. The training schools started by Tom Wintringham and others in the summer of 1940 did invaluable work in spreading an understanding of the nature of total war and an imaginative attitude towards military problems.

Even the then lack of weapons had its advantages, for it led to much experimenting in garages and machine shops, and several of the anti-tank weapons now in use are partly the result of Home Guard researches.

Socially, the Home Guard is not quite what it was at the beginning.

Membership has changed rapidly with the call-up, and its tendency has been to settle into the accepted English class pattern. This was perhaps inevitable in an unpaid army in which it is difficult to do the work of an officer without having a car and a telephone.

But if its internal atmosphere is not truly democratic, at least it is friendly. And it is very typical of Britain that this vast organisation, now three years old, has had no conscious political development whatever. It has neither developed into a People's Army like the Spanish Government militias, as some hoped at the beginning, nor into an S.A., as others feared or professed to fear. It has been held together not by any political creed, but simply by inarticulate patriotism.

Its mere existence—the fact that in the moment of crisis it could be called into being by a few words over the air, the fact that somewhere near two million men have rifles in their bedrooms and the authorities contemplate this without dismay—is the sign of a stability unequalled in any other country of the world.

2071. To John Macmurray

10 May 1943   07/ES/EB

Dear Professor Macmurray[1]

I wonder if you would like to do a short talk for the Indian Section of the B.B.C. We have a series called BOOKS THAT CHANGED THE WORLD, dealing with books which can be said to have had a direct influence on human history. The present series deals with the sacred books of the various Oriental religions, such as the KORAN, the BAGWAD GITA,° and so on. We want to round it off with a talk on THE NEW TESTAMENT and I think you would be just the person to do it if you would undertake it. We want a talk of 13½ minutes, that is, 15 or 1600 words, and we should want the script by about May 20th, or a day or two later. The talk would actually go out on Friday, May 28th, but if that date should be inconvenient to you you could easily record it beforehand. You will appreciate, no doubt, that we want a talk rather on the social, philosophical and ethical influence of the New Testament, than on the actual doctrines of the Christian religion.

I hope you will be able to do this for us. Could you be kind enough to let me know, as early as possible, whether you can or not.

Yours sincerely
[Initialled] E. A. B
George Orwell
(Talks Producer)
Indian Section.

1. John Macmurray (1891–1976), Grote Professor of the Philosophy of Mind and Logic, University of London, 1922–44; Professor of Moral Philosophy, University of Edinburgh, 1944–58. Among his many publications were *The Philosophy of Communism* (1933), *The Structure of Religious Experience* (1936), and *The Boundaries of Science* (1939). He also

contributed to *Marxism* (1934) and *Aspects of Dialectical Materialism* (1934). He served in the army, 1914–19 and was awarded the Military Cross. In this correspondence his name is regularly spelt 'MacMurray'; it has been corrected. See *531* for Orwell's review of Macmurray's *The Clue of History*.

2072. BBC Talks Booking Form, 11.5.43

George Strauss, M.P.:[1] 'The Debate Continues'; 'talk of approx. 6 minutes to come within the period The Debate Continues . . . which he will write and broadcast'; broadcast 17.5.43; fee £5.5s. Signed: E Dunstan[2] for I.P.O. Remarks: 'The title of this talk is Joint Production Committees in the Factories.'

1. George Strauss (1901–; Life Peer, 1979), Labour M.P. from 1929, was at this time Parliamentary Private Secretary to the Minister of Aircraft Production and a co-director of *Tribune*. In the post-war Labour administrations he was Minister of Supply, 1947–51, and introduced the Iron and Steel Nationalisation Bill in 1949.
2. Presumably the 'ED' who typed letters for Orwell in February 1942.

2073. 'Marrakech'

Broadcast 10 May 1943

Orwell's Source Material File (derived from his Personal File by a member of the BBC's staff at the BBC Written Archives Centre, Caversham, March 1984) states that he recorded a talk, 'Marrakech,' on 10 May 1943 at 1830 for Radio Newsreel. He was paid no fee. No mention of this talk is given in the daily PasBs for the Pacific, Eastern, African, or North American Services, 10 to 17 May 1943. No script has been traced.

2074. To V. B. Wigglesworth

12 May 1943   Handwritten draft[1]

Reply (p.c.) 12/5/43.
Many thanks for your letter of 11.5.43. I will let you know later the exact date of the talk (round about 25th July). I will arrange for you to come here a little early so that [we] shall have time for rehearsal.

E.A.B.

1. This was written in ink by Orwell on the verso of Dr. Wigglesworth's letter of 11 May; it has been ticked through with the date '12/5/43' written in pencil, indicating that Winifred Bedwell had sent the postcard.

2075. Extracts from Minutes of Eastern Service Meeting

12 May 1943

HINDUSTANI SERVICE

<u>Messages</u> Reported that as many Indians in this country were unaware of the message service, informatory circulars had been sent out. Noted that payment of expenses helped to secure good, well presented messages: Mr. Blair to discuss use of English messages in English Service: vernacular messages accommodated as far as possible in appropriate newsletters.

<u>COMPETITIONS</u>
Reported that only one entry received in April. Agreed competitions to be publicised as much as possible over the microphone: to be tried for another two/three months and if attention still lacking it was suggested that three months' prizes be pooled.

After Orwell had left the BBC, the following report was made to the Committee on 22 December 1943:

<u>COMPETITIONS</u>
E.S.D. reported that, in spite of wide publicity, only a very small number of entries had been received for monthly competitions. Entries were mainly from Anglo-Indians who represented a minority audience, and very few had been received from Indians. E.S.D. asked whether the meeting considered it was worth while continuing the competitions. It was agreed that they should be continued for the present, but that essays should be asked for on one specific programme, to be announced in advance, and not on the English Service as a whole. Also agreed that AIR should be asked to publish photograph of the winner when announcing the result. Mr. Brander to pursue arrangements with Mr. Beachcroft.

2076. News in Tamil, 4[1]

13 May 1943

The English version was written by Eric Blair. No script has been traced.

1. This is the only Newsletter in this series to be described in PasB as 'News in Tamil.' All others are called 'Newsletter in Tamil' or 'Tamil Newsletter.'

2077. To K. K. Ardaschir

13 May 1943   07/ES/EB/WMB

Dear Ardaschir

Herewith the script, I spoke to you about. I'm sorry we can't use it but it is not quite up our street.

Yours sincerely
[Initialled] E. A. B
Eric Blair
(Talks Producer)
Indian Section

2078. To the Secretary of the Royal Literary Fund

13 May 1943   Original, on BBC letterhead   07/ES/EB/WMB

Dear Sir

I understand that the Anglo-Indian writer, Cedric Dover, is applying to the Royal Literary Fund for a grant. I believe that he is in some distress through having been unexpectedly called up for service in the Armed Forces.[1] It may perhaps be useful to you if I give you some particulars about him and his work.

Cedric Dover has done a good many broadcasts in English for the Indian Section of the B.B.C. besides some for the Hindustani programme section. Several of his talks on literary and sociological subjects were of outstanding merit and three of them are being re-printed in a book of broadcasts which Allen and Unwins are publishing in a few months time. Cedric Dover is also author of the well-known book HALF-CASTE and of other books dealing with Asiatic problems. He deserves encouragement, not only as a talented writer but because writers of Anglo-Indian blood are a very great rarity and are in a specially favourable position to illuminate some of the most difficult of present day problems, in particular, the problem of colour.

Yours truly
[Signed] Geo. Orwell
George Orwell
(Talks Producer)
Indian Section

1. On 26 March, Dover wrote to Orwell about money Orwell had lent him that he had not repaid: 'In the circumstances you will understand why I have defaulted on my debt to you . . . But give me a little more time and I'll square up.'

2079. On Orwell's behalf to Arthur Wynn, Music Bookings Manager

13 May 1943   Original   EB/WMB

Contract for Mr° Narayana Menon

As usual, will you kindly arrange a contract and payment for Dr. Narayana Menon, for planning and choosing his 15 minutes programme of gramophone records, which will be broadcast on Thursday next, the 20th May, at 1130–1145 GMT, in the Eastern Service, Red Network.

Dr. Menon's address is 176 Sussex Gardens, W.2., and the programme, as usual, is a Feature Programme.

[Signed] M Bedwell
(For Eric Blair)

2080. BBC Talks Booking Form, 13.5.43

Oliver Bell: 'Women Generally Speaking,' Films of the Month; introduction by Lady Grigg; broadcast 26.5.43; fee £10.10s. Signed: E. Dunstan for I.P.O.

2081. News Commentary in English for Malaya, 33

14 May 1943

This was written and read by George Orwell. No script has been traced.

2082. BBC Talks Booking Form, 17.5.43

Sir Richard Winstedt, KBE, CMG: script and reading of Malay News Commentary in Malay language; broadcast 4, 11, 18, and 25.6.43;[1] fee £8.8s. Signed: 'For Mr Blair,' by R. Lloyd. Remarks: Please issue a studio pass on a monthly basis.

1. There was evidently confusion in preparing this and *2083*. Winstedt was responsible for the News Commentary in the Malay language but the dates given are for Orwell's Commentary to Malaya in English. Winstedt broadcast on Tuesdays, on the dates in *2083*, and he could not act as his own switch censor. The first form must, therefore, be for Winstedt to give his News Commentary in Malay, on the dates given in *2083*, and the second form must be for payment to him to act as switch censor for Orwell's English-language commentaries on the dates given in *2082*. Winstedt had stood in for Orwell on 12.2.43, writing and reading Commentary 20. For Winstedt, see *1669, n. 1*.

2083. BBC Talks Booking Form, 17.5.43

Sir Richard Winstedt, KBE, CMG: switch censoring Malay News Commentary; broadcast 1, 8, 15, 22, and 29.6.43; fee £3.3s. Signed: 'For Mr Blair' by R. Lloyd. Remarks: Please pay him the usual switch censor's fee and issue him with a pass on a monthly basis.

2084. To Norman Collins, Empire Talks Manager

18 May 1943   Original   EB/WMB

APPROACHING EMINENT SPEAKERS

We have approached[1] the following M.P.'s to do five-minute talks in the DEBATE CONTINUES series.

Wilfred Roberts, Liberal M.P. for North Cumberland
Miss Eleanor Rathbone, M.P.

We have booked these speakers for Monday, May 24th, and Monday, June 7th respectively.[2]

[Signed] Eric Blair
(Eric Blair)

1. For 'have approached,' 'propose approaching' was originally typed. The first wording is only lightly crossed through, with hyphens, and would have plainly been read by Collins.
2. Collins has annotated the memorandum 'Thursday's Talks.'

2085. To Eleanor Rathbone, M.P.

18 May 1943   07/ES/EB

Dear Miss Rathbone[1]

I understand from Princess Indira of Kapurthala that you are willing and will be able to take part, with Princess Indira, in our weekly broadcast of 'The Debate Continues' on Monday, 7th June. The actual time of this broadcast is from 1.15 to 1.30 p.m. DBST., and we should very much like you to be at 200 Oxford Street, W. 1. for rehearsal with Princess Indira in the Studio at 12.45 p.m.

Princess Indira would like her broadcast to fit in with yours—either in the form of a discussion, or so that her preliminary few minutes of speech may lead up to your broadcast. With regard to subject, you will probably have some definite ideas of what you would like to talk about in your six to eight minutes talk, but it would be helpful if you could discuss the subject matter with me on the 'phone, in the course of the next week.

We should like it if your script can be ready some time on Thursday, 3rd June, and if it is any help to you, we can send someone to collect it from you.

Yours sincerely,
[Initialled] E. A. B
Eric Blair
Talks Producer

1. Eleanor Florence Rathbone (1872–1946) was the first woman member of the Liverpool City Council; Independent M.P. for Combined English Universities, 1929–46; and a member of the Comintern-sponsored Commission of Inquiry into Alleged Breaches of the Non-Intervention Agreement in Spain, September 1936. Her publications include *The Disinherited Family: A Plea for Family Endowment* (1924), *Child Marriage: The Indian Minotaur* (1934), and *The Case for Family Allowances* (1940).

2086. To Wilfrid Roberts, M.P.

18 May 1943   07/ES/EB/ED

Dear Mr. Roberts,[1]

I understand from Princess Indira that you have kindly agreed to do a talk for us on the refugee problem on Monday next, 24th May, and we shall be glad if you could be here (at 200 Oxford Street) at 12.45 p.m. on that day.

I will arrange for a messenger to collect a copy of your script at 10.30 on Friday morning, and Princess Indira will phone you later in the day, after she has seen it.

I have instructed our Contracts Department to get into touch with you, and you will be hearing from them shortly.

Yours sincerely,
[Initialled] E. A. B
(Eric Blair)
Talks Producer

1. Wilfrid Roberts (1900–), Liberal M.P., 1935–50, joined the Labour Party in 1956. His name is spelt 'Wilfred' in this correspondence, but has been silently corrected.

2087. BBC Talks Booking Form, 18.5.43

Wilfrid Roberts, M.P.: The problem of refugees, within 'The Debate Continues'; broadcast 24.5.43; fee £5.5s. Signed: Z. A. Bokhari.[1]

1. Bokhari returned to England from his eight-month absence, mainly in India, on 13 or 14 May 1943. He probably returned to the office on Monday, 17 May. This is the first form associated with Orwell signed by him after his leave.

2088. To C. D. Darlington

19 May 1943   07/ES/EB/WMB

Dear Darlington

I am writing to you on the advice of Professor Haldane.[1] I wonder if you would like to do a talk for us in a forthcoming series to India. I should want the script in about a fortnight's time.

We nowadays do series of talks which are designed after being broadcast, to be printed as pamphlets in India. Usually there are *six* talks in a series, making a pamphlet of about 10,000 words. In most cases these talks are literary, but I want for the next one, to have a series of Scientific ones. The subjects are:— Malnutrition, Soil Erosion, Plant or Animal Breeding, Malaria, House-flies and Drinking Water. This sounds a very heterogenious° collection, but each touches on problems important to India, and if put together, they should make a readable popular pamphlet. I wonder whether you would like to do the one on "Plant or Animal Breeding." You could concentrate on Plants or Animals, whichever you prefer, but I suppose that in a talk of *thirteen-and-a-half* minutes—that is about 1500 words, it would be better to stick to one or the other. The main thing we want emphasized is the great differences that can be made in Agricultural production by breeding only from good strains.

Could you let me know as soon as possible whether you will undertake this? The date of the broadcast would be June 30th. Of course, you can always record beforehand if the date is inconvenient, but my main concern is to have the scripts in early, so that I can send them to India to be printed.

Yours sincerely,
[Initialled] E. A. B
George Orwell
(Talks Producer)
Indian Section

1. This letter was typed from a carbon copy of Orwell's letter to Haldane of 7 April 1943 (See *1998*), which Orwell altered to make appropriate for Darlington.

2089. Newsletter in Tamil, 5

20 May 1943

The English version was written by Eric Blair. No script has been traced.

2090. BBC Talks Booking Form, 20.5.43

Professor John Macmurray: 'Books That Changed the World,' 6, New Testament; broadcast 28.5.43; fee £12.12s. Signed: Z. A. Bokhari.[1]

1. On 20 May, Macmurray sent Orwell a postcard apologising for not having delivered his script, as promised, for the 19th; he said it would be ready by Saturday, 22 May. When he sent it, he apologised for its length, but, before cutting it, wished Orwell to see it in full. He said he would be coming to London, from Beaconsfield, Bucks, on Tuesday, Wednesday, and Thursday, 25, 26, 27 May, and Orwell marked at the foot of his letter, 'Fix recording.' This is crossed through and below is written, in another hand, 'Fixed Wed.'

2091. BBC Talks Booking Form, 20.5.43

Eleanor Rathbone, M.P.: The Care of Children as Citizens of the Future, within 'The Debate Continues'; broadcast 7.6.43; fee £7.7s. Signed: Z. A. Bokhari.[1]

1. On 30 May, Miss Rathbone wrote to say that she was unable to fulfil this engagement. The fee on the booking form has been crossed through and 'Cancelled' written in the lower fee-section of the form.

2092. News Commentary in English for Malaya, 34

21 May 1943

This was written and read by George Orwell. No script has been traced.[1]

1. On Sunday, 16 May, Gentry records in his diary: 'Unconfirmed report from Berne broadcast by Delhi states: King of Italy has abdicated, Cabinet resigned, an Italian has stated that Italian fleet is too weak to do anything & that Italian waters are all mined, so that invasion may be expected any moment. Italy has lost 10 divisions and 17000 air force personnel in Tunisia.' The reference to Delhi is, presumably, to All-India Radio. This could have been heard in the house of a consular official, but Gentry notes when he made visits, so the radio was probably available in the prison camp. The Italian island of Pantelleria was bombed during this week and surrendered on 11 June, but Allied troops did not land on Sicily until 10 July.

2093. On Orwell's behalf to Arthur Wynn, Music Bookings Manager

22 May 1943   EB/WMB

Contract for Mr° Narayana Menon

As usual, will you kindly arrange a contract and payment for Dr. Narayana Menon, for planning and choosing his 15 minutes programme of gramophone records, which will be broadcast on Thursday, June 3rd, at 1130–1145 GMT, in the Eastern Service, Red Network.

Dr. Menon's address is 176 Sussex Gardens, W.2., and the programme, as usual, is a Feature Programme.

[Signed] W Bedwell
(For Eric Blair)

2094. BBC Talks Booking Form, [15–22.5.43]

J. D. S. Paul: translating and reading Tamil News Commentary; broadcast 3, 10, 17, and 24.6.43; fee £5.5s each talk + railway vouchers for return journey, Cambridge–London. Signed: R. Lloyd, 'For Mr. Blair.' Remarks: Please issue Mr Paul with a railway voucher on the Thursday in each case, also a Studio Pass to cover these dates.[1]

1. Paul translated and read the Newsletters Orwell wrote each week for transmission in Tamil. This talks booking form is, unusually, undated, but the person noting the need for railway vouchers has dated this request 22 May. Thus the form may have been prepared at any time during the preceding week.

2095. Profile: Sir Richard Acland

The Observer, 23 May 1943

There is little doubt that this profile, published anonymously, was, in the main at least, written by Orwell. David Astor recalls, in a letter of 14 January 1991, that it was Orwell's work, and, in addition to the text printed in *The Observer*, a typescript survives. It was given by Ivor Brown, editor of *The Observer*, 1942–48, to Honor Balfour in the mid to late 1940s in order that she might compile a book of *Observer* Profiles. (This book was never published.) Brown identified the Profile at that time as having been written by Orwell. Moreover, as the text shows, the way Common Wealth's aims and policies are presented is akin to the way they are described in Orwell's London Letter to *Partisan Review* of c. 23 May 1943; see *2096*.

The typescript, a carbon copy, was not made by Orwell. The typewriter face and the typing style are not his and are unlike any associated with him or his secretaries at the BBC; and the use of asterisks to separate sections (placed precisely as those in the printed version) is foreign to Orwell's practice. Honor Balfour has found one other Profile typescript (of Noel Coward, 11 October 1942). This came to her from Ivor Brown. It is in precisely the same style; the lines are to the same measure and have the same indentation, and the use of asterisks is identical. The Acland typescript was, it might seem, prepared in the offices of *The Observer*, perhaps at Brown's request, for use in the preparation of the book. That is unlikely, however, because the typescript and *The Observer's* printed version are not the same. It is more probable that this typescript is a fair copy made in *The Observer* office from a rough draft submitted by Orwell, though this is not wholly convincing, because Orwell was well known at *Tribune* for providing copy that, if not typed in a totally professional manner, demanded very little amendment. A handwritten note of identification at the top of the script is in Miss Balfour's hand.

The printed version gives details about Acland's father and mother which do not appear in the typescript and omits, from about the same point, references to Acland's 'persistent advocacy of an alliance with the U.S.S.R.' and his books *Unser Kampf* (1940) and *What It Will Be Like* (1942). The printed Profile also omits the typescript's final four-line paragraph, probably in the interest of getting the copy into the space available. The passage about Acland's parents contains eighty-seven words and replaces eighty-three words (including 'safe' of 'safe seat'; both include a 'spacing asterisk' but the position of that asterisk in the typescript is far more logical than that in the printed version (where it splits the details about Acland's father and mother). These differences make it even more probable that the typed version is what Orwell submitted, whereas the printed version reproduces changes made in *The Observer* office. The typescript has, therefore, been reproduced here and the variant readings found in the printed version are given in the notes. It will be seen that the minor variants—punctuation and capitalisation—also point to the printed version having been amended by a sub-editor. In order that the nature of the text of the typescript can be assessed, no editorial alterations have been made to it here.

The Profile was illustrated by a drawing of Acland by Stanley Parker. Acland died in 1990, aged 83.

Lean, spectacled and young-looking for his thirty-six years, with an irresistible suggestion of a sixth-form boy—the kind of prefect who is not very good at games but makes up for it by force of character—Sir Richard Acland gives above all else an impression of earnestness. Even his enemies do not accuse him of insincerity. But it is not a solemn kind of earnestness either; merely the eager, buttonholing enthusiasm of a man who not only knows that he possesses the truth, but, what is more, knows that the truth is very simple and can be printed on a four-page leaflet.

If you ask Sir Richard Acland what is the central doctrine of Common Wealth, his small but growing political party, he will answer you more or less like this: Capitalism must be scrapped forthwith but Britain must "go Socialist" under her own steam and in the way that accords with her past traditions. Nationalisation of industry—yes; class warfare—no; Imperialism—no; patriotism—yes; collaboration with Russia—yes; imitation of Russian methods—no.

Simple, and even obvious, as such a programme may sound, it is original enough to have earned the hostility of the older left-wing[1] parties. And the by-election figures suggest that they have good reason to fear this youthful rival.

*

Much depends on phraseology, as Acland is well aware. Common Wealth dislikes labelling itself as "Socialist",[2] avoids the Marxist jargon and tries, not altogether successfully[3] to speak the language of the people. Acland himself has the advantage of having reached his collectivist opinions by an unusual route. A[4] landowner and fifteenth baronet, holder of a safe seat[5] at Barnstaple, for which he was elected as a Liberal, he has never passed through[6] the ordinary discipline of a left-wing[7] party.

*

In the years before the war he was known chiefly for his persistent advocacy of an alliance with the U.S.S.R. and a "firm stand" against Germany. During the period of the phoney war the "firm stand" wavered somewhat, and in his rather unbalanced book "Unser Kampf", Acland voiced the dangerous belief that the war could be won by intelligent use of a megaphone. "What It Will Be Like" is a more sober document and, politically as well as psychologically, a great advance.[8]

Acland[9] likes to explain—eagerly, and even with a tendency to bang on the table—that the existing left-wing[10] parties have ruined themselves by ignoring three obvious facts. The first is that the "dictatorship of the proletariat" is out of date. The proletariat by itself is no longer strong enough to dominate society and can only win with the help of the middle classes. Secondly, any political party which insults patriotism is doomed, at any rate in England. Thirdly, and above all, the real driving force behind the Socialist movement is and must be ethical and not economic. Hence the Common Wealth slogan, "What is morally wrong cannot be politically right"—a clumsy slogan, but one with some appeal.

Grafted on to this is a rather indeterminate immediate policy, which at times seems to promise everything to everybody. Common Wealth proposes to nationalise all the means of production, but it is also ready to pay compensation—full compensation to small property-owners, fractional compensation to big ones. It will stop exploiting the Empire, but will preserve the English standard of living. It will deal firmly with its opponents, but will permit freedom of speech. It will be anti-military, but will encourage patriotism. It will co-operate with anyone whose aims are reasonably similar.

In all this, no doubt, there is an element of Utopianism. But this much can be said: if common ownership is ever established in Britain, it will be by a party of approximately the kind that Acland is striving for, and not of the continental Marxist type.

★

Whether Sir Richard Acland will be the ultimate leader of that party is a different question. He himself says that he does not want to; he merely wants to bring a larger movement into being. His opponents, on the other hand, accuse him of a "führer complex" and declare that if Common Wealth seemed likely to be swamped by a really nation-wide movement, Acland would walk out of it sooner than play second fiddle.

This judgment is probably coloured by jealousy. It is, in fact, not easy to imagine Acland as a political figure of the very first rank, either for good or evil. He has the single-mindedness of a dictator, but not the vulgarity, perhaps not even the toughness. More plausibly, his opponents say that Common Wealth is merely a product of the electoral truce and will wither away as soon as the Labour Party is free to campaign again.

★

Meanwhile, Common Wealth fights by-elections all over the country and wins a surprising number of votes. It may finally break, as all radical movements hitherto have broken, on the rock of the trade unions. Acland claims, and can produce figures to support him, that he has a strong following in the armed forces and is gaining ground in the factories, in spite of Communist opposition. He has at least had the wisdom not to look at

Britain through pink spectacles or think in terms of that mythical animal, the "economic man".

If he fails, as so many other prophets have failed before him, he will be long remembered for that unpolitical but psychologically sound gesture of crossing out "Is it expedient?" and substituting "Is it right?"[11]

1. left–wing] Left–wing
2. "Socialist",] "Socialist,"
3. successfully] successfully,
4. Acland himself . . . unusual route. A] Acland is a
5. baronet, holder of a safe seat] baronet, but this describes only a part of his background. He comes of notable West Country Radical stock. His father, Sir Francis Dyke Acland, after holding other Government posts, was Asquith's Secretary to the Board of Agriculture in the first Coalition, and resigned office with his leader in 1916.

★

Lady Acland, a woman of singular sensibility and graciousness, who died in 1933, was a former President of the Women's National Liberal Federation and an ardent worker for the emancipation of women. Thus Richard Acland's politics are deeply rooted.
Holder of a seat
6. he has never passed through] Acland has never experienced
7. left–wing] Left–wing
8. In the years before the war . . . a great advance] *omitted from printed version*
9. Acland] He
10. left–wing] Left–wing
11. If he fails . . . "Is it right?"] *omitted from printed version*

2096. London Letter, [c. 23 May 1943]

Partisan Review, July–August 1943

Earlier London Letters were given a specific date and had a salutation. The date this Letter was written cannot be precisely established. It must have been after 15 May 1943, the day the Comintern was dissolved. If Orwell started to write on a free day, then Sunday, 16 or 23 May, would be likely. Since there seems to be a link with his News Commentary in English for Malaya transmitted on 28 May 1943 (see *2102*), in which he also speaks of the dissolution of the Comintern as a gesture, the later of these two dates is suggested here.

I begin my letter just after the dissolution of the Comintern,[1] and before the full effects of this have become clear. Of course the immediate results in Britain are easy to foretell. Obviously the Communists will make fresh efforts to affiliate with the Labour Party (this has already been refused by the LP Executive), obviously they will be told that they must dissolve and join as individuals, and obviously, once inside the Labour Party, they will try to act as an organised faction,[2] whatever promises they may have given before-hand. The real interest lies in trying to forsee the long-term effects of the dissolution on a Communist party of the British type.

Weighing up the probabilities, I think the Russian gesture should be taken at its face-value—that is, Stalin is genuinely aiming at a closer tie-up with the

USA and Britain and not merely "deceiving the bourgeoisie" as his followers like to believe. But that would not of itself alter the behaviour of the British Communists. For after all, their subservience to Moscow during the last fifteen years did not rest on any real authority. The British Communists could not be shot or exiled if they chose to disobey, and so far as I know they have not even had any money from Moscow in recent years. Moreover the Russians made it reasonably clear that they despised them. Their obedience depended on the mystique of the Revolution, which had gradually changed itself into a nationalistic loyalty to the Russian state. The English left-wing intelligentsia worship Stalin because they have lost their patriotism and their religious belief without losing the need for a god and a Fatherland. I have always held that many of them would transfer their allegiance to Hitler if Germany won. So long as "Communism" merely means furthering the interests of the Russian Foreign Office, it is hard to see that the disappearance of the Comintern makes any difference. Nearly always one can see at a glance what policy is needed, even if there is no central organisation to hand out directives.

However, one has got to consider the effect on the workingclass membership, who have a different outlook from the salaried hacks at the top of the party. To these people the open declaration that the International is dead must make a difference, although it was in fact a ghost already. And even in the central committee of the party there are differences in outlook which might widen if after a while the British Communist party came to think of itself as an independent party. One must allow here for the effects of self-deception. Even long-term Communists often won't admit to themselves that they are merely Russian agents, and therefore don't necessarily see what move is required until the instructions arrive from Moscow. Thus, as soon as the Franco-Russian military pact was signed, it was obvious that the French and British Communists must go all patriotic, but to my knowledge some of them failed to grasp this. Or again, after the signing of the Russo-German pact several leading members refused to accept the anti-war line and had to do some belly-crawling before their mutiny was forgiven. In the months that followed the two chief publicists of the party became extemely sympathetic to the Nazi weltanschauung, evidently to the dismay of some of the others. The line of division is between deracinated intellectuals like Palme Dutt and trade union men like Pollitt and Hannington.[3] After all the years they have had on the job none of these men can imagine any occupation except boosting Soviet Russia, but they might differ as to the best way of doing it if Russian leadership has really been withdrawn. All in all, I should expect the dissolution of the Comintern to produce appreciable results, but not immediately. I should say that for six months, perhaps more, the British Communists will carry on as always, but that thereafter rifts will appear and the party will either wither away or develop into a looser, less Russophile organization under more up-to-date leadership.

There remains the bigger puzzle of why the Comintern was dissolved. If I am right and the Russians did it to inspire confidence, one must assume that the rulers of Britain and the USA wanted the dissolution and perhaps demanded it as part of the price of a second front. But in Britain at any rate there has been little sign in the past dozen years that the ruling class seriously objected to the existence of the Communist party. Even during the People's Convention period they showed it an astonishing amount of tolerance. At all other times from 1935 onwards it has had powerful support from one or other section of the capitalist press. A thing that it is difficult to be sure about is where the Communists get their money from. It is not likely that they get all of it from their declared supporters, and I believe they tell the truth in saying that they get nothing from Moscow. The difference is that they are "helped" from time to time by wealthy English people who see the value of an organisation which acts as an eel-trap for active Socialists. Beaverbrook for instance is credited, rightly or wrongly, with having financed the Communist party during the past year or two. This is perhaps not less significant as a rumour than it would be as a fact. When one thinks of the history of the past twenty years it is hard not to feel that the Comintern has been one of the worst enemies the working class has had. Yet the Upper Crust is evidently pleased to see it disappear—a fact which I record but cannot readily explain.

The other important political development during these past months has been the growth of Common Wealth, Sir Richard Acland's party. I mentioned this in earlier letters but underrated its importance. It is now a movement to be seriously reckoned with and is hated by all the other parties alike.

Acland's programme, which is set forth almost in baby language in many leaflets and pamphlets, could be described as Socialism minus the class war and with the emphasis on the moral instead of the economic motive. It calls for nationalisation of all major resources, immediate independence (not Dominion status) for India, pooling of raw materials as between "have" and "have not"[4] countries, international administration of backward areas, and a composite army drawn from as many countries as possible to keep the peace after the war is done. All in all this programme is not less drastic than that of the extremist parties of the Left, but it has some unusual features which are worth noticing, since they explain the advance Common Wealth has made during the past few months.

In the first place the whole class war ideology is scrapped. Though all property-owners are to be expropriated, they are to receive fractional compensation—in effect, the bourgeois is to be given a small life-pension instead of a firing squad. The idea of "proletarian dictatorship" is specifically condemned; the middle class and the working class are to amalgamate instead of fighting one another. The party's literature is aimed chiefly at winning over the middle class, both the technical middle class and the "little man" (farmers, shopkeepers etc.). Secondly, the economic side of the programme lays the emphasis on increasing production rather than equalising consumption. Thirdly, an effort is made to synthesise patriotism with an internationalist outlook. Stress is laid on the importance of following British tradition and "doing things in our own way". Parliament, apparently, is to be preserved in much its present form, and nothing is said against the

Monarchy. Fourthly, Common Wealth does not describe itself as "Socialist" and carefully avoids Marxist phraseology. It declares itself willing to collaborate with any other party whose aims are sufficiently similar. (With the Labour Party the test is that the LP shall break the electoral truce.) Fifthly—and perhaps most important of all—Common Wealth propaganda has a strong ethical tinge. Its best-known poster consists simply of the words "Is it expedient?" Crossed out and replaced by "Is it right?" Anglican priests are much to the fore in the movement though the Catholics seem to be opposing it.

Whether this movement has a future I am still uncertain, but its growth since I last wrote to you has been very striking. Acland's candidates are fighting by-elections all over the country. Although they have only won two so far, they have effected a big turn-over of votes against Government candidates, and what is perhaps more significant, the whole poll seems to rise wherever a Common Wealth candidate appears. The ILP has been conducting a distant flirtation with Common Wealth, but the other Left parties are hostile and perhaps frightened. The usual criticism is that Common Wealth is only making progress because of the electoral truce—in other words, because the Labour Party is what it is. In addition it is said that the membership of the party is wholly middleclass. Acland himself claims to have a good nucleus of followers in the factories and still more in the Forces. The Communists, of course, have labelled Common Wealth as Fascist. They and the Conservatives now work together at by-elections.

The programme I have roughly outlined has elements both of demagogy and of Utopianism, but it takes very much better account of the actual balance of forces than any of the older Left parties have done. It might have a chance of power if another revolutionary situation arises, either through military disaster or at the end of the war. Some who know Acland declare that he has a "führer complex" and that if he saw the movement growing beyond his control he would split it sooner than share authority. I don't believe this to be so, but neither do I believe that Acland by himself could bring a nation-wide movement into being. He is not a big enough figure, and not in any way a man of the people. Although of aristocratic and agricultural background (he is a fifteenth baronet) he has the manners and appearance of a civil servant, with a typical upper-class accent. For a popular leader in England it is a serious disability to be a gentleman, which Churchill, for instance, is not. Cripps is a gentleman, but to offset this he has his notorious "austerity", the Gandhi touch, which Acland just misses, in spite of his ethical and religious slant. I think this movement should be watched with attention. It might develop into the new Socialist party we have all been hoping for, or into something very sinister: it has some rather doubtful followers already.

Finally a word about antisemitism, which could now be said to have reached the stature of a "problem". I said in my last letter that it was not increasing, but I now think it is. The danger signal, which is also a safeguard, is that everyone is very conscious of it and it is discussed interminably in the press.

Although Jews in England have always been socially looked down on and debarred from a few professions (I doubt whether a Jew would be accepted as an officer in the Navy, for instance), antisemitism is primarily a working-class thing, and strongest among Irish labourers. I have had some glimpses of working-class antisemitism through being three years in the Home Guard—which gives a good cross-section of society—in a district where there are a lot of Jews. My experience is that middleclass people will laugh at Jews and discriminate against them to some extent, but only among working people do you find the full-blown belief in the Jews as a cunning and sinister race who live by exploiting the Gentiles. After all that has happened in the last ten years it is a fearful thing to hear a workingman saying "Well, I reckon 'Itler done a good job when 'e turned 'em all out", but I have heard just that, and more than once. These people never seem to be aware that Hitler has done anything to the Jews except "turned 'em all out"; the pogroms, the deportations etc. have simply escaped their notice. It is questionable, however, whether the Jew is objected to as a Jew or simply as a foreigner. No religious consideration enters. The English Jew, who is often strictly orthodox but entirely anglicised in his habits, is less disliked than the European refugee who has probably not been near a synagogue for thirty years. Some people actually object to the Jews on the ground that Jews are Germans!

But in somewhat different forms antisemitism is now spreading among the middle class as well. The usual formula is "of course I don't want you to think I'm antisemitic, but—"—and here follows a catalogue of Jewish misdeeds. Jews are accused of evading military service, infringing the food laws, pushing their way to the front of queues, etc., etc. More thoughtful people point out that the Jewish refugees use this country as a temporary asylum but show no loyalty towards it. Objectively this is true, and the tactlessness of some of the refugees is almost incredible. (For example, a remark by a German Jewess overheard during the Battle of France: "These English police are not nearly so smart as our SS Men".) But arguments of this kind are obviously rationalisations of prejudice. People dislike the Jews so much that they do not want to remember their sufferings, and when you mention the horrors that are happening in Germany or Poland, the answer is always "Oh yes, of course that's dreadful, but—"—and out comes the familiar list of grievances. Not all of the intelligentsia are immune from this kind of thing. Here the get-out is usually that the refugees are all "petty bourgeois"; and so the abuse of Jews can proceed under a respectable disguise. Pacifists and others who are anti-war sometimes find themselves forced into antisemitism.

One should not exaggerate the danger of this kind of thing. To begin with, there is probably less antisemitism in England now than there was thirty years ago. In the minor novels of that date you find it taken for granted far oftener than you would nowadays that a Jew is an inferior or a figure of fun. The "Jew joke" has disappeared from the stage, the radio and the comic papers since 1934. Secondly, there is a great awareness of the prevalence of antisemitism and a conscious effort to struggle against it. But the thing remains, and perhaps it is one of the inevitable neuroses of war. I am not particularly impressed by the fact that it does not take violent forms. It is true that no one wants to have pogroms and throw elderly Jewish professors into cesspools, but then there is very little crime or violence in England anyway. The milder form of antisemitism prevailing here can be just as cruel in an indirect way, because it causes people to avert their eyes from the whole refugee problem and remain uninterested in the fate of the surviving Jews of Europe. Because two days ago a fat Jewess grabbed your place on the bus, you switch off the wireless when the announcer begins talking about the ghettoes of Warsaw;[5] that is how people's minds work nowadays.

That is all the political news I have. Life goes on much as before. I don't notice that our food is any different, but the food situation is generally considered to be worse. The war hits one a succession of blows in unexpected places. For a long time razor blades were unobtainable, now it is boot polish. Books are being printed on the most villainous paper and in tiny print, very trying to the eyes. A few people are wearing wooden-soled shoes. There is an alarming amount of drunkenness in London. The American soldiers seem to be getting on better terms with the locals, perhaps having become more resigned to the climate etc. Air raids continue, but on a pitiful scale. I notice that many people feel sympathy for the Germans now that it is they who are being bombed—a change from 1940, when people saw their houses tumbling about them and wanted to see Berlin scraped off the map.

George Orwell

1. The Comintern (Communist International) was established in Moscow in 1919 to promote revolution by workers against capitalist governments. It was dissolved on 15 May 1943 by Stalin. For a sympathetic interpretation of this 'gesture,' see the correspondence arising from Orwell's Malay Newsletter of 28 May, representing the official British government line, 2102.
2. faction] printed as fraction—a possible but unlikely reading
3. Rajani Palme Dutt (see 1989, n. 7) was Vice-Chairman of the Communist Party and member of the Executive Committee from 1922. Harry Pollitt (see 364, n. 2) was a founder of the British Communist Party and its General Secretary from 1929. Walter Hannington (see 274, n. 3) was author of The Problem of the Distressed Areas published by the Left Book Club (November 1937), and Ten Lean Years (1940), an account of the 1930s.
4. '"have not"' was printed as 'have "not"' by Partisan Review.
5. The massacre of Jews in the Warsaw ghetto began on 20 April 1943 and ended on 16 May. At least 56,000 people were killed and those left alive were transported to concentration camps. See 2194 Days of War, 366.

2097. To E. F. W. Mackenzie

24 May 1943   Handwritten draft[1] and typed versions
07/ES/EB/MEH

Dear Colonel Mackenzie,
Very many thanks for the script, which is just what we wanted. I suppose you do not object to this script being printed as part of a pamphlet in India? You will, in theory, get a royalty from the pamphlet, but as you can imagine this is not likely to be a large amount.

We have had to alter the dates of these talks, and yours will go out on Thursday, the 19th July, at 12.30 p.m. (standard time). If this is inconvenient we can easily record beforehand.

Yours sincerely,
[Initialled] E. A. B
Eric Blair
Talks Producer
Indian Section

1. Orwell drafted this letter on the verso of Lieutenant-Colonel Mackenzie's compliment slip accompanying the script on 22 May. Mackenzie replied on 31 May saying he had no objection to publication and would like to record his talk. Orwell annotated that reply, 'Miss Bedwell Please arrange recording. E.B.'

2098. BBC Talks Booking Forms, 25.5.43[1]

Lady Grigg: 'Women Generally Speaking'; broadcast 2, 9, 16, 23, and 30.6.43; fee £8.8s each broadcast. Signed Z. A. Bokhari.

1. Two slips were issued because the time of the broadcast, from 16 June, was changed from 1:45–2:00 P.M. DBST to 12:15–12:30 P.M. DBST.

2098A. To Dwight Macdonald, 26.5.43: see Introduction

2099. Review of *The English People* by D. W. Brogan[1]

The Listener, 27 May 1943

This is a book written about England but at America, and in consequence slightly defiant in tone. Professor Brogan was evidently travelling in the United States during the bad period of the summer and autumn of 1942, and quite obviously he is perturbed by the fact that many Americans neither like us nor know anything about us. He is anxious to explain things and perhaps, in some cases, to explain them away. And apart from the Americans, he is also to some extent writing against the English literary intelligentsia, whose sneers have to be braved by anyone speaking a good word for England, and even against certain other minority groups, as his title implies: for it is almost a political act nowadays to use the word England instead of bowing to the noisy minority who want it called Britain.

How does Professor Brogan present us? The general build-up is of an unthinking but very gentle and civilised people, obstinate in adversity, snobbish but fairly neighbourly, inefficient but with sound instincts and therefore capable of avoiding really destructive mistakes. There is no doubt that his picture is broadly true, and in places (especially in the voluminous footnotes) extremely acute. The chapter entitled 'English Religion' does a particularly difficult job with distinction. Naturally, with his eye on the American reader, Professor Brogan spends most of his time in defending the things usually regarded as indefensible—the class system, the convolutions of English democracy, the public schools, India, and such minor matters as Sabbatarianism and the dreary ugliness of English towns. Some of what he says needed saying, though from time to time, with American susceptibilities in mind, he probably says things that he does not really believe—for example, that Britain's rule in India is likely to have come to an end 'long before the second centenary of Plassy'. His defence of the monarchy as an institution is well worth reading, though perhaps he does not emphasise sufficiently the part played by hereditary monarchs in canalising and neutralising emotions which would otherwise attach themselves to real rulers with genuine powers for evil.

Witty and even exciting as this book is, it is a little spoiled by the ghostly American reader who seems to haunt every page and who forces Professor Brogan to drag in an American analogy wherever one can be plausibly said to exist. Inevitably one finds oneself appraising the book for its propaganda as well as its literary value, and this raises the question: does propaganda of this type ever make any real difference? As far as one can judge from the American press, pro-British and anti-British sentiment in the United States are constants, or at any rate are little affected by what is said and done in this country. The most one can do in the way of propaganda is to supply the pro-British faction with ammunition, and for that purpose statistics and hard facts generally are of more use than ingenious explanations of why the public-school system is not such a bad thing after all. Or on the other hand, if one is going to hit back at Britain's enemies in the United States—and Professor Brogan appears to be doing this in a few passages—any attempt to defend British institutions is useless; it would be far better to counter on *tu-quoque* lines with remarks about the American negroes, etc. To say this is not to belittle Professor Brogan's book as a book. It is most stimulating reading, the kind of book with which one can violently agree or violently disagree at almost every page. But its value is chiefly for Englishmen or for Americans who have a general knowledge of its subject matter already. In propaganda, even more than in chess and war, it is a good rule that attack is the best defence, and a book so essentially defensive as this will not make many converts among the disciples of Colonel Lindbergh or Father Coughlin.[3]

1. Orwell was paid a fee of £2.12.6 for this review.
2. Brogan was right; Robert Clive was victorious at Plassy, Bengal, in 1757; British rule in India ended in 1948.
3. For Col. Charles Lindbergh, see *908, n. 3*; for Father Coughlin, see *1106, n. 6*.

2100. Newsletter in Tamil, 6

27 May 1943

The English version was written by Eric Blair. No script has been traced.

2101. To Sir John Russell

27 May 1943   Handwritten draft[1]

Reply
(P.C.)
Many thanks for your script. We have had to alter the dates in our new schedule so this talk will now go out on Thursday the 22nd July at 1215 (standard time). If this is not convenient to you we can easily arrange to record beforehand.

[Signed] Eric Blair

1. Written by Orwell at the foot and on the verso of Sir John Russell's letter to him of 25 May 1943.

2102. News Commentary in English for Malaya, 35

28 May 1943

The script used for the broadcast of this Commentary, written and read by Orwell, has not been traced, but because objections were raised to his treatment of the story of the dissolution of the Comintern by Stalin on 15 May 1943, part of it has survived. Objection was made at the same time to a broadcast by Wickham Steed which had also referred to the dissolution of the Comintern; references to that broadcast are not reproduced here apart from the final sentence of J. B. Clark's memorandum of 31 May. The extract from Orwell's broadcast is given first, followed by the memoranda in chronological order.

EXTRACT FROM ENGLISH NEWS COMMENTARY FOR MALAYA BY GEORGE ORWELL, 11.30–11.45 GMT 28TH MAY

The items dealt with in the commentary were:—
(a) The R.A.F. raid on Dortmund.
(b) Heavy raiding in the Mediterranean, leading to the evacuation of Cagliari.
(c) The dissolution of the Comintern.
The following extract deals with the last of these items.

Five days ago it was announced from Moscow that the Third International, usually called the Comintern, or Communist International, had been dissolved. Though it is purely political in nature, this is an important piece of news, probably more important than anything that has happened on the actual battlefields since the surrender of the Axis forces in Tunisia. But to see its significance, one must remember what the history of the Comintern has been.

The Comintern was founded in 1920 under the inspiration of Lenin. It was the third attempt to form a world wide socialist organisation. The First International which was formed nearly 80 years ago was a failure, and the second° International, formed about 40 years ago, although it survived, practically ceased after 1914 to deal with anything except Trade Union affairs. When Lenin founded the Third International the Russian Revolution was in full swing and great hopes were entertained of revolutions of the same kind breaking out all over the world. The Comintern was formed with the quite frank intention of fomenting violent revolutions everywhere. Although it must be said to have failed, it did at any rate make efforts to carry out this programme and remained for about the first fifteen years of its existence a dangerous and subversive organisation.

It is easy to see the obstacle the Comintern presented to the formation of a firm alliance of Soviet Russia and the Western democracies against Fascism. When Germany, Italy and Japan signed the anti-Comintern Pact, they were not of course really concerned with fighting against Bolshevism, but with forming a military alliance with predatory aims against Russia, Britain and the United States, but they were able to say plausibly that Communism presented a great danger and there were plenty of people, particularly in the United States, who were ready to listen. Crudely, the Germans and Japanese alleged that the Soviet Government was fomenting Revolution everywhere and using the Comintern as its instrument. This is the propaganda manoeuvre generally known as the Bolshevik Bogey. It scored many successes in the United States, in the Catholic countries of Europe, and even in Britain. Now, with the dissolution of the Comintern, the Bolshevik Bogey is dead. There is not even a shadow of an organisation aiming at bloody revolution, and the last obstacle to collaboration between Soviet Russia and the Western democracies is gone.

Two days ago was the anniversary of the signature of the alliance between Great Britain and Soviet Russia. The alliance has been loyally honoured on both sides and by their victories, both Britain and Russia have contributed to one another's safety. But by dissolving the Comintern, the Russian Government appears to be making a gesture towards a closer and warmer alliance which will continue when the war is won, and it is a question of rebuilding the countries ravaged by war, and not merely of surviving the onslaughts of the common enemy.

This extract was sent by J. B. Clark, Controller, Overseas Services, to the Director General, R. W. Foot,[1] on 31 May 1943. It is annotated: 'For circulation to Output Controllers in connection with Minute 157 of Programme Policy Meeting':

As requested, I attach hereto the scripts which you wished other Controllers to see. As only the file copy existed of George Orwell's talk I have had an extract made of his complete reference to the dissolution of the Comintern. The whole talk is cast in rather simple language and is designed for those who understand English in the occupied territories of Indonesia. This weekly English commentary is broadcast on the Malayan beam and on a single frequency—employed on other days of the week for vernacular broadcasts at the same time.

The Wickham Steed talk, of which a full duplicate script is attached, was widely radiated in Overseas Services.

The Director General evidently asked the advice of his Deputy Foreign Adviser, H. R. Cummings. He reported on both scripts on 8 June to the Director General:

My comments on these scripts, neither of which was submitted to me, are as follows:

The George Orwell script: this is not, strictly speaking, contrary to policy, but I consider it inadequate and out of perspective. It misses the point that the dissolution of the Comintern was the logical consequence of Stalin's policy of 1927—the abandonment of Trotsky's doctrine of World Revolution, and the adoption of "Socialism in one Country". This is a truer and better line than emphasis on the failure of the Comintern, and it is in accordance with policy guidance. The obstacle to a firm alliance between Russia and the Western democracies presented by the Comintern might have been more prudently described, and greater emphasis laid on the exposure of the enemy's fraudulent misuse of the "Bolshevik bogey".

We were instructed not to say that the Russian Government had dissolved the Comintern, but that it had dissolved itself.

It is also a mistake, I think, to describe the dissolution as a "gesture"; this goes dangerously near substantiating the enemy's criticism of the step as a trick or propaganda bluff. It was an act of policy, not a gesture.

On 14 June 1943, Clark sent Foot the following memorandum, 'Dissolution of the Comintern,' marked 'Private & Confidential':

I hope that this memo will help to clarify some of the issues involved.

1. Having regard (a) to the facts on H.M.G. policy known to us at the time, (b) the needs, susceptibilities, and circumstances of the respective target and eavesdropping audiences, and (c) the purpose of the talks and the personalities of the speakers as broadcasters, I take full responsibility for judging these two talks as suitable for the services in which they were broadcast. I shall be glad to know if my judgment is considered to be at fault.

2. I have great respect for Cummings' sage advice on foreign affairs, but I think that his comments in this instance are on the one hand more matters of argument than of policy and on the other are somewhat academic, inasmuch as they are not related (on the choice of words and phrases for example) to the proven technique and personalities of the speakers.

3. As to the one clear point of policy about the Comintern dissolving itself, I understand that this appeared only in the P.W.E. Central Directive which is not seen in the O.S. Division. No such directive was circulated within the Corporation as far as I can discover, nor ventilated at a news meeting from which our machinery is arranged to ensure the over-all guidance of all sections of output. The following quotations from a European Service editorial broadcast in English on long and medium

waves (receivable in this country and on the continent) & on more than a dozen short wave frequencies (widely receivable outside this country) also are relevant: "The dissolution of the Comintern is perhaps the most important political event of the war. . . . Primarily it is a vote of confidence by the Soviet Government in the good faith . . . of the peoples and governments of Britain and the United States etc. . . . In fact, this development means that the Soviet Government has reached the conclusion that etc. . . ."

As to Cummings' more general observations, it must, I think, be remembered that Orwell was attempting to survey the important events of the week and that it was inevitable that from some points of view he could not deal "adequately" with any one of them. The point about the logical consequence of Stalin's policy of 1927 is a good Foreign Office plank, but I cannot think that it would be very realistic either for surreptitious listeners in occupied territory or for any free listeners. I see the point about "gesture" but I cannot see that the word is seriously objectionable.

The last two paragraphs of this memorandum are concerned with Wickham Steed's broadcast and are not reproduced here.

1. Robert William Foot (1889–1973), solicitor; General Manager, Gas, Light & Coke Company, 1928–41; adviser to the BBC on Wartime Organisation, was Joint Director General of the BBC (with Sir Cecil Graves), January 1942 and Director General, September 1943–April 1944. Graves (1892–1957) 'had been dogged by illness' and Foot 'had been in sole charge for most of the year [1943]' (Asa Briggs, *A History of Broadcasting in the United Kingdom*, 3, 552).

2103. To N. Gangulee

28 May 1943   Handwritten draft and typed versions
07/ES/EB/MEH

Dr. Gangulee wrote to Orwell on 27 May 1943, drawing his attention to the fact that the United Nations Food Conference, meeting at Hot Springs, Arkansas, had agreed upon a Five-Point Food Policy. He had obtained the full text of the U.K. Delegation's Declaration of Principles. These, he said, 'are sound and I believe they should be widely known in India.' He suggested that a talk be commissioned on this topic, although he did not propose himself as its author. He was writing an article on the subject for a Calcutta daily paper, but that would not reach India for some six weeks, and the press summaries issued were inadequate. Orwell drafted a reply on the back of Gangulee's letter; the typed version also survives. The only difference between them is that the manuscript version has no paragraph division.

Dear Dr. Gangulee,
Many thanks for your letter. How would you like to tackle the Five-point Food Policy in your 'In Your Kitchen' series, either this week or next week? It could be done in the form of a dialogue as usual, if you like.

You might perhaps ring me up about this on Monday. I don't know that I can fit it in at any other time, important though it is.

Yours sincerely,
[Initialled] E. A. B
Eric Blair
(Talks Producer)
Indian Section

2104. BBC Talks Booking Form, 28.5.43

[From Indian Programme Organiser][1] Oliver Bell: 'Women Generally Speaking,' Films of the Month; introduced etc. by Lady Grigg as usual; broadcast 23.6.43; fee 'usual fee,' £10.10s. Signed: Z. A. Bokhari.

1. Before Bokhari's return from India, talks booking forms coming within Orwell's sphere had been issued as from 'Eric Blair.' This and the two following were issued as from Bokhari. Hereafter, such forms will be reproduced without noting whether they are said to be from Bokhari.

2105. BBC Talks Booking Form, 28.5.43

'? Kingsley-Martin Esq.':[1] '13½ minute MONTHLY TALK. (Subject NOT yet definite)'; broadcast 6.7.43; fee (estimated)[2] £10.10s. Signed: Z. A. Bokhari.

1. Kingsley Martin (see 496, n. 4) had earlier rejected Orwell's review of Franz Borkenau's The Spanish Cockpit because it controverted the political policy of The New Statesman and Nation, of which he was editor; see Orwell's letter to Raymond Mortimer, 9 February 1938, 424. However, Orwell wrote twenty reviews for the journal between 1940 and 1943.
2. Uncertainty as to the fee led to further correspondence, which involved Orwell only on 30 July 1943; see 2210. For the conclusion, see 2266.

2106. BBC Talks Booking Form, 28.5.43

L. A. G. Strong: 'Calling All Students,' Literary Series, 2: Georgian Poets; broadcast 4.7.43; fee £12.12s. Signed: Z. A. Bokhari.

2107. BBC Talks Booking Forms, 29.5.43

Two for Dr. N. Gangulee: 'In Your Kitchen,' 9 and 10; broadcast 2 and 9.6.43; and 11 and 14; broadcast 17 and 24.6.43, and 1 and 8.7.43; the series 'will then end for a time'; fee £8.8s for each programme. Signed: Z. A. Bokhari.

2108. BBC Talks Booking Forms, 29.5.43

Two for Mrs. K. C. Roy: 'In Your Kitchen,' 9 and 11; reading only; broadcast 2 and 17.6.43; 'usual small appearance fee' £3.3s each broadcast. Signed: Z. A. Bokhari.

2109. BBC Talks Booking Form, 29.5.43

Miss D. Nanavati: 'In Your Kitchen,' 10; in discussion with Dr. Gangulee & Mr. Telkar;[1] broadcast 9.6.43; fee £3.3s. Signed: Z. A. Bokhari.

1. The forms *2107, 2108, 2109* mention that Shridhar Telkar will take part in programmes 9–14, but his booking forms seem not to have survived.

2110. To John Atkins
31 May 1943

10a Mortimer Crescent   London   NW 6

Dear Atkins[1]

I do not know whether you know of the existence of the New York paper, the "Partisan Review". It is one of the few intelligent politico-literary reviews left in the world. You can't buy it on the bookstalls in England, but the editors now inform me that they can take foreign subscriptions and have asked me for names of possible subscribers in this country. I have taken the liberty of giving them your name.

The "Partisan Review" is published six times a year and its address is 45 Astor Place, New York N.Y., USA. Allowing for postage the subscription is about 2 dollars, or 10 shillings a year. I can readily lend you a specimen copy if you want to see what it is like.

Yours sincerely
[Signed] Geo. Orwell
George Orwell

1. John Atkins (see *1340, n. 1*) was at this time literary editor of *Tribune*. This is evidently one of a number of similar letters (that to Atkins is a carbon copy) which Orwell sent out to attract subscribers to *Partisan Review*. A space was left after the salutation and Orwell wrote in the name 'Atkins' and signed the letter over his name typed in full, a practice he did not normally use for his personal letters, though usual at the BBC. The word 'the' was erroneously typed after 'Allowing' and was X-ed through. The layout and the way his own address is given suggest that Orwell typed the letter.

2111. BBC Talks Booking Form, 31.5.43

Sir John Russell: 'Calling All Students,' Scientific Series, 3, Soil Erosion and Soil Deterioration; broadcast 29.7.43; fee £10.10s. Signed: Z. A. Bokhari.

2112. BBC Talks Booking Form, 31.5.43

Lieutenant-Colonel E. F. W. Mackenzie, OBE: 'Calling All Students,' Scientific Series, 6, Drinking Water; broadcast 19.8.43;[1] fee £10.10s. Signed: Z. A. Bokhari.

1. The date was originally typed as 19 July; the new date was written over it.

2113. To B. H. Alexander, Copyright

1 June 1943   Original   EB/WMB

INDIAN PLAY (NO 6) THE KING OF THE DARK CHAMBER
BY RABINDRANATH TAGORE

Today, June 1st, at 1145–1200 GMT, we broadcast the Indian play—THE KING OF THE DARK CHAMBER, written and translated by Rabindranath Tagore. This play was adapted for the radio by Dr. Narayana Menon, and it was broadcast as a Feature programme in the Eastern Service (Red Network).

Will you please arrange payment for Dr. Menon accordingly. He made a free adaptation of this story for the radio, and the duration was 13 mins. 20 secs. Dr. Menon's address is 176 Sussex Gardens, London, W.2.

The rehearsal of this play took place in St. 4 (200 Oxford St.) from 10.30 am. to 1.45 pm. (DBST). It was produced by Douglas Cleverdon.

[Initialled] WB[1]
(For Eric Blair)

1. This memorandum, from Venu Chitale, is annotated '6 gns (long play).'

2114. BBC Talks Booking Form, 1.6.43

Professor E. D. Edwards, D. Litt: 'Women Generally Speaking'; 13-minute talk on Chinese Deeds of Heroism; broadcast 30.6.43; fee £10.10s. Signed: Z. A. Bokhari.

2115. Newsletter in Tamil, 7

3 June 1943

The English version was written by Eric Blair. No script has been traced.

2116. To K. K. Ardaschir

3 June 1943   Handwritten draft and typed versions[1]
07/ES/EB/WMB

Dear Ardaschir

I am very[2] sorry about the[3] delay in answering your letter.

   I am sending both scripts back, also the one[4] of the play, under separate cover. I'm afraid I can't use any of this, or anything else for some time to come. Our new schedule starts on June 13th and for three months we shall be broadcasting largely music. I can't, in any case,[5] commission any talks for it. Your talk on the Panama Canal goes out tomorrow.[6]

   If Miss [7] Margaret Taylor comes to call I shall,[8] of course, be happy to see her, but I can't arrange any more talks at present.

Yours sincerely
[Signed] Eric Blair
Eric Blair
(Talks Producer)
Indian Section

1. Orwell wrote the draft on the verso of Ardaschir's letter. The variations between the draft and what was typed show changes typically made without authority to an author's script. Though they are insignificant, they do illustrate how Orwell's letters may have been modified and are therefore recorded here.
2. very] *not in draft*
3. the] *not in draft*
4. one] ms *in draft*. The play was about Byron and called *The Pilgrim of Eternity*. It had been presented at the Duke of York's Theatre, London, in 1921.
5. I can't, in any case,] *commas added by the typist, Winifred Bedwell*
6. A date stamp on Ardaschir's letter shows it was received on 2 June 1943. Orwell probably scribbled his reply then and there, and it was typed the following day, the day it is dated. By then 'tomorrow' was 'today.' This can be deduced from Orwell's memo to Collins of 3 June. Ardaschir's Panama Canal talk was recorded on 11 May, specifically for the ice-box. From the tone of the letter it would appear that Ardaschir was becoming something of an embarrassment and that Orwell did not wish to encourage him further. This is the last letter Orwell wrote to him that has been traced. Orwell exaggerated slightly when he wrote that 'we shall be broadcasting largely music.' The schedule in *London Calling* (see *2151*) shows that there was a considerable amount of music, however. This change was brought about in part by Bokhari's visit to India. In *London Calling*, 203, 29 July 1943 (programmes 29 August–4 September), C. Lawson-Reece contributed an article, 'Planning Music of the West for Indian Listeners.' This explained that the BBC's Music Department and Bokhari had drawn up a programme to educate listeners and also to provide them with music to listen to. There were three educational programmes: Bohkari, 'The Sa Re Ga of Western Music,' Wednesdays at 15:15, on the basic materials of European music—folk song, plain song, and early musical instruments; Princess Indira, 'Music of the East and West,' Mondays at 10:00; and Hubert J. Foss (Music Editor, Oxford University Press), who explained pitch, tone colour, scales, rhythm, and melody in 'Music in the Making,' Fridays at 10:00 (all GMT). There were several programmes simply of music; the whole series was introduced by Arthur Bliss (1891–1975; Kt., 1950). Music was not Orwell's forte (as his proposals for music for his *Little Red Riding Hood* script, 9 July 1946, indicate; (see *3032*) and his letter to Alex Comfort, *2185*, where he says, 'I know nothing about music.' This development may well have added to his growing disenchantment with the BBC in its greater emphasis on music at the expense of serious talks.
7. Miss] *possibly* Mrs
8. shall,] *comma omitted in typing*

2117. To Norman Collins, General Overseas Service Manager

3 June 1943

Recorded Talk by Professor Gilbert Murray

Some time back you sent us the script of a talk entitled ESCAPE, by Professor Gilbert Murray, which was marked as having been broadcast on the Home Service on the 12th April. The disc numbers were DOX. 13070. You asked whether we could use this talk and I said I could and I think named the date. This had been scheduled for some time past as going out in our Service today. Half-an-hour before the broadcast it was discovered that the talk on the discs was not by Professor Murray, but a totally different talk which had been recorded instead. We only discovered this, more or less by chance, and had to put in an ice-box talk at short notice. I'm not sure where the responsibility lies, but I report this mishap because there is clearly a fault somewhere when the scrapping of one talk and the recording of another, under the same disc number, is not reported beforehand to the responsible producer.

[Signed] Eric Blair
(Eric Blair)

Collins (now promoted from Empire Talks Manager) took up this complaint, and a long office interchange took place indicative of the inevitable bureaucracy that the programme planners had to contend with. Collins first wrote to Mrs. W. Short of the Empire Programme Executive:

Please see the attached note from Mr. Blair. Disc number DOX 13070 was given to Mrs. Rudd by your office. I would be grateful if you could check with your present records as it may of course have been misheard on the telephone.

In any case, I would be grateful if you would return the note to me as I want to find out how it is that no steps had been taken about obtaining the discs until apparently half-an-hour before the broadcast.

She replied:

According to the records in this office, disc number DOX 13070 applies to a talk recorded from the Home Service on 12th April by Professor Gilbert Murray.

If there was a last minute alteration in the Home Service, it would appear that this office was not informed.

Her memorandum was annotated, signed, and dated, 9 June, by Collins and returned to Mrs. Short:

Pse see attached. Cd you please let me know what yr arrangements are for checking discs before b/cast—it seems that this point also arises.

Mrs. Short replied on 11 June:

In reply to your query re arrangements for checking discs before broadcast, Recorded Programmes Library check the discs for transmission from Recorded Programmes Bookings schedule, which is received the night before.

This memorandum was, in its turn, annotated by Collins on 16 June and sent to Orwell:

I'm sorry that this has bn. held up. Cd you pse find out if the R.P. check *is* being made sufficiently in advance for the Recordings to be put right if a mistake is found. Its° obviously too late now for this particular case to be taken up but the general principle is important.

The word 'Recordings' is uncertain. It looks rather like 'things' but there is something before it and the word(s) are much contracted. Collins may have written 'wretched things.'

On 20 June, Collins, having received Orwell's answer (not traced), wrote to B. Lyons (of the Recorded Programme Section?) giving Orwell's explanation:

I am anxious to clear up a matter which has been running on since the 3rd June. On that date a talk by Gilbert Murray was planned to go out in reproduction in the Eastern Service. My office gave Mr. Blair the number DOX 13070 which it had obtained from Empire Programme Ex. Half-an-hour before the broadcast it was discovered that there had been an error in numbering and that the discs in question in no way related to Gilbert Murray's talk. Could you please let me know what the arrangements are on your side for checking that the discs are in point of fact in order? Mr. Blair when asked to investigate said:

R.P. Library have no regular machinery for checking it, so that a mistake is not necessarily detected till just before the programme goes on the air, when the R.P.A. would test the discs out.

I can't believe this to be the case and would be grateful if you would let me know in point of fact what the machinery is.

Lyons replied in a handwritten response lacking a date:

The talk by Mr. Murray was supposed to be recorded from the Home Service Prog at 1945 on Ap. 12—apparently the Home programme was changed & another speaker took Gilbert Murray's place. The mistake was not in the numbering but due to the fact that the person booking the recording was not aware that the H.S. prog was altered — I feel that a check of this sort is rather beyond our scope. The numbering was quite correct & would have been the right talk if Murray had appeared. We do have to rely more on Nos. than titles since the difference between the title

given a talk on recordings & the title used for trans. so often have no apparent relation to each other.
P.S. The R.P.A.[1] did find the error when making up the discs.

No more correspondence has been traced.

1. Recorded Programme Assistant?

2118. To Mrs. Milton (Naomi Royde-Smith)

3 June 1943   07/ES/EB/WMB

Dear Mrs. Milton
I am not sure whether you have been given the correct dates for your talks. Your talk in July is on the 21st, not on the 14th. I have an impression that you may have been told it was the 14th.
Your next talk is on the 16th June. I should be obliged if I could have the script fairly soon.

Yours sincerely
[Signed] Geo. Orwell
George Orwell
(Talks Producer)
Indian Section

2119. BBC Talks Booking Form, 3.6.43

Wing-Commander [Roger] Falk: 'My Visit to the Indian Contingent in Great Britain'; 6–7-minute talk to be kept for use when needed; recorded 9.6.43; no broadcast time arranged; fee £6.6s. Signed: Z. A. Bokhari.[1]

1. Orwell initiated this talks booking form, and, on the same day, Bokhari wrote to Falk at the India Office in London, enclosing a copy of his script and arranging a time for the recording to be made. At the head of the carbon copy of his letter is a note to 'Mr. Blair's office—for information,' asking that a booking slip be prepared for Falk. The reason the talk was to be held in reserve was that, although highly recommended as a broadcaster by 'Field Marshal Wavell and others' and having done 'fairly regular work' for All-India Radio, the Director of Talks, G. R. Barnes, was 'not very greatly impressed.' In his view, 'the trouble is that Falk is accustomed to addressing an audience of pukka Sahibs and is not likely to make an effective appeal to the heterogeneous audience of B.B.C. listeners.' However, he did know 'a lot about the conditions in which troops in India are living and training,' and Barnes thought 'we may be liable to a good deal of outside pressure on Falk's behalf' (from a private & confidential memorandum, 4 June, from J. C. S. Macgregor, Assistant Controller (News), to Controller (News), A. P. Ryan, who annotated the memorandum that he thought Falk 'worth seeing for news stories'). Falk's performance was evidently such that he was asked to broadcast again on 26 June 1943; see 2163. A little later he was to give a weekly series of thirty-nine short broadcasts at the request of Norman Collins called 'Keeping in Touch' intended specifically for the 14th Army to help counter their belief that they were 'the forgotten army.' Roger Falk (1910–; Kt., 1969) worked in Bombay and Calcutta, 1932–35, and served in the RAF

throughout the war, for one year on Field Marshal Wavell's staff (private communication from Sir Roger).

2120. Literature and the Left

Tribune, 4 June 1943

"When a man of true Genius appears in the World, you may know him by this infallible Sign, that all the Dunces are in Conspiracy against him."[1] So wrote Jonathan Swift, 200 years before the publication of *Ulysses*.

If you consult any sporting manual or year book you will find many pages devoted to the hunting of the fox and the hare, but not a word about the hunting of the highbrow. Yet this, more than any other, is the characteristic British sport, in season all the year round and enjoyed by rich and poor alike, with no complications from either class-feeling or political alignment.

For it should be noted that in its attitude towards "highbrows"—that is, towards any writer or artist who makes experiments in technique—the Left is no friendlier than the Right. Not only is "highbrow" almost as much a word of abuse in the *Daily Worker* as in *Punch*, but it is exactly those writers whose work shows both originality and the power to endure that Marxist doctrinaires single out for attack. I could name a long list of examples, but I am thinking especially of Joyce, Yeats, Lawrence and Eliot. Eliot, in particular, is damned in the left-wing press almost as automatically and perfunctorily as Kipling—and that by critics who only a few years back were going into raptures over the already forgotten masterpieces of the Left Book Club.

If you ask a "good party man" (and this goes for almost any party of the Left) what he objects to in Eliot, you get an answer that ultimately reduces to this. Eliot is a reactionary (he has declared himself a royalist, an Anglo-Catholic, etc.), and he is also a "bourgeois intellectual," out of touch with the common man: therefore he is a bad writer. Contained in this statement is a half-conscious confusion of ideas which vitiates nearly all politico-literary criticism.

To dislike a writer's politics is one thing. To dislike him because he forces you to think is another, not necessarily incompatible with the first. But as soon as you start talking about "good" and "bad" writers you are tacitly appealing to literary tradition and thus dragging in a totally different set of values. For what is a "good" writer? Was Shakespeare "good"? Most people would agree that he was. Yet Shakespeare is, and perhaps was even by the standards of his own time, reactionary in tendency; and he is also a difficult writer, only doubtfully accessible to the common man. What, then, becomes of the notion that Eliot is disqualified, as it were, by being an Anglo-Catholic royalist who is given to quoting Latin?

Left Wing literary criticism has not been wrong in insisting on the importance of subject-matter. It may not even have been wrong, considering the age we live in, in demanding that literature shall be first and foremost propaganda. Where it has been wrong is in making what are ostensibly literary judgments for politics ends. To take a crude example, what Communist would dare to admit in public that Trotsky is a better writer than Stalin—as he is, of course? To say "X is a gifted writer, but he is a political enemy and I shall do my best to silence him" is harmless enough. Even if you end by silencing him with a tommy-gun you are not really sinning against the intellect. The deadly sin is to say "X is a political enemy: therefore he is a bad writer." And if anyone says that this kind of thing doesn't happen, I answer merely: look up the literary pages of the Left Wing press, from the *News Chronicle* to the *Labour Monthly*, and see what you find.

There is no knowing just how much the Socialist movement has lost by alienating the literary intelligentsia. But it has alienated them, partly by confusing tracts with literature, and partly by having no room in it for a humanistic culture. A writer can vote Labour as easily as anyone else, but it is very difficult for him to take part in the Socialist movement *as a writer*. Both the book-trained doctrinaire and the practical politician will despise him as a "bourgeois intellectual," and will lose no opportunity of telling him so. They will have much the same attitude towards his work as a golfing stockbroker would have. The illiteracy of politicians is a special feature of our age—as G. M. Trevelyan put it, "In the seventeenth century Members of Parliament quoted the Bible, in the eighteenth and nineteenth centuries, the classics, and in the twentieth century nothing"—and its corollary is the literary impotence of writers. In the years following the last war the best English writers were reactionary in tendency, though most of them took no direct part in politics. After them, about 1930, there came a generation of writers who tried very hard to be actively useful in the Left Wing movement. Numbers of them joined the Communist Party, and got there exactly the same reception as they would have got in the Conservative Party. That is, they were first regarded with patronage and suspicion, and then, when it was found that they would not or could not turn themselves into gramophone records, they were thrown out on their ears. Most of them retreated into individualism. No doubt they still vote Labour but their talents are lost to the movement; and—a more sinister development—after them there comes a new generation of writers who, without being strictly non-political, are outside the Socialist movement from the start. Of the very young writers who are now beginning their careers, the most gifted are pacifists; a few may even have a leaning towards Fascism. There is hardly one to whom the mystique of the Socialist movement appears to mean anything. The ten-year-long struggle against Fascism seems to them meaningless and uninteresting, and they say so frankly. One could explain this in a number of ways, but the contemptuous attitude of the Left towards "bourgeois intellectuals" is likely to be part of the reason.

Gilbert Murray relates somewhere or other that he once lectured on Shakespeare to a Socialist debating society. At the end he called for questions in the usual way, to receive as the sole question asked: "Was Shakespeare a capitalist?" The depressing thing about this story is that it might well be true. Follow up its implications, and you perhaps get a glimpse of the reason why Céline wrote *Mea Culpa*[2] and Auden is watching his navel in America.

Orwell's article brought a response from the Shakespeare scholar (later King Alfred Professor of English Literature, University of Liverpool), Kenneth Muir (1907–1996):

Though I agree with the main argument of Mr. Orwell's article (June 4), I would like to question his statement that "Shakespeare is, and perhaps was even by the standards of his own time, reactionary in tendency." Mr. Orwell is critically orthodox in his opinion. Apart from a few Marxists, who interpret Shakespeare as a champion of the "heroic ideals of bourgeois humanism," or as a "healthy, well-poised, sceptical melioristic, humanist, somewhat to the Left of the centre of advanced bourgeois opinion," most critics seem to believe that he was a wholehearted supporter of the Tudor despotism. Tawney, in his great book, *Religion and the Rise of Capitalism*, showed conclusively that Shakespeare's views on Order were shared by practically all political and religious thinkers.

But I do not think that it has been fully realised that after 1600, Shakespeare accepted the theory of Order with increasing reservations. *Measure for Measure* can hardly be regarded as a defence of authoritarian government. Isabella's great speeches to Angelo at the climax of the play provide a devastating criticism of authority:

> Man, proud man,
> Dressed in a little brief authority,
> Most ignorant of what he's most assured,
> His glassy essence, like an angry ape
> Plays such fantastic tricks before high heaven,
> As make the angels weep. . . .

Shakespeare returned to the subject in *King Lear*, where the mad king declares that the great image of authority is that a dog's obeyed in office. Lear's development from King to Man, leading him to a realisation of the injustice of society, shows him how justice is merely an instrument of the strong and rich to oppress the poor and weak. A year later, in *Timon of Athens*, the power of money became Shakespeare's main theme. Timon's great speech on gold, which was brilliantly interpreted in Marx's still untranslated *Political Economy and Philosophy* and also quoted in *Capital*, is a terrifying analysis of the economic basis of society.

I have deliberately refrained from discussing *Coriolanus*, which Hazlitt used to show Shakespeare's lack of sympathy for the common people. But to retain our sympathies for the hero, it was necessary to provide him with some excuse in the fickleness of the mob. If the mob had been sympathetic, Coriolanus would have been a mere traitor. Even so, when the play was last performed in Paris, it was regarded by the Fascists as an attack on dictatorship; and when I myself produced it in modern dress two years ago, it was most appreciated by the Left, who regarded it as an analysis of the Fifth Columnist mentality, and most criticised by the Right who disliked hearing such an uncompromising statement of their own views.

1. More correctly quoted in 'Imaginary Interview: George Orwell and Jonathan Swift', 2 November 1942 (*1637*); Orwell is doubtless quoting from memory as was often his custom. The correct reading is: 'When a true Genius appears in the World, you may know him by this Sign, that the Dunces are all in confederacy against him' (*Thoughts on Various Subjects, Miscellanies*, volume 1, 1728).
2. *Mea Culpa* (1936) was written after a visit to the USSR, which he found abhorrent.

2121. News Commentary in English for Malaya, 36

4 June 1943

This was written and read by George Orwell. No script has been traced.

On 14 June 1943, the Controller (Overseas Services), J. B. Clark, sent the following memorandum to the Director General of the BBC. It is marked, presumably by the Director General, 'I would like to see C(OS) about all these points. 15/6/43.' The memorandum is also marked that the matter should be brought up for discussion on 18 June; that date is crossed out and 21 June is written above it.

I must apologise for several serious errors of judgment betrayed by this talk for which I accept responsibility. The broadcast in its final form was, in fact, the result of misunderstandings which will not recur.

(a) It was the first talk of the kind censored for policy by one of the new senior members of our staff who had, with some justification, not realised properly the extent to which a talk provided for "personality" reasons in the target area should be brought into line with general policy. I make no excuse for failing to ensure that he was properly briefed, but I am satisfied that the situation in this respect is secure for the future.

(b) The accident would have been less likely to have happened if Tonkin our principal news specialist on the Far East had not been diverted from his specialist duties. This situation is not likely to recur and needless to say no blame whatever attaches to Tonkin in these circumstances.

It may be relevant to recall that these English broadcasts in what is known internally as the "Malayan Band" were started in simple English by the Chinese who was engaged for the Hokkein broadcasts. It was thought that his English and accent would be suitable for the purpose they were intended to serve, but he proved unequal to the task. They are radiated on a single frequency used on other days of the week at the same time for miscellaneous minority languages. Orwell was allowed to step into the breach because there was strong external evidence that he was well known and trusted in Burma where it was hoped we would influence an important section of the potential audience.

Apart from other considerations which were neglected in this instance, the talks have been rather carefully related to the information available to us about Japanese propaganca in the somewhat prescribed target area.

What it was that Orwell said that prompted this reaction is not known. There was relatively little news during the preceding week of the kind he might have wished to focus on. On 30 May, the island of Attu in the Aleutians was retaken, and there was much air fighting on all fronts. Gentry's diary is particularly thin for this week. For 29 May he records: 'Essen bombed—usual quantity. Our losses 23 planes. Zeiss works at Jena raided by 50 mosquito bombers which went in at a few hundred feet. Our losses small. Southern Italy bombed.' For 2 and 3 June he states 'No special news' and for 4 June, 'No special news apart frofm the usual heavy bombing.' No news is mentioned on 30 and 31 May and 1 June. It is likely that Orwell gave some general reflections on the war and, perhaps, in the light of the reference to 'a talk provided for "personality" reasons,' on what victory might imply for Malaya and the countries of Southeast Asia.

2122. To E. M. Forster

4 June 1943   07/ES/EB

Dear Forster

I cannot get a copy of Max Beerbohm's lecture,[1] partly, perhaps, because I don't know to what Society he delivered it. You said that you had written to his publishers. I don't know whether that has borne fruit yet?

If the Strachey project falls through, then I think it would be quite a good idea to do the one about Plays, particularly as most of them are of a kind which might be read, if not seen, in India. We could, after all, return to the Strachey talk another month.

I am sorry about this change to Sunday but it doesn't seem to be avoidable. The simplest way would be for you to arrange to record always on one day of the week—any day which is convenient to you, but preferably not Saturday. Could you let me have a suitable date for your recording for the 20th? It might be better to give two alternative dates and I would like the script the day before you come to record, because we have to get it censored.

I am sorry for all this change-about, but once we get into the new arrangement it will no doubt be as simple as before.

Yours sincerely
[Initialled] E. A. B
George Orwell
(Talks Producer)
Indian Section

1. This must be the Rede lecture 'Lytton Strachey' (Cambridge, 1943) by Sir Max Beerbhom (1872–1956), critic, essayist, satirist. It is reprinted in his *Mainly on the Air*, enlarged 1957 edition, a volume composed mostly of broadcast talks. Giles Lytton Strachey (1880–1932), biographer and critic, is remembered particularly for the change in the art of biography following publication of his *Eminent Victorians* (1918).

2123. To Mrs. Milton (Naomi Royde-Smith)

5 June 1943   07/ES/EB/WMB

Dear Mrs. Milton
Thank you for your letter of the 4th.

The correct dates and times of your next two broadcasts are as follows:—

Wednesday June 16th at 12.15–12.30 pm.
    ,,   July 21st at 12.15–12.30   ,,
These times are Double British Summer Time.

Your script arrived safely yesterday, for which many thanks.

Yours sincerely
[Initialled] WB
For George Orwell
(Talks Producer)
Indian Section

2124. On Orwell's behalf to W. J. Turner

5 June 1943   07/ES/EB

Dear Mr. Turner
This is just a reminder about your talk on Shakespeare, on Thursday next, June 10th, with special reference to his play MEASURE FOR MEASURE. We should be very glad to have the script by Tuesday next, the 8th. As Mr. Blair has mentioned, the script should be about 1200 words (about 10 minutes reading approximately).

The time of the broadcast is 1.30 to 2 pm. (Double British Summer Time) Could you kindly be at 200 Oxford Street, about 1 o'clock?

Yours sincerely
[Initialled] WB
(For George Orwell)
Talks Producer
Indian Section

2125. BBC Talks Booking Form, 5.6.43

W. J. Turner: 'Great Dramatists,' 7, Shakespeare, MEASURE FOR MEASURE; broadcast 10.6.43; fee £8.8s. Signed: Z. A. Bokhari. Remarks: Address to Turner at *The Spectator*, marked 'Private & Personal.'

2126. To Arthur Wynn, Music Bookings Manager

7 June 1943   Original   EB/WMB

MUSICAL INTERLUDE

With reference to our memo. of the 16th March, requesting you to issue a contract for Dr. Narayana Menon of 176 Sussex Gardens, London, W.2. for the six broadcasts in our series CALLING ALL STUDENTS—GREAT DRAMATISTS, we have decided to broadcast a further programme in this series, making 7 in all. Dr. Menon is again choosing the recorded music for the Musical interlude (approximately 5 minutes) in this programme, and we shall be grateful, therefore, if you will arrange to issue a contract to Dr. Menon for this last broadcast, which will take place on Thursday next, June 10th 1943 at 1130–1200 GMT, in the EASTERN SERVICE (RED NETWORK).

[Signed] Eric Blair
(Eric Blair)

2127. To Alan Rook

8 June 1943   Handwritten draft for postcard

P.C.
Thanks for your letter.[1] We will arrange[2] a recording for Saturday July 10th & let you know the exact time etc. when we have made the booking.

G.O.

1. Rook wrote on 7 June saying he would let Orwell have his script by 1 July. He would be in London on 10 and 11 July and could record his talk then, or he could arrange to come to London on Saturday, 3 July.
2. The draft is written on the verso of Rook's letter; for 'arrange,' Orwell originally wrote 'book.'

2128. To C. E. M. Joad

9 June 1943   07/ES/EB/WMB

Dear Professor Joad
Confirming our telephone conversation; we would like you to do a monthly talk every fourth Tuesday on a more or less philosophical subject to balance the more or less political ones which Kingsley Martin is doing. We want the first talk for Tuesday, June 22nd, at 5.15 pm. (Double British Summer Time). If we had the script in two or three days beforehand that would do. You can record beforehand if you wish.

As to the subject of the first talk: I thought that some such title as WHAT THE WEST HAS LEARNED FROM THE EAST, or something of that kind, would be about right, but you can please yourself. We want, in any case, to have some vague east-west tie-up in these talks.

The talks are all 13½ minutes—which is about 1600 words. I understand that you will get your usual fee.

Could you let me know, as early as possible, whether you can definitely undertake these broadcasts? I hope you can because, otherwise, it will leave rather a hole in our programme.

> Yours sincerely
> [Initialled] E.A.B
> George Orwell
> (Talks Producer)
> Indian Section.

Joad replied on 11 June with suggestions for five talks. Orwell annotated this:

Mr Bokhari
I have written to J. asking him to go ahead. As to the fee, I think he ought to get 20 gns. He is worth it to us. E.A.B.

2129. Newsletter in Tamil, 8
10 June 1943

The English version was written by Eric Blair. No script has been traced.

2130. News Commentary in English for Malaya, 37
11 June 1943

This was written and read by George Orwell. No script has been traced.

2131. To Balachandra Rajan
11 June 1943   Handwritten draft and typed versions
07/ES/EB/WMB

Dear Mr. Rajan[1]
Very many thanks for the copy of MONSOON. I don't know whether I shall get an opportunity of reviewing it, but I am going to pass it on to Mr. E. M. Forster, who does a monthly book talk for India. I think in his next talk, or next but one, he will be talking about books written by Indians, or having some connection with India, and in that case he might well include yours.

> Yours sincerely
> [Initialled] E.A.B
> George Orwell
> (Talks Producer)
> Indian Section

1. Balachandra Rajan (1920–) edited *Focus* (Nos. 1–5, 1945–50) with Andrew Pearse; in the second number, Orwell's essay 'Arthur Koestler' was first published; see *2548*. In the letter accompanying *Monsoon*, Rajan described it as his first volume of poems and seemed to be inviting Orwell to review it. He was to become a distinguished academic critic and interpreter, especially of Milton and Eliot, and Professor of English at the University of Western Ontario.

2132. BBC Talks Booking Form, 12.6.43

Kingsley Martin: 'The Debate Continues'; recorded 18.6.43; broadcast 19.6.43; fee £5.5s.[1] Signed: Z. A. Bokhari.

1. This was increased to £9.9s because, instead of being six minutes long, it proved to be twelve minutes long when Martin arrived with the script. It was altered and shortened, and ran 10' 20". Bokhari asked for the larger fee on 21 June, and it was offered to Martin on 23 June.

2133. Modern English Verse
Broadcast 13 June 1943

This talk was the first in the 'Calling All Students,' Modern English Verse Series. The text is reproduced from the typescript used for the broadcast. This is not professionally typed, so was probably typed by Orwell. There are no manuscript cha~ges, but at the head of the first page Orwell has written, 'As b'cast 13' E.A.B'; this is the timing also given in PasB. The script was censored by someone initialled KF. Timings for each page are written on the typescript in Orwell's hand; these have here been printed in italic within square brackets. There is no title on the typescript; that given here comes from Orwell's letter to the first prospective contributors, 13 April 1943; see *2006*. The typescript has towards the end of the first paragraph, 'we hope . . . to broadcast the poem in the its author's own voice'; 'its' has been omitted here and one or two typing errors have been silently corrected.

The six talks that follow this one are intended to give a survey of modern English poetry from about the year 1900 until the present. The speakers in the series are Desmond McCarthy, who is well known as a literary and dramatic critic and is literary editor of the Sunday Times; L. A. G. Strong, the novelist; Alan Rook, who is one of the most promising of the very young poets who have made their appearance in England since the outbreak of war; Lord David Cecil, who is well known for his life of the poet Cowper, his recent book on Thomas Hardy and other critical works; John Lehmann, who from 1936 onwards has been editing the periodical New Writing, which apart from publishing the less-known English and American writers has done a lot to introduce contemporary European and Asiatic literature to the English public; and Desmond Hawkins, the critic, whose voice is pretty well known to listeners on the Eastern service. Each of these six talks will include one poem belonging to the period, and we hope where possible to broadcast the poem in the author's own voice. After they have been broadcast these talks, like various others of the series we do in this service, will be printed and sold in India in pamphlet form for a few annas.

I don't want to anticipate what the other speakers will say, merely to give a sort of background sketch of the period they will be covering. Poetry is of all arts the most national, or I should [1¾'] rather say local, the most difficult to export or import. Whereas prose can always be adequately translated, and in some cases may actually be better in translation than in the original, poetry is almost untranslateable. And just as a poem belongs, more than a piece of music or perhaps even a picture, to a particular place, so it belongs to a particular time. It is much easier to appreciate a foreign poem, and perhaps even one in your own language, if you know something about the social, moral and religious background from which it springs. For the music of poetry depends on word-associations, and in order to appreciate it you have to share those associations to some extent, or at any rate to be able to imagine them. It isn't therefore irrelevant to try to supply a sort of historical background to the talks that will follow. The period that they will cover is only 43 years, but during that time enormous changes have happened and the prevailing mental climate has altered out of recognition. To some of the English poets who were writing in 1900, the Great Exhibition of 1851 would have been a vivid memory; those who are now beginning to publish their work don't even remember the war of 1914–18. They live in a different world, though a short lifetime would span the two dates. I am trying to indicate here the differences that have come over British society in that time.

If you put yourself into the mind of a man who was mature in 1900, you find that several pieces of mental furniture that we are very much accustomed to are missing. The first of these is what I might call the concept of the machine. We live in an age in which everyone who thinks at all, everyone who ever reads a book or newspaper or listens to the radio, is very much aware of the power of machinery [3¾'] and technology to raise our standard of living. Films, textbooks, posters, pamphlets, the speeches of political leaders, rub this into us all the time. Every educated person knows that given a reasonable amount of international co-operation, the world's wealth could be increased, health and nutrition improved, drudgery abolished, to an extent unthinkable a few decades ago. Now this fact was not in the consciousness of most of the writers who were mature in 1900, although the essential technological changes had already happened. If you look at a writer like Thomas Hardy, or Robert Bridges, or Gerard Manley Hopkins, or A. E. Housman, a thing that strikes you is that they still think of England as an agricultural country—which as a matter of fact it wasn't even in 1900. They haven't much conception of the new sort of world, now obviously possible though it hasn't arrived, in which the brute labour is done by machinery and the peasant or workman is better off than a king would have been in the Middle Ages. They still think in terms of the harsh peasant world where it is normal to work hard, to till the ground with primitive implements, to do without foreign luxuries, and to die rather young.

On the other hand, what you are not likely to find in the mind of anyone in the year 1900, is a doubt about the continuity of civilization. If the world as people then saw it was rather harsh, simple and slow-moving, it was also secure. Things would continue in a more or less recognizable pattern; life might not get appreciably more pleasant, but at any rate barbarism wouldn't return. Now here again is a great change that has occurred in these four decades. We have seen an enormous technological advance, and with it a reversion to barbarism [6'] that our grandfathers would not have believed possible. We have invented machines that would have seemed magical only a hundred years ago, and we have used them almost solely for making war. The world has grown into an economic unit, so that if you merely look round the room you are sitting in you'll see products that come from every corner of the earth; and at the same time nationalism has been erected into a sort of evil religion and the races of mankind are shut off from one another by insane hatreds. All that is in the consciousness of anyone who is writing now. All the younger writers, people like Auden or Spender, or the still younger ones like Henry Treece and Alex Comfort who have appeared more recently, have it as the background of their thoughts that the basis for a decent society is already there, and on the other hand that the very existence of civilization is menaced. If you had told the average person, and that would include most of the poets, in 1900 that it would soon be easy to fly from London to Calcutta he wouldn't have believed you; and if you had told him that before long Jews would be persecuted more fiercely than they ever were in the Middle Ages, he wouldn't have believed that either. Anyone born within this century takes both facts for granted, and that establishes a valid distinction.

However, other things have happened between 1900 and today besides scientific invention and the rise of the new kind of barbarism that we call Fascism. There was also the period of exceptional prosperity between the opening of the century and the war of 1914, there was the war itself, there was the period of exhaustion and recovery that followed the war, and there was the economic depression of 1930. Those, [8'] with the two periods I've just been speaking of, make up the background of the six talks you will hear. It's worth saying a little about each of them.

The period between about 1905 and 1914, generally referred to when one's speaking of literature as the "Georgian" period, was a very good time to be alive, at any rate in England. There was great prosperity, much of the dulness and prejudice of Victorian society had been broken down, and there was a growth of what appeared to be enlightenment and internationalism. The great nations of the world were in fact getting ready for war, but the ordinary man didn't believe that war was coming. A carefree attitude towards life was more possible then than it has been since, and also a rather shallow pantheism summed up in the then popular phrase, "Nature worship".

The war of 1914 butted into this comfortable period more unexpectedly than the present war has done. Whether it caused more or less suffering than the present war is hard to say. It killed more people than have been killed hitherto, but it probably impinged less on the lives of non-combatants. But what is unmistakeable in the characteristic literature of the 1914 war is the sense of something unprecedented and something meaningless. Whereas all the best writing of the nineteen-thirties is heavy with the sense of approaching disaster, so that it is almost a relief when the expected happens and the guns begin to shoot, the characteristic reaction in the other war is surprise and resentment. The war is thought of as a horror that has come as it were from nowhere, and for no reason, like an earthquake. It is just a purposeless slaughter—nearly all the best writing of [10'] that time expresses that feeling, which may have been mistaken but was at least subjectively true.

The war of 1914–18 left Britain much exhausted, but after it ended there was still another decade when life was well worth living, at any rate in the victorious countries. There was a worldwide revulsion from war, another seeming growth of internationalist feeling, and better contacts between the writers and artists of different countries than there had ever been before. That was the period in which for the first time the great Russian writers were fully popularised in England, and when the French writers of the past few decades had their greatest influence. It is perhaps significant that the best writers of this particular period were most of them either Americans or Irishmen. For a while it could almost be said that the headquarters of the English literary world were in Paris. In that emancipated, fairly prosperous period of the nineteen-twenties there was room for a culture and refinement that English literature had not seen since the eighteenth century. But the mental climate changed very suddenly at the beginning of the next decade, with the onset of the economic depression and the beginning of something that Britain had not experienced before—middle-class unemployment. Inevitably, after 1930, there was a far greater preoccupation with politics, with sociology, with economics than had seemed necessary in the decade before. The younger writers almost all of them turned to Karl Marx because the basis of their own existence had been shaken and Marx was the prophet who had foretold that this would happen. And then a little later came the rise of Fascism, the undisguisable drift towards world war, and [12'] the new orientation of the younger writers who find themselves in a world which has all the potentialities of peace and plenty combined with the *fact* of destruction and hatred.

I have tried to sketch in as best I could in a quarter of an hour the social background of the various literary periods you'll hear discussed in this series. I hope you'll like them, because I know they'll be good talks and well worth the six annas when they're published in pamphlet form. Remember that they're at this time—1515 Greenwich time, that's 9.45 Indian standard time—three Sundays in each month. The other Sunday E. M. Forster will give his regular monthly talk, "Some Books". He will be on the air this time next week. So the first talk in the "Calling All Students" series will be the Sunday after next, June the 27th, at this time. [13']

2134. To C. E. M. Joad

14 June 1943   07/ES/EB/WMB

Dear Professor Joad
Many thanks for your letter dated June 11th. I think the subjects of the talks you have suggested are very good and just the kind of approach we wanted. I hope you will be able to find the necessary time and that we can have the script of the first talk not later than June 20th. As to the fee—I think you will hear from the Contracts Department shortly. I am passing on your request and hope that they will be able to meet your wishes.[1]

Yours sincerely
[Initialled] E. A. B
George Orwell
(Talks Producer)
Indian Section

1. Orwell had suggested to Bokhari a fee of £21; see *2128*. On 17 June, Ronald Boswell, the Talks Booking Manager, wrote on behalf of the Programme Contracts Director offering a special fee of £18.18 (instead of the usual £15.15) because of the extra preparation involved. Joad accepted this on 22 June 1943.

2135. Newsletter in Tamil, 9

17 June 1943

The English version was written by Eric Blair. No script has been traced.

2136. To T. S. Eliot

17 June 1943   07/ES/EB/WMB

Dear Eliot
Following on our telephone conversation I want to ask whether you would do one talk in the new literary series we're starting towards the end of August. We're going to have a series dealing with English prose literature of the present century, and are calling it—MODERN MASTERPIECES. I want each talk to deal ostensibly with a single book, but in doing so to give some account of the author's work as a whole. The projected list of talks is attached.[1] Would you like to tackle the talk on JAMES JOYCE, with special reference to ULYSSES. I can't give you the exact date of the talk because I haven't yet fixed the order, in which they will appear, but it will not be earlier than the 21st August. This would be a talk of the usual length, that is, 15/1600 words. I must also ask whether, in the event of your doing the talk, you will

object to its being printed in India as part of a pamphlet. We now have a
number of our programmes printed in pamphlet form.

Yours sincerely
[Initialled] E. A. B
George Orwell
(Talks Producer)
Indian Section

1. This was accidentally omitted; see *2140*.

2137. Letter to an American Visitor by 'Obadiah Hornbooke' (Alex Comfort)

Tribune, 4 June 1943

For Orwell's answer to this satirical verse, see *2138*. See also his letter to
Comfort of 11 July (?), *2183*.

Columbian poet, whom we've all respected
   From a safe distance for a year or two,
Since first your *magnum opus* was collected—[1]
   It seems a pity no one welcomed you
   Except the slippery professional few,
Whose news you've read, whose posters you've inspected
   Who gave America Halifax, and who
Pay out to scribes and painters they've selected
     Doles which exceed a fraction of the debts
     Of all our pimps in hardware coronets.

You've seen the ruins, heard the speeches, swallowed
   The bombed-out hospitals and cripples' schools—
You've heard (on records) how the workers hollowed
   And read in pokerwork GIVE US THE TOOLS!
   You know how, with the steadfastness of mules,
The Stern Determination of the People
   Goes sailing through a paradise of fools
Like masons shinning up an endless steeple—
     A climb concluding after many days
     In a brass weathercock that points all ways.

The land sprouts orators. No doubt you've heard
   How every buffer, fool and patrioteer
Applies the Power of the Spoken Word
   And shoves his loud posterior in your ear;
   So Monkey Hill[2] competes with Berkeley Square—

The B.B.C. as bookie, pimp and vet
   Presenting Air Vice-Marshals set to cheer
Our raided towns with vengeance (though I've yet
     To hear from any man who lost his wife
     Berlin or Lubeck brought her back to life.)

You've heard of fighting on the hills and beaches
   And down the rabbit holes with pikes and bows—
You've heard the Baron's bloody-minded speeches
   (Each worth a fresh Division to our foes)
   That smell so strong of murder that the crows
Perch on the Foreign Office roof and caw
   For German corpses laid in endless rows,
"A Vengeance such as Europe never saw"—
     The maniac Baron's future contribution
     To peace perpetual through retribution . . .

You've heard His Nibs decanting year by year
   The dim productions of his bulldog brain,
While homes and factories sit still to hear
   The same old drivel dished up once again—
   You heard the Churches' cartwheels to explain
That bombs are Christian when the English drop them—
   The Union bosses scrapping over gain
While no one's the temerity to stop them
     Or have the racketeers who try to bleed 'em
     Flogged, like the Indians for demanding freedom.

They found you poets—quite a decent gallery
   Of painters who don't let their chances slip;
And writers who prefer a regular salary
   To steer their writings by the Party Whip—
   Hassall's been tipped to have the Laureateship:
Morton is following Goebbels, not St. Paul.
   There's Elton's squeaky pump still gives a drip,
And Priestley twists his proletarian awl
     Cobbling at shoes that Mill and Rousseau wore
     And still the wretched tool contrives to bore.

They found you critics—an astounding crowd:
   (Though since their work's their living, I won't say
Who howled at Eliot, hooted Treece, were loud
   In kicking Auden when he slipped away
   Out of the looney-bin to find, they say,
A quiet place where men with minds could write:
   But since Pearl Harbour, in a single day
The same old circus chase him, black is white,
     And once again by day and night he feels
     The packs of tripehounds yelling at his heels).

I say, they found you artists, well selected,
  Whom we export to sell the British case:
We keep our allied neighbours well protected
  From those who give the thing a different face—
  One man's in jail, one in a "medical place";
Another working at a farm with pigs on:
  We take their leisure, close their books, say grace,
And like that bus-conducting lad Geoff Grigson
    We beat up every buzzard, kite and vulture,
    And dish them out to you as English Culture.

Once in a while, to every Man and Nation,
  There comes, as Lowell said, a sort of crisis
Between the Ministry of Information
  And what your poor artistic soul advises:
  They catch the poets, straight from Cam or Isis:
"Join the brigade, or be for ever dumb—
  Either cash in on your artistic lysis
Or go on land work if you won't succumb:
    Rot in the Army, sickened and unwilling":
    So can you wonder that they draw their shilling?

You met them all. You don't require a list
  Of understrapping ghosts who once were writers—
Who celebrate the size of Britain's fist,
  Write notes for sermons, dish out pep to mitres,
  Fake letters from the Men who Fly our Fighters.
Cheer when we blast some enemy bungalows—
  Think up atrocities, the artful blighters,
To keep the grindstone at the public's nose—
    Combining moral uplift and pornography,
    Produced with arty paper and typography.

They find their leisure to fulfil their promise,
  Their work is praised, *funguntur vice cotis;*[3]
And Buddy Judas cracks up Doubting Thomas.
  Their ways are paved with favourable notice
  (Look how unanimous the Tory vote is).
They write in papers and review each other,
  You'd never guess how bloody full the boat is;
I shan't forgive Macneice his crippled brother
    Whom just a year ago on New Year's Day
    The Germans murdered in a radio play.

O for another Dunciad—a POPE
  To purge this dump with his gigantic boot—
Drive fools to water, aspirin or rope—
  Make idle lamp-posts bear their fitting fruit:
  Private invective's far too long been mute—

O for another vast satiric comet
   To blast this wretched tinder, branch and root.
The servile stuff that makes a true man vomit—
      Sucked from the works to which they cling like leeches,
      Those resurrection-puddings, Churchill's speeches.

God knows—for there is libel—I can't name
   How many clammy paws of these you've shaken,
Been told our English spirit is the same
      From Lord Vansittart back to pseudo-Bacon—
      Walked among licensed writers, and were taken
To Grub Street, Malet Street, and Portland Place,
   Where every question that you ask will waken
The same old salesman's grin on every face
      Among the squads of columbines and flunkeys,
      Set on becoming Laureate of Monkeys.

We do not ask, my friend, that you'll forget
   The squirts and toadies when you were presented,
The strength-through-joy brigades you will have met
      Whose mouths are baggy and whose hair is scented—
      Only recall we were not represented.
We wrote our own refusals, and we meant them.
   Our work is plastered and ourselves resented—
Our heads are bloody, but we have not bent them.
      We hold no licences, like ladies' spaniels;
      We live like lions in this den of Daniels.

O friend and writer, deafened by the howls
   That dying systems utter, mad with fear
In darkness, with a sinking of the bowels,
      Where all the devils of old conscience leer—
      Forget the gang that met you on the pier,
Grinning and stuffed with all the old excuses
   For starving Europe, and the crocodile tear
Turned on for visitors who have their uses.
      We know the capers of the simian crew.
      We send our best apologies to you.

1. There have been many guesses as to who the visiting American poet was. In a letter giving the editors permission to reprint this poem, Alex Comfort revealed that 'the visitor was imaginary' (1 August 1995).
2. At the Zoological Gardens, Regent's Park, London.
3. Comfort has slightly adapted the opening of Horace's Ars Poetica, lines 304–5, which translated say, 'I will act as a whetstone, which can sharpen steel, but which itself has no power to cut.'

2138. 'As One Non-Combatant to Another (A letter to
"Obadiah Hornbooke")'
Tribune, 18 June 1943

O poet strutting from the sandbagged portal
Of that small world where barkers ply their art,
And each new "school" believes itself immortal,
Just like the horse that draws the knacker's cart:
O captain of a clique of self-advancers,
Trained in the tactics of the pamphleteer,
Where slogans serve for thoughts and sneers for answers—
You've chosen well your moment to appear
And hold your nose amid a world of horror
Like Dr. Bowdler walking through Gomorrah.

In the Left Book Club days you wisely lay low,
But when "Stop Hitler!" lost its old attraction
You bounded forward in a Woolworth's halo
To cash in on the anti-war reaction;
You waited till the Nazis ceased from frightening,
Then, picking a safe audience, shouted "Shame!"
Like a Prometheus you defied the lightning,
But didn't have the nerve to sign your name.[1]
You're a true poet, but as saint and martyr
You're a mere fraud, like the Atlantic Charter.

Your hands are clean, and so were Pontius Pilate's,
But as for "bloody heads," that's just a metaphor;
The bloody heads are on Pacific islets
Or Russian steppes or Libyan sands—it's better for
The health to be a C.O. than a fighter,
To chalk a pavement doesn't need much guts,
It pays to stay at home and be a writer
While other talents wilt in Nissen huts;
"We live like lions"—yes, just like a lion,
Pensioned on scraps in a safe cage of iron.

For while you write the warships ring you round
And flights of bombers drown the nightingales,
And every bomb that drops is worth a pound
To you or someone like you, for your sales
Are swollen with those of rivals dead or silent,
Whether in Tunis or the B.B.C.,
And in the drowsy freedom of this island
You're free to shout that England isn't free;
They even chuck you cash, as bears get buns,
For crying "Peace!" behind a screen of guns.

In 'seventeen to snub the nosing bitch
Who slipped you a white feather needed cheek,
But now, when every writer finds his niche
Within some mutual-admiration clique,
Who cares what epithets by Blimps are hurled?
Who'd give a damn if handed a white feather?
Each little mob of pansies is a world,
Cosy and warm in any kind of weather;
In such a world it's easy to "object,"
Since that's what both your friends and foes expect.

At times it's almost a more dangerous deed
Not to object; I know, for I've been bitten.
I wrote in nineteen-forty that at need
I'd fight to keep the Nazis out of Britain;
And Christ! how shocked the pinks were! Two years later
I hadn't lived it down; one had the effrontery
To write three pages calling me a "traitor,"
So black a crime it is to love one's country.
Yet where's the pink that would have thought it odd of me
To write a shelf of books in praise of sodomy?

Your game is easy, and its rules are plain:
Pretend the war began in 'thirty-nine,
Don't mention China, Ethiopia, Spain,
Don't mention Poles, except to say they're swine;
Cry havoc when we bomb a German city,
When Czechs get killed don't worry in the least,
Give India a perfunctory squirt of pity
But don't enquire what happens further East;
Don't mention Jews—in short, pretend the war is
Simply a racket "got up" by the Tories.

Throw in a word of "anti-Fascist" patter
From time to time, by way of reinsurance,
And then go on to prove it makes no matter
If Blimps or Nazis hold the world in durance;
And that we others who "support" the war
Are either crooks or sadists or flag-wavers
In love with drums and bugles, but still more
Concerned with cadging Brendan Bracken's favours;
Or fools who think that bombs bring back the dead,
A thing not even Harris[2] ever said.

If you'd your way we'd leave the Russians to it
And sell our steel to Hitler as before;
Meanwhile you save your soul, and while you do it,
Take out a long-term mortgage on the war.
For after war there comes an ebb of passion,

The dead are sniggered at—and there you'll shine,
You'll be the very bull's-eye of the fashion,
You almost might get back to 'thirty-nine,
Back to the dear old game of scratch-my-neighbour
In sleek reviews financed by cooli labour.

But you don't hoot at Stalin—that's "not done"—
Only at Churchill; I've no wish to praise him,
I'd gladly shoot him when the war is won,
Or now, if there were someone to replace him.
But unlike some, I'll pay him what I owe him;
There was a time when empires crashed like houses,
And many a pink who'd titter at your poem
Was glad enough to cling to Churchill's trousers.
Christ! how they huddled up to one another
Like day-old chicks about their foster-mother!

I'm not a fan for "fighting on the beaches,"
And still less for the "breezy uplands" stuff,
I seldom listen-in to Churchill's speeches,
But I'd far sooner hear that kind of guff
Than your remark, a year or so ago,
That if the Nazis came you'd knuckle under
And peaceably "accept the status quo."
Maybe you would! But I've a right to wonder
Which will sound better in the days to come,
"Blood, toil and sweat" or "Kiss the Nazi's bum."

But your chief target is the radio hack,
The hired pep-talker—he's a safe objective,
Since he's unpopular and can't hit back.
It doesn't need the eye of a detective
To look down Portland Place and spot the whores,
But there are men (I grant, not the most heeded)
With twice your gifts and courage three times yours
Who do that dirty work because it's needed;
Not blindly, but for reasons they can balance,
They wear their seats out and lay waste their talents.

All propaganda's lying, yours or mine;
It's lying even when its facts are true;
That goes for Goebbels or the "party line,"
Or for the Primrose League or P.P.U.
But there are truths that smaller lies can serve,
And dirtier lies that scruples can gild over;
To waste your brains on war may need more nerve
Than to dodge facts and live in mental clover;
It's mean enough when other men are dying,
But when you lie, it's much to know you're lying.

That's thirteen stanzas, and perhaps you're puzzled
To know why I've attacked you—well, here's why:
Because your enemies all are dead or muzzled,
You've never picked on one who might reply.
You've hogged the limelight and you've aired your virtue,
While chucking sops to every dangerous faction,
The Left will cheer you and the Right won't hurt you;
What did you risk? Not even a libel action.
If you would show what saintly stuff you're made of,
Why not attack the cliques you *are* afraid of?

Denounce Joe Stalin, jeer at the Red Army,
Insult the Pope—you'll get some come-back there;
It's honourable, even if it's barmy,
To stamp on corns all round and never care.
But for the half-way saint and cautious hero,
Whose head's unbloody even if "unbowed,"
My admiration's somewhere near to zero;
So my last words would be: Come off that cloud,
Unship those wings that hardly dared to flitter,
And spout your halo for a pint of bitter.[3]

1. The *Tribune* printed this footnote: 'In fairness to "Mr. Hornbooke" it should be stated that he was willing to sign his name if we insisted, but preferred pseudonym.—EDS., *Tribune*.'
2. Sir Arthur Harris (1892–1984; Kt., Bt., 1953), Commander-in-Chief, Bomber Command, 1942–45. He organised mass bombing of Germany earning the soubriquet, 'Bomber Harris.'
3. Names in *2137* and *2138* are not indexed.

2139. News Commentary in English for Malaya, 38

18 June 1943

This was written and read by George Orwell. No script has been traced.[1]

1. Gentry's diary for 18 June 1943 shows he had contrasted a 'B.B.C. commentary' with news from other sources: 'A Jap air attack on Guadalcanal resulted in their losing 77 machines for a loss of 6 American planes, only B.B.C. commentary refers to this action as a victory of great importance & state that American "Lightning" fighters were used. Thought that this machine even faster than Spitfire.' The use of 'commentary' here may or may not be significant. *If* it is deliberate, it suggests that Orwell's broadcast was heard (and the entry is for the date of the broadcast). *2194 Days of War* records for 16 June: 'About 120 Japanese aircraft attack Guadalcanal and shipping . . . losing nearly a hundred of their aircraft.' This may refer to Orwell's broadcast, for the 'news' was two days old. The Spitfire Mk IX had a top speed at 21,000 feet of 404 mph; the P-38 Lightning had a top speed of 415 mph.

2140. To T. S. Eliot
18 June 1943   07/ES/EB/WMB

Dear Eliot
With reference to my letter yesterday I very much regret the list of projected talks was omitted but am sending you one herein.[1]

I hope very much you will be able to do the talk on JAMES JOYCE.

Yours sincerely
[Not signed/initialled]
George Orwell
(Talks Producer)
Indian Section

1. A copy of the schedule is not filed with this letter, but see *2141*.

2141. To William Plomer
18 June 1943   07/ES/EB

Dear Plomer[1]
I wonder whether you would like to do a talk for the Indian Section. I can't give you an exact date but it would be some time in September.

We're going to start a series called MODERN MASTERPIECES, dealing with English prose works of this century. We want each talk to deal ostensibly with a single book but in doing so to give some account of the author's work as a whole. I attach a list of the projected talks. If you would like to do E. M. FORSTER, I think it might be better to concentrate on HOWARDS END, because any Indian audience likely to listen in to a talk of this type would know about A PASSAGE TO INDIA already.

These are talks of 13½ minutes, that is, 15/1600 words. I assume that you would not object to your talk being afterwards printed as part of a pamphlet in India. We do this with some of our literary talks. In theory you get a royalty but in practice the profits are negligible. Could you let me know whether you will undertake this?[2]

Yours sincerely
[Initialled] E. A. B
George Orwell
(Talks Producer)
Indian Section

On a separate sheet:

MODERN MASTERPIECES

List of Projected Talks

T. S. ELIOT	JOYCE — (ULYSSES)
E. M. FORSTER	STRACHEY — (QUEEN VICTORIA)
V. S. PRITCHETT	WELLS
H. G. WELLS	SHAW
WILLIAM PLOMER	FORSTER — (HOWARDS END)
RAYMOND MORTIMER	VIRGINIA WOOLF[3]

1. William Charles Franklyn Plomer (1903–1973), South African poet and novelist educated in England (Rugby), edited *Voorslag* in Durban, 1926–27, with Roy Campbell (opposing racial discrimination), and spent some time in Japan before settling in England in 1929. In 1943 he published an autobiography, *Double Lives*. By then he had published the novels *Turbott Wolfe* (1926), *The Case is Altered* (1932), *The Invaders* (1934), the collection *I Speak of Africa* (1927), and edited *Kilvert's Diary* (3 vols., 1938–40). His *Collected Poems* appeared in 1960.
2. Plomer declined on 24 June, saying he was too busy and could not add anything to Peter Burra's essay on Forster's novels (presumably 'The Novels of Forster,' *Nineteenth Century and After*, vol. 116 (1934)).
3. 'Virginia Woolf' is a handwritten emendation by Orwell for the typist's 'WOLFF.'

2142. To Raymond Mortimer

18 June 1943   07/ES/EB/WMB

Dear Mortimer

Would you like to do another talk for the Indian section. I can't give you an exact date but it would be some time in September.

We're going to start a series called MODERN MASTERPIECES, dealing with English prose works of this century. We want each talk to deal ostensibly with a single book but in doing so to give some account of the author's work as a whole. I attach a list of the projected talks. If you would like to do Virginia Wolff° you could choose whichever of her books you like to centre your talk upon, bearing in mind that you are speaking to the Indian public which would probably find some books more intelligible than others.[1]

Yours sincerely

[Not signed/initialled]

George Orwell

(Talks Producer)

Indian Section

1. The final paragraph, as for Plomer (see *2141*), is not reproduced here, and the schedule has not survived. Mortimer answered, 22 June 1943, by postcard, saying he was prepared to talk about Virginia Woolf. He selected *Orlando* as being 'most suitable as a focus,' but sought Orwell's opinion.

2143. To V. S. Pritchett

18 June 1943   07/ES/EB/WMB

Dear Pritchett

This is to follow up our hurried conversation in the canteen. The new series we're going to start towards the end of August will be called MODERN MASTERPIECES and will deal with English prose works of this century. We want each talk to deal ostensibly with a single book but in doing so to give some sort of idea of the writer's work as a whole. I attach a list of the projected talks. If you will undertake H. G. Wells you could choose what book of his you like to drape your talk round, but it would be better to choose one which the Indian public will have heard of and would find intelligible. I should therefore be inclined to steer clear of books like "MR. POLLY" and take something more like the "TIME MACHINE", or perhaps the "OUTLINE OF HISTORY", but use your discretion.

Yours
[Initialled] E. A. B
George Orwell
(Talks Producer)
Indian Section

1. The final paragraph, as for Plomer (see 2141), is not reproduced here. The schedule has not survived.

2144. Z. A. Bokhari to Orwell

18 June 1943

The Indian Programme Organiser produced this scheme of lectures. The memorandum was addressed to Orwell, and copies were sent to Rushbrook Williams (Eastern Service Director), Lawson-Reece (Eastern Service Organiser), and Brander, Eastern Intelligence Officer. Although some of Bokhari's categories are curious (Spender as a military poet and Wintringham as a centrist politician, for example), and despite uncertainties in spelling names, which combine to suggest he was not fully in command of the details of his scheme, his enthusiasm is plain. Brander's reaction is in line with his demand for a better-organised service, and his support for Lady Grigg (given his criticisms of her elsewhere) is interesting. Bokhari's spellings have been left as typed, but they are marked ° and the correct spellings are given in n. 1.

I think I have hit upon an idea. I will just give you the outlines of it. Please work it out and let us discuss it. I am sick of having unconnected talks; frankly I don't like living from day to day. Here is an idea for our new schedule:—

"THE WORLD WE HOPE FOR"

Politicians, scientists, religious leaders, poets, writers, workers, employers, painters, sculptors, architects, editors and newspaper owners, film and theatre directors, philosophers, radio chiefs, economists, farmers, soldiers, sailors, ad nauseam.

Politicians	Extreme Right	Douglas Jerrold
		Ernest Benn, Lord Hankey
	Right	Grigg or Herbert Williams
	Liberal	Lloyd George, Megan, or Sinclair
	Independent	Vernon Bartlett, W. J. Brown
	National Liberal	Attlee or Bevin or Morrison
	Moderate	Maxton or Brockway
	Communist	Pollitt or Dutt
	Centre	Ackland,° Winteringham°
Scientists	Accepted	Eddington (dead?)[2]
	Controversial	Huxley
	Rebellious	Haldane
	Provocative	Bernal
	Popular	A. M. Low
Religion	Established	Canterbury or Whale
	Subversive	Lincoln or Bradford or Birmingham
	Secular	Middleton Murray°
	Provocative	Macleod or Mervin° Stockwood
	Austere	Alexander Miller
	Iconoclastic	Father Grosier[3]
	Militant Pacifist	Donald Soper
Poets	Military	Stephen Spender
	Un-military	Osbert Sitwell
	Neutral	William Plomer
	Satirical	Sagittarius
	Common-sensical	V. Sackville-West, Roy Campbell and Cecil Day Lewis etc.
Writers	Hard Patriotic	Rebecca West, Rose Macaulay, Arthur Bryant
	Soft Patriotic	E. M. Forster, or Rosamund Lehmann, Clemence Dane
	Romantic	Graham Green,° Ethel Manning°
	Sentimental	J. B. Priestley, Beverly° Nichols
	Jingoistic	Noel Coward
Workers		Must be found in factories
Employers		Sir Archie Rowlands will help us
Painters		Epstein, John, Nevinson
Sculptors		(Raymond Mortimer will be able to suggest more names)
Architects		Raymond Mortimer will be able to suggest some names

Editors and Newspapers° Owners	J. J. Astor, Lord Astor, Burlington Ward, E. H. Carr, Gerald Barrie° etc.
Film Directors	Margery Lockett will help
Theatre Directors	Binkee° Beaumont or John Gieulgud° will help
Women	A mother A married girl A factory worker Writer, Actress Politicians etc.
Economists	Keynes, Beveridge. (Laski might be able to help)
Philosophers	Bertrand Russell, Joad, etc.

This list can go on indefinitely and give us real thought-provoking talks. We can always ask the speakers to suggest a play, a feature, a story or a poem to illustrate their point of view. Such features, plays, poems, etc., can be broadcast after or before the talk and cross-referenced.

I am sending a copy of this to E.S.D., and E.S.O., and Mr. Brander. They will I am sure help us to plan these series.

Laurence Brander, the Eastern Intelligence Officer, responded on 22 June sending copies to Orwell and the Eastern Service Director and Organiser:

An excellent idea. Audience reaction suggests that it is a mistake to run a long series of talks on one theme. The six talks series run by Blair seem to be about right.

For the Indian audience the six speakers I should choose (having consideration also for the categories in which you place them) would be:—

Politician	Vernon Bartlett
Scientist	Huxley
Poet	Osbert Sitwell
Writer	E. M. Forster
Economist	Laski
Philosopher	Joad

The only way I can suggest for a lengthening of the discussion of this topic would be to run a parallel series by women. Not just mothers and factory workers, but members of the professions.

Such a series would give Lady Grigg a chance. A fortnight ago she was talking to me on this very subject. If she is going to run another series after her holiday, I am sure she would tackle this one with great enthusiasm.

1. Sir Richard Acland, John Middleton Murry, the Right Reverend Mervyn Stockwood, Graham Greene, Ethel Mannin, Beverley Nichols, Sir Gerald Barry, Hugh (Binkie) Beaumont, John Gielgud.
2. Sir Arthur Eddington (1882–1944) was still alive.
3. The Reverend St John Groser (1891–1966), born in Australia, served as a chaplain in World War I and was awarded the Military Cross. He gave forty years of service to the people of

London's East End, where he was known as 'Father.' A strong-minded Christian Socialist, who had actively supported trade unionists, especially in the Depression, he was injured in a police baton charge during the General Strike of 1926. He gave a memorable performance as Beckett in the film of T. S. Eliot's *Murder in the Cathedral*, 1950.

2145. To Philip Unwin

21 June 1943   Handwritten

Dear Mr Unwin,

I return a copy of the proofs of "Talking to India", duly corrected. The other copy is with Cedric Dover, who had asked to be sent one. He hasn't returned it. If he doesn't do so soon I don't think it is worth waiting, as he is not likely to make any alterations that matter much. He merely wanted a copy to make sure typing errors, etc. had not slipped in, & I had already been over the MS. to make sure of that. I understand you also sent a copy to Reginald Reynolds who will return it independently.

I wonder when the book will be coming out?[1] I saw an advance notice in the "Times Lit. Supp". As to complimentary copies, I think every oriental contributor should have a copy, & there are one or two people in the office here who should have copies, so if I had a dozen to hand out that would about cover it. You will know what to do about review copies, but I should emphasise that it is important to get as many as possible to *India*, also the U.S.A.

Yours sincerely
Geo. Orwell

On the same day, Orwell sent Unwin this handwritten postcard:

I am sending separately Cedric Dover's copy of the proofs of "Talking to India". He has only made minor alterations, but he says it is *particularly important* that the word "Negro" (pp. 17–21) should *always* be given a capital.

Geo. Orwell

1. On 22 June, Allen & Unwin informed Orwell that Reginald Reynolds's proofs had arrived; on 26 June, Orwell was informed that, although it would be possible to get the book out in August, 'a somewhat dead month,' they proposed holding it over until September. It was published on 18 November 1943.

2146. BBC Talks Booking Form, 22.6.43

Oliver Bell: 'Women Generally Speaking,' Films of the Month; broadcast 28.7.43; fee £10.10s. Signed: Z. A. Bokhari.

2147. Newsletter in Tamil, 10

24 June 1943

The English version was written by Eric Blair. No script has been traced.

2148. Norman Collins, General Overseas Service Manager, to Mrs. C. V. Salmon[1]

24 June 1943   Copy to Mr. Blair

I have just read V. S. Pritchett's talk on Thomas Hardy. It occurs to me that it would be a good thing to ensure that Mr. Blair should see these scripts. As you know Eastern Service take up[2] fairly "high-brow" attitude on literary talks, and you could afford to omit any scripts which seem definitely more popular.

1. Mrs. C. V. Salmon had, until recently, been Winifred Craig. She was a talks producer in the General Overseas Service.
2. Probably an error for 'take a,' or 'take up a.'

2149. BBC Talks Booking Form, 24.6.43

Lord David Cecil: 'Calling All Students,' 4, 'talk on Poetry and the poet T. S. Eliot'; recorded 24.6.43; broadcast 25.7.43; fee £10.10s. Signed: Z. A. Bokhari. Remarks: 'Suggested fee as estimated: £12.12.0d.'

2150. BBC Talks Booking Form, 24.6.43

Alan Rook: 'Calling All Students,' 5, War Poets of 1914–1918; recorded 10.7.43; broadcast 11.7.43; fee £10.10s. Signed: Z. A. Bokhari. Remarks: 'Suggested fee as estimated: £12.12.0d.'

2151. *London Calling*

London Calling was published weekly and advertised the BBC's overseas programmes. It cost ten shillings a year if payment was made to BBC Publications, Wembley, England, but arrangements were made for remittances to be sent to various addresses abroad: $2.00 per annum in the USA; Can.$2.50 in Canada; 12s 6d in Australia and New Zealand; and 10s 0d in South Africa. There were no local arrangements for India. Issue 198 for 25–31 July 1943 (printed 24 June 1943) gave the schedule illustrated for India and the Far East. The periodical also included a number of articles each week.

A typical selection of special BBC programmes for India and the Far East that affected Orwell's work is given below. The prominent role of music is apparent. This followed changes made after Bokhari's return from his visit to India. See Orwell's letter to K. K. Ardaschir, 3 June 1943, *2116, n. 6.*

10.00–10.30   English programme for Indian Listeners $\left\{\begin{array}{l}\text{— \ \ 15.42 Mc/s \ 19.46 m.} \\ \text{GSG 17.79 Mc/s \ 16.86 m.}\end{array}\right.$

         Sun: Music
         Mon: Music programme presented by Princess Indira of Kapurthala
         Tues: Orchestral concert
         Wed: Music, followed by 'Women Generally Speaking'
         Thurs: Music, followed by a talk
         Fri: Music
         Sat: Feature programme

13.45–14.00   Broadcasts in Indian regional languages $\left\{\begin{array}{l}\text{GRV 12.04 Mc/s \ 24.92 m.} \\ \text{— \ \ 15.42 Mc/s \ 19.46 m.}\end{array}\right.$

         Sun: Sinhalese newsletter
         Mon: Gujerati newsletter
         Tues: Sinhalese newsletter
         Wed: Hindustani message programme
         Thurs: Marathi newsletter
         Fri: Hindustani message programme
         Sat: Hindustani programme

14.00–14.30   Hindustani News and programme $\left\{\begin{array}{l}\text{GRV 12.04 Mc/s \ 24.92 m.} \\ \text{— \ \ 15.42 Mc/s \ 19.46 m.}\end{array}\right.$

14.30–14.45   Broadcasts for Indonesia.... $\left\{\begin{array}{l}\text{GRV 12.04 Mc/s \ 24.92 m.} \\ \text{— \ \ 15.42 Mc/s \ 19.46 m.}\end{array}\right.$

         Sun: Hindustani programme
         Mon: Burmese newsletter
         Tues: Malay newsletter
         Wed: Burmese newsletter
         Thurs: Tamil newsletter
         Fri: Malay newsletter
         Sat: Bengali newsletter

15.15–15.45   English programme for Indian listeners $\left\{\begin{array}{l}\text{GRG 11.68 Mc/s \ 25.68 m.} \\ \text{— \ \ 15.42 Mc/s \ 19.46 m.}\end{array}\right.$

         Sun: Poetry reading.   Music
         Mon: New discs reviewed by Spike Hughes.   Music
         Tues: Talk.   Music.
         Wed: Music feature
         Thurs: Talk by J. B. Priestley.   Music
         Fri: Wickham Steed on 'World Affairs'.   Music
         Sat: 'The Debate Continues': talk by Princess
                     Indira of Kapurthala.   Music

2152. News Commentary in English for Malaya, 39

25 June 1943

This was written and read by George Orwell. No script has been traced.[1]

1. Gentry recorded in his diary for 20 June: 'Wavell appointed Viceroy of India — [General] Auchinleck C in C.' These appointments Orwell would surely have mentioned in this broadcast.

2153. To J. C. Drummond

25 (or 26) June 1943[1]   07/ES/EB/WMB

Dear Dr. Drummond

I understand from Robert Westerby that you might be willing to do a talk for the Indian Section of the B.B.C. We have a series dealing with popular science and we want to start it with a talk on MALNUTRITION. This is perhaps a rather awkward subject when speaking to India, because in India the primary causes of malnutrition are no doubt poverty and, at the moment, actual shortages of certain food stuffs. But there is also great ignorance of dietetics and it is that that we would like you to deal with. Of course there is no harm in saying plainly at the outset that poverty is a cause of malnutrition. These talks are 13½ minutes, that is to say, 15/1600 words. I have no power of fixing a fee but I believe it would be 10 guineas. We want this talk to be broadcast on Thursday, the 15th of July, which would mean that we should like to have the script not later than July 12th, at the very latest. The time of broadcasting is 5.15 pm. but if this is inconvenient you can easily record beforehand. The other speakers in this series are Sir John Russell, Dr. Darlington, Sir Philip Manson-Bahr, Dr. Wigglesworth and Colonel Mackenzie. Could you be kind enough to let me know, as early as possible, whether you would like to do this.[2]

Yours truly
[Initialled] E. A. B
Eric Blair
(Talks Producer)
Indian Section

1. The carbon copy shows that the date has been overtyped. Because Winifred Bedwell typed a batch of letters on Friday, 25 June, this letter has been sorted with those.
2. Drummond, Scientific Adviser to the Ministry of Food and Agriculture (see *1504, n. 1*) wrote to Orwell on 1 July 1943 to say he could let him have a script by 12 July.

2154. To T. S. Eliot

25 June 1943   Handwritten draft and typed versions
07/ES/EB/WMB

Dear Eliot

It doesn't matter greatly which order these talks are done in, so how about Sunday the 19th[1] September for you? (As it is a Sunday there is no need to do it LIVE—you could[2] record any time beforehand.) We should want the script by about the 10th September. If that doesn't suit you could have September 5th or 26th. Please let me know.

Yours sincerely
[Initialled] E. A. B[3]
(George Orwell)
Talks Producer
Indian Section

1. Orwell wrote '25th' in the draft and crossed it through, substituting '19th.' Two other dates were wrongly calculated in the draft.
2. Orwell wrote 'can.'
3. Orwell signed the draft 'Geo. Orwell' but initialled it E. A. B.; this variation is common in the few instances where original and carbon copies survive.

2155. To Desmond Hawkins

25 June 1943   07/ES/EB/WMB

Dear Desmond

I am writing to ask whether you would like to undertake a weekly programme which Bokhari proposes starting at the beginning of August? The projected title is REMEMBER THIS? (incidentally this is a rotten title and you might be able to think of a better one).[1] The idea is to make a sort of re-hash programme out of our programmes of the preceding week. For example, one can re-play bits of the music that have been put out or from other works of the same composer, and similarly, where we have talks on literary subjects, as we do every week, you could put in readings from the works of the authors dealt with. The idea is to try to make the listener guess the context of each passage of literature or music before being told. This is a half-hour programme but ought not to entail a great deal of work. Miss Chitale would help you with compiling the stuff, i.e. by giving you details of the programme[s] but you would have to jazz it up and make it into an attractive programme. What is aimed at is a sort of mosaic of words and music. Could you let me know, at once, whether you would like to do this because we have only got about a month in which to start it going?

Yours
[Initialled] E. A. B
George Orwell
(Talks Producer)
Indian Section

1. For Hawkins's suggestion, see Orwell's postcard of 29 June 1943, *2165.* Fifty years later this is the basis of a regular and popular radio programme: 'Pick of the Week.'

2156. To Stephen Spender

25 June 1943   07/ES/EB/WMB

Dear Stephen

Would you like to do another talk for the Indian section? We have a series starting about the end of August on MODERN ENGLISH PROSE WRITERS. The way we intend to do it is to make each talk deal ostensibly with one particular book, but in doing so, to give, if possible, some idea of the writer's work as a whole. I thought you might like to do the talk on E. M. FORSTER. The book I would like you to drape it round is HOWARDS END, as a° PASSAGE TO INDIA will be already well-known to our audience. These talks are of 13½ minutes, which means 15/1600 words. I can't yet give you an exact date, but it would probably be a Sunday about the beginning of October. You could record it any time beforehand. Could you let me know whether you would like to do this?

Yours
[Initialled] E. A. B
(Eric Blair)
Talks Producer
Indian Section

2157. BBC Talks Booking Form, 25.6.43[1]

John Lehmann: 'Calling All Students,' 5, Literary Series; '13½ mins. talk on W. H. Auden & others which he will write and broadcast'; broadcast 1.8.43; fee £10.10s. Signed: Z. A. Bokhari.[2] Remarks: 'Suggested fee as estimated— £12.12.0.'

1. These (and later) talks booking forms, though initiated by Bokhari, were for programmes Orwell organised—as is clear from the action Orwell took in following up on this programme; see *n. 2*.
2. Lehmann sent his script, with a covering letter dated 18 July 1943. Orwell annotated this: 'Miss Bedwell Please send a p.c. acknowledging this. E.A.B.' Miss Bedwell sent a postcard erroneously dated 17 July. Lehmann's letter is annotated in shorthand, presumably by Miss Bedwell. That Orwell frequently wrote out letters in full was, therefore, not because his secretary was unable to write shorthand.

2158. BBC Talks Booking Form, 25.6.43

Lieutenant-Colonel E. F. W. Mackenzie, OBE: 'Calling All Students,' Scientific Series, 6 Drinking Water; broadcast 19.8.43; no fee proposed. Signed: Z. A. Bokhari.[1]

1. On 18 June, Mackenzie wrote to Orwell to say that he understood a recording was to be made of this talk and that any day in July except the 2nd, 12th, 21st, or 30th would be convenient. His letter is annotated in pencil, but not in Orwell's hand, 'Ackd p.c. 19/6/43.'

2159. BBC Talks Booking Form, 25.6.43

Mrs. K. C. Roy: 'In Your Kitchen,' 13 and 14; with Dr. Gangulee and Shridhar Telkar; broadcast 1 and 8.7.43; fee £3.3s each broadcast. Signed Z. A. Bokhari.

2160. BBC Talks Booking Form, 25.6.43

Sir John Russell: 'Calling All Students,' Scientific Series, 3: Soil Erosion and Soil Deterioration; broadcast 29.7.43; no fee proposed. Signed: Z. A. Bokhari.

2161. BBC Talks Booking Form, 25.6.43

Dr. V. B. Wigglesworth: 'Calling All Students,' Scientific Series, 5 The House Fly; broadcast 12.8.43;[1] fee £10.10s. Signed: Z. A. Bokhari.

1. Wigglesworth wrote to Orwell on 29 July to say that he would be unable to broadcast on 12 August; he preferred to make a recording in advance.

2162. To E. M. Forster

28 June 1943   07/ES/EB/WMB

Dear Forster
We have fixed a recording for you for Friday, the 16th July, at 3 to 3.30 pm. In Studio 6.

We are sending you THE ENGLISH PEOPLE by D. W. Brogan. I have another book at home, (a Penguin) by a man called Hancock,[1] an Australian. It is written from a more or less Imperialistic standpoint, but I will send it along to you later this week.

Yours
[Signed] Geo. Orwell
George Orwell
(Talks Producer)
Indian Section

1. W. K. Hancock (1898–1988), born in Melbourne, Australia, was at this time Professor of History, University of Birmingham, and Supervisor of Civil Histories for the War Cabinet, the series of which he edited. Orwell must have had in mind *Argument of Empire* a Penguin Special, S130 (June 1943). West: *Broadcasts*, 261, suggests his *Survey of British Commonwealth Affairs*. This work, more than 1,000 pages, published in May 1937 and July 1940, was outside the scope of a Penguin publication in those days, especially with the wartime paper shortage.

2163. BBC Talks Booking Form, 28.6.43

(Retrospective) Wing Commander Roger Falk: interview with an officer of the Indian Air Cadets; 5' talk he had written and previously broadcast; broadcast 26.6.43; fee £4.4s.

2164. To R. R. Desai

29 June 1943   07/ES/EB/MB

Dear Desai

We have just had an Airgraph from one of your listeners in Bombay, requesting that you should broadcast something about the measures for the Restriction of Dividends and the Compulsory Saving.[1] I believe you were already contemplating doing something on this subject. Do you think you could do *five minutes* or more if you like, on Monday week, that is to say the 12th July? In that case, you could announce this Monday that in response to requests from listeners you were going to deal with this subject next week. I think it is better to give them at any rate a week's notice.

Yours sincerely
Eric Blair
Talks Assistant.
Dictated by Eric Blair &
despatched in his absence
by: [Initialled] MB

1. A portion of income tax payable was only temporarily collected and spent by the government. It was allowed as a 'Post-War Credit,' and such amounts were paid back after the war.

2165. To Desmond Hawkins

29 June 1943   Handwritten draft of postcard

Hawkins replied to Orwell's letter of 25 June 1943 on the 28th saying he liked the idea of 'Remember This?' and would be glad 'to have a shot at it.' As an alternative title to the one Orwell thought 'rotten' he suggested 'Return Ticket.' At the foot of Hawkins's letter Orwell wrote the following note for his secretary. At the top is typed 'Replied 1/7/43.'

<u>Miss Bedwell</u>

Send Mr Hawkins a pc. asking him to make his date with us as early as possible after his return from Ireland, as we have only about 3 weeks in which to arrange this.

Eric Blair 29/6/43

2166. To Sir John Russell

30 June 1943   07/ES/EB/MB

Dear Sir John

Thank you very much for your letter of the 29th June.

We have arranged to record your 13½ minute talk on 'Soil Erosion' on

Tuesday, 13th July, at 200 Oxford Street, W.1. From 10.0 to 10.30 a.m. We do hope that this appointment will suit you and we shall be glad if you can be here promptly at 10.0 a.m., so that we may have a run-through in the Studio before the actual Recording starts.

Yours sincerely,
[Initialled] E. A. B
Eric Blair
Talks Producer

2167. Newsletter in Tamil, 11

1 July 1943

The English version was written by Eric Blair. No script has been traced.

2168. To E. M. Forster

1 July 1943   07/ES/EB

Dear Forster

I have seen Mr. Rushbrook Williams about Brailsford's book.[1] He says that it is not officially banned in India and that it will be all right to talk about it on the air but that to balance it one should have some book giving the opposite viewpoint. He suggests Professor Coupland's book called, I think, INDIAN CONSTITUTIONAL PROBLEMS, and issued by the Nuffield Trust.[2] I will endeavour to get it for you, as quickly as possible. I am afraid all this is rather short notice as you are due to record your talk on the 16th, but if I can procure the book within the next day or two that will give you, at any rate, ten days to consider it. I think it will be safe to go ahead now with, of course, the normal precautions.

Yours
[Initialled] E. A. B
George Orwell
(Talks Producer)
Indian Section

1. Henry Noel Brailsford (see *424* and *1293*) described by Kingsley Martin in the *DNB, 1951–60* as 'one of the most eminent of British journalists,' who was 'convinced . . . that war in this epoch is the result of the economic rivalry of the great Powers.' After World War I he had travelled through Eastern Europe and Germany (bitterly attacking the Allied war blockade that had led to widespread hunger). He learned Russian and visited Russia, describing what he saw, first with hope and then critical of the effects of Stalin's rule. A friend of Gandhi and Nehru, he wrote two books advocating Indian independence: *Rebel India* (1931) and *Subject India* (1943). The latter is the book to which Orwell probably refers; he reviewed it in *The Nation*, 20 November 1943; see *2365*. At this time he was chief leader writer for *The New Statesman and Nation*.
2. Sir Reginald Coupland (1884–1952), historian, especially of the British Empire and the

Commonwealth, was at the time Beit Professor of Colonial History, University of Oxford. Among his books on India are *The Cripps Mission* (1942), *The Indian Problem 1833–1935* (1942), *Indian Politics 1936–1942* (1943) (which, according to the *DNB*, includes 'the first serious treatment in English of the idea of Pakistan'), *The Future of India* (1943), and *India, a Re-statement* (1945). In his reply, Forster remarked, 'A short Coupland is always more welcome than a long one' (West: *Broadcasts*, 262).

2169. To Alan Rook

1 July 1943   07/ES/EB/EB/WMB°

Dear Major Rook
Very many thanks for the script, which is just the kind of thing we wanted. It is just possible that it is a bit too long but if we find it to be so when we rehearse we can no doubt cut out a paragraph somewhere. It might perhaps be better to have Owen's poem read in a different voice, and I will arrange for that. You are down to record at 10.45 am. It might be well if you got here at 10.15 which would give us time to rehearse. I suppose you know the place—*200 Oxford Street*, which used to be Peter Robinson's Menswear Department. Ask for Mr Blair. Perhaps you will like to have lunch with me afterwards.

Yours sincerely
[Initialled] E. A. B
(George Orwell)
Talks Producer
Indian Section

2170. News Commentary in English for Malaya, 40

2 July 1943

This was written and read by George Orwell. No script has been traced.

It was the last News Commentary Orwell prepared and broadcast to Malaya, but there was, in effect, no break in the sequence of his work so far as he was concerned. From the next Friday, 9 July 1943, he wrote and read an English Newsletter for Indonesia, which was, like Malaya, occupied by the Japanese at this time. The Newsletter was broadcast at 1330 GMT on Fridays, the time previously allocated to the English-language Newsletter for Malaya. These broadcasts and the English versions of the Tamil Newsletters Orwell was also preparing continued until he left the BBC's service on 24 November 1943. The last broadcasts in each series were given on his behalf one and two days after his departure.

2171. To E. M. Forster

2 July 1943   07/ES/EB

Dear Forster

I understand that the library have sent you off Volume 1 of Professor Coupland's book, which, I imagine, is no use in itself. The one I intended them to send you was Volume III, which I understand is still being printed. But, they mistook my directions. If you can't make a talk out of the books you now have, what about reverting to our original idea and having one on NEW WRITING. A similar anthology has just been published called NEW ROAD,[1] containing mostly the work of the writers who have come on since the New Writing group. If you would like this I can send it to you, and I think you said you already had a copy of NEW WRITING. Please let me know as early as possible. I am sorry that there has been so much fuss.

Yours sincerely
[Initialled] E. A. B
(George Orwell)
Talks Producer
Indian Section

1. See letter to Alex Comfort, 26 August 1942, *1420*, and headnote to 'Looking Back on the Spanish War,' *1421*, which was Orwell's contribution to the first number of *New Road*.

2172. To V. S. Pritchett

2 July 1943   07/ES/EB/WMB

Dear Pritchett

I have put your talk on H. G. Wells down for Sunday, the 22nd August. As it is a Sunday you will no doubt prefer to record beforehand. Would you please let us know a suitable date? I would like the script in not later than August 15th,—the usual length, i.e. 13½ minutes (15/1600 words.) I think we fixed that you should choose which book of his you liked to deal with, but would like something that was not too much tied down to the local English scene.

Yours
[Initialled] E. A. B
George Orwell
(Talks Producer)
Indian Section

2173. BBC Talks Booking Form, 2.7.43

J. D. S. Paul; Translating and Reading Tamil News Commentary; broadcast 1, 8, 15, 22, 29.7.43; fee £5.5s each talk plus railway fare. Signed: Eric Blair. Remarks: 'Issue Mr Paul with a railway voucher to travel on the Thursday in each case, also Studio Pass to cover these dates. (Please refund him with railway fare, which he paid yesterday.)' The form is marked URGENT.

2174. BBC Talks Booking Form, 2.7.43

Professor J. C. Drummond; 'Calling All Students,' Scientific Series: Malnutrition; broadcast 15.7.43; fee £10.10s. Signed: Z. A. Bokhari.

2175. On Orwell's behalf to E. M. Forster

    3 July 1943   07/ES/EB/WMB

Dear Mr. Forster

Your letter of the 2nd has just arrived. Mr. Orwell is away from the Office this morning, but I have obtained the pamphlet BRITAIN AND INDIA,[1] which you mentioned, and am sending it on right away, though I don't know whether it will be of any use without the copy of the larger volume (III) which we were unable to send. If you are unable to use it could you kindly return it some time?

Yours sincerely
[Initialled] WB
Secretary to George Orwell
Talks Producer
Indian Section

1. Forster, in his letter to Orwell of 2 July 1943, referred to a pamphlet by Coupland costing sixpence called *Britain & India 1600–1941* (West: *Broadcasts*, 262).

2176. To E. M. Forster

    5 July 1943   07/ES/EB

Dear Forster

Thanks for your letter. We cannot send the third volume of Coupland's book, as I understand it is not out yet. We are sending you the short pamphlet on the Cripp's Mission[1]—a very painful subject, as you will appreciate.

As for stuff about Coupland, I really know little about him but on looking him up in WHOSE WHO,° find that he is a Fellow of ALL SOULS,[2] Editor for some time of THE ROUND TABLE, and has held a number of official positions and seats on Royal Commissions in England and India. He sounds thoroughly dull all round, but perhaps you can make something of him. I am told that John S. Hoyland's book on India[3] just published is good, and am

endeavouring to procure that for you, as well. I hope you will find time to
deal with all this.

Yours
[Initialled] E.A.B
George Orwell
(Talks Producer)
Indian Section

1. Coupland had been attached to Sir Stafford Cripps's mission to India and the pamphlet
referred to, *The Cripps Mission* (1942), was a product of that experience.
2. His chair carried with it a professorial fellowship at All Souls.
3. John Somervell Hoyland (1887–1957) had been an educational missionary in India, 1922–28,
and was awarded the Kaiser-i-Hind Gold Medal for public service. He wrote a number of
religious books, including *Book of Prayers for an Indian College* (1920). Orwell probably refers
to his *The Indian Crisis: The Background* (June 1943).

2177. BBC Talks Booking Form, 5.7.43

Miss Cherry Cottrell;[1] Great Poetry; producer Eric Blair; broadcast 14.7.43; fee
£6.6s + repeat fees. Initialled S.F.A. for Programme Contracts Department.

1. Cherry Cottrell (1909–), an actress who made her debut in 1928, played Ophelia and Titania
(twice) at the Old Vic in 1937 and at Regent's Park, 1940, 1942. She was a member of the BBC
Repertory Company during the war.

2178. To P. Chatterjee

6 July 1943   07/ES/EB/WMB

Dear Mr. Chatterjee
I am very sorry to have to send this talk[1] back and still more sorry to have
kept it so long. I put it by me hoping we might be able to make use of it some
time, but I find we cannot, so I am returning it. Please forgive me.

Yours sincerely
[Initialled] E.A.B
Eric Blair
(Talks Producer)
Indian Section

1. Not identified.

2179. Extract from Minutes of Eastern Service Meeting

7 July 1943

Pamphlets   Mr. Blair reported production of pamphlets on talks series in the English period for India for publication in India progressing; two pamphlets already completed[1] and two more in prospect. At the present rate, one pamphlet will probably be published every six or eight weeks.
[Optimum broadcast timings]
Mr. Hayes stated that the technical optimum period for India throughout the year was 1100–1330 GMT, with a later period of fair or good reception from 1430 onwards. The period 1330–1430 GMT was not very satisfactory during summer and was definitely poor in winter for the U.K.–India circuit: Mr. Hayes reported that the Engineering Division could not recommend placing important broadcasts to India within this period.[2]

1. *Books and Authors* and *Landmarks in American Literature*; they were not published until 29 October 1946; see *3101*. Only these two pamphlets were published. One on medical science was evidently proposed; see Orwell's letter to Bryan Brooke, 23 July 1943, *2197*.
2. In a letter to R. R. Desai, 17 January 1942, William Empson explained that to ensure clarity in shortwave broadcasting to India, speech in English should be at about 120 words a minute.

2180. Newsletter in Tamil, 12

8 July 1943

The English version was written by Eric Blair. No script has been traced.

2181. English Newsletter for Indonesia, 1

9 July 1943

This is the first in the series of Newsletters in English beamed to Japanese-occupied Indonesia. Most of these were written and read by Orwell under that name. On this occasion, he did not read the Newsletter. The record states: 'Service for Indonesia: News Commentary written in English by George Orwell (SNF) [Staff No Fee] and read by John Morris (SNF).' No script has been traced.

2182. To E. C. Bowyer

9 July 1943   Handwritten draft and typed versions
07/ES/EB/EB/WMB°

Dear Mr. Bowyer
Very many thanks for the copy of THE FUTURE OF BRITISH AIR TRANSPORT,[1]
which I shall read with great interest.

Yours sincerely
[Initialled] E.A.B
George Orwell
(Talks Producer)
Indian Section

1. This was a memorandum prepared by the Society of British Aircraft Constructors. Orwell
had evidently asked for a copy, but the first print run was small owing to the shortage of
paper. Bowyer had been able to arrange 'a small reprint,' one copy of which was sent to
Orwell.

2183. To Alex Comfort

Sunday 11 [?] July 1943   Typewritten

10a Mortimer Crescent   London   NW 6

Dear Comfort,
Very many thanks for sending me the copy of "New Road". I am afraid I was
rather rude to you in our "Tribune" set-to,[1] but you yourself weren't
altogether polite to certain people. I was only making a *political* and perhaps
moral reply, and as a piece of verse your contribution was immensely better,
a thing most of the people who spoke to me about it hadn't noticed. I think no
one noticed that your stanzas had the same rhyme going right the way
through. There is no respect for virtuosity nowadays. You ought to write
something longer in that genre, something like the "Vision of Judgement".[2]
I believe there could be a public for that kind of thing again nowadays.

As to "New Road". I am much impressed by the quantity and the general
level of the verse you have got together. I should think half the writers were
not known to me before. Appropos of Aragon[3] and others, I have thought
over what you said about the reviving effect of defeat upon literature and also
upon national life. I think you may well be right, but it seems to me that such
a revival is only *against* something, ie. against foreign oppression, and can't
lead beyond a certain point unless that oppression is ultimately to be broken,
which must be by military means. I suppose however one might accept defeat
in a mystical belief that it will ultimately break down of its own accord. The
really wicked thing seems to me to wish for a "negotiated" peace, which
means back to 1939 or even 1914. I have written a long article on this for
"Horizon" appropos° of Fielden's book on India, but I am not certain
Connolly will print it.[4]

I am going to try to get Forster to talk about "New Road", together with the latest number of "New Writing", in one of his monthly book talks to India. If he doesn't do it this month he might next. There is no sales value there, but it extends your publicity a little and by talking about these things on the air in wartime one has the feeling that one is keeping a tiny lamp alight somewhere. You ought to try to get a few copies of the book to India. There is a small public for such things among people like Ahmed Ali[5] and they are starved for books at present. We have broadcast quite a lot of contemporary verse to India, and they are now doing it to China with a commentary in Chinese. We also have some of our broadcasts printed as pamphlets in India and sold for a few annas, a thing that could be useful but is terribly hard to organise in the face of official inertia and obstruction. I saw you had a poem by Tambimuttu. If you are bringing out other numbers you ought to get some of the other Indians to write for you. There are several quite talented ones and they are very embittered because they think people snub them and won't print their stuff. It is tremendously important from several points of view to try to promote decent cultural relations between Europe and Asia. Nine tenths of what one does in this direction is simply wasted labour, but now and again a pamphlet or a broadcast or something gets to the person it is intended for, and this does more good than fifty speeches by politicians. William Empson has worn himself out for two years trying to get them to broadcast intelligent stuff to China, and I think has succeeded to some small extent. It was thinking of people like him that made me rather angry about what you said of the BBC, though God knows I have the best means of judging what a mixture of whoreshop and lunatic asylum it is for the most part.

Yours sincerely
Geo. Orwell

1. See the Obadiah Hornbooke exchange, *2137, 2138.*
2. When George III died, Robert Southey, the poet laureate, wrote a conventional elegy, *Vision of Judgement* (1821). To this, Byron wrote a devastating rejoinder, *The Vision of Judgement.* Its satire was so biting that John Murray refused to take the risk of publishing it, and when Leigh Hunt, editor of *The Liberal*, printed it in 1822, he was fined £100.
3. Louis Aragon (Louis Andrieux) (1897–1982), French writer associated with innovatory artistic modes and with communism, came to the fore after the collapse of France, through his patriotic poems—*Le Crève-coeur* (1941) and *Les Yeux d'Elsa* (1942) among them. See Orwell's review of *New Writing and Daylight, 2208.*
4. Lionel Fielden (1896–1974), after serving in World War I (including Gallipoli) and working for the League of Nations and the High Commission for Refugees in Greece and the Levant, joined the BBC in 1927. He was Head of the General Talks Department, 1930–35, and Controller of Broadcasting in India, 1935–40. Back in England, he was Indian Editor for the BBC for seven months and then worked for the Ministry of Food and Aircraft Production until he joined the editorial staff of *The Observer* in 1942. He served as a staff officer in Italy in 1943 and was Director of Public Relations for the Allied Control Commission in Italy, 1944–45. It has been suggested that the successful Talks Department of the BBC was deliberately broken up in 1935 by John Reith, Director-General, 1927–38, and the Prime Minister, Stanley Baldwin because of its alleged radicalism. In *Good Listening* (1948), Elkan and Dorotheen Allan state that 'a team unmatched in any department [except possibly Features at the time of the book's publication] was broken up. Lionel Fielden was sent to India . . . Joe Ackerley to *The Listener.* . . .' Covert government interference was then and thereafter an ever-present

threat to the supposed independence of the BBC. Orwell contributed a long review article to *Horizon*, September 1943, on Fielden's 'ironical attack on British imperialism in India,' *Beggar My Neighbour*, all royalties of which went to support the Indian Freedom Campaign with which Reg Reynolds was associated (see his *My Life and Crimes*, 210).

2. Ahmed Ali (1908–), author and academic, was at this time the BBC's Listener and Research Director in India; see *1103, n. 3*.

2184. To Alan Rook

12 July 1943   07/ES/EB/JEL[1]

Dear Rook,

Following on our conversation of two days ago I will give you some information about those of our programmes which are likely to interest your friends in Cairo. We have two transmissions, the first at 1000–1030 GMT and the other at 1515–1530 GMT, i.e. they go out at 12 noon and 5.15 clock time.[2] I am not certain how Cairo time compares, but I think it is 3½ hours ahead of GMT. The wavelengths are 16.86 and 19.46 for the 1000 transmission and 25.68 and 19.46 for the 15.15.°

The 1000–1030 transmission is all music except on Wednesdays and Fridays when half of it is talk, we try to get good music into this period. The 1515 period is mostly talks, the ones, I think, likely to interest your friends go out on Sundays. I will give you a full list of the forthcoming speakers up to early October:—

> 25th July — Lord David Cecil
> 1st August — John Lehmann
> 8th August — Desmond Hawkins
> 15th August — E. M. Forster
> 22nd August — V. S. Pritchett
> 29th August — Raymond Mortimer
> 5th September — Sean O'Casey
> 12th September — E. M. Forster
> 19th September — Stephen Spender
> 26th September — T. S. Eliot
> 3rd October — E. M. Forster
> 10th October — E. M. Forster

We shall no doubt be doing other literary programmes as well later. I should be much obliged if you could send an airgraph passing this information on to G. S. Fraser[3] or anyone else in the Middle East who you think would be interested, or alternatively if you could let me know whom to write to giving the information. I cannot write out of the blue because I do not know these people and also do not know their addresses. I believe our stuff is picked up quite successfully in the Middle East and the times of day do not seem too hopeless. You might be kind enough to let me know whether you are taking any steps about this.

Yours sincerely,
[Initialled] E.A.B
(George Orwell)

1. JEL was June Elizabeth Light (later Mrs. Knight). This is the first letter which has survived that she typed for Orwell. By 26 July she had fully taken over from Winifred Bedwell. Her letters can be distinguished from Miss Bedwell's because she fully punctuated the addresses, whereas Miss Bedwell used hardly any punctuation marks. She worked for Orwell until he left the BBC.
2. '12 noon and 5.15' allow for Double British Summer Time. Orwell gives the hours for English-language programmes. See *2151*.
3. This is 'Frazer' in the original. George Sutherland Fraser (1915–1980), poet, critic, and academic, served throughout the war, and much of his poetry was drawn from that experience: *Home Town Elegy* (1944), *The Fatal Landscape* (1948), *The Traveller Has Regrets* (1948). He also wrote in Lallans (Broad Scots). In 1958 he was appointed to a lectureship at Leicester University and later was Professor of English Literature. His critical works include *The Modern Writer and His World* (1953, rev. 1964) and *Vision and Rhetoric* (1959).

2185. To Alex Comfort

13 July 1943   Typewritten

10a Mortimer Crescent   London   NW 6

Dear Comfort

Many thanks for your letter. I have given a copy of "New Road" to Forster, who will talk about it on the air on Sunday the 7th August, together with the current issue of "New Writing". He does these literary talks for us once a month. We have a literary talk which I try to make a good one every Sunday, and though these things are aimed at India it recently occurred to me that we have a possible audience in the Middle East with all the troops that are there. I believe G. S. Fraser[1] is in Cairo and he was at any rate till recently running a little magazine there. The other day when Alan Rook was broadcasting for us I asked him to write to any friends in the Middle East who might be interested in our stuff, and he undertook to do so. Do you know anyone serving in those parts who might care to listen to literary talks occasionally instead of the usual Forces programme? If you gave me the name etc. of anyone I could send him an airgraph with the wavelengths etc. At the moment we are only doing rather stodgy literary talks (intended to be printed afterwards) but a little while back we were b'casting fragments of plays which got a certain amount of response from the Indian students, and we shall do so again in the autumn. We also put out musical programmes which I am told are fairly good tho' I know nothing about music. As the times of day are fairly favourable (Cairo time would only be about an hour ahead of British summer time) I know that our Hindustani b'casts get an audience among the Indian troops in Egypt, and I would like to work up a parallel audience among British intellectuals now with the Middle East Forces. But it is a question of establishing contact with a few people and letting them know that these b'casts exist in addition to the usual muck.

I have got a young Indian at work translating a story by the Urdu novelist Prem Chand.[2] How good he really is I don't know, but the only story of his that has been translated hitherto ("The Shroud", which appeared in an Indian review in 1938) was very good, and if the others are up to sample he would be quite a discovery. If this story when done seems worth while I will send it along for you to look at in case you would like it for a later number of New Road. I have told the Indians about the existence of New Road and I hope Narayana Menon, who I think is about the most gifted of the younger ones, will send you something. As to publishing your poem and mine together, it might be a good idea but it isn't fair as it stands because I had the last word. Perhaps some time somebody will write another in approximately the same vein but not adopting either viewpoint, and then one could print all three together.

I'll let you know whether the Hindustani story comes to anything.

Yours sincerely
Geo. Orwell

1. This is 'Frazer' in the original.
2. Prem Chand (or Prem Cand or Premchand) was Dhanpat Rāy Śrīvāstav (1880–1936), novelist and short-story writer in Urdu and Hindi. His stories, now available in English, are chiefly concerned with the peasants of India, and his work, though not the earliest of its kind in India, was a precursor of contemporary writing. He had at one time been a teacher and government inspector, but in 1921, influenced by Gandhi, he devoted himself to vernacular writing.

2186. To C. D. Darlington

13 July 1943   07/ES/EB/WMB

Dear Darlington

We are sending you a copy of your script for your talk next week, so that you will be able to run over it before then. The actual time of your broadcast is at 12.15 to 12.30 (Double British Summer Time) on Thursday next, the 22nd July. Could you manage to be here (200 Oxford Street) at about 11.45 am. so that we may have a short rehearsal beforehand?

Yours sincerely
[Initialled] E.A.B
George Orwell
(Talks Producer)
Indian Section

2187. To Samuel Runganadhan

13 July 1943   07/ES/EB/WMB

Dear Sir Samuel,

This is just to remind you that we should be very much obliged if you could give us the addresses of the two Burmese students mentioned in your talk, Maung Hla Myint and Maung Tha Hla.[1]

Yours sincerely
[Initialled] E.A.B
(Talks Producer)
Indian Section

1. Sir Samuel Runganadhan, High Commissioner for India, gave a monthly talk, usually arranged by Bokhari. This is probably the one for 13 July 1943 in the series 'Indians in Great Britain.' Burmese affairs were then overseen by him. The first name appears in the faint carbon copy to be 'Rla' for 'Hla' and is followed by a comma.

2188. Newsletter in Tamil, 13

15 July 1943

The English version was written by Eric Blair. No script has been traced.

2189. English Newsletter to Indonesia, 2

16 July 1943

This was written and read by George Orwell. No script has been traced.

2190. To James Stephens

16 July 1943   07/ES/EB/WMB

Dear Stephens

I wonder whether you would like to do a talk on BERNARD SHAW. I am not sure whether he is up your street, but if he is I would like to have the talk on him done by another Irishman. We have got a series coming on shortly dealing with modern prose writers to balance the one we have now got going dealing with MODERN POETS. These talks are of 13½ minutes, and *unlike the* one you did before don't include an acted extract. The date of this talk would be early in September. If you would like to do it would you let me know and I will send you further particulars.

Yours sincerely
[Initialled] E.A.B
George Orwell
(Talks Producer)
Indian Section

2191. To C. E. M. Joad

16 July 1943   07/ES/EB/WMB

Dear Professor Joad

We have booked a recording session for Friday, July 30th, at 3.30 to 4 pm. in Mixer 2, 200 Oxford Street, for your third talk for the Indian Service on "Why the West has not taken kindly to Indian Philosophy." We hope this time is quite convenient.

Yours sincerely
[Initialled] E. A. B
(George Orwell)
Talks Producer
Indian Section

P.S. We are returning your original manuscript, as requested.

2192. To Bryan Brooke

19 July 1943   07/ES/EB/WMB

Dear Mr. Brooke[1]

Mr. Anthony Weymouth has told me that you might be willing to help me with some programmes which we propose starting round about the middle of August. From time to time, we do series of talks for India on popular science, and I am contemplating having a series of six talks on recent developments in drugs. I have sketched out a very rough programme but I would like to get some expert advice both as to the arrangement and as to speakers. If you are interested in taking part in this series I would be much obliged if you could let me know and we could perhaps make an appointment and meet. I think I understood Mr. Weymouth to say that you are up in London on Wednesdays.

Yours sincerely
[Initialled] E. A. B
Eric Blair
(Talks Producer)
Indian Section

1. Bryan Nicholas Brooke (1915–; FRCS, 1942), an expert in gastroenterology, from 1946 taught successively at Aberdeen, Birmingham, and Cambridge Universities; he became Hunterian Professor, Royal College of Surgeons in 1951. He is always addressed by Orwell as 'Brian'; his name has been silently corrected.

2193. To George Allen & Unwin

21 July 1943   Original postcard   WMB/VL/EB/WMB

On 14 July, Allen & Unwin wrote to Orwell to tell him that blocks had been made for the illustrations for *Talking to India*, and they were returning six photographs. On 20 July, they wrote to check Tambimuttu's initials and the correct spelling of Hsiao Ch'ien's name. Orwell's response was:

With reference to your letter Tambimuttu's initials are J. M. The name Ch'ien should be so spelt with the apostrophe.

[Signed] Geo. Orwell
(George Orwell)

On 11 August, Allen & Unwin wrote to say a fault had been found in the block of 'Sending Messages to India' and Orwell was asked to return the photograph. Orwell evidently sent all six photographs, for on 27 August Allen & Unwin wrote that the fault had been corrected and they were returning six originals.

2194. Newsletter in Tamil, 14

22 July 1943

The English version was written by Eric Blair. No script has been traced.

2195. BBC Talks Booking Form, 22.7.43

Kingsley Martin: 'Topic of the Month'; recording date not yet fixed; broadcast 3.8.43; 'estimated fee: £10.10.0d.'[1] Signed: Z. A. Bokhari.

1. Martin complained again (see *2105*) that his fee was too low. This led to extensive internal correspondence. For the conclusion, see Bokhari's letter to him of 4 September 1943, *2266*.

2196. English Newsletter to Indonesia, 3

23 July 1943

This was written and read by George Orwell. No script has been traced.

2197. To Bryan Brooke
         23 July 1943   07/ES/EB/WMB

Dear Mr. Brooke
This is to confirm what we agreed upon in our conversation two days ago.
This series of talks will begin on Thursday, the 26th August, and continue for
six Thursdays at 12.15 pm. The subjects will be:—

> The Sulphonomide° Group
> Penicillin
> Plasma
> Anaesthetics
> Insulin
> Synthetic Vitamins

You will do the third talk yourself and will help by picking speakers and will
receive a fee as adviser in addition to the fee for your talk. These talks will be
afterwards printed in India in pamphlet form and I shall explain this to the
speakers and get their permission. I would like it if we can get this swinging
fairly soon because the sooner I have all the scripts in the sooner I can send
them to India to be printed.[1] I will do all the necessary letter writing if you
will just let me have the speakers° names and addresses.

Yours sincerely
[Initialled] E.A.B
Eric Blair
(Talks Producer)
Indian Section

1. For a proposal that a third series of talks on medical science should be published by Oxford
   University Press in Bombay, see 2179.

2198. To R. R. Desai
         23 July 1943   07/ES/EB/WMB

Dear Desai
I send herewith some cuttings passed on to me by Mr. Tonkin.[1] These appear
to deal chiefly with the Pacific Front, which, I believe, was what you wanted
material about. There is also a wad of news bulletins of July 22nd, which
Tonkin passed on to me. I don't know whether he means to send you the
bulletins daily, I presume not, but I suppose that there is something in this
particular lot that he wanted you to see.
    Will you please return this documentation when you come on Monday.

Yours sincerely
[Initialled] E.A.B
Eric Blair
(Talks Producer)
Indian Section

There had been some confusion about sending cuttings to Desai. An undated and unsigned memorandum was sent to Ronald Boswell, the Talks Booking Manager, which led to Boswell's contacting Orwell the day before the letter. The memorandum states:

Mr. Boswell.

re Mr. Desai

Mr. Blair's office would like you to hold the letter you are sending to him. Also that as he is to receive copies of our News Bulletins, it will not be necessary to pay him the expenses for his time spent in London, as he will not have to come to London for collecting material for his scripts.

Boswell annotated this:

Rang Blair 22/7 afternoon. He says he knows nothing of above message. He told me that in spite of new arrangement sending Desai News Bulletins it wd. still be necessary in the interests of the programme for him to come to London on Sundays to look at papers & to be in time for censorship etc.

RB

Boswell wrote to Desai on 23 July to say that the proposed new arrangements had been reviewed and it was agreed to continue the former system, paying him an expense allowance of £1 when he stayed in London overnight.

1. Tonkin was described by J. B. Clark as 'our principal news specialist on the Far East' in a memorandum to the Director General on 4 June 1943.

2199. To James Stephens

23 July 1943   07/ES/EB/WMB[1]

Dear Stephens

Following on our hurried conversation in the entrance hall, I will explain just what kind of talk we want you to do on Bernard Shaw. We have a series coming on called MODERN MEN OF LETTERS, dealing with modern English prose writers. In this case we are not having any extract from the writer's work as in the series you took part in before, but we just want a talk with such illustrations as you think necessary. The way we want to do it is to make each talk give some idea of the writer's work as a whole but to revolve ostensibly round one book or play in particular. You can choose whichever of Shaw's plays you like to talk about but I'd rather you did not choose ARMS AND THE MAN because we had that on the air fairly recently. The date of your talk would be Sunday, the 5th September, which means that I want the *script in* before the end of August. As it is a Sunday you can record it beforehand and we will fix up later a date convenient to you. These talks go out at 5.15 pm. They are of 13½ minutes, which means 15/1600 words.

Yours sincerely
[Initialled] E.A.B
George Orwell
(Talks Producer)
Indian Section

1. This is the last letter typed for Orwell by Winifred Bedwell to be traced. From Monday, 26 July 1943, his secretary was J. E. Light; see *2184, n. 1*. For details of Orwell's secretaries, see memorandum to E. W. D. Boughen, 1 December 1942, *1707, n. 1*.

2200. To Indian Programme Organiser

26 July 1943   Copy to E. Lawson-Reece (ESO)   EB/JEL

"SCIENCE AND THE PEOPLE"—Series No 2

In connection with our "Science and the People" No. 2 series which begins in week 34 we are employing Dr. Bryan Brooke in the capacity of Adviser as well as to deliver one of the talks. His job is to help me by arranging the scheme of subjects, furnishing names of suitable speakers and where possible contacting them before hand.° I think he should have a fee for this in addition to the fee for his talk and I would be obliged if you could let me know what to do about a contract for him.

[Signed] E. A. Blair
(Eric Blair)

Bokhari replied to Orwell on 27 July:
Thank you for your memo of 26th July in connection with the employment of Dr. Bryan Brooke. I am getting in touch with the Contracts Department, and am asking them to help you. I have a feeling that you have committed yourself to Dr. Brooke for the task: if so, I wish you had done it after you had consulted me.

The carbon copy bears the handwritten annotation: 'I.P.O. May we speak about this, please? C. Lawson-Reece.' On 29 July, Bokhari wrote to the Talks Booking Manager, marking his note 'Private & Confidential':
Mr. Blair wishes to get Mr. Bryan Brooke of 34 Church Crescent, N.20[1] to advise him in planning a series of six talks on Science, and finding suitable speakers. One of these talks will be given by Mr. Brooke himself. It is suggested that Mr. Brooke should be paid £5/5/– for this advisory work, and the usual fee of £10/10/– for his talk. His advisory work begins from Week 34 and continues for 6 weeks.
    I think the fee of £5/5/– is too small, but Blair (bless him!) thinks it will be all right.

1. By mistake, Bokhari has given the address of Dr. C. M. Fletcher, also engaged for this series.

2201. Georges Kopp to Orwell and His Wife

26 July 1943

Orwell's former commander in Spain, Georges Kopp, wrote to him and Eileen from Occupied France. He was working, he said, as 'a sort of Consulting Engineer' with the French Ministry of Industrial Production: 'it is not a full time job and does not prevent me from performing my other duties; far from it.'

These duties included espionage for British Naval Intelligence. Very shortly after writing, he was betrayed to the Gestapo, but the British managed to fly him out of France to England in September 1943. He wrote the day after Mussolini was overthrown, which followed the taking of Sicily by Allied forces. There were hopes of a rapid end to the war, especially in Italy, though this was not to be, for Mussolini was captured by partisans and shot only on 28 April 1945. Kopp writes about prospects for the ending of the war in cautious terms:

We have just learned to day° the fall of Mussolini; I suppose that Italy will collapse soon and I expect it might have an influence upon the duration of the war, although I remain rather pessimistic as for the length of German resistance; people reckon it in months or even weeks, but I persist to think the bastards will fight desperately for another couple of years; this is a political sort of war and everybody in Germany who is holding any sort of post, from dictator down to postman, knows he will loose° it when Germany capitulates and the régime changes; it is something akin to what happened in republican Spain; they will all refrain as long as they can from avowing they are beaten.

1. For details of Georges Kopp and the degree to which he was what he purported to be, see *359, n. 2, 535, n. 1.*

2202. BBC Talks Booking Form, 27.7.43

J. D. S. Paul: translating script and reading Tamil News Commentary; broadcast 5, 12, 19, and 26.8.43; fee £5.5s each talk + railway vouchers for travel from Cambridge and studio pass for each date. Signed: A. C. Smith.[1]

1. From this date onwards, A. C. Smith, a talks producer in the Indian Section, made the bookings in this series.

2203. BBC Talks Booking Form, 28.7.43

V. S. Pritchett: 'Modern Men of Letters,' 1—H. G. Wells; recorded 18.8.43; broadcast 22.8.43; fee £10.10s + 11s fare. Signed: Z. A. Bokhari.[1]

1. Apart from the series of Newsletter bookings, made by A. C. Smith, Bokhari seems from hereon to have reserved to himself the function of initiating as well as signing the booking forms. This might have been the result of a rearrangement of duties, or Bokhari may have been edging Orwell out of this limited area of control.

2204. BBC Talks Booking Form, 28.7.43

Oliver Bell: Film Talk; 13½ minutes; broadcast 25.8.43; fee £10.10s. Signed: Z. A. Bokhari.

2205. Newsletter in Tamil, 15

29 July 1943

The English version was by Eric Blair. No script has been traced.

2206. To C. M. Fletcher

29 July 1943   07/ES/EB

Dear Dr. Fletcher,[1]

Mr. Bryan Brooke suggested to me that you might be willing to do a talk for the Indian Section of the BBC. We do, from time to time, series of popular scientific talks and we wish shortly to do a series on recent discoveries in drugs and recent advances in medical practice generally. We would like you, if you would, to do us a talk on penicillin. This follows on a talk on the sulphonomide° group by Professor L. P. Garrod. These talks are aimed at the English speaking Indian students. In drafting the talk you can assume that you are speaking to an educated audience, but not to people with much scientific knowledge. These talks are of 13½ minutes, which means 15 or 16 hundred words. We usually have them printed afterwards in India in pamphlet form. I suppose you would not object to that? In addition to the fee for the talk you would in theory get a royalty on the pamphlet, but you can imagine that this is not likely to amount to much. The date of your talk would be Thursday, 2nd September at 11.15 a.m., and I would like to have the script by the 15th August. Could you be kind enough to let me know fairly soon whether you would care to undertake this.

Yours truly,
[Initialled] E.A.B
(Eric Blair)

1. Charles Montague Fletcher (1911–) was assistant physician, Emergency Medical Service, 1943–44; Director, Medical Research Council's Pneumoconiosis Research Unit, 1945–52; Physician to Hammersmith Hospital, 1952–76. In 1941 he wrote many papers whilst a Nuffield Research Student at Oxford on the first use of penicillin, and later 'The First Clinical Use of Penicillin,' *British Medical Journal*, 289, 22–29 December 1984, 1721–23. In 1955–70 he played a major role in introducing televised medical programmes. Like Brooke and Garrod, he had worked at St Bartholomew's Hospital. In a letter to the editor, 19 June 1990, Fletcher recalled clearly 'Blair, as I think I then called him, dashing in to the studio to correct some error of presentation in my script,' which indicates Orwell's close involvement in the transmission of these talks.

2207. To L. P. Garrod

29 July 1943   07/ES

Dear Professor Garrod,[1]

Mr. Bryan Brooke suggested to me that you might be willing to do a talk for the Indian Section of the BBC. We do, from time to time, series of popular scientific talks and we wish shortly to do a series on recent discoveries in drugs and recent advances in medical practice generally. We would like you, if you would, to do us a talk on the sulphonomide° group. These talks are aimed at the English speaking Indian students. In drafting the talk you can assume that you are talking to an educated audience, but not to people with much scientific knowledge. These talks are of 13½ minutes which means 15 or 16 hundred words. We usually have them printed afterwards in India in pamphlet form. I suppose you would not object to that? In addition to the fee for the talk you would in theory get a royalty on the pamphlet but you can imagine that this is not likely to amount to much. The date of your talk would be Thursday, 26th August at 11.15 a.m., and I would like to have the script by the 15th August. Could you be kind enough to let me know fairly soon whether you care to undertake this.

Yours truly,
[Initialled] E.A.B
(Eric Blair)

1. Lawrence Paul Garrod (1895–1979), Professor of Bacteriology, University of London, was later Honorary Consultant in Chemotherapy, Royal Postgraduate Medical School. He served as a surgeon in the Royal Navy in World War I and was an adviser on antibiotics to the army in World War II

2208. Review of *New Writing and Daylight* [Summer 1943], edited by John Lehmann[1]

The Spectator, 30 July 1943

At a time when verse is flourishing, at any rate so far as quantity is concerned, while imaginative prose languishes, it is no surprise to find that in the latest number of *New Writing* the critical essays are better than the stories. But there is one notable exception, and that is Henry Green's brilliant short story, *The Lull*. Describing life in a fire-station which has not seen a blitz for eighteen months, this story accurately pins down one of the minor horrors of war, and does it almost entirely in dialogue with barely a word of comment.

As for the critical essays, Josef Kodicek's remarks on the Czech theatre will be of value to anyone interested in production, and Derek Hill's description of a theatre in Peking is a delicate and amusing sketch. Demetrios Capetanakis and Henry Reed between them sum up the achievements and failures of the Auden-Spender school and of the new literary movements which have appeared since the war. Although it generalises too freely about the latest generation of writers, who are very numerous and by no means all alike, Henry Reed's essay contains some valuable remarks on the dangers of group literature. But the best contribution of all is Raymond Mortimer's essay, *French Writers and the War*. This is a painstaking attempt at something which was badly needed and which had hitherto only been fragmentarily done in various American magazines—an exact account of how the better-known French writers are behaving under Vichy and the Germans. After sifting the rather scanty evidence that has accumulated in the last three years, Mr. Mortimer finds that French writers have behaved better than might have been expected and, more significant, that on the whole the best writers have behaved best. Everyone who cares for the freedom of the intellect should read this essay with attention. If the Nazis had got to Britain we, too, should have had our "collaborators," and the whole subject of the relationship between Fascism and the intelligentsia needs all the investigation it can get. Mr. Mortimer strikes no moral attitudes and says that he looks forward to the execution of Montherlant and Drieu la Rochelle with regret. He also performs a public service by printing a poem of Aragon which had not previously been published in England.

Aragon also appears in two translations by Louis MacNeice, the first of them a very good one. There is also a translation of a long poem by the Czech writer Nezval, interesting in its subject-matter but very difficult to read. Roy Fuller contributes four sincere but rather laboured poems, and Robert Graves some partially successful facetiae.

1. From 12 July 1943 to 31 December 1945, Orwell kept a log of his earnings from writing. The first entry shows £2 12s 6d paid for this review and dated 12 July. The full log is given in *2831*. From here on, where a fee was recorded it is given after the item, in square brackets. The dates are those Orwell delivered his copy.
2. Pierre-Eugène Drieu La Rochelle (author of *Fascist Socialism*, 1934) committed suicide in April 1945; see *913, n.8*. Henry de Montherlant (1896–1972) was a notorious collaborator (*Oxford Companion to French Literature*) despite Martin Seymour-Smith's claim that this 'has no foundation, and the perpetuation of the accusation has become scandalous' (*Guide to Modern World Literature* (1986), 455). He was elected to the Académie Française in 1960. Fearing he was going blind, he committed suicide.

2209. English Newsletter to Indonesia, 4

30 July 1943

This was written and read by George Orwell. No script has been traced.

2210. To Ronald Boswell, Talks Booking Manager

30 July 1943   Handwritten

Attached is the contract referred to in our telephone conversation. It was definitely agreed that Mr Martin was to receive £15. 15. 0 for each of his monthly talks, & I understand he received that sum for his first talk on July 6th. I assume therefore that the attached contract was made out in error.[1]

Eric Blair   30/7/43

1. Kingsley Martin had complained on 22 July 1942 that his fee was less than he had expected. The problem originated in the 'estimated' £10.10s in the talks booking form of 28.5.43 signed by Bokhari; see *2105*. On 3 August, K. F. Lowe apologised to Martin and offered £15.15s. For the outcome of such misunderstandings and other problems associated with Martin, see Bokhari's letter to him of 4 September 1943, *2266*. This memorandum to Boswell seems to be Orwell's only written involvement in the long saga.

2211. 'Those Seaside Postcards'

Strand Magazine, August 1943

This is a shortened and bowdlerised version of Orwell's 'The Art of Donald McGill,' *Horizon*, September 1941. Details of cuts and changes follow the original article; see *850*. Orwell was paid £8.8s for allowing publication. From the nature of the alterations, it is unlikely that he was responsible for them.

2212. To B. H. Alexander, Programme Copyright

2 August 1943   Original

Recording of Poem by Dylan Thomas

Will you please arrange for payment to be made to Mr. Dylan Thomas (Strand Film Co., 1 Golden Square, W. 1)[1] for his recording of a poem written by himself entitled "A Saint about to Fall" (the first line). The duration of the recording was 3′38″ and it took place on Saturday, July 31st, in St. 2, Oxford Street, in the period 12.15 to 12.45 pm. (DBST).

This poem will be transmitted on Sunday, August 8, at 1515–1530 GMT, in the Eastern Service (Purple Network) in our series CALLING ALL STUDENTS (Literary Series No. 6) a talk on THE APOCALYPTIC POETS by Desmond Hawkins.

[Unsigned]

1. The address in parentheses is crossed out in ink. The memorandum is annotated 'RNM 5g'— presumably indicating that the fee was £5.5s.

2213. To Alex Comfort

3 August 1943   Original   07/ES/EB/JEL

Dear Comfort,
I will be dispatching the translations of the two stories by Prem Chand[1] in a few days time. Now that they are translated I am rather disappointed with them, at any rate they are not so good as the one which was in that Indian review I told you about, but you might care to have a look at them.

Forster is doing his broadcast on Sunday, 15th August at 4.15 p.m. standard time. You might be able, if you are some distance from London, to pick him up on the 19.46 wavelength, but it is not usually easy to pick up these broadcasts at all in England. He is going to talk about New Road, the latest New Writing and Maurice Bowra's book on symbolism.[2]

Yours truly,
[Signed] Geo. Orwell
(George Orwell)

1. Evidently one was unsatisfactory for 'The Resignation' and 'The Shroud' were published in *New Road: New Directions in European Art and Letters*, edited by Alex Comfort and John Bayliss (1944), 199–213 (see *2228*). A note preceding the first story explained that Prem Chand (see *2185, n. 2*) had 'moved from Romanticism into a form of Social Realism,' but 'never wholly forfeited his Romantic background.' It was stated that 'for fear of political reprisals, the translator of this story asks to remain anonymous.'
2. This issue of *New Road* (June 1943) included Orwell's 'Looking Back on the Spanish War'; see *1421*. *New Writing* was edited by John Lehmann. The book by Sir Maurice Bowra (1898–1971), classical scholar, author, and Warden of Wadham College, Oxford, was *The Heritage of Symbolism* (1943; New York, 1961).

2214. To L. P. Garrod

3 August 1943   07/ES/EB/JEL

Dear Professor Garrod,
Many thanks for your letter of the 30th July. I am glad that you are able to do the talk. The six subjects arranged for this series are:

     sulphonomide° group
     penicillin
     plasma
     anaesthetics
     insulin
     synthetic vitamins.

As you suggest it might be better to have a general introductory talk on chemotherapy, but that would bring the number of talks up to seven which is just too long for the purpose of the pamphlet, or it would mean cutting out one of the other subjects. From the fact that the talk following yours will be on penicillin you can perhaps infer how far you ought to go.

These talks are not meant to be propaganda of a very direct kind. We are addressing in the Indian students a difficult and hostile audience and one can probably best approach them by keeping up what one might call an atmosphere of intellectual decency. For that reason we do a great many programmes on literary and scientific subjects not having any direct connection with war, but of course wherever we can give Britain or the other United Nations a bit of a boost, without being too obvious about it, naturally we do so.

I do not fancy that your lack of experience of broadcasting will present any difficulty, but it might be as well, on the actual day of the broadcast, to come at least half an hour before the time so as to put in a little rehearsal.

Yours truly,
[Initialled] E.A.B
(Eric Blair)

2215. To Diana Wong

3 August 1943   07/ES/EB/JEL

Dear Miss Wong,

Many thanks for your letter of July, 26th. I am afraid I cannot arrange a talk at present because I have no space in my schedule for some time to come. But I think it is just possible that the North American service would like you to do a talk for them, so I have passed your letter over to them.[1]

Yours sincerely,
[Initialled] E.A.B
(Eric Blair)

1. The letter is annotated (but not in Orwell's hand) 'letter to Mr Macalpine 3/8/43,' indicating that Orwell passed it on. She had spoken about her escape from France in June 1942; see *1148*. J. W. Macalpine was North American Talks Organiser according to the Staff List for 21.8.43.

2216. BBC Talks Booking Form, 3.8.43

Professor L. P. Garrod: 'Calling All Students,' 2nd Scientific Series: No. 1, Sulphonomide° group; broadcast 26.8.43; fee £10.10s. Signed: Z. A. Bokhari.

2217. To C. M. Fletcher

4 August 1943   07/ES/EB/JEL

Dear Dr. Fletcher,

Many thanks for your letter of August 3rd and for the specimen article, which I am returning herewith.

I think Professor Garrod will probably have made a few brief introductory remarks on chemotherapy in his talk about the sulphonomide° group. At any rate I should plan your talk as though he had done so. If necessary we can always make a few last-minute modifications.

I think the article you sent is at about the right level for our audience, except that we ought not to assume that they have [a] working knowledge of the various groups of bacteria.

I look forward to seeing your script.

Yours truly,
[Initialled] E.A.B
(Eric Blair)

2218. To V. S. Pritchett

4 August 1943   07/ES/EB/JEL

Dear Pritchett,

I have arranged for you to record your talk on H. G. Wells on Wednesday, 18th August from 2.0–2.30 p.m. at 200 Oxford Street. I hope this will be convenient for you.

Yours
[Initialled] E. A. B
(George Orwell)

2219. Replacement of P. Chatterjee for Bengali Newsletter

4 August 1943

Orwell prepared the English version of the Bengali Newsletter from 18 July 1942 until 27 February 1943. The composition of the Newsletter was then taken over by Dr. P. Chatterjee. On 2 August 1943, Chatterjee wrote to Bokhari to say he had been commissioned into the Indian Army and suggested that Dr. H. C. Mukerji (who lived at the same address as Chatterjee) take over. On 4 August, Miss Joyce M. Rainbow of the Programme Contracts Department formally reported Chatterjee's imminent departure to the Overseas Service Division. On 12 August Bokhari invited Mukerji to come to see him.

2220. BBC Talks Booking Form, 4.8.43

Bryan Brooke: 'Calling All Students,' 2nd Scientific Series, No. 3, 'Plasma'; approx. $13\frac{1}{2}$ minutes; broadcast 9.9.43; fee £10.10s. Signed: Z. A. Bokhari. Remarks: 'Mr. Brooke is acting as advisor for the other five talks in this series.'

2221. Newsletter in Tamil, 16

5 August 1943

The English version was written by Eric Blair. No script has been traced.

2222. Mary Blackburn to Desmond Hawkins

5 August 1943

Following the first 'Backward Glance' programme, Mary Blackburn, who had been Bokhari's secretary since 1940, wrote this letter as 'Assistant (Programmes).' Her name does not appear in the Staff List for 21.8.43; the Assistant

(Programmes) is shown as I. B. Sarin. Miss A. L. Bateman is listed as Bokhari's secretary.

Dear Mr. Hawkins

Thank you for your P.C. Here is A Book—"The Royal Observatory Greenwich—its History & Work".[1] I do hope this will be of some use to you.

"Backward Glance" No. 1 went off well and was really slick and entertaining. The only sad thing was that while Mr. Blair's secretary was actually typing the script for Mr. Cleverdon to produce, she murmured vaguely that she thought that the Recording of L. A. G. Strong's talk had been destroyed! And it had! The script was altered (only slightly) accordingly, and we didn't actually refer to L. A. G. Strong's voice, as though he were himself speaking again. This won't happen again. We have already carefully checked that all the talks which have been sent to you, marked "As Recorded" are actually recorded and the discs really available.

1. This was by Sir Harold Spencer Jones and was published in 1943.

2222A. To Dwight Macdonald, 6.8.43: see Introduction

2223. BBC Talks Booking Form, undated

Dr. Edith Summerskill, M.P.: 'The Debate Continues'; recorded 5.8.43; broadcast 7.8.43; fee £5.5s. Signed: Z. A. Bokhari.

2224. English Newsletter to Indonesia, 5
6 August 1943

This was written and read by George Orwell. No script has been traced.[1]

1. In his diary, Gentry noted for 5 August, 'B.B.C. have announced that Bangkok [where he was held prisoner] will be bombed as soon as weather permits.'

2225. To Oliver Bell
6 August 1943   07/ES/EB/JEL

Dear Mr. Bell,

Many thanks for your letter of August 4th. I think it would be *possible* for you to do your talk from Glasgow or Edinburgh, but it isn't easy. The trouble is about the announcements which have to be done this end. If possible it would be better if you could arrange to record it before hand.° I don't know when you are leaving for Scotland, but if you record it as much as a week before hand I don't suppose your stuff would be very much out of date by the day of transmission. Could you let me know what you think about this?[1]

Yours sincerely,
[Initialled] E.A.B
(Eric Blair)

1. Bell replied by postcard on 6 August, to say that this was the obvious solution. On the verso, Orwell wrote, in pencil: 'Please arrange recording & let B. know. E.A.B'.

2226. BBC Talks Booking Form, 6.8.43

Dr. C. M. Fletcher: 2nd Scientific Series, Penicillin, talk No. 2; broadcast 2.9.43; fee £10.10s. Signed: Z. A. Bokhari.

2227. BBC Talks Booking Form, 6.8.43

Kingsley Martin: 'Topic of the Month'; recording to be arranged; broadcast 31.8.43 [handwritten alteration of 3 August]; fee £15.15s. Signed: Z. A. Bokhari.

2228. To Alex Comfort

10 August 1943   Original   07/ES/EB

Dear Comfort,
Thanks for your letter of the 9th August. I am glad you succeeded in picking up Hawkins's broadcast. Forster's will be at the same time etc. The BBC retain copyright of broadcast material for 28 days, after which it reverts to the author, so you have only to fix it up with Hawkins about reprinting. I can let you have a copy if Hawkins hasn't got one.

Our audience in India, i.e. for English language stuff, is very small, a question of thousands at most, but we do find that literary stuff is more listened to than anything else, except of course the news and some of the music. I try to aim exclusively at the students, but I fancy there is a possible subsidary audience among the British troops which is why I am circularising people likely to be interested. In my experience it is no use trying to push this kind of broadcast on to the Home Service—they will never look at any of our stuff.

I have sent the two Prem Chand stories, but am also procuring the one which was previously printed (in India only) and will send that.

Yours sincerely,
[Signed] Geo. Orwell
George Orwell

2229. BBC Talks Booking Form, 10.8.43

James Stephens: 'Modern Men of Letters,' 3, Bernard Shaw; recording 'not yet fixed'; broadcast 5.9.43; fee £10.10s; 'Amended £12.12s + 19s 0d fare.'[1] Signed: Z. A. Bokhari.

1. Stephens wrote to the Programme Contracts Director on 15 August complaining that the fee offered was too little. He had, he wrote, been reading in preparation for the talk for eight hours a day for two weeks, and travel from Cirencester to make the broadcast involved standing in a crowded train corridor for six hours. He asked for £15.15s. K. F. Lowe replied for the Programme Contracts Director on 24 August offering £12.12s. Stephens accepted that on 30 August, though he said he still felt 'badly treated' since the talk had taken him nearly a month to write.

2230. 'Crainquebille' by Anatole France, adapted by George Orwell

BBC Eastern Service, 11 August 1943

Orwell's adaptation of Anatole France's short story 'Crainquebille' is the first of his attempts at a sub-genre that particularly interested him—the 'featurised story' (see 2247). Its influence on his adaptation of *Animal Farm* is discussed in *CW*, VIII, Appendix III, 115–22. It is reproduced here from what looks like a professionally-prepared typescript, although the typewriter is not dissimilar to that used by Mrs. Miranda Wood for typing one of the drafts of *Nineteen Eighty-Four*; see the *Facsimile*, 183. It is unlike the BBC machines used by Orwell's secretaries, and its short comma and small-dot 'i' are different from those of the machine Orwell used to type personal letters in July and August 1943, which he took to Jura. It is possible that it was the second typewriter owned by the Orwells, left in London for Mrs. Wood to use when Orwell sublet the flat to her whilst he was in Scotland; see Appendix 12, *3735*. The typing is too good to be Orwell's, but it just might be Eileen's. All but one single-letter amendment to the typescript is in a hand other than Orwell's, which also added the names of the actors, sound effects, and directions. The script is marked 'Not checked with broadcast.' Two replacement passages given here are from carbon copies, far more blurred than the clear-cut typeface of the main text, reproduced from a wax stencil, but the machines could be the same. The amendments probably stem from the producer, Douglas Cleverdon, and almost certainly had Orwell's approval.

Cleverdon (1903–1987) was a bookseller, 1925–39, then joined the BBC. With Howard Thomas he initiated the very successful programme 'The Brains Trust'; after the war he was a particularly fine producer for the Third Programme, notably the 1953 dramatisation of *Under Milk Wood*, by Dylan Thomas, narrated by Richard Burton.

In the text of the broadcast below, except in the cast list, italic is used to represent manuscript additions and emendations. The notes record alterations and cuts except for insignificant slips. The few words underlined in the typescript are similarly printed here, not italicised.

CAST: CRAINQUEBILLE *Carleton Hobbs*
       MADAME BAYARD *Molly Rankin*
       CONSTABLE 64 *Allan Jeayes*
       MAITRE LEMERLE *Leonard Sachs*
       PRESIDENT BOURRICHE ⎫
       SECOND POLICEMAN ⎰ *Deryck Guyler*
       NARRATOR *Richard Williams*
       3 others[1]
  PRODUCER: *Douglas Cleverdon*

Fade up market noises

Crainquebille: *Cabbages, Turnips, Carrots . . . (Fade out)*

Narrator: Jerome Crainquebille, 60 years of age, was a vegetable-seller in the Rue Montmartre in Paris. Every day of his life he went up and down the street, pushing his barrow in front of him and crying:

Crainquebille: "Cabbages! Turnips! Carrots!"

Narrator: When he had leeks he cried: "Asparagus!", because leeks are the asparagus of the poor. Now it happened that one day, just about noon, he was going down the Rue Montmartre when Madame Bayard, the shoe maker's wife, came out of her shop. She went up to Crainquebille's barrow, and *picked*[2] up a bundle of leeks with a disdainful air[3]:

Mde. Bayard: These leeks aren't much good, are they? How much are they a bundle?

Crain: 15 sous, Ma'am. Best leeks on the market!

Mde. Bayard: What! 15 sous for three miserable leeks?

Narrator: And she flung the bundle of leeks back on to the barrow with a gesture of disgust. It was just at this moment that a policeman,[4] Constable No. 64, arrived on the scene and said to Crainquebille:

C. 64: Move on, there. Keep moving.

Narrator: Now, Crainquebille had been moving on from morning till night for the last 50 years. To be told to move on didn't seem in the least unnatural to him. He was quite ready to obey, but he did stop and urge Madame Bayard to take whatever vegetables she wanted. Madame Bayard said sharply that she must have time to choose, and with great care she felt all the bundles of leeks over again. Finally *she*[5] picked out the one she thought best, *and*[6] held it clasped against her bosom, rather as the saints in sacred pictures hold the palm of victory.

Mde. B: I'll give you 14 sous. That's plenty. But I'll have to fetch the money out of the shop, because I haven't got anything on me.

Narrator: Still clasping the leeks, she went back into the cobbler's shop. At this moment Constable 64 *spoke*[7] to Crainquebille for the second time:

C. 64: Move on, there. Didn't you hear me tell you to keep moving?

Crain: But I'm waiting for my money!

C. 64: Never mind about waiting for your money. I'm not telling you to wait for your money. I'm telling you to move on.

Narrator: Meanwhile in the cobbler's shop Madame Bayard had thrown the leeks onto the counter and was busy fitting a pair of slippers onto a child whose mother was in a hurry. Crainquebille had a profound respect for authority. He had acquired it during the 50 years in which he had been pushing his barrow through the streets. But at this moment he was in a peculiar position, and his mind was not adapted to complex problems. Pehaps he attached too great an importance to the 14 sous that Madame Bayard owed him, and too little to his duty of moving on when a policeman told him to. At any rate, instead of moving on as he had been told to do, he simply stood still. Constable 64 quietly and calmly *spoke to him again.*[8]

Constable 64:   *For the third time, move on will you?*

[*Narrator:*][9]   Crainquebille merely shrugged his shoulders and looked sadly at the police constable. Now it happened that at this moment the block of traffic in the Rue Montmartre was just at its worst. (*Crowd noises up*) Carriages, drays, carts, buses and trucks were jammed one against another in such a tangle that it looked as though they would never be sorted out again. There was an uproar of shouting and swearing. (*Crowd noises*) Cabmen and butcher bo[th] exchanged insults at long range and the bus conductors, who considered Crainquebille to be the cause of the traffic jam, *called him*[10] "silly turnip". The crowd on the pavement were pressing round to listen to the dispute. Constable 64, finding himself the centre of attention, felt that it was time to display his authority. With a solemn air he took a stump of pencil and a greasy notebook out of his pocket. Crainquebille wasn't moving; all he could think of were those 14 sous. Besides, he couldn't move. The wheel of his barrow had got jammed with that of a milkman's cart. At the sight of the notebook he tore his hair under his cap and cried:

Crain: But didn't I tell you that I'm waiting for my money? How can I go away without getting my money? It's a bloody shame!

Narrator: Those words expressed despair rather than rebellion; but Constable 64 felt that he had been insulted. Now, according to Constable 64's ideas, every insult inevitably took the form of a shout of "Down with the police!" In his experience all rioters, demonstrators, anarchists, in general, all enemies of society invariably shouted "Down with the police!" "Down with the police!" was the regular, traditional, classical insult. Consequently it was in this time-honoured form that he heard what Crainquebille said.

C. 64:   Ah! that's enough! "Down with the police!", you said. Very well, then. Come along with me.

Narrator: Crainquebille was stupified:

Crain: What! me? I said, "Down with the police?" Why should I say that?

C. 64:   That'll do! D'you think I didn't hear you? Come along with me.

Narrator: It was no use. Constable 64 had it firmly in his head that "Down with the police" was what Crainquebille had said. He began to lead him away. Even as he was doing so Madame Bayard, the shoemaker's wife, came out of the shop with the 14 sous in her hand.

Mme Bayard: *Mon Dieu!* . . .

Narrator: But Constable 64 already had Crainquebille by the collar. Madame Bayard promptly decided that one does not need to pay money to a man who is being taken to the police station and put her 14 sous back in her[11] apron pocket. Crainquebille was taken before the Commissioner of the Police, and spent the night in the lock-up.[12]

Crainquebille: It's a queer place, this. I've never been in jug before. I wonder what they did with my barrow? Doesn't seem much sense to shut a man up in a stone cell all by himself. And doesn't the time go slowly! Of course they have to do it. There's some people that have to be locked up, otherwise nobody'd[13] be safe. But it's not what I'd call home-like. It's all so clean! They must swab these walls down every morning. And fancy chaining that stool to the wall! It isn't as if you could take it away with you. And it's so quiet! Makes every minute seem like an hour. I wonder what they did with my barrow?

[*Narrator:*] On the third day he received a visit from his lawyer, Maitre Lemerle, one of the youngest members of the Paris bar. Crainquebille endeavoured to tell his story. But this wasn't easy. Crainquebille was no conversationalist, and the lawyer didn't give him much help, but merely twiddled his fair moustaches in a bored manner while he listened.

Crain: You see, Monsieur, it was like this—I didn't insult him, you understand that? He just took it into his head that I'd said it. Besides he was in a bad temper because of the way the bus drivers were carrying on. But I couldn't go away without my 14 sous, could I? You couldn't expect a man to go away without his money?

Lemerle: You say definitely that you did not insult this man? Are you perfectly certain that you did not say, "Down with the police?"

Crain: Of course I didn't, Monsieur. That is to say I did say it, but—

Lemerle: You did say it?

Crain: In a manner of speaking I said it, Monsieur. But not the way he meant. And what about my 14 sous? Madame Bayard had taken the bunch of leeks. Besides, how could I move on when my barrow was jammed against the milk cart?

Lemerle: This is a complicated business, Crainquebille. I don't find anything about a milk-cart in my brief; nor about a bunch of leeks.

Crain: You see Monsieur, it's all a little difficult to explain.

Lemerle: Crainquebille, let me give you a piece of advice. It would be in your own interest to plead guilty.

Craine: *Guilty.*

Lemerle: If you persist in denying it, it will create a bad impression. If I were you I should confess.

Crain: Very well, Monsieur. But just tell me. What *is it*[14] that I have to confess?

Narrator: Next morning Crainquebille was taken before the magistrates. Monsieur Bourriche, the president of the court, devoted six whole minutes to examining him. The examination would have been more useful if Crainquebille had answered the questions that were asked of him. But he was not used to discussions, and he was too much overawed by the ceremonious atmosphere of the court to be able to speak freely. So he was silent. The president solved the problem by answering his own questions himself. He concluded solemnly:

President: And, so, prisoner at the bar, you admit to having said, "Down with the police."

Crain: Monsieur, I did say, "Down with the police", but only after he said it, if you understand me. He said, "Down with the police", and so then I said, "Down with the police", don't you see?

President: Are you seriously trying to maintain that this policeman shouted, "Down with the police" himself?

Narrator: Crainquebille gave up trying to explain. It was too difficult. The President took this as a *sign*[15] of guilt.

President: So you do not persist in your statement. Quite right. That is the wisest course you can take.

Narrator: The president then had witnesses called. Constable 64, by name Bastien Mátra, was called and gave evidence in the following terms:

C. 64:   I promise that what I say shall be the truth, the whole truth and nothing but the truth. On the 20th of October at noon, I was on my beat when I noticed in the Rue Montmartre a person who appeared to be a coster- monger unduly blocking the traffic with his barrow opposite No. 328. On three occasions I gave him the order to move on, but he refused to comply. I then gave him warnings that I was about to charge him. He retorted by shouting, "Down with the police!" I saw that this was intended as an insult, and took him in custody.

Narrator: Constable 64's evidence was delivered in a firm and moderate tone. It made an excellent impression on the magistrates. After the calling of other witnesses Maitre Lemerle, Crainquebille's lawyer, made a speech in which he endeavoured to show on the one hand that Crainquebille had not shouted "Down with the police", and on the other that he had shouted it, but had not meant it seriously.

Lemerle: Your worship, my client is accused of having shouted "Down with the police". Now we all know that this expression is frequently shouted in the streets by a certain class of people. So the question resolves itself into this: in what spirit did Crainquebille say it? And on the other hand did he say it at all? Permit me to doubt it, gentlemen.

Gentlemen, I will say no word against the police force. A finer body of men does not exist. I would be far from suspecting Constable 64 of any evil intention. But we know that a police officer's profession is an arduous one. He is often tired, harassed, overworked. Is it not possible, gentlemen, that in such circumstances Constable 64 may have suffered from some kind of aural hallucination and merely imagined that my client uttered the words attributed to him? And on the other hand, let us suppose that Crainquebille did shout "Down with the police". It still remains to be proved whether, on his lips, such words can be regarded as contempt. Crainquebille is the natural child of a coster-monger, ruined by years of drinking and other evil courses. Crainquebille was born alcoholic. You have only to look at him to see how completely he has been brutalised by 60 years of poverty. Gentlemen, you must conclude that he is not responsible for his actions.

Narrator: Maitre Lemerle sat down. His speech had accomplished nothing. Monsieur Bourriche, the president of the court, immediately pronounced a sentence condemning Crainquebille to pay 50 francs fine and to go to prison for a fortnight. The evidence of Constable 64 had been too strong. Crainquebille was led away to prison.

When he had gone back to his cell Crainquebille sat down with a feeling of wonder and admiration on the stool which was chained to the wall.[16]

Crainquebille: There's something gone wrong somewhere. Or is it me that's wrong? I *didn't* shout "Down with the police", that's certain. Or did I? The funny thing is, you couldn't imagine those gentlemen on the bench making a mistake. They were all of them clever men, they understood all about the law and all that, you could see that with half an eye. And they were very fair, I must say that. They didn't try to stop you speaking up for yourself. How could they make a mistake? Maybe I *did* shout "Down with the police"? Could you shout out a thing like that without knowing you'd done it? Or maybe I just forgot about it afterwards. I don't believe that [a] magistrate would make a mistake. A regular learned man he looked, with his spectacles and his black gown. He had a way of holding his head down and looking at you over his spectacles—it kind of made you feel that he was looking right through you and knew all about you. And yet I didn't shout "Down with the police", I could swear to that. It's all a puzzle.

[*Narrator:*] On the next day his lawyer came to visit him:

Lemerle: Well, Crainquebille, things didn't turn out so badly after all, did they? Don't be discouraged, a fortnight is soon over. We haven't much to complain of.

Crain: I must say, Monsieur, that the gentlemen were very kind, very polite. Nobody called me any names. It was quite different from what I expected. Did you see the white gloves the officers were wearing?

Lemerle: All things considered, Crainquebille, I think we did well to plead guilty.

Crain: Perhaps, Monsieur. You know best.

Lemerle: Now, I have some good news for you, Crainquebille. A charitable person whom I managed to interest in your case has sent me 50 francs for you. That will just do to pay your fine, you see.

Crain: And when do I get the fifty francs?

Lemerle: It will be paid into the clerk's office, don't bother about that.

Crain: Thank you, Monsieur. I'm very grateful to this person. This is a queer business that's happened to me, isn't it Monsieur?

Lemerle: Not so queer, really. Things like this are happening every day, you know.

Crain: There's one other thing, Monsieur. I suppose you couldn't tell me where they put my barrow?

Narrator: A fortnight later Crainquebille was discharged from prison. Once again he was back in the Rue Montmartre, pushing his barrow and shouting "Cabbages! Turnips! Carrots!" He was neither ashamed nor proud of his adventure. The memory of it was not even painful. It was merely a mysterious interval like a dream. But above all he was glad to be once again tramping over the mud and the cobbles, and to see overhead the rainy sky as dirty as the water in the gutter, the familiar sky of Paris where he had been born. At every corner he stopped for a glass of red wine, and then with an invigorated feeling he would spit on his horny hands, seize the shafts and push his barrow on again. Meanwhile the flocks of sparrows flew away at the sound of the familiar cry.

Crain: Cabbages, turnips and carrots!

Narrator: Like Crainquebille the sparrows were poor and got up early, and like him they sought their living in the streets. When *he met his customers*—[17]

Woman: Where have you been all this time, Crainquebille? We haven't seen you for three weeks.

Crain: Oh, I've[18] been in prison.

Narrator: There appeared to be no change in his life except that he went oftener to the pub, because coming out of prison had given him the feeling of being on holiday. He came back to the garret where he slept a little bit the worse for drink. Stretching himself on his mattress, he drew over him the sacks which he had borrowed from the chestnut seller at the corner, and which served him as blankets; and he thought to himself:

Crain: Well really, prison isn't so bad. You've got everything you want there. It's clean, there's enough to eat and they keep you warm. They give you clothes to wear, and you don't have to worry about the rent either. But all the same, there's no place like home.

Narrator: However, Crainquebille did not remain long in this contented frame of mind. Very soon he noticed that his old customers were looking askance at him. All kinds of people who had previously flocked round his barrow when it was piled with fresh green vegetables, now turned away when they saw him coming. He went round to Madame Bayard, the cobbler's wife, who owed him the 15 sous which had started the whole trouble. But when he reminded her about the 15 sous Madame Bayard, who was sitting at her counter, did not even deign to turn her head.

The fact was that the whole of the Rue Montmartre knew that Crainquebille had been in prison. As a result the whole quarter gave him the cold shoulder. It ended with Crainquebille having a disgraceful wrangle in the street with Madame Laure, an old customer of his, whom he found buying vegetables from somebody else's barrow. The two of them stood there shouting insults at one another in the street, while a group of idlers looked on. It might even have come to something worse if a policeman had not suddenly appeared on the scene. The policeman did not do anything, but by his mere appearance he reduced both of them to silence. So they separated. But this quarrel was the final touch and had the effect of discrediting Crainquebille once and for all in the eyes of everyone in the Rue Montmartre.

It was the same with all of them. They all avoided him as though he had the plague. Even his old friend the chestnut seller would no longer have anything to do with him. Crainquebille felt himself an outcast. He used to muse to himself about the injustice of it *all*.

Crain: It isn't fair, that's what I say, it isn't fair! I get put away for a fortnight and after that I'm not even thought good enough to sell leeks. Do they call that justice? Where's the sense of making a *fellow*[19] die of starvation just because he once got into a bit of trouble with the police? What's to become of me if I'm not allowed to sell vegetables? I'd like to give a few of the people in this quarter a bit of my mind, the hypocrites![20]

Narrator: In fact, he did give several people a bit of his mind, and in no uncertain terms. He got into a number of quarrels at the wine shop. People said that old Crainquebille was turning into a regular porcupine, and they were right; he was becoming disagreeable, foul-mouthed and abusive. The fact was that for the first time in his life he was discovering the imperfections of society; but not having the equipment of a philosopher he expressed his thoughts in hasty and ill-judged words. Misfortune made him unjust. He took his revenge on people who wished him no evil and sometimes on people weaker than himself. One day Alphonse, the wine seller's little boy, innocently asked him what it was like in jail. Crainquebille smacked him on the ear and said:

Crain: You dirty little brat! It's your father who ought to be in jail instead of filling his pockets by selling poison.

Narrator: It was an unworthy action, for as the chestnut seller rightly pointed out, a child does not choose his own parents and ought not to be blamed for them. Crainquebille was also beginning to drink too much. The less money he earned the more brandy he drank. This was a great change in his habits, for before he went to prison he had always been thrifty and sober. He himself noticed these changes. Often he blamed himself severely for his bad habits and his laziness.

Crain: It's funny. I never used to be one for the drink. The fact is you don't get any better as you get older. Nowadays it seems I'm no good for anything except boozing. But then I just[21] have to have a pint or two *now and then* to put a bit of strength into me. It's like as if I had a fire burning in my inside and there's nothing except[22] drink will put it out. I can't do without it, that's the trouble.

Narrator: Nowadays Crainquebille often missed the auction at the vege-table market in the morning, and had to pick up inferior fruit and vegetables on credit. One day, with discouragement at his heart and a tired feeling in his legs, he left his barrow in the shed and spent the whole day hanging round the tripe stall and lounging in and out of the wine shops near the vegetable market. In the evening, sitting on a basket, he meditated on the deterioration which had overtaken him. He remembered how strong he had been in his early years, how hard he used to work all day, and how happy he had been in the evenings. He remembered the innumerable days, swiftly passing, all alike and all full of labour. He remembered the darkness of the early mornings, when he waited in the cobbled yard for the auction to begin; he remembered how he used to carry the vegetables in armfuls and arrange them artistically on his barrow; and then the little cup of black coffee swallowed standing at one gulp, and then the shafts grasped vigorously and then his own loud cry of "Cabbages! Turnips! Carrots!", piercing as a cock- crow, rending the morning air as he passed through the crowded streets. The rough, innocent, useful life, like that of a human pack horse, which he had led for 50 years—it all came before his eyes. He sighed:

Crain: No, I can't go on any longer. I'm done for. Nobody lasts for ever. Besides, ever since that time I was had up by the police it seems as if I haven't the same character any longer. No I'm not the man I used to be.

Narrator: The fact is Crainquebille had given up hope, and when a man reaches that state he might as well be lying on his back in the mud. Every passer by treads him under foot.

Poverty came to him, black, grinding poverty. The old coster-monger who used once to come back from Montmartre with a bag full of five franc pieces now had not a single copper to his name. It was winter now. Driven out of his garret, Crainquebille slept under some carts in a shed. It had been raining for days, the gutters were overflowing , and the shed was flooded.

As he squatted in his barrow to get away from the filthy water, amid spiders, rats and half starved cats, he meditated. [H]e had had nothing to eat all day and he no longer had the chestnut seller's sacks for a covering. At this moment he remembered that fortnight in prison when the government had provided him with food and shelter. He found himself actually envying the prisoners' fate:

Crain: After all, it isn't so bad in jail. At any rate you aren't cold and you aren't hungry. They're better off in there than I am out here. And it's easy enough to get inside. It didn't take much to make them lock me up last time. I'll do it! Why didn't I ever think of it before?

Narrator: Crainquebille got up and went out into the street. It was a little past eleven on a cold dark night. A drizzling mist was falling, colder and more penetrating than rain. The few passers by crept along under cover of the houses.

Crainquebille turned into the Rue Montmartre. It was deserted. A solitary policeman was standing under a street lamp outside a church, while all around him fell a fine rain which looked reddish in the gas light. The policeman was standing so still that he looked scarcely human. The reflection of his boots on the wet pavement,[23] prolonged his shape downwards and gave him, from a little distance, the appearance of some amphibious monster half out of the water. Seen closer to, with the hood of his water-proof cape covering his head, he had more the appearance of a monk.[24] The coarse features of his face, magnified under the shadow of the hood, were sad and by no means aggressive. He was an old policeman,[25] with a thick grey moustache. Crainquebille went up to him, halted and summoned up his courage. Then in a weak, quavering voice he cried out:

Crain: Down with the police!

Narrator: Nothing happened. Crainquebille waited for the terrible words[26] to take their effect. Still nothing happened. The policeman remained motionless and silent, his arms folded beneath his short cloak. His eyes were wide open, they glistened in the darkness and regarded Crainquebille with a mixture of sorrow, watchfulness and scorn. Crainquebille was astonished, but he was still resolute. He tried again:

Crain: Down with the police! Didn't you hear me? Down with the police!

Narrator: There was a long silence in the chill darkness and the fine penetrating rain. At last the policeman spoke:

Policeman: You mustn't say things like that. Don't you know better at your age? You'd better get along home.

Crain: Why don't you arrest me? Didn't you hear me shout. "Down with the police"? They arrested me last time.

Policeman: Listen, if we were to take up all the fools who say things they oughtn't to, we'd have our work cut out. Besides what would be the use of it?

Narrator: Crainquebille was defeated. The policeman's magnanimous attitude was something he had never bargained for. For a long time he stood stupefied and silent, with his feet in the gutter. He was about to make off, but before going he tried to explain:

Crain: Listen, I didn't mean any harm. I wasn't saying "Down with the police" to you, you understand. Not you more than anyone else. It was only an idea, if you understand me.[27]

Policeman: Maybe it was an idea, maybe it wasn't but it's not a thing you ought to say. Because when a man does his duty and has a lot to put up with there's no sense in calling him names. Now, you go home to bed.

Crain: And you're not going to arrest me?

Policeman: No. Why should I? What is there to arrest you for? Go home.

Narrator: So Crainquebille, with his head bowed and his arms hanging limply from his body, slouched away into the rain and the darkness.

1. Written to left of cast list; 3 was orginally 2.
2. *picked*] pciking° *ts* (typescript)
3. 'she said' originally followed 'air' in *ts*.
4. The *ts* shows a number of typing errors—here, 'ahat° a policaman°'; these have been corrected silently. 'Policemen' is on other occasions spelt with an 'a'—not one of Orwell's idiosyncracies.
5. *she*] having   *ts*
6. *and*] she   *ts*
7. *spoke*] said   *ts*
8. Constable 64 quietly and calmly *spoke to him again*] For the third time Constable 64 quietly and calmly ordered him to move on   *ts*

9. '[*Narrator:*]' is an editorial insertion. There are two others.
10. *called him*] abused him under the name of   *ts*
11. '14 sous back in her'] is repeated in *ts* and crossed through by same hand that made other deletions and additions.
12. Apart from 'and spent the night in the lock-up,' Orwell indicates that all the original typescript between 'Commissioner of the Police' and 'On the third day' should be deleted, though it has two sentences not crossed through: 'Next morning he was taken to the police court in a prison van' and 'Being in prison did not seem to Crainquebille particularly painful or humiliating.' These lines may have been restored, or it may have been intended to retain them as well as 'and spent the night in the lock-up' (shown in italic in the passage reproduced below). A similar confusion occurs later; see *n. 16.* For the deleted passage, Orwell substituted Crainquebille's speech, 'It's a queer place, this . . . what they did with my barrow?' The section to be deleted is indicated by the following typed slip:

PAGE FOUR

DELETE   "At the Commissioner's office . . . . under arrest".
DELETE   "Next morning he was takne° to the police court in a prison van."
DELETE   "Being in prison . . . done with my barrow? AND SUBSTITUTE: 'At the Commissioner's office an onlooked° who had watched the whole incident came forward and testified that Crainquebille had not shouted, "Down with the police", and in fact had not insulted Constable 64 in any way whatever. It turned out that this onlooked° was chief physician at one of the leading Paris hospitals. At another time his evidence would have been quite enough for the Commissioner of Police, but unfortunately it happened that just at that time men of science were regarded in France with suspicion. So it was no use. Crainquebille continued under arrest [*and spent the night in the lock-up.*] Next morning he was taken to the police court in a prison van.

'Being in prison did not seem to Crainquebille particularly painful or humiliating. He was well aware that society has need of prisons. What chiefly struck him was the extreme cleanness of his cell, and also the fact that the stool was chained to the wall. This last detail surprised him very much. He sat down and twiddled his thumbs, and in the silence of his cell the time seemed very long. Many times he thought anxiously of his barrow, which had been confiscated with its load of vegetables. If he asked himself any question in the night, it was only: "What have they done with my barrow?"'

13. The 'd' of 'nobody'd' is a handwritten addition in what seems to be Orwell's hand.
14. *is it*] it is   *ts*
15. *sign*] sing   *ts*
16. In the original typescript, narration continued after 'chained to the wall,' but Orwell gave typed instructions that this should be deleted. There is a conflict between the typed instructions and the passage marked for deletion, 'certain that the magistrates had made a mistake. The' not being crossed out. Crainquebille's speech beginning 'There's something gone wrong somewhere' is substituted for:

'By this time he was not at all certain that the magistrates had made a mistake. The imposing ritual of the court had concealed its essential weakness from him. It was impossible for him to conceive that anything could go wrong in so elaborate a ceremony. It was true that he was still perfectly aware that he had *not* shouted "Down with the police"; but to be sentenced to a fortnight's imprisonment for having shouted it appeared to him as a kind of mystery, unintelligible, but not actually unjust. Indeed, since he had been condemned for shouting "Down with the police" he had a feeling that perhaps he *had* shouted it in some mysterious manner unknown to himself. Nearly everything was mysterious in the world which *he had* now entered.'

17. *he met his customers—*] his customers asked him,   *ts*
18. *Oh, I've*] he explained freely that he had
19. *fellow*] bloke   *ts*
20. hypocrites] dirty hypocrites   *ts*
21. then I just] then I just to have it now and then. I just   *ts*
22. except] except to   *ts*
23. pavement,] pavement, which looked like a pool of water,   *ts*
24. monk] mink   *ts* (ms. alteration)

25. policeman,] policeman, perhaps 40 years old, *ts*
26. words] words, which on the previous occasion had got him into so much trouble, *ts*
27. In *ts*, Crainquebille's speech is followed by: 'Narrator: The policeman answered sternly but kindly.' This is crossed through.

2231. Newsletter in Tamil, 17

12 August 1943

The English version was written by Eric Blair. No script has been traced.

2232. To Oliver Bell

12 August 1943   07/ES/EB/JEL

Dear Bell,
About your talk on August 25th, I suppose you will be able to do that one live—it will be at 11.00 a.m. BST. As to the music, I think you said that you were going to see Miss Lilian Duff[1] about it for us and find out whether it would be possible to use the film music. I should be glad to know how this is progressing because we have to get our stuff scheduled some days in advance, and if we cannot have the film music for your next talk I shall have to fill up the quarter hour in some other way.

Yours sincerely,
[Initialled] E.A.B
(Eric Blair)

1. Lilian Duff was a programme announcer in the Home Division Presentation Department. She arranged a popular programme, 'French Cabaret,' based on gramophone records and presumably, from this reference, film music.

2233. To F. R. Daruvala

12 August 1943   07/ES/EB/JEL

Dear Mr. Daruvala,
We held this script[1] up for some time in hopes of being able to find a place for it, but I am sorry to say we have not been able to do so. My schedule is in fact full up for some months to come. I am therefore returning your script with many thanks for giving me the opportunity of seeing it. Please forgive the delay.

Yours sincerely,
[Initialled] E.A.B
(Eric Blair)

1. The script has not been identified. Daruvala also had tried to have a script in Gujarati accepted in 1942; see Orwell's letter to him, 29 December 1942, *1780*. Unfortunately, Hilton Brown of the Home Division Talks Department had returned to him his script 'The Problems Confronting the New Viceroy' on 6 August 1943. Daruvala was in the Royal Army Service Corps and was apparently posted at MI5 headquarters as a driver.

2234. To L. P. Garrod

c. 12 August 1943   Handwritten draft for postcard

On 11 August, Professor Garrod wrote to Orwell to say that if he wanted the script he had written altered, he would be glad to do that. He particularly mentioned his references to Hitler, gonorrhoea, and vivisection. At the top of the letter, Orwell has written in pencil, 'Answered 12.8.43' and at the bottom, 'P.T.O.' On the verso is his draft for a postcard to Garrod:

Please answer: (pc)
Very many thanks for an excellent script. I have no wish to alter anything in it. The time and date are Thursday 26th at 11 am (I may have told you 12.00 but the clock will have changed by then[1]). Do you wish to deliver your talk live or record it beforehand?

Eric Blair

1. The change was from Double to Single Summer Time, when the clock would be put back one hour, from DBST's two hours in advance of Greenwich Mean Time. For the confusion caused by this change, see letter to Garrod, 20 August 1943, *2244, n. 1.*

2235. English Newsletter to Indonesia, 6

13 August 1943

This was written and read by George Orwell. No script has been traced.

2236. Review of *Red Moon Rising* by George Rodger; *A Million Died*, by Alfred Wagg

The New Statesman and Nation, 14 August 1943

Very little worth-while news has come out of Burma since the Japanese occupation, and even about the campaign itself extraordinarily little has been published. The competent authorities have simply kept their mouths shut (rumour has it that even Mr. Wagg's book, which is notably pro-British was published only against official opposition), and no newspaper correspondent with a background knowledge of Burma seems to have been present during the crucial period. The result has been a crop of rumours and a widespread misconception of the reasons for which Burma was lost. It is because they help to put the Burma campaign in perspective, and because they agree with the meagre verbal information that is obtainable, that these two books are worth reading.

It cannot be said that they are good books. Both are by Americans, and though Mr. Wagg is more recognisably the tough guy reporter, both have the characteristics we have learned to expect in the books that roving correspondents throw off between journeys. Mr. Rodger is more inclined to misspell names and mistranslate phrases, but makes up for it by having better photographs (incidentally anyone who cares for photography should have a look at the picture of Indian refugees opposite page 55), while Mr. Wagg shows more awareness of Burma's political and economic development, and of the sources of Burmese nationalism. Between them they add to our knowledge on two very important subjects—the extent of the Burmese fifth column, and the attitude of the Burmese towards the Indians.

There is, of course, very little question as to why Burma was lost. More numerous, better armed, greatly superior in the air, the Japanese were bound to win, and the British and Indian troops achieved a great deal in getting out of the country as an organised force. The idea prevalent at the time, that it would somehow have been different if Burma had been promised independence, was a sentimentality. The Burmese could not have resisted the Japanese even if they had wished to. But the Japanese had grasped one fact which the British had ignored, and are still ignoring in India, namely, that an unarmed peasant who is little use as a regular soldier can do a lot of damage as a guerrilla or saboteur. Long before the war they had made contact with the Thakin party (the extreme nationalists), and as soon as fighting broke out they formed the Burma Independence Army, which was used for creating diversions, cutting communications, and supplying guides and interpreters. The Thakin party overlapped with the dacoits, from whose ranks several of the leading Burmese politicians had graduated, and the Burma Independence Army probably started off with a good supply of stolen weapons, mostly shotguns. The Japanese do not seem to have taken the risk of distributing modern arms in large quantities, and it is known that the partisans suffered heavy casualties. This presumably did not distress the Japanese, who would have their own troubles with the Nationalists to settle later. It is impossible to get from either Mr. Wagg's or Mr. Rodger's book any definite idea of the number of Burmese who were actively anti-British, but both give the impression that it was a large number, perhaps scores or even hundreds of thousands. This somewhat contradicts other accounts of the campaign, which suggest that not more than ten thousand Burmese actually fought on the Japanese side. All accounts that have appeared agree that the mass of the population were indifferent or merely frightened, fleeing into the jungle when the bombers came but not intervening on either side. Only the wild tribes of the far north were reliably pro-British.

Both Mr. Wagg and Mr. Rodger have much to say about the exodus of the Indians, an appalling tragedy of which too little has been heard in this country. Between a hundred and two hundred thousand Indians, something over a third of the Indian population of the country, fled from Burma when the Japanese came, thousands perishing of hunger in the mountains between Burma and Assam, or at the hands of dacoits. For years past anti-Indian feeling had been rampant, not unjustifiably, because in many parts of Lower Burma the Indian moneylenders were gradually eating up the peasants. However, the long columns who set out on the thousand-mile march to India, unarmed and almost without food, were composed not of money-lenders but of wretched Dravidian coolies whose chief crime was their willingness to work for low wages. All the way they were robbed and murdered by gangs of dacoits and systematically overcharged by the villagers. Mr. Rodger gives a revealing little description of a mixed gang of criminals and policemen setting up a road-block and charging a toll from every refugee who passed. The Forest Department, the Assam tea-planters and various missionary organisations set up rest camps and distributed such food as they could lay hands on, but many of the refugees were caught by the monsoon and isolated in places where they were bound to starve to death. At the time it was widely rumoured that the Europeans had saved their own skins and left the Indians to their fate. Allowing for the fact that the person with money is the person who gets a seat in an aeroplane, this charge does not seem to have been true, and probably it was merely a by-product of the agitation against the Cripps mission. It would, of course, have been quite impossible to evacuate all the Indians in Burma by air. Altogether less than ten thousand people escaped by air, and many Europeans left Burma on foot; on the other hand some fifty thousand Indians were successfully repatriated by the British and Indian navies.

Both of these books give valuable eye-witness accounts of the effects of bombing on a helpless and uninterested population. Rangoon was almost emptied of inhabitants by a week or so of bombing which by our standards would hardly have seemed like bombing at all. There did not seem to have been much panic; the people saw that they could do nothing, and walked out. Most of the towns and villages of Burma are built of wood, and as this was the dry season the most terrible devastation was caused by fire bombs, Mandalay and other towns in Upper Burma being reduced to mere piles of ashes. This kind of thing is going to happen all over South Asia when the war gets into its stride at that end of the world. Meanwhile, Burma is under Japanese rule, and of its real condition we know next to nothing. Whoever is interested in this subject should look out for a little-known book, *What Happened in Burma*,[1] shortly to be published here, which begins where Mr. Wagg and Mr. Rodger leave off, and on the whole bears out what they say.

[Fee: £3.14s; 5.8.43]

1. Maung Thein Pe, *What Happened in Burma. The Frank Revelations of a Young Burmese Revolutionary Leader Who Has Recently Escaped from Burma to India*, published by Kitabistan Press, Allahabad, in April 1943 and reprinted in July 1943. The introduction, by Edgar Snow, is datelined Delhi, September 1942. The back cover says the author was from 1935 to 1939 'No. 1 on the Burma Police list of anti-British agitators. He was the Joint Secretary of the extreme nationalist party of which a section bargained with Japan. In 1936 he organised All Burma° Student Strikes and took part in 1938–39 mass movement of peasants and workers and was imprisoned.' He was also an author and journalist. His most famous book was said to be *Tetpongyi*, which satirised the Buddhist monks of Burma. The biographical note concludes, 'out of the clutches of the Japanese Gestapo, he is now residing in India.' Maung Thein Pe was twenty-seven in 1943. See Orwell's note to G. E. Harvey, 18 August 1943, *2240*, and 'As I Please,' 39, 25 August 1944, *2537*.

2237. Review of *The New Age* by Edward Hulton

The Observer, 15 August 1943

To know where to go and to know how to get there are two different mental processes, all too seldom combined in any one person. Political thinkers, in general, can be divided into two classes, the Utopian with his head in the clouds and the realist with his feet in the mud. Mr. Edward Hulton, in spite of the shrewdness that brought *Picture Post* into being at the exact moment when the potential demand for it had begun to exist, is nearer to the first class and more successful at pointing out desirable objectives than at surveying the actual political scene.

The new world that Mr. Hulton wants is, broadly speaking, the kind of world that every sensible man wants, but the comparative powerlessness of sensible men is something that he is inclined to ignore. Throughout his book called "THE NEW AGE" (George Allen and Unwin, 7s. 6d.), the phrases "we must," "we should," "the Government must," "the Government should," recur again and again, on every subject from foreign policy to town planning and from finance to educational reform, with the implied assumption that if "we" know what we want "we" shall get it. But there is also the working-class assumption that "they" (the higher-ups) will invariably prevent you from getting what you want, and though this is often over-pessimistic it contains much truth.

Mr. Hulton has not much use for the orthodox Socialist, and particularly for the Marxist doctrinaire. Now it is true that Marxism in the form in which it is usually preached makes a false estimate of the balance of forces, but it does keep sight of the fundamental truth that "where your treasure is, there will your heart be also." The social changes that Mr. Hulton desires would only entail a diminution of power and privilege for a few people, but those few people are not easily removable, and what is more, are not teachable. For as Marx rightly pointed out, the rich man will not only cling to his riches, but will construct philosophies to justify him in doing so.

But if Mr. Hulton has his blind spots, his boldness and generosity more than make up for them. For five years he has acted as a sort of catalyst on public opinion, and what he writes is nearly always stimulating, even when it is silly. He stands for a number of things which no society has yet succeeded in combining but which the ordinary thinking man in our age instinctively feels to be compatible. He stands for a world of plenty and a simple way of living, for a planned economy and individual freedom, for a European Federation and local autonomy, for democracy without uniformity, and for religion without dogma.

Though he is definitely to be classified as "left," he is a disbeliever in the class war, does not believe nationalisation to be the cure for everything, thinks the British ruling classes have their points, and is not notably anti-imperialist. The dinginess and out-of-dateness of contemporary England, its unenterprising business methods, its worship of stupidity, its ravaged countryside, its joylessness (Mr. Hulton is markedly anti-puritan) fill him with considerable fury, but he has a mystical belief in the destiny of his own country and is quite certain that Britain must be the paramount influence in western Europe after the war. In a slightly guarded way he is pro-Russian, and he is also—perhaps this is only a temporary phenomenon, arising out of recent events—anti-American.

Now this epitomises the outlook of some millions of youngish people who are well aware that the present evils of the world are largely unnecessary, and Mr. Hulton has done a great service, both here and in *Picture Post*, by acting as a sort of one-man Brains Trust. The best quality of his mind is that he is genuinely anti-totalitarian, and no respecter of orthodoxy of any kind. In his search for remedies he flits blithely to and fro between democracy, aristocracy, Socialism, currency reform, federalism, imperialism, consumers' co-operatives, compulsory labour service, Youth Movements, and even—tentatively—polygamy. And there is little doubt that with his eclectic approach he gets nearer to the truth than he could get by clinging to some obsolete "ism."

Against the Conservative he maintains that "sound finance" is nonsense, class privilege indefensible, and national sovereignty an anachronism. Against the Socialist he maintains that the class war is out of date, hedonism a danger, and pacifism a delusion. Above all, he insists on the need for common decency and an abandonment of the Machiavellianism practised by politicians and defended by intellectuals. As a statement of what the ordinary decent person under fifty *wants*, his book is adequate, and it is not even so shallow as its hurried slipshod writing makes it appear. It is merely that, like most Liberals, he underestimates the gulf between "what" and "how."

Perhaps, after all, Mr. Hulton could learn something from the doctrinaires whom he too lightly dismisses. At present there is a gap in his intellectual ladder. Commonsense and good will are not enough; there is also the problem of overcoming ill will and invincible ignorance. Mr Hulton might do us all a service if he would turn his optimistic and inquiring mind towards that problem.

[Fee: £5.5s; 9.8.43]

2238. To Oliver Bell

17 August 1943   07/ES/EB/JEL

Dear Bell,
Many thanks for your letter. I am sorry to hear about your accident. Do you think it will be possible for you to get in touch with Miss Duff and arrange about the music in time? The broadcast is on the 25th August and we must have all the details by the 21st. Could you let me know about this as otherwise I shall have to make other arrangements for that particular half hour.

Yours sincerely,
[Initialled] E.A.B
Eric Blair[1]

1. Orwell's secretary first typed 'George Orwell' below 'Yours sincerely'; that was erased and
'Eric Blair' typed in its place. Bell replied on 27 August saying that Lilian Duff had made
arrangements for the inclusion of the film music he required.

2239. To Bryan Brooke

18 August 1943   07/ES/EB

Dear Mr. Brooke,
Many thanks for the script which is just the kind of thing we wanted. I don't
think I would write in something simply in order to expand it as that always
gives an impression of padding. But I thought that where you made in
passing a mention of blood-groups it might be as well to insert a paragraph
explaining about the division of human blood into four different groups (or
however many it is) as we cannot assume that our audience would know this.
The date of your talk is Thursday September 9th at 11.15 a.m. so perhaps you
could come here not later than 10.45 that morning.

Yours sincerely,
[Initialled] E.A.B
(Eric Blair)

2240. To G. E. Harvey[1]

18 August 1943   Handwritten postcard

10a Mortimer Crescent NW. 6.

Many thanks for your interesting letter. "What Happened in Burma" (by Mg
Thein Pe, who used to be a leading light in the Nationalist movement) was
published by the KITABISTAN press, Allahabad. So far as I know there are at
present only 2 copies in this country, but I *hope* it is to be republished here as a
pamphlet. I am now trying to pull strings to bring that about.[2]

Geo. Orwell.

1. Godfrey Eric Harvey (1889–) served in the Indian Civil Service, 1912–35, for the first twenty
years in Burma, and was lecturer in Burmese at the University of Oxford, 1935–40. He was
the author of *A History of Burma* (1925; reissued 1969) and *British Rule in Burma 1824–1942*
(1946), in which he defended British policy in Burma. On 31 July 1935 he had written to
Orwell (as Richard Orwell) asking when they could meet; his excuse was that he had 'never
come across so necessary a book as *Burmese Days*, which represents exactly what so many of us
experienced yet nobody cared to describe.' It is not known whether or not they met. Nothing
in this postcard suggests they did.
2. It would seem that Orwell was unsuccessful. No English or U.S. edition has been traced
except for a typewritten reproduction found in a few American libraries prepared in the
United States by the International Secretariat of the Institute of Pacific Relations, 1944; copies
are marked, 'Not for publication.'

2241. Newsletter in Tamil, 18

19 August 1943

The English version was written by Eric Blair. No script has been traced.

2242. English Newsletter for[1] Indonesia, 7

20 August 1943

This was written and read by George Orwell. No script has been traced.

1. From this date on, 'for' is used, instead of 'to,' before 'Indonesia.'

2243. To T. S. Eliot

20 August 1943   Handwritten draft and typed versions
07/ES/EB/JEL

Dear Eliot,
Very many thanks for the talk which will do very well and covers the ground we wanted. I will ring up your secretary and find out a day convenient to you for recording. If you come here half an hour before the actual recording time that would be all right for rehearsal, I should say. It is about the right length.

Yours sincerely,
[Initialled] E. A. B
(George Orwell)

2244. To L. P. Garrod

20 August 1943   Handwritten draft and typed versions[1]
07/ES/EB/JEL

Dear Professor Garrod,
It does not make much difference whether the talk is done live or recorded. I merely suggested a recording in case the date did not suit you. Other things being equal we prefer a live talk.

I am sorry you were told the wrong time. The exact time of the broadcast is 11.15 a.m. If you could be here by 10.30 a.m. this would give us enough time for rehearsal.

Yours truly,
[Initialled] E.A.B
(Eric Blair)

1. These versions differ slightly. The draft, on the verso of Garrod's letter to Orwell of 17

August and dated 19 August, has, after 'the wrong time,' an additional sentence: 'We had not allowed for the change back to single summer time'; see postcard to Garrod, 12 August 1943, *2234, n. 1.*

2245. On Orwell's behalf to Desmond Hawkins
21 August 1943   07/ES/EB/JEL

Dear Desmond,
I am enclosing another batch of scripts for the next Backward Glance programme to be broadcast on Wednesday, September 1st. I shall be glad if you will include an extract from the featurised short story "Crainquebille" broadcast on the 11th August.

Yours,
[Not signed/initialled]
for George Orwell

2246. To B. H. Alexander, Copyright Department
24 August 1943   Original   EB/JEL

COPYRIGHT FOR "THE FOX" BY IGNAZIO SILONE

On Wednesday, 8th September we intend to broadcast a featurised adaptation of the short story "The Fox" by Ignazio Silone which is published in Penguin New Writing, No. 2. This programme will go on the air in the Purple Network, Eastern Service, between 1000–1030 GMT.
    Would you kindly cover the copyright for this story.

[Signed] Eric Blair
(Eric Blair)

2247. To Rayner Heppenstall
24 August 1943   Handwritten on BBC letterhead

Dear Rayner,
Thanks for yours. I hope your new post isn't too bloody. I'll try & fit in a talk for you in our next literary lot, but that will be 6 weeks or more from now— schedule is full up till then.
    I wonder would you feel equal to featurising a story? We do that now about once in 3 weeks. I featurised the first 2 myself, choosing Anatole France's "Crainquebille" & Ignazio Silone's "The Fox" (these are ½ hour programmes). I am probably going to hand the job of featurising future ones over to Lionel Fielden, but he won't necessarily do it every time. The chief difficulty is picking suitable stories, as they must be *a*. approximately right length, *b*. have a strong plot, *c*. not too many characters & *d*. not be too local,

as these are for India. Have you any ideas? I could send you a specimen script & no doubt you could improve on my technique of featurisation.

Re. cynicism, you'd be cynical yourself if you were in this job. However I am definitely leaving it probably in about 3 months. Then by some time in 1944 I might be near-human again & able to write something serious. At present I'm just an orange that's been trodden on by a very dirty boot.

Yours
Eric

2248. To C. E. M. Joad

c. 24 August 1943   Original postcard

I have arranged a recording for your next talk on Monday, 30th August at 4.0 p.m. at 200 Oxford Street. I hope this will be convenient for you.[1]

[Signed] Geo. Orwell
(George Orwell)

1. Joad annotated this card to say that the time was convenient but that because he would be away from London until Friday, the 27th, he could not have his script typed until then. He would not, therefore, be able to deliver the script until Monday, the 30th. This annotation was initialled 'CEMJ,' and the original card was returned to Orwell.

2249. BBC Talks Booking Form, 25.8.43

Capt. the Hon. Quintin Hogg, M.P.: 'The Debate Continues'; 'talk of approx. 7 mins'; recorded 28.8.43; broadcast 4.9.43; fee £6.6s. Signed: Z. A. Bokhari.

2250. BBC Talks Booking Form, 25.8.43

Stephen Spender: 'Modern Men of Letters,' 4, E. M. Forster; recording not yet fixed; broadcast 19.9.43; fee £10.10s. Signed: Z. A. Bokhari.

2251. Newsletter in Tamil, 19

26 August 1943

The English version was written by Eric Blair. No script has been traced. Orwell was on holiday from Thursday, 3 September, to Sunday, 20 September, 1943. The English version of the Newsletter in Tamil for 2 September was written by M. Phatak, who worked on the Malayan Newsletters, and for 9 and 16 September by John Morris, who later replaced Rushbrook Williams as Eastern Service Director. The translator, J. D. S. Paul, and the switch censor, the Reverend G. Matthews, remained the same. Since Orwell wrote the

Newsletter for Indonesia transmitted on 3 September (read by John Morris), it is surprising that he did not prepare the English version of the Tamil Newsletter for 2 September.

2252. To Desmond Hawkins

26 August 1943   07/ES/EB/JEL

Dear Desmond,

I suggest the following might be suitable for the September anniversary:

General Wolfe (died at Quebec—13.9.1759)

Buffon (naturalist) (born—7.9.1707)

Zola (died 29.9.1902)

The Nuremburg Laws (passed—15.9.1935)

G. D. Fahrenheit (thermometers) (died 16.9.1736)

Rudolf Diesel (diesel engines) (died 30.9.1913)

Torquemada (died 16.9.1498)

Could you let me know fairly soon which one you fix on.

Yours sincerely,

[Initialled] E.A.B

(George Orwell)

2253. BBC Talks Booking Form, 26.8.43

Oliver Bell: Monthly Film Talk; broadcast 22.9.43; fee £10.10s. Signed: Z. A. Bokhari.

2254. News Commentary in English for Indonesia, 8

27 August 1943

This was written and read by George Orwell. No script has been traced.[1]

1. On the date of this broadcast, Gentry records in his diary, 'Forecast that we shall shortly land 2 million men on N. France or Low Countries. Men & transports massed on N. African coast for attack on Mediterranean coast of Europe.' No indication is given of the source of this information. The second sentence may refer to Operation Avalanche, the landing of the main invasion force under U.S. General Mark Clark on 9 September at Salerno, Italy, following a diversionary attack by the British Eighth Army on 3 September on the Calabrian coast. The first sentence could well have come from one of the disinformation campaigns to mislead the Germans about where Allied invasion forces would land in Europe.

2255. To Ivor Brown

31 August 1943   Typewritten

On 28 August, Ivor Brown, on behalf of *The Observer*, wrote to Orwell saying he had heard he was leaving the BBC and he wondered whether he would like to go to Algiers and Sicily, 'accredited' by the War Office, though not as 'a regular war correspondent.' It might mean writing for other newspapers as well as *The Observer*, in order to share costs, 'but primarily you would be "The Observer" man.' See Orwell's letter to L. F. Rushbrook Williams, 24 September 1943, *2283* and *n. 2*.

10a Mortimer Crescent   London NW 6

Dear Mr Brown,
Many thanks for your letter. I would, of course, like very greatly to go to North Africa for you if it can be arranged. If it *can*, however, I wonder if it would be possible to have some idea of the date. I have not put in my formal resignation to the BBC but have informed my immediate chiefs that I intend to leave them, and when resigning formally I am supposed to give 2 months' notice. This however would not be insisted on so long as I could give at any rate a few weeks° notice. Meanwhile I have arranged to go on my annual holiday (for a fortnight) at the end of this week. Of course I would throw this up if the opportunity of going to North Africa occurred immediately, but otherwise I am not anxious to miss my holiday as I have not had one for 14 months and am rather in need of one. So I should be greatly obliged if you could give me some idea of when this scheme is likely to materialise, supposing that it does so.

Yours sincerely
Geo. Orwell

2256. To Samuel Runganadhan

31 August 1943   07/ES/EB/JEL

Dear Sir Samuel,
I understand that there is some doubt as to whether you will continue to do the monthly talks to India, but that you will at any rate be doing the one on this coming Tuesday, that is to say September 7th. We intend to put in during this period a short message of thanks to Ceylon which was recorded by a W.A.A.F.[1] in reply to a gift made by the inhabitants of Ceylon to one of the R.A.F. funds. This will come immediately after your talk and with announcements will take about 4 minutes 15 seconds, so your talk should take not more than nine minutes or twelve hundred words.

Yours truly,
[Initialled] E.A.B
(Eric Blair)

1. A member of the Women's Auxiliary Air Force.

2257. Gandhi in Mayfair. Review of *Beggar My Neighbour* by Lionel Fielden

Horizon, September 1943

This review was reprinted in *Partisan Review*, Winter 1944, with the same heading. It follows the styling of the original unusually closely, but there are three verbal variants. These may have been introduced by *Partisan Review*, although in that case more styling variation would be expected. The changes may thus be Orwell's. They have been incorporated here and noted.

If you compare commercial advertising with political propaganda, one thing that strikes you is its relative intellectual honesty. The advertiser at least knows what he is aiming at—that is, money—whereas the propagandist, when he is not a lifeless hack, is often a neurotic working off some private grudge and actually desirous of the exact opposite of the thing he advocates. The ostensible purpose of Mr. Fielden's book is to further the cause of Indian independence. It will not have that effect, and I do not see much reason for thinking that he himself wishes for anything of the kind. For if someone is genuinely working for Indian independence, what is he likely to do? Obviously he will start by deciding what forces are potentially on his side, and then, as cold-bloodedly as any toothpaste advertiser, he will think out the best method of appealing to them. This is not Mr. Fielden's manner of approach. A number of motives are discernible in his book, but the immediately obvious one is a desire to work off various quarrels with the Indian Government, All-India Radio and various sections of the British Press. He does indeed marshal a number of facts about India, and towards the end he even produces a couple of pages of constructive suggestions, but for the most part his book is simply a nagging, irrelevant attack on British rule, mixed up with tourist-like gush about the superiority of Indian civilization. On the fly-leaf, just to induce that matey atmosphere which all propagandists aim at, he signs his dedicatory letter 'among the European barbarians', and then a few pages later introduces an imaginary Indian who denounces Western civilization with all the shrillness of a spinster of thirty-nine denouncing the male sex:

'. . . an Indian who is intensely proud of his own traditions, and regards Europeans as barbarians who are continually fighting, who use force to dominate other peaceful peoples, who think chiefly in terms of big business, whisky, and bridge; as people of comparatively recent growth, who, while they put an exaggerated value on plumbing, have managed to spread tuberculosis and venereal disease all over the world . . . he will say that to sit in the water in which you have washed, instead of bathing yourself in running water, is not clean, but dirty and disgusting; he will show, and I shall agree with him absolutely, that the English are a dirty and even a smelly nation compared with the Indians; he will assert, and I am not at all sure that he is wrong, that the use of half-washed forks, spoons and knives by different people for food is revoltingly barbaric when compared with the exquisite manipulation of food by Indian fingers; he will be confident that the Indian room, with its bare walls and beautiful carpets, is infinitely superior to the European clutter of uncomfortable chairs and tables', etc. etc. etc.

The whole book is written in this vein, more or less. The same nagging, hysterical note crops up every few pages, and where a comparison can be dragged in it is dragged in, the upshot always being that the East is Good and the West is Bad. Now before stopping to inquire what service this kind of thing really does to the cause of Indian freedom, it is worth trying an experiment. Let me rewrite this passage as it might be uttered by an Englishman speaking up for his own civilization as shrilly as Mr. Fielden's Indian. It is important to notice that what he says is not more dishonest or more irrelevant than what I have quoted above:

'. . . an Englishman who is intensely proud of his own traditions, and regards Indians as an unmanly race who gesticulate like monkeys, are cruel to women and talk incessantly about money; as a people who take it upon themselves[1] to despise Western science and hence[2] are rotten with malaria and hookworm . . . he will say that in a hot climate washing in running water has its points, but that in cold climates all Orientals either wash as we do or as in the case of many Indian hill tribes—not at all; he will show, and I shall agree with him absolutely, that no Western European can walk through an Indian village without wishing that his smell organs had been removed beforehand; he will assert, and I am not at all sure that he is wrong, that eating with your fingers is a barbarous habit since it cannot be done without making disgusting noises; he will be confident that the English room, with its comfortable armchairs and friendly bookshelves, is infinitely superior to the bare Indian interior where the mere effort of sitting with no support to your back makes for vacuity of mind', etc. etc. etc.

Two points emerge here. To begin with, no English person would now write like that. No doubt many people think such thoughts, and even utter them behind closed doors, but to find anything of the kind in print you would have to go back ten years or so. Secondly, it is worth asking, what would be the effect of this passage on an Indian who happened to take it seriously? He would be offended, and very rightly. Well then, isn't it just possible that passages like the one I quoted from Mr. Fielden might have the same effect on a British reader? No one likes hearing his own habits and customs abused. This is not a trivial consideration, because at this moment books about India have, or could have, a special importance. There is no political solution in sight, the Indians cannot win their freedom and the British Government will not give it, and all one can for the moment do is to push public opinion in this country and America in the right direction. But that will not be done by any propaganda that is merely anti-European. A year ago, soon after the Cripps mission had failed, I saw a well-known Indian nationalist address a small meeting at which he was to explain why the Cripps offer had been refused. It was a valuable opportunity, because there were present a number of American newspaper correspondents who, if handled tactfully, might cable to America a sympathetic account of the Congress Party's case. They had come there with fairly open minds. Within about ten minutes the Indian had converted all of them into ardent supporters of the British Government, because instead of sticking to his subject he launched into an anti-British tirade quite obviously founded on spite and inferiority complex. That is just the mistake that a toothpaste advertiser would not make. But then the toothpaste advertiser is trying to sell toothpaste and not to get his own back on that Blimp who turned him out of a first-class carriage fifteen years ago.

However, Mr. Fielden's book raises wider issues than the immediate political problem. He upholds the East against the West on the ground that the East is religious, artistic and indifferent to 'progress', while the West is materialistic, scientific, vulgar and warlike. The great crime of Britain is to have forced industrialization on India. (Actually, the real crime of Britain during the last thirty years has been to do the opposite.) The West looks on work as an end in itself, but at the same time is obsessed with a 'high standard of living' (it is worth noticing that Mr. Fielden is anti-Socialist, Russophobe and somewhat contemptuous of the English working class), while India wants only to live in ancestral simplicity in a world freed from the machine. India must be independent, and at the same time must be de-industrialized. It is also suggested a number of times, though not in very clear terms, that India ought to be neutral in the present war. Needless to say, Mr. Fielden's hero is Gandhi, about whose financial background he says nothing. 'I have a notion that the legend of Gandhi may yet be a flaming inspiration to the millions of the East, and perhaps to those of the West. But it is, for the time being, the East which provides the fruitful soil, because the East has not yet fallen prone before the Golden Calf. And it may be for the East, once again, to show mankind that human happiness does not depend on that particular form of worship, and that the conquest of materialism is also the conquest of war.' Gandhi makes many appearances in the book, playing rather the same part as 'Frank' in the literature of the Buchmanites.

Now, I do not know whether or not Gandhi will be a 'flaming inspiration' in years to come. When one thinks of the creatures who *are* venerated by humanity it does not seem particularly unlikely. But the statement that India 'ought' to be independent, *and* de-industrialized, *and* neutral in the present war, is an absurdity. If one forgets the details of the political struggle and looks at the strategic realities, one sees two facts which are in seeming conflict. The first is that whatever the 'ought' of the question may be, India is very unlikely ever to be independent in the sense in which Britain or Germany is now independent. The second is that India's *desire* for independence is a reality and cannot be talked out of existence.

In a world in which national sovereignty exists, India cannot be a sovereign State, because she is unable to defend herself. And the more she is the cow and spinning-wheel paradise imagined by Mr. Fielden, the more this is true. What is now called independence means the power to manufacture aeroplanes in large numbers. Already there are only five genuinely independent States in the world, and if present trends continue there will in the end be only three. On a long-term view it is clear that India has little chance in a world of power politics, while on a short-term view it is clear that the necessary first step towards Indian freedom is an Allied victory. Even that would only be a short and uncertain step, but the alternatives must lead to India's continued subjection. If we are defeated, Japan or Germany takes over India and that is the end of the story. If there is a compromise peace (Mr. Fielden seems to hint at times that this is desirable), India's chances are no better, because in such circumstances we should inevitably cling to any territories we had captured or not lost. A compromise peace is always a peace of 'grab what you can'. Mr. Fielden brings forward his imaginary Indian to suggest that if India were neutral Japan might leave her alone; I doubt whether any responsible Indian nationalist has said anything quite so stupid as that. The other idea, more popular in Left-wing circles, that India could defend herself better on her own than with our help, is a sentimentality. If the Indians were militarily superior to ourselves they would have driven us out long ago. The much-quoted example of China is very misleading here. India is a far easier country to conquer than China, if only because of its better communications, and in any case Chinese resistance depends on help from the highly-industrialized states and would collapse without it. One must conclude that for the next few years India's destiny is linked with that of Britain and the U.S.A. It might be different if the Russians could get their hands free in the West or if China were a great military power; but that again implies a complete defeat of the Axis, and points away from the neutrality which Mr. Fielden seems to think desirable. The idea put forward by Gandhi himself, that if the Japanese came they could be dealt with by sabotage and 'non-co-operation', is a delusion, nor does Gandhi show any very strong signs of believing in it. Those methods have never seriously embarrassed the British and would make no impression on the Japanese. After all, where is the Korean Gandhi?

But against this is the *fact* of Indian nationalism, which is not to be exorcised by the humbug of White Papers or by a few phrases out of Marx. And it is nationalism of an emotional, romantic, even chauvinistic kind. Phrases like 'the sacred soil of the Motherland', which now seem merely ludicrous in Britain, come naturally enough to an Indian intellectual. When the Japanese appeared to be on the point of invading India, Nehru actually used the phrase 'Who dies if India live?'[4] So the wheel comes full circle and the Indian rebel quotes Kipling. And nationalism at this level works indirectly in favour of Fascism. Extremely few Indians are at all attracted by the idea of a federated world, the only kind of world in which India could actually be free. Even those who pay lip-service to federalism usually want only an Eastern federation, thought of as a military alliance against the West. The idea of the class struggle has little appeal anywhere in Asia, nor do Russia and China evoke much loyalty in India. As for the Nazi domination of Europe, only a handful of Indians are able to see that it affects their own destiny in any way. In some of the smaller Asiatic countries the 'my country right or wrong' nationalists were exactly the ones who went over to the Japanese—a step which may not have been wholly due to ignorance.

But here there arises a point which Mr. Fielden hardly touches on, and that is: we don't know to what extent Asiatic nationalism is simply the product of our own oppression. For a century all the major Oriental nations except Japan have been more or less in subjection, and the hysteria and shortsightedness of the various nationalist movements may be the result simply of that. To realize that national sovereignty is the enemy of national freedom may be a great deal easier when you are not being ruled by foreigners. It is not certain that this is so, since the most nationalist of the Oriental nations, Japan, is also the one that has never been conquered, but at least one can say that if the solution is not along these lines, then there *is* no solution. Either power politics must yield to common decency, or the world must go spiralling down into a nightmare of which we can already catch some dim glimpses. And the necessary first step, before we can make our talk about world federation sound even credible, is that Britain shall get off India's back. This is the only large scale decent action that is possible in the world at this moment. The immediate preliminaries would be: abolish the Viceroyalty and the India Office, release the Congress prisoners, and declare India formally independent. The rest is detail.*

But how are we to bring any such thing about? If it is done at this time, it can only be a voluntary act. Indian independence has no asset except public opinion in Britain and America, which is only a potential asset. Japan, Germany and the British Government are all on the other side, and India's possible friends, China and the U.S.S.R., are fighting for their lives and have little bargaining power. There remain the peoples of Britain and America, who are in a position to put pressure on their own Governments if they see a reason for doing so. At the time of the Cripps mission, for instance, it would have been quite easy for public opinion in this country to force the Government into making a proper offer, and similar opportunities may recur. Mr. Fielden, by the way, does his best to throw doubt on Cripps' personal honesty, and also lets it appear that the Congress Working Committee were unanimously against accepting the Cripps proposals, which was not the case. In fact, Cripps extorted the best terms he could get from the Government; to get better ones he would have had to have public opinion actively and intelligently behind him. Therefore the first job is—win over the ordinary people of this country. Make them see that India matters, and that India has been shamefully treated and deserves restitution. But you are not going to do that by insulting them. Indians, on the whole, grasp this better than their English apologists. After all, what is the probable effect of a book which irrelevantly abuses every English institution, rapturises over the 'wisdom of the East' like an American schoolmarm on a conducted tour, and mixes up pleas for Indian freedom with pleas for surrender to Hitler? At best it can only convert the converted, and it may de-convert a few of those. The net effect must be to strengthen British imperialism, though its motives are probably more complex than this may seem to imply.

On the surface, Mr. Fielden's book is primarily a plea for 'spirituality' as against 'materialism'. On the one hand an uncritical reverence for everything Oriental; on the other a hatred of the West generally, and of Britain in particular, hatred of science and the machine, suspicion of Russia, contempt

---

* Of course the necessary corollary would be a military alliance for the duration of the war. But it is not likely that there would be any difficulty in securing this. Extremely few Indians really want to be ruled by Japan or Germany [Orwell's footnote].

for the working-class conception of Socialism. The whole adds up to Parlour Anarchism—a plea for the simple life, based on dividends. Rejection of the machine is, of course, always founded on tacit acceptance of the machine, a fact symbolised by Gandhi as he plays with his spinning-wheel in the mansion of some cotton millionaire. But Gandhi also comes into the picture in another way. It is noticeable that both Gandhi and Mr. Fielden have an exceedingly equivocal attitude towards the present war. Although variously credited in this country with being a 'pure' pacifist and a Japanese agent, Gandhi has, in fact, made so many conflicting pronouncements on the war that it is difficult to keep track of them. At one moment his 'moral support' is with the Allies, at another it is withdrawn, at one moment he thinks it best to come to terms with the Japanese, at another he wishes to oppose them by non-violent means—at the cost, he thinks, of several million lives—at another he urges Britain to give battle in the west and leave India to be invaded, at another he 'has no wish to harm the Allied cause' and declares that he does not want the Allied troops to leave India. Mr. Fielden's views on the war are less complicated, but equally ambiguous. In no place does he state whether or not he wishes the Axis to be defeated. Over and over again he urges that an allied victory can lead to no possible good result, but at the same time he disclaims 'defeatism' and even argues that Indian neutrality would be useful to us in a *military* sense, i.e. that we could fight better if India were not a liability. Now, if this means anything, it means that he wants a compromise, a negotiated peace; and though he fails to say so, I do not doubt that that is what he does want. But curiously enough, this is the *imperialist* solution. The appeasers have always wanted neither defeat nor victory but a compromise with the other imperialist powers; and they too have known how to use the manifest folly of war as an argument.

For years past the more intelligent imperialists have been in favour of compromising with the Fascists, even if they had to give away a good deal in order to do so, because they have seen that only thus could imperialism be salvaged. Some of them are not afraid to hint this fairly broadly even now. If we carry the war to a destructive conclusion, the British Empire will either be lost, or democratised, or pawned to America. On the other hand it could and probably would survive in something like its present form if there were other sated imperialist powers which had an interest in preserving the existing world system. If we came to an understanding with Germany and Japan we might diminish our possessions (even that isn't certain: it is a little-noticed fact that *in territory* Britain and the U.S.A. have gained more than they have lost in this war), but we should at least be confirmed in what we had already. The world would be split up between three or four great imperial powers who, for the time being, would have no motive for quarrelling. Germany would be there to neutralize Russia, Japan would be there to prevent the development of China. Given such a world system, India could be kept in subjection almost indefinitely. And more than this, it is doubtful whether a compromise peace *could* follow any other lines. So it would seem that Parlour Anarchism is something very innocuous after all. Objectively it only demands what the worst of the appeasers want, subjectively it is of a kind to irritate the possible friends of India in this country. And does not this bear a sort of resemblance to the career of Gandhi, who has alienated the British public by his extremism and aided the British Government by his moderation? Impossibilism and reaction are usually in alliance, though not, of course, conscious alliance.

Hypocrisy is a very rare thing, true villainy is perhaps [as] difficult as virtue. We live in a lunatic world in which opposites are constantly changing into one another, in which pacifists find themselves worshipping Hitler, Socialists become nationalists, patriots become quislings, Buddhists pray for the success of the Japanese army, and the Stock Market takes an upward turn when the Russians stage an offensive. But though these people's motives are often obvious enough when seen from the outside, they are not obvious to themselves. The scenes imagined by Marxists, in which wicked rich men sit in little secret rooms and hatch schemes for robbing the workers, don't happen in real life. The robbery takes place, but it is committed by sleepwalkers. Now, one of the finest weapons that the rich have ever evolved for use against the poor is 'spirituality'. If you can induce the working-man to believe that his desire for a decent standard of living is 'materialism', you have got him where you want him. Also, if you can induce the Indian to remain 'spiritual' instead of taking up with vulgar things like trade unions, you can ensure that he will always remain a coolie. Mr. Fielden is indignant with the 'materialism' of the Western working class, whom he accuses of being even worse in this respect than the rich and of wanting not only radios but even motor-cars and fur coats. The obvious answer is that these sentiments don't come well from someone who is in a comfortable and privileged position himself. But that is only an answer, not a diagnosis, for the problem of the disaffected intelligentsia would be hardly a problem at all if ordinary dishonesty were involved.

In the last twenty years Western civilization has given the intellectual security without responsibility, and in England, in particular, it has educated him in scepticism while anchoring him almost immovably in the privileged class. He has been in the position of a young man living on an allowance from a father whom he hates. The result is a deep feeling of guilt and resentment, not combined with any genuine desire to escape. But some psychological escape, some form of self-justification there must be, and one of the most satisfactory is transferred nationalism. During the nineteen-thirties the normal transference was to Soviet Russia, but there are other alternatives, and it is noticeable that pacifism and Anarchism, rather than Stalinism, are now gaining ground among the young. These creeds have the advantage that they aim at the impossible and therefore in effect demand very little. If you throw in a touch of Oriental mysticism and Buchmanite raptures over Gandhi, you have everything that a disaffected intellectual needs. The life of an English gentleman and the moral attitude[3] of a saint can be enjoyed simultaneously. By merely transferring your allegiance from England to India (it used to be Russia), you can indulge to the full in all the chauvinistic sentiments which would be totally impossible if you recognized them for what they were. In the name of pacifism you can compromise with Hitler, and in the name of 'spirituality' you can keep your money. It is no accident that those who wish for an inconclusive ending to the war tend to extol the East as against the West. The actual facts don't matter very much. The fact that the Eastern nations have shown themselves at least as warlike and bloodthirsty as the Western ones, that so far from rejecting industrialism, the East is adopting it as swiftly as it can—this is irrelevant, since what is wanted is the mythos of the peaceful, religious and patriarchal East to set against the greedy and materialistic West. As soon as you have 'rejected' industrialism, and hence Socialism, you are in that strange no man's land where the Fascist and the pacifist join forces. There is indeed a sort of apocalyptic truth in the statement of the German radio that the teachings of Hitler and Gandhi are the same. One realizes this when one sees Middleton Murry praising the Japanese invasion of China and Gerald Heard proposing to institute the Hindu caste system in Europe at the same time as the Hindus themselves are abandoning it. We shall be hearing a lot about the superiority of Eastern civilization in the next few years. Meanwhile this is a mischievous book, which will be acclaimed in the Left-wing Press and welcomed for quite different reasons by the more intelligent Right.

[Fee: £6.6s; 5.7.1943]

1. themselves] them   Horizon
2. hence] consequently   Horizon
3. attitude] attitudes   Horizon
4. 'Who stands if Freedom fall?/Who dies if England live?' ('For All We Have and Are,' 1914).

2258. Toothpaste in Bloomsbury
November 1943

Lionel Fielden wrote a long reply, which was published in *Horizon*.

If you compare rape with seduction, one thing that strikes you is its relative intellectual honesty. The raper at least knows what he is aiming at—that is, satisfaction—whereas the seducer, when he is not an impotent trifler, is often a neurotic working off a Freudian grudge against his grandmother. This proposition seems not less nonsensical than Mr. Orwell's glorification of the 'intellectual honesty' of commercial advertising compared with the (according to him) lifelessness or neurosis or grudgery of his own adopted profession, political propaganda. All propaganda, commercial or political, is biased: it gives one side of the picture, and therefore not the whole truth. To praise (as Mr. Orwell does) the 'honesty' of the toothpaste advertiser because he 'cold-bloodedly' uses the most effective means to his one end, money, and to condemn the political propagandist because (again according to Mr. Orwell) 'when he is not a lifeless hack, he is often a neurotic working off a private grudge' seems, apart from rather wild generalizing, to show a confusion of ideas between what is right and what is expedient. Ruthless money-grubbing, however efficient, is not more 'intellectually honest' than non-money-grubbing conviction, however personal: and you don't, at any rate in the long run, 'sell' political ideas by methods successfully employed for toothpaste. The argument with which Mr. Orwell crowns his dialectical house of cards is that *Beggar My Neighbour* fails to 'sell' Indian freedom to its potential buyers, the British public, because it contains a passage which may offend them. To this there are three replies, technical, factual and ethical. Technically, shocks and even insults may be first-rate advertising: witness body-odour, halitosis, and queries on every bus as to whether you have cleaned your teeth. Factually, with the exception of Mr. Orwell I have not so far found among my English audiences or readers a single soul who was 'offended' by comparisons between the Indian way of life and ours: on the contrary, such details never fail to arouse great interest. Ethically, while it may be commercially inexpedient to reveal the ingredients of a toothpaste, it is politically wise and even necessary to reveal the feelings of a subject race. And the feelings of a subject race are necessarily more sensitive than those of a dominating one. The wealthy landlord can afford to be amused at Socialist gibes: if the gibe is the other way round, there is an uproar. When Mr. Orwell re-writes the passage in which I compared Indian ways favourably with English ones, and makes it vice-versa (adding that Englishmen, although nowadays they don't write such things, still think them), his words will undoubtedly offend Indians in a way that mine could never offend Englishmen. Cats looking at kings are not kings looking at cats.

Mr. Orwell has fired a great number of arrows at me, and he is a skilful shot. I ought by rights to be bleeding as tragically as any St. Sebastian. Actually, the arrows give me a pleasing—here Mr. Orwell would say masochistic—glow. That is partly because I am glad that my book should be noticed at such length by so brilliant a writer in such an admirable publication: partly because so violent a protest does some honour to my arguments. I suspect that Mr Orwell, who agrees exactly, and says so, with my conclusions about India, hates my methods of approach to those conclusions and is infuriated because he cannot find better ones: at least, that is how his argument strikes me. And it is worth considering this point, if only because Mr. Orwell, occupying a position in the Indian section of the B.B.C., is directly concerned with methods of approach. I should dearly like to wean him from his belief in the intellectual honesty of toothpaste. But before making this attempt, I must try to remove the poison from some at least of his many arrows.

I am, it seems, Russophobe, anti-Socialist, and contemptuous of the 'working-class conception of Socialism': I am 'uncritically reverent' of everything Oriental: I do not want Indian independence: I desire to work off quarrels with All-India Radio, the Government of India, and the British Press: not only do I want a negotiated peace, but I plead for 'surrender to Hitler': I am in a 'comfortable and privileged position': and I am a 'parlour Anarchist', whatever that may be. It is a formidable indictment. Russophobe. I went to Russia nine years ago because I was fascinated by the Soviet experiment: I had a whale of a time, was treated with the greatest hospitality and kindness, and so fell in love with the beauty and exhilaration of Moscow that for two pins I'd have chucked my Indian assignment in order to stay there. The two pins were withheld partly because, while admiring the Kremlin, I was near as a toucher annihilated by a string of black-windowed cars, issuing from the great gate at forty miles an hour to the accompaniment of a red light and a clanging bell, and containing, so I understood, Mr. Stalin and others. If I found some things in Russia repellent and some comic, I also found quite as many charming and intelligent people as elsewhere. Anti-Socialist? As far as I know, the 'working-class conception of Socialism' ranges from extreme Conservatism down to a desire to grab any property in sight: between lie infinite gradations. My conception of Socialism is something which gives as much importance to the Indian coolie starving in Calcutta as to the Beveridge plan: a working-class of one country which lives on the exploitation of the working-class of another is doing the same thing as the capitalist one step above. Uncritically reverent of everything Oriental: am I? I have said in my book that I hold no brief for Indians, that many of them treated me abominably, that India has her full share of rogues and robbers, and that she will not be happy in a moment because she is free. But Mr. Orwell is partly right, because he has not read my book carefully. I wrote in it that it was a biased book, and so it is. In writing *Beggar My Neighbour* I did my best to get inside the skin of an Indian and to write, though still as an Englishman, what he might feel. I may have done it badly; I still feel that it is something that needs doing. I will gladly confess to Mr. Orwell that, personally, I have always disliked, and felt uncomfortable in, India and the Orient: that does not prevent me from thinking that an Indian has a perfect right to revere Oriental ways and habits, and that those may be as good as, even better than, our own. Do I desire to 'work off quarrels'? Perhaps to some extent we all do. I had the privilege of building and naming A.I.R.; its personnel are, I hope, my friends—at least I am theirs; the feeling I have for it, as far as I can judge, is one of affectionate interest. I certainly fought with the Government of India for every penny I spent and every inch of progress we made: I think (as does apparently Mr. Orwell) that it would be better swept away in favour of a National Government: I don't think I have any quarrel with it—after all, it gave me a superb chit, as well as the C.I.E., when I left it. As for the British Press, I have a quarrel with those sections of it which persistently ignore or twist the Indian problem, thus furthering ignorance and misunderstanding: but perhaps it isn't their fault: in the logic of the toothpaste-advertiser, India isn't 'news'.

These are unimportant, because personal, arrows. But the questions of negotiated peace and privileged position, mixed up with parlour anarchy and Mr. Orwell's pet obsession, the intellectual unconsciously or mischievously playing into the hands of the imperialist—these raise wider issues. In discussing whether Gandhi will be 'an inspiration', Mr. Orwell uses a striking phrase. 'When one thinks of the creatures who *are* venerated by humanity it does not seem particularly unlikely.' Words are elastic, and I may mistake Mr. Orwell's intention. But his use of the word 'creatures' suggests that humanity's veneration is wrongly directed, and the word 'veneration' usually attaches to men of ideas—Christ, Buddha, Socrates, Shakespeare, whom you will. If he considers that humanity's veneration has been mistaken in the past, as it will be mistaken in the case of Gandhi, I do not know whom he would wish us to venerate: perhaps none, or maybe the toothpaste advertiser. But the great adventure of humanity, greater than any war, is the adventure of ideas: intelligent men and women the world over have been and will be preoccupied above all by the search for a better society and a better way of life. We can hardly say that we have discovered it. And those who contribute ideas whose fundamental goodness can be recognized, even though the ideas may seem impossible to reconcile with society as we know it, will be venerated. We recognize the essential rightness of the Sermon on the Mount, or, if you like, the Ten Commandments: we know well-enough that if we put them into practice, if we do not covet, if we are meek, if we truly love our neighbour, we make a perfect society. It is true that neither Eastern nor Western man has been able to do so: it is also true that this type of thinking has mainly come *to* the West *from* the East. Mr. Orwell and others of his persuasion are at pains to prove that the East is as bad as the West, and that to extol the East is an infallible sign of Fascism and pacificism. It is as easy in wartime to stick these damaging labels on to anyone you don't like, as to smear a Jew's robe with yellow. The East is, at the moment, a convenient illustration, because over a fairly long period of history the best and biggest wars have been conducted by Europeans, inside or outside Europe: tomorrow the reverse may be the case. The mythos, as Mr. Orwell calls it, is not of the East because it is the East, but of a set of challenging ideas, embraced and rejected by humanity throughout history, of which Gandhi happens to be (as I think at least) the most sincere exponent in our time.

Those ideas will not be dispelled by any number of Orwells. Equally, any number of Fieldens may believe in them but fail to practise them. That I am in a comfortable and privileged position is Mr. Orwell's sharpest arrow: I grant the wound. Detachment from possession is, I am convinced, the best, possibly the only, way for humanity to avoid war: I suspect that it may also be the key to the most satisfactory way of living. But I was brought up to like possessions, and I like them. Must I, even if on the wrong side of the camel's eye, remain dumb? I may get through it some day. Meanwhile I admire Gandhi, not in the least because he is Indian but because he is a human being who has made himself a world figure without force or weapons, and is indifferent to possessions and comfort and even life itself. And if I am asked whether I want a negotiated peace, I cannot do better than to quote the penultimate paragraph of the Congress Resolution of 1939:

'The working Committee wishes to declare that the Indian people have no quarrel with the Japanese people, or the German people, or any other people, but they have a deep-rooted quarrel with the systems which deny freedom and are based on violence and aggression. They do not look forward to the victory of one people over another, or to a dictated peace, but to a victory of real democracy for all people in all countries, when the world is freed from the nightmare of violence and imperialist oppression.'

That is an expression of something which most decent men feel, more or less, according to their circumstances and associations and the amount of propaganda that they swallow. Democracy, if it is to be any good at all, must be world-wide: and world-wide democracy cannot be born of the totalitarian conception of Victory, of Might, of the Dictate. A peace treaty may be bad or good: its endurance depends not upon whether it is negotiated or dictated, but upon whether it takes place at a moment when fair dealing and foresight can function freely. Mr. Orwell whips himself up into such a pet over words like negotiation and disaffection that his pen flies from insinuation to sheer misrepresentation, and he has the effrontery to state that *Beggar My Neighbour* contains 'pleas for surrender to Hitler'. It doesn't: that's all there is to be said. But why all this foam and fury? Mr. Orwell is, I am sure, sincere: he is also a brilliant writer and an influential propagandist. Therefore, it is worth asking what has brought his eloquent lance into such irritable action, and whether by any chance he is tilting at windmills.

His main targets seem to be four. First, Parlour Anarchy: the plea for the simple life, based on dividends. Second, the mischief of any propaganda not conducted on toothpaste-advertising lines. Third, the 'disaffected' intellectual who has (according to Mr. Orwell) so many complexes— including guilt, privilege, resentment, transferred nationalism, chauvinism, scepticism and 'no desire to escape' (qualities not perhaps confined to intellectuals)—that he lands up as pacifist *and* Fascist. Fourth, the hideous alliance of, as he calls it, 'impossibilism' and reaction: the fact, as Mr. Bernard Shaw put it, that the further Left you go, the nearer you get to the Right.

These ninepins can be shied at. A simple life based on dividends is what ninety-nine per cent of humanity naturally and rightly desires: dividends is only one name for security. And security is available to all if a simple life is lived: not, however, if life is complicated by advertising rackets of the toothpaste kind, and twisted into a hideous game of grab and envy, in which abysmal poverty must compensate colossal wealth. The 'intellectual honesty' of commercial advertising is a ninepin which never stood up at all. The 'disaffected intellectual'—and not he alone by any means—is merely the man or woman who struggles to discover a better conception of society and looks beyond the temporary and fanciful scales of values imposed— perhaps inevitably—by war and war propaganda. The intellectual is seldom either Fascist or pacifist: intellectuals are conspicuous by their absence in the ranks of both. The intellectual may choose to fight with bayonet or with brain or to stand apart: he cannot choose but *think*. And in thinking he must probe the values, however temporarily sacrosanct, which have led human nature to condone and practise mass murder. As to 'impossibilism', what is it? A hundred years ago it would have been a man speaking through the air to the whole world, or photographs taken in darkness, or Russia an equalitarian State. And in the flux of today nothing, surely, is impossible: not even Christian living—though that, for Mr. Orwell, may be 'reactionary'.

But, when all that is said, there remains in Mr. Orwell's writing a rancour which is hard to explain. The labels which he himself fabricates, infuriate him. Can it be that, compromising between his principles and his bread-and-butter, he has a special envy of those who don't or needn't? He tells us, bravely enough, that England must get off India's back, that the Viceroy must go, the India Office be wound up: it is 'the only decent gesture'. But, he adds, this can't be done because the Government (for which he himself does propaganda) won't have it. So what? So, says Mr. Orwell, you must not frighten or shock anyone (except of course the 'disaffected intellectual'), you must 'win over' the British public gradually and politely, as toothpaste advertisers do, and all will be well. So might some phantom George Orwellski, Russian Government propagandist of 1916, have written, urging that Lenin would be welcomed back to Petrograd and political prisoners crowned with laurels, if only everyone were perfectly polite about it.

No, Mr. Orwell, it does not work that way: you cannot hunt and run. I am not, and never was, under any illusion that books like *Beggar My Neighbour* stir more than the faintest of faint ripples: I wrote it because I felt impelled to say what I sincerely felt about India, and for no other reason. My book will leave as indifferent the indifferent British public as Orwell's literary broadcasts the starving people of Bengal. Words don't fill bellies or alter arrogant minds. Yet words as they accumulate do modify opinion, the quicker if their impact be sharp and timely. I can assure Mr. Orwell that the mass of British opinion is already converted to his views and mine: that is, it wants to see India free: but it does not and cannot act because the situation is distorted and obscured by the powers which propaganda serves. Amery plays down the famine, plays up the crimes of a Provincial Government: Cripps declares that constitutional changes are 'impossible' in wartime: Churchill states that Congress does not represent the Hindu masses. The average man, already preoccupied by the complications of his daily life and the immediate issues of war, takes such pronouncements as expert, and dismisses India as something that must, by its nature, unhappily drift. And in such an opinion he is no doubt strengthened by Mr. Orwell. To me it seemed more necessary to say, even if with only a small, small voice, that the drift was to chaos: and present conditions in India bear out that view. Neither our war effort nor our prestige will gain by Indian famine: and Indian famine is a direct result of the policy of drift. Mr. Orwell, subscribing as it seems to me to the policy of drift, condemns my book as a mischievous one, which will be acclaimed by the Left and welcomed, for different reasons, by the Right. He puts it, I think, too high. But his own article, from a pen so much better-known and eloquent than mine, will certainly show all Indians who read it how profoundly Mr. Orwell despises them: and that, I imagine, while it may be acclaimed by his fellow-propagandists, is a service which will be greatly welcomed in Berlin.

2259. Roy Walker to George Orwell

28 September 1943

One of those who objected to the tenor of Orwell's review of Fielden's book, and especially to his attitude to Gandhi, was Roy Walker[1] of the Peace Pledge Union. This important letter from him survives—important because it quotes from a lost letter Orwell had written to him, and also because what Walker said may have played a part in the later development of Orwell's interpretation of Gandhi's character and role in Anglo-Indian affairs (as expressed, for example, in 'Reflections on Gandhi,' January 1949; see *3516*). Walker's letter mentions that Orwell 'may be in poor health.'

Dear Mr. Orwell,

So what you've got against Gandhi is that some "big capitalists" show "veneration" for him! It seems to me that you might just as well speak slightingly of Stalin's "financial background" because his present policy happens to coincide with the immediate interests of the capitalist countries in the West. By this criterion Stalin went wrong the moment the Times started to call him "Mr. Stalin."

Moreover you strangely leave out of account the veneration of the masses for Gandhi, which he has earned by fighting for them for nearly half a century with a devotion that puts most socialists to shame. Nehru has protested vigorously about the slanders of "parlour socialists" against Gandhi, and himself does not exactly look on the Mahatma as a pawn in the capitalist game. From the time when he led the Ahmedabad mill-workers in their strike in 1917 Gandhi has fought on the side of the people. He does not accept all the socialist party cries, truly. But that doesn't put him in the fascist-imperialist camp.

Of course the British officials think Gandhi is useful in some ways, and he is. At first they thought he was merely simple-minded in preaching non-violence and that this was equivalent to giving them no trouble. Later not a few of them have literally prayed that he might fail, that the violent elements (Bose & Co[2]) might triumph, because of the disastrous consequences of applying oppression to people who did not hit back, which had made our name mud in America and a good many other places. Also, the apparently innocuous hand-spinning campaign gave Lancashire a nasty shock in the thirties, and the Government did a lot of propaganda against it.

My own very wobbly *ahimsa*[3] almost gives way altogether when you say cheerfully that "one length of railway line torn up achieves more than a lot of soul-force." If this isn't just back-chat it means that if the Indian nationalists had resorted to violence during the last thirty years, instead of Satyagraha,[4] they would have achieved, or would be nearer achieving, real independence. You may think so. I don't. If Amritsar[5] had been answered by a counter-massacre, everyone would cheerfully have supported Dyerism without end, and Gandhi would have been hung out of hand.

Your summary of Gandhi's pronouncements since the outbreak of this war is full of mistakes and inaccuracies. (1) He said at first he gave moral support to the British cause and held Hitler responsible for the war *because he had refused arbitration*. (2) He advocated attempting to reach agreement with Japan by negotiation, just as he advised Britain to negotiate with Hitler, and had himself negotiated with boundless patience with Britain. This is not inconsistent at all. Negotiation does not mean surrender. Gandhi contended that if honourable terms could not be got there must be struggle; only if he could influence India it must be non-violent struggle. (3) So far from being willing to "support the war again tomorrow" if certain concessions were made, he has set his face against such bargaining, which is why he retired from the field during the negotiations with Cripps. (4) While he himself would try to raise a non-violent force, Congress wished India to be defended by force. He explained that *Congress* would not object to the Anglo-American army remaining. Where Gandhi and Congress agreed was that political power should be handed over to a representative Indian Cabinet. (5) Gandhi has said repeatedly that "cowardice is worse than violence." Therefore he always admires bravery, and in this sense has praised the Poles and others. He would rather India fought by military means than surrendered. But he would still say, quite consistently, that in all of these cases the 'higher' alternative of "non-violence" was open, and that the highest courage would have been to adopt that means of struggle. (6) He said candidly to a Pressman (I think) that the theoretical possibility was that the Japanese might kill the whole population of India in an attempt to subdue the country. If they did so, and the Indians died without returning violence for violence, that would have been the triumph of Satyagraha. He then said that it was not in the least likely that that would happen, for the Japanese and other terrorists relied on the panic produced by a few atrocities to smash the morale of the mass. If they failed to do so they would give up terrorism.

The White Paper was published over here. The "Times" said that it showed an unfortunate eagerness to make debating points, and the "New Statesman" which is by no means tender to Gandhi described it as from first to last an indictment of Gandhi. I have read it carefully, and find nothing in it which upsets any of the points I have briefly made above.

You sneer a little at Gandhi's description of Chinese resistance against Japan as "almost non-violent." (I knew he said that about Poland, and it is quite likely he did say it of China too, although what comments of his I have seen about China were not quite so magnanimous.) I have partly explained this point already. Resistance to evil is essential, Gandhi believes. Courage and the willingness to suffer for a cause are the backbone of any morality. He can admire these qualities wherever they are found. In some cases, as where the small Polish forces stood up to the overwhelming mass of Nazi machinery, the element of courage is so much greater than the element of violence that, almost, such action must be classed with the ideal Satyagrahi who also would stand against the oppressor but would not return violence at all. To tear the phrase from its context and pretend it represents only a confusion of thought is unfair and unconvincing.

Don't you think that you should try to go into the evidence before you circulate dirt about "the sham austerities of the ashram"? And what is it in his whole career that makes you think him "a bit of a charlatan?"

I don't want to involve you in a correspondence about this, because I expect you are busy, as I am.[6] Also I hear from a friend that you may be in poor health—and at the risk of being thought to practise pacifist technique I send my good wishes for your recovery.

But I do think you were grossly unfair to Gandhi in your review, and that your defence of your attitude in your letter to me only underlines your bias towards him. I would like to think that you will, if you have time, go into the question more thoroughly. You may come back with a more imposing indictment of Gandhi. I prefer to believe that if you are really concerned to find the truth about him you will want to write again in "Horizon" or elsewhere and make him some amends. I don't make the kind of assumption about you that you made about Gandhi; I don't judge you by the fact that your gospel is a White Paper (which I think you have not read) and that your bark belongs to the India Office pack. I think you are just in a muddle and are angry with pacifists. You will be a more formidable critic of pacifism if you do us justice.

Every good wish,
Roy Walker

1. Roy Oliver Walker (1913–1992), pacificist and prominent member of the Peace Pledge Union, for which he worked, 1937–46, was a frequent contributor to *Peace News*. He took a special interest in the effects of the food blockade, famine, and food relief; he was Secretary of the Food Relief Campaign of the PPU and during and after the war wrote several pamphlets and a book, *Famine Over Europe* (1941), on these topics. He also wrote on PPU meetings (1939 and 1940). He was later dismissed by the Executive from service with the PPU, a statement in *Peace News* for 22 February 1946 stating that a majority had voted that he should no longer be employed at Head Office, partly to reduce expenditure and partly because 'for some time he has not been found an easy person to work with' even though it was recognised that the PPU was much indebted to him for his services over the preceding eight years, particularly in connection with food relief. He was three times prosecuted and twice imprisoned for refusing to be medically examined for national service. His selection called *The Wisdom of Gandhi in His Own Words* was published in 1943, and in 1945 his *Sword of Gold: A Life of Mahatma Gandhi*. He wrote a book on card tricks (1933) and studies of *Hamlet* (1948) and *Macbeth* (1949). See also 2372.
2. For Subhas Chandra Bose, Indian nationalist leader, see Wartime Diary, *1081, 3.4.42, n. 1.*
3. *ahimsa* means non-violent creed, often used particularly with respect to sparing animal life.
4. Satyagraha is usually interpreted as 'passive resistance,' for example, civil disobedience, suffering police charges without responding to physical attack, lying down on the track in front of advancing trains. It was evolved by Gandhi in South Africa. In 'Reflections on Gandhi' (see 3516), Orwell notes that Gandhi objected to the translation 'passive resistance.' In Gujarati, he said, it seemed that Satyagraha meant 'firmness in the truth': literally, 'holding on to truth'.
5. On 13 April 1919, General R. E. H. Dyer (1864–1927) ordered troops under his command to open fire on unarmed protestors, of whom 379 were killed. Although condemned generally and by court-martial, the Guardians of the Golden Temple of Amristar invested him as a Sikh in gratitude for his action and a London newspaper, the *Morning Post*, raised £26,000 for him by public subscription (*DNB*). On 13 March 1940, at the Caxton Hall, London, one of the survivors of the massacre, Udham Singh, assassinated the man who had been Lt. Governor of the Punjab at the time and General Dyer's superior, Sir Michael O'Dwyer. Udham Singh was hanged on 31 July 1940. His remains were returned to India in 1974, where he is still revered.

6. Orwell and Walker continued to correspond in 1943 but none of Orwell's letters have been traced. See Walker's letter to Orwell of 25 November 1943, *2372*.

2260. Extract from Minutes of Eastern Service Meeting

1 September 1943

Mr. Blair suggested that the present scientific series "Calling All Students" which had dealt principally with health and medicine should be followed by a series on psychology as applied to modern conditions. The suggestion was approved and it was agreed that Mr. Blair should consult Mr. Norman Collins and Mr. Weymouth regarding the expert guidance necessary.

Mr. Blair suggested that to follow the existing "Modern Men of Letters" series there should be a fresh series of "Great Dramatists". The former series under this title had proved popular in India; and there was plenty of material. The suggestion was accepted.

2261. To Desmond Hawkins

2 September 1943   03/ES/EB

Dear Hawkins,

I am going away this week for a fortnight's holiday so I shall not be here for the next Backward Glance. Your anniversary programme will also be coming off just after I get back. Could you please let us have the scripts a bit earlier. In the case of today's programme I didn't get the script until yesterday—only one day before production. This can make a lot of trouble: if there is any censorship difficulty or in the case of today's cast when they had to come and do their stuff live unexpectedly. I am gong to try and make quite sure that in future it is quite clear whether the scripts are recorded or live. If it is a live script it is better not to write the programme so that people have to do their piece again, which entails paying them over again as well as bringing them to the studio at short notice.

Yours sincerely,
[Initialled] E.A.B
(George Orwell)

[On verso]
I shall be glad if you will return the books on Greenwich Observatory[1] as soon as possible.

1. One was *The Royal Observatory Greenwich—Its History and Work* by Sir Harold Spencer Jones (1943); see Mary Blackburn's letter, 5 August 1943, *2222*.

2262. To C. E. M. Joad

2 September 1943   Original   07/ES/EB/JEL

Dear Joad,
I wonder if it would be possible for you to do your talk on Tuesday, October 12th, live. Could you let me know about this? I should like, in any case, to have the script not less than a week in advance of the broadcast date.

Yours sincerely,
[Signed] Geo. Orwell
(George Orwell)

Joad annotated this letter and returned it to Orwell. He would be speaking elsewhere on 12 October and hoped to record the talk on the 7th or 8th. He would provide the script by 2 or 4 September. He concluded, 'Is this the last talk?' When the script arrived, Orwell was on holiday; it was read by Bokhari. He found it very much above his head (as he wrote to Joad, 14 September), and felt that 'people of average intelligence, like myself, in India, will be rather disappointed.' He continued at length—there are eleven subsections—to show Joad, one of the great popularisers of philosophy, how to talk to a general audience. Though Joad might find his 'long rigmarole' fit only for the wastepaper basket, Bokhari said, he had written 'just in order to tell you what India will be most interested in.' Joad's response is not known. Despite its ironical aspects, Bokhari's serious intent does come through. See also Bokhari's letter to Oliver Bell, 14 September 1943, 2273.

2263. Orwell's Annual Leave

3 September 1943

Orwell took annual leave from Friday, the 3rd, to Monday, 20 September 1943. For arrangements for the production in his absence of the Newsletters in Tamil and in English for Indonesia, see notes to these Newsletters of 26 August and 3 September, 2251 and 2264.

2264. English Newsletter for Indonesia, 9

3 September 1943

This was written by George Orwell, and read by John Morris. No script has been traced.
    Whilst Orwell was on leave, John Morris wrote and read the Newsletters for Indonesia on 10 and 17 September.[1]

1. Gentry records in his diary for 28 August, 'Details of American repatriation [of prisoners] given on Wireless news. British repatriation said to be still under negociation°!' This might have been heard on local, Bangkok, radio. However, on 5 September, a BBC service was heard: 'B.B.C. gave a weather report covering the English Channel—the first since the war started!' This indicated that all danger of invasion was over.

2265. On Orwell's behalf to E. M. Forster

3 September 1943   07/ES/EB/JEL

Dear Mr. Forster,
I have arranged a recording for your next "Some Books" talk on Friday,
10th September at 3.00 p.m. and I shall be very glad if you could be here at
2.30 to run through and time it. I am enclosing The Making of the Indian
Princes by Edward Thompson and Reflections on the Revolution of our
Time by Harold Laski.[1]

Yours sincerely,
[Not signed/initialled]
for George Orwell

1. Orwell was to review *Reflections on the Revolution of Our Time* in *The Observer*, 10 October
1943; see *2309*. The letter was sent by Miss J. E. Light.

2266. Kingsley Martin and the BBC Eastern Service

There had been a number of disagreements about the fee Kingsley Martin was to
be paid for broadcasting. On 28 May 1943, Bokhari made the mistake of offering
Martin an *estimated* fee of £10.10. This was resolved by his being offered a fee of
£15.15 (see Orwell's memorandum of 30 July 1943, *2210*). However, there were
also doubts about Martin as an appropriate speaker, and though this surfaced
over a particular issue, those doubts ran deeper. On 30 July, he was to talk, in
'Education in England,' on the Norwood Report (on secondary schools), but he
did not mention that report. Instead, he talked about education in general, and,
according to J. B. Clark, Controller, Overseas Services, had 'far too much to say
about Public Schools,' did not put secondary schools 'into the right perspective,'
and was confused about 'purely denominational aspects of the religious
background to the teaching in schools' (memorandum of 5 August 1943 to L. F.
Rushbrook Williams). Rushbrook Williams replied 11 August, in a memorandum marked 'Private and Confidential.' He explained that Martin had
changed his topic without consulting his staff. Orwell was then brought into the
picture:

Blair (instructed by E.S.O. [C. Lawson Reece] at, I understand, your
instance) immediately got into touch with A.C.(H) [Assistant Controller,
Home Division, R. N. Armfelt[1]]: but was uncertain in what capacity
A.C.(H) entered the picture at all. A.C.(H), according to Blair, could not
be induced to surmount an initial objection to Kingsley Martin being asked
to deal with an educational topic. Blair tried in vain to explain that
Kingsley Martin had not been selected as an educational expert: but as a
writer on current political affairs whose topic on this occasion happened to
be an educational one. The exchange between A.C.(H) and Blair never
recovered from the initial misunderstanding: although Blair did succeed in
elucidating A.C.(H)'s principal objections to some of Kingsley Martin's
expressions, which were modified in the "as broadcast" script (this had

further been "touched up" by Weymouth). Blair has expressed his regrets that his treatment of A.C.(H) lacked the normal courtesies: but pleads that he did, under conditions of great urgency, find it very difficult indeed to reach a common basis of approach.

I agree that the script is disappointing in its balance. The stress laid upon denominational difficulties, and the personal reminiscences, are in fact just right for the particular audience: but I admit that this may be the result of accident rather than of *expertise*!

In future, I have arranged that the scripts of this series shall come to me personally in ample time to ensure that the agreed topic is in fact dealt with, and dealt with as we should like.

J. B. Clark replied on 15 August:

Thank you for your memo of August 11th. Experience in this instance does, as I am sure you will realise, yield valuable guidance for the future over one or two important principles;

(a) As you know, I am constantly emphasising the extreme importance of clear briefs to speakers. These are essential if we are, in fact, to direct and control our own services and if we are to choose the right speakers for a given subject. It is one thing for a journalist of distinction, like Kingsley Martin, to deal in a topical talk with a published report (for example the Norwood Report) but the changing of the brief or subject as in this case must not recur. I am glad to have your assurance on this point in your final paragraph, but of course the same principle does apply to all talks or series.

(b) I made it quite clear in my short manuscript note to E.S.O. that A.C.(H) should be consulted "as an expert within the B.B.C. on education". Blair should therefore, have been under no misapprehensions as to the capacity in which he was to consult A.C.(H). There was nothing new about this and I was merely re-stating a situation explained to the Oxford Street Services many months ago. Just as it is valuable for people in other services to consult your Department on Eastern and Far Eastern affairs, it is from a Corporation angle justifiable for A.C.(H) to be consulted on all doubtful matters in broadcasts about education in this country, or on other educational questions where expert advice is necessary.

Rushbrook Williams annotated this memorandum for Lawson Reece's attention on 16 August:

Please see C(O.S.)'s note above. Would you please keep a fatherly eye on this matter of briefing?

We cannot risk any more trouble over Kingsley Martin: and I'd be grateful if you would get Blair's cooperation to ensure that the suggested precautions are in fact observed.

There is considerably more internal correspondence (and some is reproduced in

'West: *Broadcasts*,' 294–99, though it should be noted that the final note is addressed to Lawson-Reece, not Sir Malcolm Darling, who does not appear to have been involved). Both fee and subject matter were resolved finally on 4 September 1943 when Bokhari wrote to Kingsley Martin:

Dear Martin,
We are exceedingly grateful to you for your most interesting monthly talks. Owing to some changes in the programme planning, it may be necessary for us to drop your talks from the 28th September. Of course you will hear from us definitely in due course.

1. Roger Noel Armfelt (1897–1955) served as Assistant Secretary and then Secretary to Buckinghamshire and Devon Educational Committees, 1928–41; and from 1945 was Secretary to the Central Council for School Broadcasting and Educational Adviser to the BBC. He is given as A.C.(H) in the Staff List dated 21.8.43. For Martin, see *496, n. 4* and talks booking form, 28.5.43, *2105, ns. 1* and *2*.

2267. On Orwell's behalf to Desmond Hawkins

6 September 1943   07/ES/EB/JEL

Dear Mr. Hawkins,
I am enclosing a copy of the Radio Times which gives some information about the six pips.[1]
  With regard to the Anniversary of the Month programme on September 21st. Mr. Cleverdon is going to Bristol on the 13th and will be producing it from there. I understand you will be in Bristol during that time, so perhaps you could get in touch with him there and let him know about the cast etc. Could you also give him a copy of the script and let us have one too, if possible by Monday the 13th.

Yours sincerely,
[Initialled] JEL
for George Orwell

1. Short, high-pitched sounds marking the time, the sixth coinciding with the hour, still used by BBC radio.

2268. On Orwell's behalf to Oliver Bell

8 September 1943   07/ES/EB/JEL

Dear Mr. Bell,
I have arranged a recording for your next Film talk on Monday, 20th September, 1943 at 11.45 a.m. I hope this will be convenient for you. Could you be at 200 Oxford Street at 11.15 a.m. to run through and time the talk?[1] I shall be glad if I can have the script by the 15 September.
  Miss Blackburn has got the BBC recording of all the film music from

Malta G.C.[2] and will arrange a presentation script with the relative parts of music to run for fifteen minutes after your talk on Wednesday, 22nd September. The script will be on the lines suggested by you.

Yours sincerely,
[Initialled] JEL
for George Orwell

1. Bell replied on 9 September to 'J. E. Light Esq.'—Miss Light, Orwell's secretary, who had evidently written her name in full on the top copy of the letter—to say that he had forgotten he would be travelling to Scotland on 19 September. He suggested a number of times when he might record his talk and promised the script by Monday the 15th—though the 15th was a Wednesday.
2. Malta was awarded the George Cross to mark the fortitude of its people when the Axis powers attempted to bomb them into submission. A nineteen-minute documentry film, *Malta G.C.*, was made by the Army, RAF, and Crown Film Units for the Ministry of Information in 1942. The music was written by Sir Arnold Bax and played by the RAF Orchestra. The commentary was spoken by Laurence Olivier, then a lieutenant in the Royal Naval Reserve.

2269. BBC Talks Booking Form, 8.9.43

Dr. P. Chatterjee: To write and broadcast Bengali Newsletter and supply an English version for censorship; 13½ minutes each week; broadcast 18 and 25.9.43; fee £10.10s each broadcast. Signed: Z. A. Bokhari.[1]

1. Despite Chatterjee's imminent departure, Bokhari was unwilling to engage his predecessor, S. K. Das Gupta, to broadcast. Chatterjee had suggested that his replacement be Dr. H. C. Mukerji (see *2219*). On 22 September, Bokhari wrote to Das Gupta, in reply to his letter of the preceding day, saying 'We regret that we do not find it possible at present to offer you an engagement in our Bengali Service.' However, talks booking forms for 18 and 22 December 1943 show that Das Gupta was asked to translate and read the Bengali Newsletters for 18 and 25 December (at a fee of £5.5s per broadcast). The form for 22 December gives the author of the English version as Charlotte Haldane (staff). P. H. Chatterjee rose to the rank of major in the Indian army; he died, aged thirty-four, in April 1947.

2270. Orwell's Adaptation of 'The Fox' by Ignazio Silone

BBC Eastern Service, 9 September 1943

The text for Orwell's adaptation for radio of Ignazio Silone's story 'The Fox' survives in the BBC's Play Library. The typescript does not appear to have been made by Orwell (it splits 'onto' into two words, for example, though he was not always consistent in typing it as a single word), and it has been fairly heavily amended. None of the emendations are in Orwell's hand, nor are a number of directions indicating how passages should be spoken. There are also a few technical directions. The script shows detailed timing indications—about every thirty seconds—and a few revised timings. The thirty-second intervals were probably introduced in rehearsal, which was timed for a run of 25 minutes 40 seconds; the timing 26.30 probably gives the performance time as broadcast.

This text is not marked 'As broadcast,' nor has it been marked as passed by the censor.

The text reproduced is that of the version amended for broadcasting. Timings have not been included because they are so regular and are so frequent as to be distracting. Handwritten substitutions and additions are printed in italic; if they are technical or production directions, they are also placed within square brackets. Three words underlined in the typescript are also underlined here, not italicised, to avoid confusion (see notes *7, 28, 29*). Passages cut and the originals of passages substituted are given in the notes. A few slight changes are made silently. It is not always possible to place production directions precisely, since they are usually scrawled in the margin. Some are difficult to decipher; if doubtful, this is mentioned in a note. '*F*' stands for 'Flash Cue' indicating that a light is flashed to tell the actor when to speak at the start of the programme or after an effects noise that might have been added outside the studio where the broadcast was taking place.

The play was produced by Douglas Cleverdon, who was probably responsible for certain sections of narrative being recast as dialogue. Originally Cyril Gardiner was to have read the narration and Richard Williams was to have played Agostino. There are some phrasing marks written into Agostino's and, to a lesser degree, the Narrator's speeches. These have not been reproduced. Their appearance in these two roles might suggest that they were the work of Richard Williams, who started by being cast as Agostino, changed to the Narrator, and after starting to mark up this copy of the script, marked up his own copy, formerly Cyril Gardiner's copy. This script has a large 'M' written at the top of the first page, which might suggest Terry Morgan, but see headnote to 'A Slip Under the Microscope,' 6 October 1943, *2297*.

The cast names are written into this script: Narrator: Richard Williams; Daniele: [Not named]; Agostino: Terry Morgan; Luca: Brian Powley; The Engineer: Cyril Gardiner; Caterina: Jean Anderson; Silvia: Lucille Lisle; Luisa: Jane Burrell.

(PIG EFFECTS)

Narrator: [*F*] Daniele *was* a peasant of the Ticino, in Switzerland,[1] just over the border from Italy. *One morning when he* was busy in the pig-sty helping the sow to litter, his daughter Silvia came a little way down the path from the house and called to him:

Silvia: Father! there's someone here that says she wants to speak to you.

Daniele: Go away, child. I can't see anyone now. Didn't I say I wasn't to be disturbed? I'm too busy looking after the sow.

(PIG EFFECTS)

Narrator: [*F*] Daniele had taken every care to see that the birth should go off successfully, but with a sow you can never be absolutely certain. He had put her on a strict diet the day before and as an extra precaution had given her a stiff dose of castor oil. Agostino, a young Italian who had been living in the Ticino for some years, was helping him. Agostino was a builder by trade but he did odd jobs of all kinds in the off season.

The birth started well and three little pigs hardly bigger than rats had already come into the world. There was practically nothing for Agostino to do except to find a suitable name for each little pig as it appeared. There was some trouble with the fourth one, but after that it went well and there were seven altogether. Agostino held up the fourth pig, the one which had not wanted to be born.

Agostino: That's a very poor pig. We'll call this one Benito Mussolini.

Daniele: Impossible. I'm going to sell these pigs in Italy.

Silvia: Father! Didn't you hear me calling you? There's somebody here who wants to talk to you.

Daniele: Go away, child. I'm busy. (*To Agostino*) Now we must wrap these young pigs up warmly. You can't be too careful with them their first day. *Help me put them in this box, Agostino. The straw will keep them warm. . . . Now, this blanket on top . . .*[2] There, they ought to be all right now. We'll have to take care that the fox doesn't get hold of them, though.

Agostino: Do you get many foxes round here?

Daniele: Lots of them. And they're cunning brutes, too. It takes a lot of catching, a fox does. A farmer's life is just one trouble after another. When it isn't bad weather it's birds, or weeds, or plant disease, or vermin. But a fox is the worst of all.

Agostino: Here's Silvia coming down the path with some one.

Daniele: Who is it?

Agostino: Looks like Caterina.

Daniele: Caterina! That dried-up, old chatter box, she'll go on for hours if she once starts talking. Quick. Come on down to the orchard, Agostino.

Silvia [calling]: Father!

Caterina: Signor Daniele!

Agostino: Too late, Daniele—you're cornered.[3]

Caterina: Signor Daniele, I want your advice about something. An Italian gentleman came to see me yesterday afternoon.

Daniele: Well, what about it?

Caterina: You'll hardly believe it. He asked me to become a spy!

Daniele: A spy!

Caterina: Yes. He wants me to spy on the Italian workers who go to and fro between Italy and Switzerland. He said to me, "*You're a dressmaker.* [quicker] With your work you must go into hundreds of houses and hear all kinds of conversations. And besides, you're an old maid and nobody takes any notice of you. You could pick up all kinds of information if you cared to." Well, he went on talking like this for some time, and then he said straight out: "If you're prepared to gather information about the activities of certain Italian anti-Fascists living in the Ticino, we can make it worth your while. In fact, you could look forward to making something to lay aside for your old age." That's what he said to me, Signor Daniele.

Daniele: Why do you come to me with this story? I'm not an Italian. I'm not interested in your Italian affairs.

Caterina: But I want your advice.

Daniele: What kind of advice? Advice about what?

Caterina: Why, whether to accept the gentleman's offer or not. I don't know what to do. I've never been so upset and worried in all my life. If I do accept I shall earn a lot of money, but only by doing harm to people who've never done any harm to me. But it's dangerous to refuse too. If I refuse they'll put me down as an anti-Fascist and then I shall be persecuted in all kinds of ways. You know me, you know I'm neither a Fascist nor an anti-Fascist. I don't know anything about politics, all I want is to be able to earn my living and be left alone. *I'm so upset about it.*[4]

Daniele: You know I don't meddle in politics either. But don't be afraid, it'll be all right. Tell Agostino what you've just told me and then do what he tells you.

Caterina: Are you working against the Fascists too, Signor Daniele?

Daniele: If I was, I shouldn't talk about it. The trouble with all you Italians is that you talk too much. Now you go along and tell Agostino all about it, and remember to do exactly what he tells you. I must get back to my pigs.

Narrator: Some days later Daniele was at work in the orchard with Silvia. *He*[5] had a free morning and was using it to disinfect his vines against disease. He was going over the affected places with a small metal brush *and* Silvia *was* follow*ing* him with a can of boiling water, *when* Agostino *appeared* driving a lorry loaded with bricks.[6]

[Lorry slows down and stops]

Agostino: [F] Hi! *Daniele!* That business of ours is going ahead.

Daniele: What business?

Agostino: You know well enough what I mean.

Daniele: I know nothing about it.

Silvia: Father, I <u>know</u>[7] you're really working against the Fascists, aren't you? Although you don't talk about it. I would like so much to help you!

Daniele: Then take these rotten twigs up to the house[8] and burn them, that's the only way you can help me at the moment. *Very well [back].*[9] All you people talk too much.

Agostino: Did you hear that there's another fox at work in the neighbourhood? It got into a chicken-run the night before last and nearly fifty chickens were found with their necks broken.

Daniele: We'll have to be careful with our chickens. We'll set the trap tonight. But it's a difficult job trapping a fox. The brutes are so sly that they won't touch the bait even when they're starving.

Agostino: A bit of poisoned meat is better than a trap.

Daniele: Even that doesn't always work. No one knows just the right amount of strychnine to kill a fox. If you put too little the fox only gets a belly-ache, and if you put too much he merely vomits it up again.

Agostino: Listen, Daniele. *Now that Silvia's gone,*[10] I'll tell you about the other fox we are trying to catch, the fox on two legs, I mean. Caterina's doing just as I told her. The Italian spy went to see her again yesterday, and after a lot of sobbing and sighing she agreed to do the work. You see the idea. Caterina's the bait. We'll make use of her to bring the spy here, and then we've got him. He's told her to find out the names of all the Italian workers who cross the frontier every day and come in contact with political refugees in this country. *[more incisive]* He also told her that it would be worth a big sum of money to her if she could help him to find out who are the people who are smuggling revolutionary books and pamphlets into Italy.

Daniele: Did he tell her that they suspected anyone in particular?

Agostino: No. She herself doesn't know anything in any case.

Daniele: Does Caterina know that I have anything to do with the Italian revolutionaries?

Agostino: No, she thinks you have nothing to do with politics. *Here's Silvia coming back . . .*

Daniele: It's rain we need; the land's caked as dry as a bone.[11]

Narrator: Every evening Daniele set the steel trap outside the hen house and scattered poisoned scraps of food. But the fox did not put in an appearance. And Agostino's fox, the two-legged one, *the spy—he didn't*[12] seem in any hurry to be caught either. At any rate Daniele heard no more of the matter for some days. Then one morning Agostino arrived.[13]

[Open][14]

Agostino: [F] The trap is set, Daniele. The fox will be caught tonight.

Daniele: How are you going to set about it?

Agostino: Caterina has written to the spy and told him that she has some important information for him. She has arranged to meet him at nine o'clock tonight near the lake, outside the old San Quirico chapel. [*try overacting*] Only, you see, Caterina won't be alone. I and two others are going to keep the appointment too.

Daniele: Don't you think it would be better to tell the police and have the man arrested? After all, he is an Italian spy.

Agostino: No, that would be stupid. The consulate would hear about it and the fox wouldn't turn up. You leave it to us. We'll make the man sorry he was ever born.

Narrator: That evening Daniele took a train to Locarno and strolled along the lake to the place where he had arranged to wait for Agostino. However, at about half past ten it was not Agostino who turned up but Luca, another Italian who worked in Switzerland, a carpenter by trade. He explained why Agostino had not appeared.

Luca: Agostino has *hurt* his hand *a bit.*[15] He didn't want *people* to *notice*[16] his bandage.

Daniele: But what about the spy?

Luca: Oh, we left him lying there. He turned up at the meeting place and met Caterina, while we stayed in hiding behind the chapel. Caterina began sobbing and sighing as usual and then told the spy a lot of absolute rubbish. Among other things she told him that the revolutionary books[17] which are being smuggled into Italy came from the Franciscan monastery at Locarno.

Daniele: That was a good idea!

Luca: Well, Agostino went across to the spy and left us behind the church. We had agreed that Agostino should only draw his revolver if the man showed any sign of using his own revolver first. Agostino walked up to him as though he was passing that way by chance, then he lit a cigarette and recognised him by the light of the match. "Ah, I[18] think I've seen you before!

You're the Italian spy!" and then the fight started. We came out of our hiding place and Caterina took to her heels.

Daniele: Did you join in too?

Luca: There was no need to. We only kept a look-out to make sure no one was coming. Agostino had got the spy down in a moment and then he punched his head so hard it would have broken a stone. It quite surprised me. I always knew Agostino was strong, but I didn't know he hated the Fascists so much as all that.

Daniele: They killed his brother, don't forget. But how did he hurt his hand?

Luca: The spy bit it. He got Agostino's left hand between his teeth.[19] Agostino punched his jaw like a mad-man° with the other hand, but he wouldn't let go. So Agostino took him by the throat and throttled him.

Daniele: You don't mean to say he finished him off?

Luca: It looked like it. At any rate we left the man for dead.

Daniele: That's a bad business! Agostino must disappear at once. He'll have to get out of the country—to France perhaps. I'd better stay the night at Locarno and see what arrangements I can make.

Narrator: As Daniele was going to spend the night away from home he thought he had better let his family know where he was, so he went into the nearest cafe and telephoned. Silvia answered the telephone.

[*Phone*]

Silvia: *Hallo, oh it's you father.* It's a good thing you rang up. I've been trying everywhere to find you for the last hour.

Daniele: What's the matter?

Silvia: There's been a bad motor accident; two cars collided near here on the road to Gordola. A man has been badly hurt. The doctor said he was too bad to be moved far so they made enquiries and all the neighbours said that ours was the only house where there would be room for him. Mother didn't want to take a stranger into the house while you were away, but I knew you'd agree.

Daniele: Of course. Where have you put him?

Silvia: On the first floor, in my room. I'll sleep with Luisa. The doctor is sending a nurse along tonight. We don't know who the man is or where he comes from. He's still unconscious. But we think he must belong to a rich family because the doctor wanted to give mother money in advance.

Daniele: Now listen, I can't come home tonight. But take good care of this man, and do everything the doctor tells you. Tell him to make quite free with my house till the man gets better. I wouldn't like to feel we hadn't done our best for him.

Narrator: Next morning Daniele learned that the injured man was an Italian engineer named Umberto Stella, who had come to Switzerland to study electric power production. Meanwhile, Daniele was trying to find out how far the police had got with their enquiries into the attempted murder the night before. He was far too clever to start talking about it himself, but he waited for others to begin, and bought several morning papers. However, he could hear nothing about it, not even when he made an excuse to go and see his lawyer and settle some formalities. In the end he decided that Luca must have exaggerated the whole business. These Italians, he said to himself, are fine people but they all talk too much. But he was glad that the spy had not been killed after all, otherwise Agostino and Caterina might have had to leave Switzerland.

As soon as he got home Daniele went up to the first floor to see the injured man. At the door of the room he found Silvia barring the way. She put her fingers to her lips.

[up]

Silvia: Sh! You mustn't make such a noise. He's got to be kept absolutely quiet. He must have no visitors, and there must be no talking. The doctor said that there must be nothing that would excite him in any way.

Daniele: So there's nothing I can do, then?

Silvia: Yes. You can take off your boots before you go downstairs, so as not to make any noise.

Narrator: Daniele took his boots off and went downstairs and out into the garden. Even then, when he started chopping some wood, Silvia came running out to tell him not to make so much noise. Daniele kept as quiet as possible, and then presently, when he saw Silvia leave the house, he went indoors again, took off his boots and crept upstairs. The nurse let him peep into the sickroom. All he could see in the bed was an enormous head completely covered with bandages. Although it was nothing to laugh at he could not help being reminded of a snowman. It was nothing but a great big white ball with a little hole for one eye and [a] slightly bigger one for the mouth. Nothing else of the man's face was visible.

For a long time after this Silvia was completely wrapped up in looking after the patient, especially when he began to get a little better and the regular nurse was discharged. For days together *Silvia*[20] hardly went out of doors, except now and then to gather a few flowers for the sickroom. Daniele went in to see the patient once or twice, but only for a few moments. He seemed a decent fellow enough, but there was always something to attend to on the farm. Even so Daniele could not help noticing the change in his daughter, and he was worried about it. The fact was he suspected that Silvia had fallen in love with the Italian engineer. Daniele took her out for a long walk and tried to talk to her, but she would not say anything. At last the engineer was well enough to leave his room and lie in a chair in the orchard. It happened that that morning Caterina and Daniele were coming back together from Gordola. They were just getting near the orchard when *on the other side of the hedge* they heard *someone*[21] calling out.

Engineer: [*floor*[22] *mike*] Signorina Silvia! [*back   upstage*][23]

Caterina: *Who's that?*

Daniele: *That's Umberto Stella, the Italian engineer. The doctor said he could come and sit out of doors this morning.*

Caterina: *Wait . . . let me have a look at him through the hedge . . . Yes, I thought so.*[24] Do you know who that is? It's the spy! That man in the orchard there is the Italian spy I told you about.

Daniele: You're mad! That man is an engineer. He was hurt in a motor accident while I was away and they brought him into my house.

Caterina: I know it's the man! I'd know him anywhere. I must get away before he sees me.

Daniele: My God.[25] Well listen, tell Agostino to come here tomorrow at the same time. *Yes, yes* I'll take care the man doesn't see him.

Narrator: Daniele said nothing to the others. The patient was now so much better that Silvia suggested they should all have their midday dinner together. At dinner the situation was almost intolerable. They talked uncomfortably about this and that. In order to make conversation Daniele started telling them about a railway accident that had just been reported in the newspapers.

Daniele: *And they say* hundreds of people have been killed.

Silvia: *How terrible.*[26]

Engineer: *Ah, Signor Daniele.* Just consider the hundreds of people who were killed in that accident yesterday. They were all kinds of people, students, [*little quicker younger*] peasants, commercial travellers, officers, doctors, lawyers—everything. They were in the same train and yet they were not in the same train. The peasants were thinking about market prices, the lawyers were thinking about the cross of the Legion of Honour, the officers were thinking about finding themselves rich brides, the students were day dreaming about the new ties they had just bought. It was as if they were all travelling in different trains. And then suddenly all of them were put into the same train, the train of death. They were just a lot of corpses mixed up together. They were all in the same train without knowing it. Death is the only unity.

Daniele: *Still* the railway authorities took care to destroy that unity.[27] They had the corpses in fur coats laid out separately from the others.

Silvia: Then people must continue to be enemies even after death?

Daniele: Present day society is based entirely on the antagonism of man to man. [*less voice   quiet*] The great majority of mankind are separated from the results of their labour. The product of their labour has hardly left their hands when it no longer belongs to them, but to their enemies. Some day it will be different.

Engineer: I see that you're an idealist. I also used to look forward to a better society than the one we live in. Nowadays I've grown more realistic in my views.

Narrator: Daniele went outside again and continued digging in the orchard. Spring was near and there was a great deal of work to do. It troubled him to have this man in his house—a spy and an enemy, and yet a human being with whom it was possible to talk. That evening they had another long conversation. They started talking about Tolstoy's "War and Peace" and ended by talking about the moon. The trouble was that Daniele could not bring himself to hate the spy as bitterly as he ought to have done. Next day Agostino arrived as had been arranged. When Daniele saw him coming he went out to meet him and took him into the house through the door on the side away from the orchard, where the so-called engineer was lying in the sun. From behind a curtain Agostino had a good look at the spy without any danger of being seen.

Agostino: That's him! That's the man right enough.

237

Daniele: You're sure?

Agostino: Perfectly. And now we've got him. He won't get away alive this time!

Daniele: You don't mean that seriously, do you?

Agostino: I do mean it. The fox is in the trap, and I'm not going to let him out of it.

Daniele: But you can't murder a man in cold blood!

Agostino: You know who that man is, don't you? He's one of those dirty Fascists who murder our comrades in Italy and shut them up in prison and on the islands. Now he's in our power. Do you think we're going to let him go?

Daniele: But he's lived in my house for weeks. He's my guest.

Agostino: He's a spy!

Daniele: He was[28] a spy, but now he's my guest. He was brought in here half dead and we've nursed him back to life. He's eaten my salt.

Agostino: [stronger] Don't you understand that we can't afford these scruples when we're fighting against Fascists? They[29] don't have scruples.

Daniele: I know. That's why I'm not a Fascist.

Agostino: Daniele, you're old fashioned.° It was just because we had scruples that the Fascists beat us in the first place. When your enemy is down, smash him. Do you remember that bit in the Bible where King Agag was captured by the Israelites? [up] Saul wanted to let him off but the prophet Samuel knew better. I've always remembered the words: "And Samuel said, [quicker] As thy sword hath made women childless, so shall thy mother be childless among women.[30] And Samuel hewed Agag in pieces before the Lord."

Daniele: That was five thousand years ago. Don't be so bloody-minded.

Agostino: You have[31] to be. Anything else isn't fair to your[32] own side. But you'll change your mind before long. Tell me, how much longer is this man staying here?

Daniele: I should think he'll be here another week. He's still very feeble.

Agostino: Oh, that's all right, then. There'll be time enough to talk this over before he gives us the slip.

Narrator: Daniele decided to say nothing about all this to the family. He did not want to worry them. And he took care to see that his guest noticed nothing either. It happened that one of his wife's sisters had recently had a baby and Daniele decided to go over and see her with his wife and Silvia. So Luisa, his younger daughter, was left alone with the invalid. Luisa was only a young girl and very anxious to entertain him. She took a childish pride in showing him all over the house and garden. She even showed him the store-room where the potatoes, onions, fruit and gardening tools were kept. Then she showed him the room on the first floor in which she and Silvia now slept. [get door set][33] When they got there something immediately attracted the engineer's attention. It was a framed picture on the wall decorated with two red paper carnations. In reality it was a picture of Matteotti, the Italian socialist deputy who was murdered by the Fascists in 1927.

Engineer: Whose picture is that?

Luisa: That's Matteotti.

Engineer: And who is Matteotti?

Luisa: He was a man who stood up for the poor and so he was murdered by Mussolini.

Engineer: [less Italian] Do you hate Mussolini? Are you an anti-Fascist?

Luisa: Of course.

Engineer: And Silvia?

Luisa: She's even more anti-Fascist than I am.

Engineer: And how about your Father?

Luisa: He's more anti-Fascist than any of us. But Father doesn't talk about it. He never talks about anything. He just acts.

Engineer: This is a very nice house that you live in. You've showed me all of it except for one room. What is that room on the second floor next to your parents' room?

Luisa: Oh, nobody's allowed in there. Father forbids it. It's his private room. All I know is that there are lots and lots of papers in there.

Engineer: Papers?

Luisa: Yes, and Father's ever so careful of them. He won't let any of us touch them. I suppose he doesn't want them untidied.

Engineer: Those must be his business papers—bills and receipts and so on.

Luisa: I expect so.

Narrator: Luisa and the engineer went back to the garden. *The engineer*[34] paced up and down the garden path for some time and seemed to be thinking. Then he asked Luisa to send off a telegram for him, and having given her the message and the money he said he was tired and was going straight to bed.

Next morning Silvia took up the engineer's breakfast. There was no answer when she knocked at his door. *She knocked again, more loudly. There was still no answer.* Immediately Silvia was certain that something was wrong. She cried out for the others:

Silvia: Father! Father! I think there's something the matter here. He doesn't answer, and the door's locked.

Daniele: One moment, I'll get the door open for you.

(SOUND OF DOOR BEING FORCED)

Silvia: He's gone!

Luisa: He's gone without even saying good-bye.

Silvia: And the bed hasn't been slept in.

Narrator: In fact, the room was empty, and what was more, the engineer's luggage had disappeared. A sudden thought struck Daniele, and in two bounds he was on the second floor.[35]

Daniele: Thief! Spy! Traitor! He's taken all my papers, Come up here! Look at this!

Luisa: What is it?

Daniele: Look, all the drawers have been emptied on to the floor. It's that Italian.

Agostino: [calling] Anyone at home?

Silvia: Agostino, is that you? Come on up here quick.

Agostino: What is it?[36]

Daniele: Look at this! Look what that dirty spy has done! He cleared off last night and he's taken nearly all my secret papers with him. He's taken all the papers dealing with the traffic across the frontier. We've got to warn the men involved at once. There's not a moment to lose.

Agostino: So that explains it. Do you know that twenty workers were arrested at Luino station early this morning? They were all men who come into Switzerland to work for the day and go home to Italy at night.

Silvia: No! no! no! It isn't true. It can't be true. I can't believe it of a man like that. Not after he'd lived in this house for weeks![37]

Daniele: What[38] we've got to think of is the ones who haven't been caught yet.

Agostino: Come on. There'll be time to warn a few of them, anyway.

Narrator: Daniele and Agostino hurried away. Daniele did not return until late that evening. His wife Filomena and Luisa were sitting by the stove. Silvia was sitting on a box at the back of the dark kitchen.

Daniele: Well, it's all up. The people who smuggle our pamphlets for us were arrested early this morning. A book depot was raided at mid-day. The police have been to Caterina's place and Agostino seems to have been arrested. If he has, he'll probably be expelled from Switzerland. Haven't the police been here yet?

Silvia: No.

Daniele: They soon will, then.

Narrator: Daniele sat down on the door-step. The night came and the stars appeared. The cock crowed for the first time, but no one thought of going to bed. No one wanted to set foot on the first floor, where until yesterday the spy who called himself an engineer had slept. The cock crowed a second time. Filomena and Luisa remained sitting by the stove, Silvia remained sitting on the box at the back of the dark kitchen and Daniele sat at the threshold. It was like a death-watch, as though somebody had died. The cock crowed a third time.

Just then an[39] animal cry broke the silence.

(FOX[40] HOWLING FOLLOWED BY CACKLE OF CHICKENS)

Silvia: [F] Listen, what's that? It's like a dog that's been hurt.

Luisa: And listen to the noise the chickens are making.

Daniele: It's the fox! He's in the trap.

Narrator: [F] Daniele sprang to his feet and dashed down the garden towards the hen house. Sure enough, there was a fox with its paw caught in the trap. The animal[41] was pulling with its three free legs trying to *loose*[42] the captured limb. When it saw Daniele approaching it started jumping frantically from side to side, though it was hampered by the chain which held the trap.

Daniele: At last! I've got him!

Narrator:[43] He seized an axe which was lying near the hen house and struck at the fox as though he were felling an oak tree. He struck at its head, its back, its belly and its legs, and went on striking long after he had hacked the carcase to pieces and reduced it to a bloody pulp.

The first reading is that of the text as amended; the second reading is that of the typescript before amendment, unless otherwise indicated.

1. Switzerland] Italian Switzerland

2. *Help me . . . on top . . .*] Narrator: Daniele carefully placed the little pigs in a big box lined with straw and covered it with a woollen blanket while Agostino cleaned up the sty.

3. *Agostino: Here's Silvia . . . you're cornered*] Narrator: At this moment Silvia, who was Daniele's elder daughter, and was aged twenty, came down the path towards the pig sty. With her was Caterina, an elderly spinster who earned her living by dress-making. Daniele tried to move off when he saw them coming, because Caterina was known as a great talker and would go on for hours. But the two of them cornered him and almost at once Caterina started on her story:

4. *I'm so upset about it*] Narrator: Daniele remained deep in thought for a moment while Caterina walked on sobbing. After a moment he followed her.

5. *Silvia. He*] Silvia when Agostino appeared. Danielle

6. *metal brush . . . bricks*] metal brush while Silvia followed him with a can of boiling water. Agostino was driving a lorry loaded with bricks; he slowed down and shouted to Daniele.

7. know] *underlined in original; not an addition*

8. *take . . . house*] pick up those diseased twigs

9. *[back]*] *spoken with the head turned away from the microphone to give the effect of distance or* sotto voce. *Since ribbon microphones would then be in use, this effect could be achieved with quite a slight turn of the head and upper body.*

10. *Now that Silvia's gone*] Silvia's out of hearing

11. *Here's Silvia . . . as a bone*] Narrator: At this moment Silvia came back into the orchard. As she approached the two men changed the subject and began talking about the weather.

12. *the spy—he didn't*] did not

13. *arrived.*] arrived and remarked casually

14. *[Open]* means open microphone; *if the audio engineer is preoccupied, a microphone might be left active at a time when, for example, there is music or sound off, and when those near it might think it safe to talk or move about. Its significance here is not clear.*

15. *hurt* his hand *a bit*] injured his hand slightly

16. *people* to *notice*] to attract attention with

17. books] books and papers

18. "*Ah, I*] "Ah," he said, "I

19. teeth] teeth and wouldn't let go

20. *Silvia*] she

21. *on the other side . . . someone*] they heard the engineer

22. *floor*] *this reading is uncertain*

23. *[back   upstage]*] *the reading* 'upstage' *is uncertain; for* 'back' *see n. 9*

24. *Caterina: Who's that? . . . Yes, I thought so,*] Narrator: Caterina heard his voice and stood rooted to the spot. Then she went and peeped through the hedge that separated the orchard from the road.

25. *My God*] All right. My God what a thing to happen!

26. *Daniele: And they say . . . How terrible*] [Narrator: . . .] Hundreds of people have been killed. The so-called engineer seemed interested and began philosophising about the railway accident in his own way:

27. unity] unity, however.

28. was] *underlined in original; not an addition*

29. They] *underlined in original; not an addition*

30. *women*] men

31. *You have*] One has

32. *your*] one's

33. *[get door set]*] *this direction gives advance warning to the effects men to provide the noise of a door being forced later in the action. Such 'anticipatory directions' are found as far back as playhouse texts of the sixteenth century.*

34. *The engineer*] He

35. floor] floor. A door was swung open, and the next moment they heard him raging and shouting like a mad-man.

36. *Luisa: What is it? . . . Agostino: What is it?*] Narrator: The women hurried upstairs. The whole room was in disorder. The drawers had been emptied on to the floor. Papers were scattered everywhere. It was at this moment at° Agostino appeared. He did not know anything yet but he was pale and agitated:

The new text—the dialogue—has been written over the original, typed, narration and the latter has not all been crossed through. A few words of the original typescript are intended to be taken into the revision (as reproduced here). The text is marked with a scrawled 'Quicker'; this may refer to the narration and not the new dialogue. In the amended form, 'Luisa' is spelt 'LOISA.'

37. weeks!] weeks! Agostino, tell me it isn't true.
38. What] We haven't time to bother about that now. What
39. an] a piercing; 'an' editorially changed from 'a'
40. FOX] DOG
41. The animal] The animal, with humped back, 'The animal' was mistakenly crossed through; its restoration here is editorial.
42. loose] free
43. 'F' was written in after 'Narrator' and then crossed through.

2271. Review of *Order of the Day* by Thomas Mann

Tribune, 10 September 1943

It is an open question whether the prospects of Liberalism—I use the word in its wider sense—are blacker now than they were two years ago. This collection of Thomas Mann's political essays and speeches covers nearly two decades, but nothing in it was written later than 1941—nothing, therefore, since the tide of the war began to turn. From his standpoint as a Liberal humanist Thomas Mann watches the European tragedy with an unshakable certainty that his horror will come to an end and common decency will ultimately triumph, but within the span of this book he has nothing to record except defeats: the assassination of Rathenau and the growth of German nationalism; the inflation and the meteoric rise of the Nazis; the reoccupation of the Rhineland, Abyssinia, Spain, Austria, Munich, and the outbreak of war. In the first two essays, dated 1923 and 1930, he is still inside Germany; then he is in Switzerland, a Cassandra vainly trying to persuade Britain and France that Hitler is dangerous; then an exile in the United States. So far as he takes the story it is a downward spiral, and though the fortunes of war have changed dramatically, it is doubtful whether the kind of world that Mann is fighting for is much nearer now than it was when the German tanks rolled into Paris.

It is important to notice that Mann never alters his fundamental opinions, and makes little or no concession to the age he is living in. He never pretends to be other than he is, a middle-class Liberal, a believer in the freedom of the intellect, in human brotherhood; above all, in the existence of objective truth. All the cruel theories of totalitarianism, based on an utter contempt for the human intellect, he rejects with a confidence which would be difficult to a younger man. This is not to say that he is the kind of Liberal who sees no further than political "freedom" and is quite content to leave western society in its capitalist shape. He sees clearly the need for Socialism, is pro-Russian, and is even over-optimistic about the chances of co-operation between the U.S.S.R. on the one hand and Anglo-America on the other. But he never budges from his "bourgeois" contention that the individual is important, that freedom is worth having, that European culture is worth preserving, and that truth is not the exclusive possession of one race or class. He dismisses the modern yearning for authority as "a perpetual holiday from the self." And it must be said that from his humanistic angle he makes shrewd political prophecies. As early as 1923 he has grasped the implications of Fascism and of the German "blood and soil" philosophy. One has only to compare his remarks on Hitler and Mussolini with, say, those of Bernard Shaw to see that respect for common decency is not a bad guide, even in international politics.

It must have needed obstinacy to stick so firmly to the concepts of the French Revolution, when for 20 years the tide of European thought has been running in the opposite direction. Perhaps the most significant thing in the whole book is Mann's repeated remarks in the first essay—this is a verbatim transcript of a lecture delivered to University students—that the audience is stamping and booing. This was back in 1923, and Mann was speaking in defence of the Weimar Republic and against militarism, authoritarianism and nationalism. Here, then, you have a man of fifty saying, in effect, "Stay alive," and an audience of youths crying out, in effect, "We want to be killed!" The middle-aged man is for liberty, the young are for authority; and though we have not had a precisely similar development in Britain—because Britain was not a defeated and bankrupt country, and therefore the particular conditions necessary for Fascism did not exist—the general tendency in every country of the world has been the same. Till very recently, nationalism and militarism were everywhere on the up-grade, democracy and liberty on the down-grade; in general, the young were more totalitarian in outlook than the old. Finally, came the triumphs of the Nazi war machine, seemingly the most complete debunking of the western conception of life that could have been imagined. "We came into the world to destroy the ideas of the French Revolution," said Dr. Goebbels, and for several years they looked like bringing it off. No one understood the danger better than Thomas Mann, as his essay *Europe Beware*, written in 1935, shows. Yet there is no sign even in the black years 1940 and 1941, or even after Munich, of his wavering in his belief that truth and justice *must* conquer in the end.

And curiously enough he was right, or may have been right. One dictatorship is in the dust and another is not likely to last very much longer in its existing form. We do not know what has happened to the young men who uttered cat-calls when Thomas Mann suggested that war is not glorious, but such of them as are still alive will have seen reason to reconsider their opinions. The trouble is that it is uncertain how deep the roots of totalitarianism lie. In this book Mann hardly pursues this question, though, of course, he avoids the folly of supposing that German wickedness is the explanation of everything. We do not know what the European young are thinking. Possibly totalitarianism has sufficiently discredited itself by the massacre to which it has led, possibly it is simply going to reappear in new forms and different places. Judging from the mental atmosphere in Britain and America, the omens are not good; but, at any rate, Thomas Mann, the nineteenth century intellectual, was right about the Nazis and Fascists. That particular dragon is almost certainly slain.[1]

[Our reviewer is, of course, fully aware that Thomas Mann has not always held the opinions expressed in this book. The aim was to discuss the book on its merits alone, without reference to what had gone before. —Eds., *Tribune*.]

[Fee: £2.2s; 16.8.43]

1. One factor among many leading to Orwell's decision to leave the BBC may have been his conviction that this 'particular dragon' had only a limited life.

2272. Review of *France Is a Democracy* by Louis Lévy

The Observer, 12 September 1943

Even if Mr. Louis Lévy's book had no other quality it would perform a useful service in reminding the average English reader that Paris is not France. To our grandfathers France meant cheap champagne, Sunday theatres, and the novels of Paul de Koch. That legend has almost passed away, but in recent years there has been an equally dangerous tendency to notice nothing in France except the antics of a few Paris politicians. In the pre-war years, even after Munich, most observers in this country took the *Front Populaire* at its face value and ignored the strong pacifist tendencies inside the Labour movement; in 1940 and even later, on the other hand, the belief was almost general in this country that the whole of France was ready to "collaborate." France was supposed to be ripe for either Communism or Fascism, and the strong democratic traditions of the mass of the people were forgotten. It is to correct this mistaken view and bring the provinces back into the Englishman's picture of France that Mr. Lévy's book is written.

Nearly half the book is a sort of topographical survey which runs over the French departments one by one and indicates the political colour of their inhabitants. Although the main object of this is to show that radicalism and republicanism have deep roots nearly everywhere, it has the added value of reminding English readers that France is a big country with considerable regional variations, Mr. Lévy does not even mind turning aside from time to time to throw in a few notes on the local wines and cheeses. But he is concerned above all to give a background to his chapters on political history and thus to show why France fell so easily, and why the overthrow of French democracy cannot possibly be permanent.

France was defeated in a military sense, but it is admitted that the treachery of the ruling classes played its part, and there can be little doubt that the attitude of the common people made their treachery easier. Pacifism of a sort was extremely widespread, and its effect was to make both preparation for war, and a firm system of alliances, almost impossible. The small French birth-rate, and the terrible losses suffered by France in the last war, made it nearly inevitable that war should seem the worst of all evils to a people who had quite obviously gained no benefit from their victory of 1918. The industrial workers, for instance, were anti-Fascist, but they were also traditionally anti-military; the school teachers were anti-Fascist, but inclined towards "pure" pacifism; the peasants were republican, but they knew that war does not pay—and besides, so many of their fathers and uncles had been killed at Verdun.

Thus at every point at which the Fascist advance might have been stopped, even when the Popular Front was in power, it was possible to damp down the enthusiasm of the common people by the threat that a firm attitude "might mean war." When war actually came the Government could show no good reason for standing firm after a long series of retreats, and in addition the Communist Party, particularly powerful in the Paris area, had by this time changed sides owing to the Russo–German pact.

Having shown just why the French peasant, the factory worker, the petty functionary, and the shopkeeper allowed themselves to be pushed into a suicidal policy by their natural enemies, Mr. Lévy draws on the background he has established earlier to show what kind of revulsion is bound to occur in each case. There is no popular basis for any regime that either Pétain or the Germans could set up. Respect for the individual and for democratic processes are ineradicable, for, as Herriot said, "Liberty cannot die in the country in which it was born."

Mr. Lévy does not profess to know with certainty what regime will follow the German collapse. Of course, it will be a Socialist regime; partly because no other will work, partly because the rich have discredited themselves by "collaborating," and the systematic plundering carried out by the Germans will have simplified the task of nationalising industry. He also hopes that it will be a democratic regime, but has his fears about the possibilities of interference from outside. He is not an uncritical follower of General de Gaulle, and is not happy to see men like Charles Vallin, the ex-Fascist, in the general's camp. "Frenchmen," he says, "have endorsed political 'Gaullism' because it had been presented to them as a democratic movement, but they are suspicious. All the more so, as they particularly fear military dictatorships and political generals."

Various quotations from the underground Press show that the forces of resistance inside France, while willing to accept General de Gaulle as an interim leader until a constitutional government can be set up, are not struggling against one dictatorship in order to set up another. And Mr. Lévy places near the end of his book the significant warning:—

> Anyone who tries to force upon French democracy a Government not in accordance with its wishes will find that he has let loose the bloodiest and most terrible of civil wars.

The point is hammered home by Professor Laski, who contributes a brilliant introduction and voices his doubts about the political complexion of the Gaullist movement a good deal more forcibly than does Mr. Lévy.[1]

[Fee: £6.6s; 30.8.43]

1. On 19 September 1943, Louis Lévy wrote to Orwell a letter of grateful thanks for this review; author and critic, he wrote, were joined in a common cause.

2273. Z. A. Bokhari to Oliver Bell

14 September 1943

Dear Mr. Bell,

I have just finished reading your script. I regret to tell you that I was rather disappointed. I frankly do not think that this script will be listened to with interest by our listeners in India. Dismissing "Watch on the Rhine" as you do in the middle of your deliberations about "Dear Octopus" is puzzling, if not misleading; and your long, rather elementary discourse on the director on pages 2, 3 and 4 is not, in my opinion, either interesting or illuminating to our listeners. People who are film-fans and understand English are much more "educated" in India in such matters than the man in the street in Great Britain. I must hastily add that to them "French Without Tears" means nothing and "Alice in Wonderland" does not form the basis of their education. Again, on page 5, the process of portraying somebody crossing the room is not exactly thought-provoking. Most of my remarks apply also to pages 6 and 7.

By the way, we haven't said a word about the author of "Dear Octopus", or the author of "Watch on the Rhine". I wonder if the records of Marie Tempest in "Dear Octopus" are available? If so, you might have included these in the talk. E. M. Forster has written something about "Watch on the Rhine" in particular and about propaganda plays in general: don't you think it would have been worth while to quote him?

My own feeling is that the script should be re-written, and I request you to do so. But if, on the other hand, you don't think it should be re-written, very reluctantly we will have to drop this talk.[1]

1. Bell replied on 17 September, sending a script he hoped would be more suitable. He commented that when he was doing these talks for Lady Grigg, he had a pretty clear idea of what was required. He was now left without guidance, and he suggested that he and Bokhari have lunch so they could talk over the policy of these talks. It is not clear whether this lack of guidance reflects on Orwell or Bokhari. See the summary of Bokhari's advice to C. E. M. Joad in *2262*, endnote to Orwell's letter to Joad of 2 September 1943. Lillian Hellman's *Watch on the Rhine* had its first London production at the Aldwych, April 1942. *Dear Octopus*, by Dodie Smith, was first performed in London in September 1938 and revived at the Adelphi in July 1940; it starred Dame Marie Tempest (1864–1942). *French Without Tears*, like the other two originally a stage play, was by Terence Rattigan and was first performed in London in 1936.

2274. On Orwell's behalf to Desmond Hawkins

17 September 1943   07/ES/EB/JEL

Dear Mr. Hawkins,

Thank you for the Anniversary script which has just arrived. I have sent a copy off to Mr. Cleverdon at Bristol which will reach him this evening. I

am enclosing copies of scripts for the next Backward Glance programme
which goes on the air on Wednesday, 29th September.

Yours sincerely,
[Not signed/initialled]
for Eric Blair

2275. BBC Talks Booking Form, 21.9.43

(Correcting slip of 18.9.43; not traced). Dr. George Yeh;[1] The World I Hope
For; time, 8' 40"; recorded 20.9.43; fee £3.3s. Signed: Z. A. Bokhari. Remarks:
for icebox; the "script of this talk, which we translated and broadcast in the
Hindustani service on 16th Sept. has been paid for by Copyright Department."

1. Dr. George Yeh, of the Chinese Ministry of Information, had declined an invitation to
broadcast in 1942 because he was too busy; see 2 September 1942, *1440*.

2276. Laurence Brander to Eastern Service Director

22 September 1943   Copies to E.S.O., I.P.O., Mr. Blair[1]

PREFERENCES OF THE ENGLISH SPEAKING° INDIAN AUDIENCE

One of the clearest impressions I got from my contacts with Indian
listeners last year was that when they tuned in to the BBC, they did so to
hear Englishmen and not Indians speak English. It was interesting,
therefore, to hear the view expressed by the Bombay journalist Tata that in
his part of the country, Indian listeners were more enthusiastic about some
of our Indian broadcasters than about any other BBC programme.

This seemed worth checking, so with the help of the Empire Audience
Research Unit a questionnaire was prepared. The results have just come
back. The questionnaire was despatched in Bombay, Bengal, Bihar, the
Punjab, the C.P.,[2] Hyderabad and South India. The actual number of
questionnaires returned was too few to form a firm conclusion. This
questionnaire is being circulated again and the following results may,
meantime, be taken as indicative if not conclusive.

1. The question has arisen whether our listeners prefer to hear Indians or
   Englishmen speak English on the radio. What are the views of your
   contacts on this?

	%
a) Prefer Englishmen	55
b) Prefer Indians	13
c) Indians or English	16
d) No Opinion	16

2. Which of these personalities are enjoyed?

	%			%
George Orwell	16	Dr. C. E. M. Joad	...	56
Shridhar Telkar	0	Dr. Gangulee	...	8
Priestley	68	E. M. Forster	...	52
Venu Chitale	12	Princess Indira	...	40
Kingsley Martin	16	Sir Azizul Haq°	...	28
Bokhari	32	Wickham Steed	...	76
Lady Grigg	20	S. Lall	...	12

3. Should news bulletins be read by Englishmen or Indians?

	%
a) Englishmen	80
b) Indians	5
c) No Opinion	15

1. Eastern Service Director: L. F. Rushbrook Williams; Eastern Service Organiser: C. Lawson-Reece; Indian Programme Organiser: Z. A. Bokhari; Brander was the Eastern Service Intelligence Officer. The carbon copy of this survey was among Orwell's papers at his death.
2. Central Provinces, now (with Berar) Madhya Pradesh.

2277. Newsletter in Tamil, 23

23 September 1943

The English version was written by Eric Blair. No script has been traced.

2278. Contract for *The English People*

23 September 1943

On 23 September 1943, Orwell signed a contract with W. J. Turner[1] as editor of the series 'Britain in Pictures,' to be published by Collins. Orwell was to provide a contribution of approximately 14,000 words and was to receive £50 as outright payment for the copyright within fourteen days of publication. The copy of the contract in the possession of Clive Fleay is annotated 'pd advance.' In his Payments Book, Orwell notes for 22 May 1944 that he is to provide 15,000 words on this topic and shows a nil payment, adding a note, 'Payment to be made later.' The entries in the Payments Book run from 12 July 1943 to 31 December 1945, and no advance is noted as being paid in this period. *The English People* was published in August 1947. See *2475* and *3253*

1. W. J. Turner had given a talk to India for Orwell on *The Book of Job*, 29 January 1943. On 24 September 1943, Orwell asked him to talk on Čapek's play *R.U.R.*; see *2284*. For Turner, see telegram to Edmund Blunden, c. 16 December 1942, *1743*, n. 1. The series, 'Britain in Pictures', was the inspiration of Hilda Matheson (1888–1940), then working for the Ministry of Information, as a propaganda medium for putting Britain and what it stood for to the world. The series was launched in March 1941, four months after Hilda Matheson's death, and by 1950, when the last book was published, 126 titles had been issued. Each volume was

of 48 pages and well illustrated in colour and monochrome. W. J. Turner (who died in 1946) took over the direction of the series, which proved an artistic and publishing success. See Michael Carney, *Britain in Pictures: a History and Bibliography* (1995).

2278. A and B. See Vol. XX, Appendix 15 for Lord David Cecil's letters to W. J. Turner condemning *The English People*.

2279. English Newsletter for Indonesia, 12

24 September 1943[1]

1. This was written and read by George Orwell. No script has been traced. Gentry records in his diary that on 18 September he listened to Delhi (All-India Radio) at the house of a Siamese, Ro Thas, in Bangkok. Prisoners were allowed out of the camp under escort by the Siamese under certain conditions.

2280. To R. R. Desai

24 September 1943   07/ES/EB/JEL

Dear Desai,

Following on Tonkin's suggestion last week I am sending some hints[1] which may be useful to you in compiling Monday's newsletter. I am not trying to force these suggestions on you, but merely to indicate the headings that seem most important. I enclose a few cuttings that Tonkin gave me, but I don't know that they will be much use.

Yours sincerely
[Initialled] E. A. B (Eric Blair)

1. G. R. Tonkin was the Eastern Service News Editor. The hints have not been traced.

2281. To V. S. Pritchett

24 September 1943   07/ES/EB

Dear Pritchett,

Would you like to do us a ten minute talk on Ibsen for Sunday, October 24th. We are going to start again the series we were running before called Great Dramatists. These are half hour programmes, consisting of an acted interlude from a play and a short talk on the author with special reference to this particular play. The play we have chosen is "An Enemy of the People" which you no doubt know. (N.B. I suppose it might have another name in some of the translations. It is the one about a doctor who discovers that the medicinal waters from which a little town makes its livelihood are poisoned.) Your talk would come before the acted extract, and what you would have to do is to give a sort of general criticism of Ibsen, using this play as the pretext. We usually start by broadcasting a few lines from the play as a trailer and that gives you your cue to start off "Those lines you have just heard come from 'An Enemy of the People' by Henrik Ibsen." Could you let me know as soon as possible whether you will do this? I should want the script by October 17th.[1]

Yours sincerely,
[Initialled] E.A.B
(George Orwell)

1. Pritchett replied in a letter also dated 24 September saying he was 'hopelessly bogged in work' and asking whether there was any chance of the date being changed. Orwell annotated Pritchett's letter: 'P.C. Sorry—can't alter the date. Another time perhaps. G.O.'

2282. To Herbert Read

24 September 1943   07/ES/EB

Dear Read,

Would you like to do us a ten minute talk on Macbeth for Sunday, October 17th? I should want to have the script by about October 10th. We are going to start again the series we were running before called Great Dramatists. These are half hour programmes consisting of an acted interlude from the play and a talk on the dramatist's work with special reference to this particular play. In the case of Macbeth I fancy that what we shall broadcast will be the last act. Your talk would precede this and would give a general criticism of Shakespeare while using Macbeth as the pretext. I think we shall do, as we did before, and start the programme with a few lines from the play as a trailer which would give you a cue to start by saying "Those lines you have just heard come from Macbeth by William Shakespeare". Could you let me know as early as possible whether you can undertake this?

Yours sincerely,
[Initialled] E.A.B
(George Orwell)

Read evidently declined, because Orwell himself wrote and delivered a talk on *Macbeth* on 17 October.

2283. To L. F. Rushbrook Williams

24 September 1943   Original

B.B.C.

Dear Mr Rushbrooke-Williams,[1]

In confirmation of what I said to you earlier in private, I want to tender my resignation from the BBC, and should be much obliged if you would forward this to the proper quarter.

I believe that in speaking to you I made my reasons clear, but I should like to put them on paper lest there should be any mistake. I am not leaving because of any disagreement with BBC policy and still less on account of any kind of grievance. On the contrary I feel that throughout my association with the BBC I have been treated with the greatest generosity and allowed very great latitude. On no occasion have I been compelled to say on the air anything that I would not have said as a private individual. And I should like to take this opportunity of thanking you personally for the very understanding and generous attitude you have always shown towards my work.

I am tendering my resignation because for some time past I have been conscious that I was wasting my own time and the public money on doing work that produces no result. I believe that in the present political situation the broadcasting of British propaganda to India is an almost hopeless task. Whether these broadcasts should be continued at all is for others to judge, but I myself prefer not to spend my time on them when I could be occupying myself with journalism which does produce some measurable effect. I feel that by going back to my normal work of writing and journalism I could be more useful than I am at present.

I do not know how much notice of resignation I am supposed to give.[2] The "Observer" have again raised the project of my going to North Africa. This has to be approved by the War Office and may well fall through again, but I mention it in case I should have to leave at shorter notice than would otherwise be the case. I will in any case see to it that the programmes are arranged for some time ahead.

Yours sincerely
[Signed] Eric Blair
Eric Blair

1. Rushbrook Williams signed his name over this misspelling of his name, without a hyphen and an 'e'; both errors were Orwell's. Although sent as from the BBC, Orwell typed this letter himself on plain paper.
2. Orwell had informed Ivor Brown of *The Observer* on 31 August (see *2255*) that he had to give two months' notice. In a footnote to this passage, West says that there was no possibility that Orwell could make such a journey; he would not be cleared on grounds of health. He suggests that this venture was, perhaps, 'a ploy to enable him to leave immediately' (*Broadcasts*, 58, n. 113). As the invitation from Brown makes clear, however, the proposal was genuine. On 29 September, Sir Guy Williams, Overseas Services Establishment Officer, wrote to Orwell, accepting his resignation 'with much regret.' Whilst recognising that he should normally work his two months' notice, Sir Guy wrote: 'if, as you say, you may have to leave at shorter notice, the Corporation would be prepared to allow you to do so'; Orwell's resignation would take effect from 24 November 1943 'unless you inform me that you wish to leave at an earlier date.' On 7 October 1943, Brown wrote to Orwell saying he had heard he would be free at the end of November and he would be glad if he could come over to see him at *The Observer* to discuss the amount of reviewing and other writing he could do for that paper. He mentioned also that he much appreciated Orwell's review 'of Laski' (of *Reflections on the Revolution of Our Time*), 10 October 1943; see *2309*.

2284. To W. J. Turner

24 September 1943   07/ES/EB

Dear Turner,
I wonder if you would like to do another talk in the series Great Dramatists
which we are reviving. What I would like is a ten minutes talk on Carel°
Capek's play "R.U.R."[1] You know the formula of these programmes, I
think. They are half hour programmes, and consist of an extract from the
play in question preceeded by a ten minutes talk on it. I should want you to
say something about Capek and his work generally, using this particular play
as a pretext. The date of the broadcast would be Sunday, 7th November,
which means I would want the script by the end of October. Perhaps you
would let me know about this.

Yours sincerely,
[Initialled] E. A. B
(George Orwell)

1. *R.U.R.* by Karel Čapek (1890–1938) was first performed in 1921. It is in the dystopian
tradition to which Orwell contributed *Nineteen Eighty-Four. Rossum's Universal Robots* (1920)
is concerned with the production of a man-like machine more efficient than man himself and
so able to take over the world. The word 'robot' was introduced into English through this
play although it was coined by Čapek's brother, Josef, three years before *R.U.R.* was
published (see William Harkins, *Karel Čapek*, New York, 1962). The Czech word *robota* is
usually defined as compulsory or statute labour; perhaps 'forced labour' aptly conveys the
sense.

2285. BBC Talks Booking Form, 24.9.43

Wing Commander Roger Falk: Talk on the 4th Indian Division; 13½ minutes;
broadcast 26.9.43; fee £10.10s. Signed: Z. A. Bokhari. Remarks: 'Will the
Contracts Department please find out whether this talk is connected with W/C
Falk's job [at India Office] or not.'

2286. BBC Talks Booking Form, 25.9.43

Oliver Bell: Monthly film talk; 13½ minutes; broadcast 20.10.43; fee £10.10s.
Signed: Z. A. Bokhari.

2287. To E. M. Forster

27 September 1943   07/ES/EB/JEL

Dear Forster,
Thank you for your letter and post-card. It will be quite all right for you to do
the Lytton Strachey talk live on Sunday, 3rd October. I have arranged a

recording for the Some Books talk on Friday, 8th October at 3.0 p.m. I am enclosing copies of Huckleberry Finn and Tom Sawyer.

Yours sincerely,
[Initialled] E.A.B
(George Orwell)

2288. On Orwell's behalf to Desmond Hawkins

28 September 1943   07/ES/EB/JEL

Dear Mr. Hawkins,
I am enclosing scripts for the next Backward Glance programme for transmission on Wednesday, 13th October.

Yours sincerely,
[Initialled] JEL
for George Orwell

2289. To Stephen Spender

28 September 1943   07/ES/EB/JEL

Dear Spender,
This is to confirm the telephone conversation this morning. We are doing a series called Great Dramatists, which are half hour programmes consisting of an acted extract from a play preceded by a ten minutes talk on it. I want you to say something about Ibsen's work in general, using The Enemy of the People as a pretext. We usually start by broadcasting a few lines from the play as a trailer and that gives you your cue to start off "Those lines you have just heard come from An Enemy of the People by Henrik Ibsen". The date of the broadcast is Sunday, October 24th, at 4.15 p.m. I shall want the script by October 17th.

Yours sincerely,
[Initialled] E.A.B
(George Orwell)

2290. Newsletter in Tamil, 24

30 September 1943

The English version was written by Eric Blair. No script has been traced.

2291. Extract from Minutes of Eastern Service Meeting

30 September 1943

Series of Talks on Psychology   This series to start in Week 40, and to consist of nine talks.[1] Subsequently to be published in pamphlet form in India by Oxford University Press, contents being condensed to six talks.[2]

1. On 27 September, Frederick Laws sent Orwell a 'rough scheme' for a set of nine talks for this series, which they had discussed 'the other day.' He proposed the following speakers (there is no number 9 in his list): 1: Oct. 14, Prof. T. H. Pear; 2: Oct. 21, Prof. J. C. Flugel; 3: Oct. 28, Dr. Susan Isaacs; 4: Nov. 4, Prof. C. W. Valentine; 5: Nov. 11, Dr. Philip E. Vernon; 6: Nov. 12 [for 18], Dr. Mary Smith; 7: Nov. 26, Prof. Cyril Burt; 8: Dec. 2, R. S. Lynd. Various problems arose in confirming this list. Burt could not give a talk; Vernon thought the Admiralty would object to his contributing; Lynd had gone to America. On 17 October, Laws suggested the following alternative speakers: Angus Macrae, Dr. S. J. F. Philpott, Eric Farmer, Prof. A. W. Wolters (which he spelt Walters), and Dr. Alan Maberley. On 3 November, he sent Orwell Marie Jahoda's address and asked if he could have copies of all the talks. Laws (1911–) was a journalist; art critic, *News Chronicle*, 1938–39; radio critic, *News Chronicle*, 1942–47; and, under the name John Aubrey, ran a feature, 'Personal Problems,' for that paper, 1945–46. Among his publications were *Made for Millions* (1947) and *Radio and the Public* (1947). On 7 October, Bokhari asked the Talks Booking section for a fee of £5.5s per talk for Laws for his work in arranging the series.
2. For the proposed pamphlet, Laws suggested telescoping talks 3 and 4 and talks 8 and 9. This pamphlet, like that to be devoted to medical topics, was not published.

2292. English Newsletter for Indonesia, 13

1 October 1943

This was written and read by George Orwell. No script has been traced.

2293. To Norman Collins

4 October 1943   Original   EB/JEL

APPROACHING M.P.s

When Parliament reopens we shall be approaching some more M.P.s for The Debate Continues series, and would like to know whether Aneurin Bevan and Sir Richard Acland are off the black list yet. When we proposed to approach Acland before I was told that he had a vote of censure tabled *and* that we could not use him while this was still sub judice.

[Signed] Eric Blair
(Eric Blair)

2294. To T. H. Pear

4 October 1943   07/ES/EB

Dear Professor Pear,[1]

Many thanks for your letter of October 1st.[2] I believe you had a telegram from us on Saturday. It will be quite all right to fix the date of broadcast as October 14th. We will fix a date for you to record, probably Monday 11th, and let you know the exact time. I hope that will suit you. If you can manage it, I would like you to send me the script here, by Friday 8th, but I think in practice it will be all right if I receive it by the morning of Monday 11th. In this case there will I suppose be time for you to send a rough draft to Mr. Laws. I have to have the final copy of the script here before the time of recording, however, in order to get it censored.

> Yours truly,
> [Initialled] E. A. B
> (Eric Blair)

1. Professor Tom Hatherley Pear (1886–1972) was, in 1943, President of the British Psychological Society and Professor of Psychology, University of Manchester. Among his large number of publications were *Remembering and Forgetting* (1922), *Fitness for Work* (1928), *The Art of Study* (1930), *The Psychology of Effective Speaking* (1933), *Religion and Contemporary Psychology* (1937), *English Social Differences* (1955). He edited *Psychological Factors of Peace and War* (1950), and, with Sir Grafton Elliot Smith, wrote *Shell Shock and its Lessons* (1917).
2. Frederick Laws (see *2291, n. 1*) had written to Pear asking him to give the first broadcast in the series on psychology, to be called 'The Uses of Psychology.' On 1 October, Pear wrote to Orwell to say he would be delighted to contribute.

2295. BBC Talks Booking Form, 4.10.43

Professor T. H. Pear: '[The Uses of] Psychology,' 3rd Scientific Series—Calling all Students; 13½ minutes (first in series); recorded 11.10.43; broadcast 14.10.43; fee (suggested): £10.10s. Signed: L. B. [A. L. Bateman?] for Z. A. Bokhari. Remarks: 'This cancels booking slip of 30.9.43 [not traced] for broadcast of talk on 7.10.43.'

2296. To T. H. Pear

5 October 1943   07/ES/EB/JEL

Dear Professor Pear,

I have arranged a recording for your talk on Monday, 11th October at 2.15 p.m. Could you be at Broadcasting House, Piccadilly, Manchester not later than 1.45 p.m. on Monday to run through and time the talk. I am writing to Mr. Wilkinson, who is Director of Programmes at Manchester, giving him details of the recording. I shall be glad to receive the script as soon as possible.[1]

Yours sincerely,
[Signed] Eric Blair
(Eric Blair)

1. On 8 October, Pear sent Orwell the typescript for his talk. He wrote that Frederick Laws had seen his original, lengthy, draft and the cuts and modifications he had made were along lines suggested by Laws. He was sending a copy to Wilkinson and to Professor Flugel.

2297. 'A Slip Under the Microscope' by H. G. Wells, Adapted by George Orwell

BBC Eastern Service, 6 October 1943

'A Slip Under the Microscope' has been reproduced from a copy surviving in the BBC Play Library. This is virtually unmarked. The few changes (one an obvious oversight) have been made in a hand other than Orwell's. The typing is professional. There are a few typing slips, which, if insignificant, have been silently corrected, as have slight variations in abbreviated forms of the speech heading 'Fair-Haired Student.' A large 'M' has been written at the top of the first page of the typescript (see headnote to 'The Fox,' 9 September 1943, 2270). The script is marked 'Not checked with broadcast.' Given the number of changes made to 'The Fox' during production it is likely that this script was also amended. There are no censorship stamps. A few abbreviated speech headings have been expanded.

The play was produced in Bristol by Douglas Cleverdon. There is a cast list, but the names of the actors have not been added. Those taking part have been recovered from Programmes as Broadcast, but they are not identified with the roles they played. The cast: Hill, Wedderburn, Miss Haysman, A girl student, A fair-haired student, A hunchbacked student, Professor Bindon, Narrator. The actors were: Jane Barrett and Rosamund Barnes (Schools' Representatives), Charles Stidwell, Lockwood West, George Holloway, Miles Rudge, William Eldridge, and Wilfred Fletcher. What is meant by Schools' Representatives is obscure. This term does not appear in Wells's short story, nor in Orwell's adaptation, and it is curious that it is related here to the two actresses who must have played Miss Haysman and the other girl student.

NARRATOR: It was an autumn morning, forty years ago. The grey London fogged° against the windows of the College of Science, but inside the laboratory there was a close warmth and the yellow light of gas lamps. On the tables were glass jars containing the mangled remains of crayfish, frogs and guinea-pigs on which the students had been working, and a litter of handbags, boxes of instruments and anatomical drawings. And on one table there lay—looking rather incongruous in its surroundings—a prettily-bound copy of William Morris's "News from Nowhere". The clock had struck eleven and the lecture in the adjoining theatre had just come to an end. The students were arriving in the laboratory by ones and twos and getting their dissecting instruments ready amid casual conversation.

(*FEET — VOICES*)

GIRL STUDENT: Have you been reading "News from Nowhere"?

MISS HAYSMAN: Yes. I borrowed it from Mr. Hill. I brought it to give back to him.

GIRL STUDENT: It's about Socialism, isn't it? It must be terribly dull.

MISS HAYSMAN: It's a wonderful book. Only there's so much in it that I don't understand.

GIRL STUDENT: There's Mr. Hill over there. He's having an argument as usual. He's a terribly self-assertive young man, isn't he? I think Mr. Wedderburn is really much cleverer in a quiet way. Of course he inherits it. His father is the famous eye-specialist, you know. These classes are terribly mixed, aren't they, with all these scholarship people? Do you see that tall man with the beard? They say he actually used to be a tailor! Now I think Mr. Wedderburn is really nice-looking.

MISS HAYSMAN: Mr. Hill has an interesting face, too.

GIRL STUDENT: But you couldn't call him good-looking, could you? And he's so badly dressed. Just look at his collar! It's all frayed along the top.

NARRATOR: Hill was a sturdily-built young man of twenty, with a white face, dark grey eyes, hair of an indeterminate colour, and prominent, irregular features. His clothes were obviously ready-made and there was a patch on the side of his boot near the toe. At the moment he was standing beside the laboratory sink with two other students, a tall fair-haired youth and a little hunchback, and arguing—a little more loudly than was necessary—about the lecture they had just been listening to.

HILL: You heard what he said: "From ovum to ovum is the goal of the higher vertebrate." I agree with him entirely. There is no world except this world—no life except bodily life.

FAIR-HAIRED STUDENT: I admit that science can't demonstrate the existence of any other kind. But there are things above science.

HILL: I deny that. Science is systematic knowledge. An idea has no value unless it can be scientifically tested.

HUNCHBACK: The thing I can't understand is whether Hill is a materialist or not.

HILL: Of course I am. There is only one thing above matter, and that is the delusion that there is something above matter.

FAIR-HAIRED STUDENT: So we have your gospel at last. It's all a delusion, is it? All our aspirations to lead something more than dogs' lives, all our work for anything beyond ourselves—just a delusion. But look how inconsistent you are. Your socialism, for instance. Why do you trouble about the interests of the race? Why do you concern yourself about the beggar in the gutter? Why are you bothering to lend William Morris's "News from Nowhere" to everyone in this laboratory?

HILL: Why not? Materialism isn't the same thing as selfishness. There's no reason why a man should live like a brute because he knows of nothing beyond matter, and doesn't expect to exist a hundred years hence.

FAIR-HAIRED STUDENT: But why shouldn't he?

HILL: Why *should* he?

257

FAIR-HAIRED STUDENT: What inducement is there to live decently if death ends everything?

HILL: Oh, inducements! You religious people are always talking about inducements. Can't a man seek after righteousness for its own sake?

FAIR-HAIRED STUDENT: And what would be your definition of righteousness?

NARRATOR: The question disconcerted Hill. The fact was that he could not have said exactly what he meant by righteousness. At this moment, however, the laboratory attendant came in, carrying a batch of freshly-killed guinea-pigs by their hind legs. He slapped down a couple of guinea-pigs on each table, and the students took their instruments out of the lockers and got ready for work.

Hill was the son of a cobbler. He had entered the College of Science by means of a scholarship and was living in London on an allowance of a guinea a week, which paid not only for his board and lodging but also for ink and paper. It even covered his clothing allowance—an occasional water-proof collar, that is. He had learned to read at the age of seven, and had read omnivorously ever since, in spite of the fact that he had gone to work in a boot factory immediately after passing the seventh standard at the Board School. He had a considerable gift of speech—indeed he was a leading light in the College Debating Society—a serene contempt for clergy of all denominations, and a fine ambition to reconstruct the world. He regarded his scholarship as a brilliant opportunity. As for his limitations, except that he knew that he knew neither Latin nor French, he was completely unaware of them.

He was in his first year at the College of Science. So far his interest had been divided equally between his biological work and those vague rambling arguments on generalities which are so dear to students everywhere. At night, when the museum library was shut, he would sit on the bed in his Chelsea room, with his coat and muffler on, writing out his lecture notes and revising his dissection memoranda; and then presently his friend Thorpe, the physics student, would call him by a whistle from the pavement, and the two of them would go prowling through the gaslit streets, talking endlessly about God and Righteousness and Carlyle and the Reorganisation of Society. It was only recently that he had become aware of a competing interest—Miss Haysman, the girl with brown eyes, who worked at the next table to him and to whom he had lent the copy of "News from Nowhere".

She was a paying student. Socially, she and Hill belonged in totally different worlds. Hill could never forget this, he could never feel at ease with her. Indeed it was not often that he had an opportunity of speaking to her. But he found himself thinking of her more and more.

HILL: I'm not much good at talking to girls. I suppose that young Wedderburn would be more her style. He's got the proper clothes and manners—he's good-looking too. His father's the famous eye-specialist, she told me. I must say, though, she didn't seem surprised when I told her that *my* father was a cobbler. I oughtn't to have said that; it almost looked as though I was jealous. Of course she knows all sorts of things that I don't, poetry and music and so forth. She must have learnt French and German at school, perhaps Latin too. But when it comes to Science I'm ahead of her. She had to come and ask me about the alisphenoid of the rabbit's skull. And she'd hardly heard of socialism until I told her about it.

NARRATOR: Miss Haysman had also thought about Hill—more frequently, perhaps, than he imagined.

MISS HAYSMAN: He told me he went to work in a factory at fourteen and won his scholarship years afterwards. I do admire him for that. But it's terrible to think of all the things he's missed. He seemed almost suspicious when I offered to lend him that book of Browning's poems. I remember he told me that he'd never "wasted[1] time" on poetry. What an idea! But what I do admire about him is that he doesn't seem to care about money or success in the ordinary sense. He seems quite ready to live all his life on less than a hundred a year. But he does want to be famous, and he does want to make the world a better place to live in. The people he admires, people like Bradlaugh[2] and John Burns,[3] all seem to have been poor. Somehow a life like that seems so terribly bare. But I've started him reading poetry. That's something.

NARRATOR: In fact, Hill spent much of the Christmas holiday in reading poetry. The examinations were over and the results would be announced at the beginning of the next term. There were no scientific textbooks in the public library of the little town where his father lived, but there was plenty of poetry, and Hill read everything he could lay hands on—except Browning, because he hoped that Miss Haysman might lend him further volumes later on. On the day that the term opened he walked to the College with the volume of Browning in his bag, turning over in his mind various neat little speeches with which he might return it. In the entrance hall, however, a crowd of students was pressing round the notice board. The results of the biology examination had just been posted up. For a moment Hill forgot all about Browning and Miss Haysman and pushed his way to the front. There on the board was the list:

Class 1: 1st H. J. Somers Wedderburn
2nd William Hill

There were no other names in the first class. Hill backed out of the crowd amid the congratulations of his friends.

FAIR-HAIRED STUDENT: Well done, Hill!

GIRL STUDENT: Congratulations on your first class, Mr. Hill.

HILL: It's nothing.

GIRL STUDENT: We poor folks in the second class don't think so.

FAIR-HAIRED STUDENT: You'd think he'd be more pleased at being in the first class, wouldn't you?

HUNCHBACK: He wants to be top of it.

GIRL STUDENT: Of course he's terribly jealous of Mr. Wedderburn, you know.

NARRATOR: In fact, Hill was jealous, a little. A moment earlier he had felt generously enough towards Wedderburn. He had been ready to shake him by the hand and congratulate him on his victory. But when he entered the laboratory the first thing he saw was Wedderburn leaning gracefully against the window, playing with the tassel of the blind, and talking to no less than five girls at once. This was too much for Hill. He could talk confidently and even overbearingly to one girl, and he could have made a[4] speech to a roomful of girls, but to exchange light conversation with five of them simultaneously was beyond him. Moreover, one of the girls in question was Miss Haysman. Hill decided to put off returning the volume of Browning. He sat down at his table and took up his notebooks, just as a stout heavy man with a white face and pale grey eyes passed down the laboratory, rubbing his hands together and smiling.

FAIR-HAIRED STUDENT: Who's that old fellow?

GIRL STUDENT: That's professor Bindon, the professor of botany. He comes up from Kew Gardens for January and February. He's going to take the botany course this term.

NARRATOR: In the term that was now beginning Hill worked harder than ever. But he was in a curious emotional state. Wedderburn, whom he had hardly noticed a term ago, was more and more in his consciousness. He was growing less shy of Miss Haysman. They talked a great deal about poetry and socialism and life in general, over mangled guinea-pigs in the laboratory, or at lunch-time in the comparative privacy of the museum. One day, however, she told him casually that she had met Wedderburn socially, "at the house of some people she knew". She hardly realised what a pang of jealousy that sent through Hill. It infuriated him to think of that remote upper-class world to which she and Wedderburn both belonged, and from which he himself was excluded.

HILL: He meets her in a drawing-room, and they talk the same language: I can only meet her here in the laboratory among a crowd of people. And I suppose she notices when my collars are frayed. He's always so well dressed. I hate these snobs! He beat me in the last exam, but look at his background and look at mine! He has a comfortable study to work in, all the books he wants, good food, servants and tailors and barbers to look after him, and a famous man for his father. I have to work in a bedroom and wear my overcoat to keep warm. But I'll beat him next time, I swear that.

NARRATOR: It seemed to Hill absolutely necessary that he should beat Wedderburn in the forthcoming examination. And Wedderburn, in his quieter way, obviously returned his rivalry. As the time of the examination drew nearer Hill worked night and day. Even in the teashop where he went for lunch he would break his bun and sip his milk with his eyes intent on a closely-written sheet of memoranda. In his bedroom there were notes on buds and stems pinned round his looking-glass, and over his washing basin, there was a diagram to catch his eye, in case the soap should chance to spare it. Everyone knew about the rivalry between the two men—the Hill-Wedderburn quarrel, it was called. Miss Haysman was perhaps not altogether sorry to feel that she was the cause of it. Wedderburn had been paying her much more attention than Hill[5]—indeed, he made rather a point of joining in conversations in which Hill was taking part. He had an irritating trick of intervening when Hill was in the middle of a speech, and uttering some neat little sneer about Socialism or atheism which Hill found difficulty in answering.

HILL: I tell you Socialism is the only hope of the human race. As I was saying at the Debating Society last night—

WEDDERBURN: Still talking about Socialism, Hill? I'm afraid I find your belief in it rather hard to share. My impression is that if you divided the money up on Tuesday it would all be back in the same places on Wednesday.

HILL: Who's talking about dividing the money up? Have you ever made a serious study of Socialism?

WEDDERBURN: I've made a serious study of Socialists, my dear fellow. That's equally enlightening.

(*LAUGHTER*)

HILL: Anybody can make cheap jokes. Why don't you come down to the Debating Society one evening and have it out?

WEDDERBURN: What time does this debating society of yours meet?

HILL: Half past seven.

WEDDERBURN: Impossible. I always dine at eight.

HILL: Socialism means common ownership of the means of production. If you'd read Karl Marx—

WEDDERBURN: Nobody has read Karl Marx, my dear fellow. He is unreadable.

(*LAUGHTER*)

NARRATOR: Hill was no good at this kind of conversation, and he knew it. It seemed to him cheap, unfair and connected in some subtle way with Wedderburn's well-cut clothes, manicured hands and generally sleek and monied exterior.

HILL: He's got such a mean, sneering way of talking. He never really argues, only tries to raise a laugh. How I wish he'd come to the Debating Society one night! Then I'd smash him. Of course that class are all the same. Millionaires, cabinet ministers, generals, bishops, professors—they're all the same. Just hiding behind their money and their little social tricks. He's not a man, he's only a type. Wait till the exam, though. This time I'll wipe the floor with him.

NARRATOR: At last the day of the examination arrived. The professor of botany, a fussy, conscientious man, had rearranged all the tables in the long narrow laboratory to make quite sure that there should be no cheating. All the morning from ten till one Wedderburn's quill pen shrieked defiance at Hill's, and the quills of the others chased their leaders in a tireless pack, and so it was also in the afternoon. Wedderburn was a little quieter than usual, and Hill's face was hot all day, and his overcoat bulged with textbooks and notebooks against the last moment's revision. And the next day, in the morning and in the afternoon was the practical examination, when sections had to be cut and slides identified. It was in this part of the examination that the mysterious slip occurred.

The professor of botany had placed on the table a microscope holding a glass slide, in which there was a preparation from some portion of a plant. The test for the students was to identify the preparation. The professor explained clearly that the slide was not to be moved.

PROF. BINDON: Will you please make quite sure, all of you, not to move the slide under that microscope. I want each of you in turn to go to the table, make a sketch of the preparation, and write down in your answer book what you consider it to be. And once again, *do not* move the slide. I want you to identify the preparation in that position, and no other.

NARRATOR: The professor's reason, of course, was that the preparation— actually it was a lenticel[6] from the elder tree—was difficult to recognise in this particular position, but easy enough in certain others. But it was a foolish stipulation to make, because it offered opportunities to a cheat. To move the slide under a microscope takes only a second and can be done accidentally; and besides, it would be quite easy for anyone to move the slide and then move it back.

When it came to Hill's turn to go to the table, he was already a little distraught. He had just had a struggle with some re-agents° for staining microscopic preparations. He sat down, turned the mirror of the microscope to get the best light, and then—

HILL: My God! I've moved the slide!

NARRATOR: In fact, he had moved it from sheer force of habit. And even as he did so he remembered the prohibition, and with almost the same movement of his fingers he moved it back again. All the same, he had had time to see what the preparation was. Slowly he turned his head. Nobody had seen—nobody was looking. The professor was out of the room and the demonstrator was reading a scientific journal. Hill's eyes roved over[7] his fellow-students, and Wedderburn suddenly glanced over his shoulder at him with a queer expression in his eyes. Hill sketched the preparation under the microscope, but he did not as yet write down the answer. He went back to his seat and tried to think it over.

HILL: I *did* move the slide. It was cheating, I suppose. No, because I didn't do it intentionally. Of course, when I moved the slide I recognised the thing at once. It was a bit of elder. But then I'd probably have recognised it in any case. What ought I to do? Own up at once? No! Why should I? Of course, I don't have to write down the answer. I could leave a blank and get no marks for that question, and then if I did cheat I shan't have profited by it. But if I do that Wedderburn will probably beat me again. I *must* beat him! After all, it was only a chance. I didn't move it on purpose. I don't see why I should throw those marks away. It's no more unfair than a lot of other things.

NARRATOR: Hill watched the clock until only two minutes remained. Then he opened his book of answers, and with hot ears and an affectation of ease, he wrote down the answer. When the results of the examination were announced, the previous positions of Hill and Wedderburn were reversed. Hill was now top of the first class, Wedderburn second. Everyone congratulated him warmly.

FAIR-HAIRED STUDENT: Well done, Hill. Jolly good!

GIRL STUDENT: Congratulations, Mr. Hill. Do you know that you're just one mark ahead of Mr. Wedderburn on the two exams. You've got 167 marks out of 200, and he's got 166. The demonstrator told me so.

MISS HAYSMAN: I *am* so glad you were top this time, Mr. Hill.

HUNCHBACK: Well done, Hill! We were all hoping you'd take him down a peg or two.

NARRATOR: But unfortunately Hill did not get much pleasure from their congratulations, not even from Miss Haysman's. The feeling of triumph that he had had at first soon wore off. Once again he was working very hard, he made brilliant speeches at the Debating Society in the evenings, he borrowed yet more books of poetry from Miss Haysman. But there was a memory that kept coming into his mind, and curiously enough it was a memory that grew more and not less vivid as time went on: it was a picture of a sneakish person manipulating a microscope slide.

HILL: I *did* move that slide, I can't get away from that. And I suppose it was unfair to take advantage of it, even though I hadn't done it on purpose. But why should I worry about it? Nobody will ever know. But a lie is a lie, whether it's found out or not. The trouble is, that it's no satisfaction now to have beaten Wedderburn. Perhaps he'd have beaten me again if we'd both started fair. Why *did* I move that slide? Perhaps it was partly because I was so keen to beat him. The queer thing is that I'm not even certain any longer that it *was* an accident. Could you intend to do something without knowing that you intended it, I wonder.

NARRATOR: Perhaps Hill's state of mind was becoming morbid. He was overworked, and unquestionably he was also underfed. The memory of what he had done even poisoned his relations with Miss Haysman. He knew now that she preferred him to Wedderburn, and in his clumsy way he tried to reciprocate her attentions. Once he even bought a bunch of violets and carried them about in his pocket all day before finally presenting them to her when they were dead and withered. But most of all he was tormented by the feeling that he had not beaten Wedderburn fairly. To feel himself superior to Wedderburn—that, really, was what he wanted most of all. And at last— moved, curiously enough, by the very same motive force that had resulted in his dishonesty he went to Professor Bindon—to make a clean breast of the whole affair.

HILL: I want to speak to you, sir. I've been wanting to for some weeks. I— well, there's something I feel it's my duty to say. You remember that slide under the microscope in the botany examination?

BINDON: Yes?

HILL: Well—I moved it.

BINDON: You moved it!

NARRATOR: And then out came the whole story, just as it had happened. As Hill was only a scholarship student, Professor Bindon did not ask him to sit down. Hill made his confession standing before the professor's desk.

BINDON: It's a curious story—a most remarkable story. I can't understand your doing it, and I can't understand this confession. Why did you cheat?

HILL: I didn't *cheat*.

BINDON: But you have just been telling me you did.

HILL: I thought I explained—

BINDON: Either you cheated or you did not cheat.

HILL: But my movement was involuntary!

263

BINDON: I am not a metaphysician. I am a servant of science—of fact. You were told not to move the slide, and you did move it. If that is not cheating—

HILL: If I was a cheat, should I come here and tell you about it?

BINDON: Of course your repentance does you credit, but it doesn't alter the facts. Even now you have caused an enormous amount of trouble. The examination list will have to be revised.

HILL: I suppose so, sir.

BINDON: Suppose so? Of course it must be revised. And I don't see how I can conscientiously pass you.

HILL: Not pass me? Fail me?

BINDON: Of course. What else did you expect?

HILL: I never thought you would fail me. I thought you would simply deduct the marks for that question.

BINDON: Impossible! Besides, it would still leave you above Wedderburn. I have no choice. The Departmental Regulations distinctly say—

HILL: But this is my own admission, sir.

BINDON: The Regulations say nothing whatever of the manner in which the matter comes to light. I must fail you, and there is an end of it.

HILL: But it will ruin me, sir. If I fail this examination they won't renew my scholarship. It's the end of my career.

BINDON: You should have thought of that before. The Professors in this College are machines. Possibly the Regulations are hard, but I must follow them.

HILL: If I'm to be failed in the examination I might as well go home at once.

BINDON: That is for you to decide. As a private person, I think this confession of yours goes far to mitigate your offence. But—well, you have set the machinery in motion. I am really very sorry that this has happened—very.

NARRATOR: For a moment a wave of emotion prevented Hill from answering. Suddenly, very vividly, he saw the heavily-lined face of his father, the cobbler. His father had been so proud of his success and of the brilliant career which seemed to be opening before him. Already in many a public house he had made himself unpopular by boasting about "my son, the professor". And now Hill would have to go home, confessing that he was a failure and his scientific career was at an end.

HILL: My God! What a fool I have been!

BINDON: You have certainly been very foolish. I hope it will be a lesson to you.

NARRATOR: But, curiously enough, they were not thinking of quite the same indiscretion.

Next day Hill's place was vacant and the laboratory was buzzing with the news.

GIRL STUDENT: Have you heard?

WEDDERBURN: Heard what?

GIRL STUDENT: There was cheating in the examination.

FAIR-HAIRED STUDENT: Cheating!

HUNCHBACK: Who cheated!

MISS HAYSMAN: Cheating? Surely not![8]

WEDDERBURN: Cheating! But I—how?[9]

GIRL STUDENT: That slide—

WEDDERBURN: Moved? Never!

GIRL STUDENT: It was. The slide we weren't to move—

WEDDERBURN: Nonsense! How could they possibly find out? They can't prove it. Who do they say—?

GIRL STUDENT: It was Mr. Hill.

FAIR-HAIRED STUDENT: Hill!

MISS HAYSMAN: Not *Mr. Hill!*

WEDDERBURN: Not—surely not the immaculate Hill?

MISS HAYSMAN: I just don't believe it! How do you know?

GIRL STUDENT: *I* didn't believe it. But I know it now for a fact. Mr. Hill went and confessed to Professor Bindon himself.

WEDDERBURN: By Jove! Hill of all people. But I must say I always was inclined to distrust these high-minded atheists.

MISS HAYSMAN: Are you quite sure?

GIRL STUDENT: Quite. It's dreadful, isn't it? But what else can you expect? His father is a cobbler.

MISS HAYSMAN: I don't care. I just don't believe it. I will not believe it until he has told me so himself—face to face. I would scarcely believe it even then.

GIRL STUDENT: It's true all the same.

MISS HAYSMAN: I just don't believe it. I'm going to find him and ask him myself.

NARRATOR: But she never did ask him, because Hill had packed up his textbooks and boxes of instruments on the previous day, and had already left London.

1. wasted] *typed as 'wated' with handwritten insertion of* 's'
2. Charles Bradlaugh (1833–1891), radical freethinker, lecturer, and editor of the *National Reformer*, spoke and wrote in a variety of causes, opposing religion, advocating birth control and individual liberty. He was prosecuted for blasphemy, sedition, and indecency. He was elected an M.P. in 1880 but wished to affirm rather than take the oath. This was not allowed until 1886, when he at last took his seat. He was opposed to socialism. He is mentioned in Wells's short story.
3. John Elliot Burns (1858–1943), labour leader, socialist, M.P., 1892–1918, was tried for sedition in 1886 but acquitted. In 1888 he was imprisoned following the 'Bloody Sunday' riot in Trafalgar Square, London, and was a leader of the great London dock strike of 1889. He was the first working-class man to become a member of a Cabinet—that of the Liberal government of 1905. In early 1914 he was appointed President of the Board of Trade, but he resigned in protest at the outbreak of World War I. He abandoned public life in 1918. He is mentioned in Wells's short story.
4. a] *handwritten insertion*
5. than Hill] *to Hill in typescript*
6. lenticel] *lentical in typescript; the error is probably the typist's; Wells's original has* 'lenticel' *(a breathing pore in bark)*
7. over] *handwritten insertion*
8. Surely not!] *followed in typescript by:* 'NARRATOR: Wedderburn's face had suddenly turned red,' *which is crossed through*
9. But I—how?] *handwritten insertion*

2298. To J. C. Flugel

6 October 1943   07/ES/EB

Dear Professor Flugel,[1]
I am so glad to hear that you are willing to do a talk in our Psychology series; I think Mr. Laws has given you an idea of the type of thing we want, but please let me know whether there are any points you want me to make clear. Your talk will be on the 21st October, which means that I should like to have the script by October 14th. It would be a good arrangement if you could send Mr. Laws a duplicate copy at the same time, as he is more or less editing the series. The script should not be longer than 1500 words as they have to be 13½ minutes on the air and scripts of this kind are often very difficult to cut down if they are too long. I suppose Mr. Laws explained to you that we hope to reprint these talks afterwards in India as pamphlets. The time of your talk will be 11.15 a.m. BST so could you be here (200 Oxford Street) on the 21st at 10.30, which would give us plenty of time?

Yours truly,
[Initialled] E. A. B
(Eric Blair)
Talks Producer
Indian Section

1. John Carl Flugel (1884–1955), on the staff of University College London from 1909; as Assistant Professor of Psychology, 1929–43; Special Lecturer in Psychology thereafter. He was President of the British Psychological Society, 1932–35, and Assistant Editor of the *International Journal of Psycho-analysis*, 1920–37. His publications included *The Psycho-Analytic Study of the Family* (1921), *The Psychology of Clothes* (1930), *Man, Morals and Society* (1945), *Population, Psychology and Peace* (1947).

2299. To Leonard Moore

6 October 1943   Typewritten

10a Mortimer Crescent London NW 6

Dear Mr Moore,
Are the Penguin people doing anything about "Burmese Days", which they were going to issue? I can't remember what date the contract said, but as far as I remember it was about now.[1]

The book "Betrayal of the Left" on behalf of which you forwarded me a small cheque[2] was a composite book in which Gollancz reprinted two essays of mine that had appeared in "Left News".

I think I am probably going to do a book for the "Britain in Pictures" series.[3] If I do, I will refer them to you.

Yours sincerely
E. Blair

1. It was not published until May 1944.

2. This book was published in March 1941. Orwell records in his Royalty Receipt Book that he received 10s.6d (52½p). He gives no date, but notes that it was 'earlier' (than 12 July 1943).
3. See contract for *The English People*, 23 September 1943, *2278*.

2300. To W. J. Turner

6 October 1943   07/ES/EB

Dear Turner,
I don't suppose you have started on your talk on R.U.R. yet, but it has been suggested that it might be better to do this in the form of a dialogue between you and Noel Iliffe[1] (this won't affect the financial aspect from your point of view). If it is to be in the form of a dialogue you don't need to write it up fully before hand as it will have to be broken down in any case, so could you instead of writing an ordinary talk just let me have a script of about the same length saying what you think about this play and we will put in a few remarks for Iliffe and do our best to make the thing sound like a genuine conversation.

Yours sincerely,
[Initialled] E.A.B
(George Orwell)

1. Noel Iliffe was a Presentation Assistant in the Overseas Services Division. As a member of the BBC's staff he would not be paid a fee, so Turner's fee would not be affected.

2301. BBC Talks Booking Form, 6.10.43

Professor J. C. Flugel: Calling All Students; Psychology; 2nd talk in series; broadcast 21.10.43; fee £10.10s. Signed: Z. A. Bokhari.

2302. Newsletter in Tamil, 25

7 October 1943

The English version was written by Eric Blair. No script has been traced.

2303. To Susan Isaacs

7 October 1943   07/ES/EB

Dear Dr. Isaacs,[1]
Mr. Frederick Laws has forwarded the letter you sent him.[2] I don't think the dates of these talks need be regarded as unchangeable. We could quite easily put your talk in towards the end, for instance, as number five or six, this would give you time to get it ready about the beginning of November. I shall

see Mr. Laws today and confirm this with him. He will then give you any further information you may need.

Yours truly,
[Initialled] E.A.B
(Eric Blair)

1. Susan Sutherland Isaacs (1885–1948), Head of the Department of Child Development, University of London Institute of Education, was extremely influential in the training of teachers of young children, particularly through her books *Intellectual Growth in Children* (1930), *The Nursery Years* (1932) (see letter to her 22 October 1943, *2330, n. 1*), *The Children We Teach* (1932), and *Social Development of Young Children* (1933). She also wrote *An Introduction to Psychology* (1921).
2. Dr. Isaacs had written to Laws on 5 October saying she would be delighted to contribute if the date could be put back a little.

2304. English Newsletter for Indonesia, 14
8 October 1943

This was written and read by George Orwell. No script has been traced.

2305. To T. S. Eliot
8 October 1943   07/ES/EB

Dear Eliot,
With reference to our brief conversation yesterday. I do not know whether you would like to do another talk in the Great Dramatists series, similar to the one you did before. The date of the talk would [be] November, 21st, which would mean having the script in about November 14th. It would be a ten minutes talk.

You probably remember how these programmes go. They are half hour programmes consisting of an extract from a play and a talk about the play and as far as possible about the author's work. We haven't yet fixed the play for November 21st, and you could choose anyone you like, but I would prefer it to be a contemporary play because we are doing these more or less in chronological order. The other five in the series are Macbeth, An Enemy of the People, Doctor's Dilemma, Cherry Orchard, and R.U.R.

Yours sincerely,
[Initialled] E.A.B
(George Orwell)

2305A, 2317A, 2341A, 2349A: this sequence of four letters will be found in Volume XX, pp. 312–4.

2306. To C. W. Valentine

8 October 1943   07/ES/EB/JEL

Dear Professor Valentine,[1]

Mr. Frederick Laws has passed your letter on to me. I think we shall have to put your talk third instead of fourth on the list, because Dr. Susan Isaacs says she cannot get hers done, which will mean having her later on; in that case yours will be broadcast on October 28th instead of November 4th. I wonder whether you could let me have the script by about October 21st. It would help if you could let Mr. Laws have a copy of the script at the same time, as he is more or less editing the series. Your script should be not more than 1600 words at the outside as these talks are 13½ minutes, and it is very [h]ard to cut material of this kind down if it is too long.

Yours truly,
[Initialled] E. A. B
(Eric Blair)

1. Charles William Valentine (1879–1964), Professor of Educational Psychology, University of Birmingham and editor of the *British Journal of Psychology*. His many publications included: *Experimental Psychology of Beauty* (1913), *Experimental Psychology in Relation to Education* (1914), *New Psychology of the Unconscious* (1921), *The Reliability of Examinations* (1932), *Principles of Army Education* (with special reference to small-arms training, 1942), *Parents and Children: Two Broadcast Talks* (1945).

2307. To Frederick Laws

[8–10? October 1943]   07/ES/EB

Dear Mr. Laws,

We have heard from Professor Pear, who thinks he would rather do his talk on the 14th. I think it is much better not to rush him, so that will mean each of the talks will be a week later than as scheduled. Professor Pear will send you a copy of his talk, or at any rate a rough draft. We shall arrange for his recording and let him know the time and date. I hope the others are coming in all right.

Yours sincerely,
[Initialled] E. A. B
(Eric Blair)

2308. On Orwell's behalf to Oliver Bell

9 October 1943   07/ES/EB/JEL

Dear Mr. Bell,

This is just to confirm that your next film talk will be on Wednesday, 20th October, at 11.00 a.m. BST. May I take it that you will be doing it live? I shall be glad to have the script as soon as possible. Could you let me know whether you will be talking about any film of which we can get the music to play in the fifteen minutes following your talk? If there is not any appropriate music we can play the records from Malta G.C.[1]

Yours sincerely,
[Initialled] JEL
for Eric Blair

1. See *2268, n.2*

2309. Review of *Reflections on the Revolution of Our Time* by Harold J. Laski

The Observer, 10 October 1943

This book is an impressive and courageous attempt to disentangle the intellectual muddle in which we are now living. In defining what is meant by Socialism and Fascism, and in proclaiming the ends we ought to aim at and the dangers that lie ahead, Professor Laski avoids mere propaganda as completely, and states unpopular views as boldly, as anyone who is personally involved in politics could well do. He has the advantage that his roots lie deeper than those of the majority of left-wing thinkers; he does not ignore the past, and he does not despise his own countrymen. But the position of someone who is a Socialist by allegiance and a Liberal by temperament is not easy, and though he never states it in those words, Professor Laski's book really revolves round this problem.

This is most apparent in his chapter on the Russian Revolution, and in the long chapter towards the end, entitled "The Threat of Counter-revolution." Professor Laski is rightly concerned with the danger that totalitarianism may soon extend itself to the countries which now call themselves democracies. He sees clearly enough that the war has made no structural change in Britain or the U.S.A., that the old economic problems will recur in more pressing forms the moment that the fighting stops, and that the inroads on privilege that might have been accepted in the moment of national danger will be resisted when there is no enemy at the gate. He is probably right, therefore, in saying that if we do not put through the necessary reforms during the war, when general consent is at any rate thinkable, we shall soon have them imposed on us by violence and at the cost of a long period of dictatorship. Professor Laski knows pretty well what reforms he wants, and few thinking men will disagree with him: he wants centralised ownership, planned production, social equality and the "positive state." Much too readily, however—indeed with an almost Nineteenth Century optimism—he assumes that these things not only can but certainly will be combined with democracy and freedom of thought.

All through his book there is apparent an unwillingness to admit that Socialism has totalitarian possibilities. He dismisses Fascism as simply monopoly capitalism in its last phase. This is the habitual left-wing diagnosis, but it seems to have been adopted on the principle of *extra ecclesiam nulla salus*,[1] and a false inference has followed from it. Since Fascism was evidently not Socialism, it followed that it must be a form of capitalism. But capitalism, by definition, cannot "work"; therefore Fascism cannot "work"—or at best it can only, like any capitalist economy, solve the problem of surplus production by going to war.

Fascist States, it has been assumed, are inherently and inevitably warlike. Professor Laski repeats this over and over again—"the counter-revolution," he says, "is bound to make war." In reality one has only to look at the map to see that most counter-revolutions don't make war and avoid it at almost any cost. Germany, Italy, and Japan bear out Professor Laski's thesis; for the rest, one country after another, in Europe and America, has gone through a counter-revolutionary process and adopted a Fascist economy, without engaging in foreign war. Does General Franco want war, for instance, or Marshal Pétain, or Dr. Salazar, or half a dozen petty South American dictators? It would seem that the essential point about Fascism is not that it solves its problems by war but that it solves them non-democratically and without abolishing private property. The assumption that every totalitarian system must finally wreck itself in meaningless wars is therefore unjustified.

Needless to say, Professor Laski is very unwilling to admit a resemblance between the German and Russian systems. There is much in the Soviet regime that he does not like, and he says so with a boldness that will get him into serious trouble with the Left. He is, perhaps, even too hard on the "oriental" worship accorded to Marshal Stalin—for, after all, Stalin is not praised more slavishly than a king or a millionaire. But he does defend the purges, the GPU, and the crushing of intellectual liberty by saying that they result from the U.S.S.R.'s backwardness and insecurity. Let Russia be really safe from foreign aggression, he says, and the dictatorship will relax. This is a poor answer, because the Russian dictatorship has evidently grown tighter as the U.S.S.R. grew stronger, militarily and economically.

What the Soviet regime has demonstrated is what the Fascist States have demonstrated in a different fashion: that the "contradictions" of capitalism can be got rid of non-democratically and without any increase in individual liberty. Economic insecurity can be abolished at the price of handing society over to a new race of oligarchs. This is not in itself an argument against the Soviet system, for it may well be that the Western conceptions of liberty and democracy are worthless. But if they are not worthless, then certain features in Russian policy are not defensible. One cannot have it both ways. Professor Laski does show signs of wanting to have it both ways, and therein is the chief weakness of his book.

Clearly his own instincts are all for liberty, and even for an old-fashioned version of liberty. His remarks on education point to an individualist outlook hardly compatible with any kind of "positive state." All the more ought he to realise that Socialism, if it means only centralised ownership and planned production, is not of its nature either democratic or equalitarian. A hierarchical version of Socialism (Hilaire Belloc's "Servile State"[2]) is probably just as workable as the other, and at this moment is much likelier to arrive. Times beyond number Professor Laski repeats that victory in the present war will achieve nothing if it leaves us with the old economic problems unsolved, and without doubt he is right. But it is a pity he did not say more forcibly that to solve our economic problems will settle nothing either, since that, like the defeat of Hitler, is only one step towards the society of free and equal human beings which he himself so obviously desires.[3]

[Fee: £6.6s; 4.10.43]

1. *Salus extra ecclesiam non est*: No salvation exists outside the church (St Augustine).
2. Hilaire Belloc (1870–1953), humorist, essayist, Roman Catholic apologist; Liberal M.P. 1906–10. *The Servile State* was first published in 1912, and in 1913 and 1927 with new prefaces. It was published in New York in 1946, introduced by C. Gauss. It is concerned with, amongst other things, the price the individual must pay in terms of personal freedom for social security.
3. On 29 September 1943 a letter from the *Observer*, almost certainly from Ivor Brown, asked for copy for this Laski review as soon as possible and asked Orwell if he would like to review Douglas Reed's *Lest We Forget* and Sidney Dark's *I Sit and I Think and I Wonder*, Orwell reviewed these (see 2347). On 7 October, another unsigned letter, also doubtless from Brown, said he 'much appreciated' the Laski review; he understood that Orwell would be free at the end of November and he wished to discuss with him further work for the *Observer*.

2310. Orwell's Sick Leave

The BBC Staff Record shows that Orwell was on sick leave from Monday, 11 October, to Friday, 15 October, 1943. This was logged as four days. He wrote to Professor Valentine on 14 October, but the letter may not have been signed until the 15th. By then he was certainly back on duty, because he read the newsletter to Indonesia on that day.

2311. Guy Wint to Orwell

11 October 1943

Guy Wint[1] wrote from Oxford on Saturday, 9 October 1943 to say that he had read Orwell's 'admirable review' in *Horizon* of Fielden's *Beggar my Neighbour* and, because he was interested in India, he would like to meet him. He was to be in London on thursday and Friday (14 and 15 October) and would call on Orwell at any time he suggested. This is annotated (not by Orwell). Probably Wint's letter was read to Orwell over the telephone, and this is the message Orwell gave to whoever called—perhaps Miss Light. The annotation reads: 'Sorry, ill can't be in until Friday at earliest[.] Look in Fri—on a chance.'

1. Guy Wint (1910–1969) had written with Sir George Schuster, *India and Democracy* (1941). He also published *The British in Asia* (1947), *South-east Asia and its Future* (1951), and books on Japan, China and Korea.

2312. On Orwell's behalf to Desmond Hawkins

12 October 1943   07/ES/EB/LB[1]

Dear Mr. Hawkins,
I am enclosing scripts for the next Backward Glance programme, for transmission on Wednesday 27th October.

Yours sincerely,
[Not signed/initialled]
for George Orwell

1. Probably Bokhari's secretary, Miss A. L. Bateman.

2313. Newsletter in Tamil, 26

14 October 1943

The English version was written by Eric Blair. No script has been traced.

2314. To Philip Rahv

14 October 1943   Typewritten

On 30 July 1943 Philip Rahv wrote to Orwell to say that Dwight Macdonald was resigning from *Partisan Review*. 'His resignation is involuntary, being forced upon him by his failure to swing us to his anti-war line, and, in general, to his orthodox reading of the old texts.' Rahv said that *Partisan Review*'s policy would remain primarily cultural and, though Marxism would be influential, 'We won't try . . . to settle the world's hash, à la Macdonald, in each issue.' Orwell was asked to continue his London Letter, 'which has been enormously successful,' three times a year, copy to be received around 20 October, 20 February, and 20 June for the November, March, and July issues. Rahv also asked Orwell for names of writers whose work might be featured in *Partisan Review*. He went on: 'The Alex Comfort gang keeps on sending in stuff, but we're pretty tired of their shennanigans. They're an ambitious lot, but their lack of talent is all-too-apparent.° And politically they are beyond the pale.' Macdonald wrote to Orwell on 22 October, and Orwell replied on 11 December; see *2392*.

10a Mortimer Crescent   London   NW 6

Dear Philip Rahv,
I have thought over your request for the names of possible contributors, but I must tell you that it is extremely difficult to think of any at present. No new people who are worth much seem to be coming along, and nearly everyone is either in the forces or being drained dry by writing muck for one of the ministries. You say the Comfort crew have been plaguing the life out of you, which I can well imagine, but I don't know which of them you have actually contacted. I think the best of this lot are Comfort himself, Treece, Alun

Lewis, Allan° Rook, William Rodgers, G. S. Frazer,° Roy Fuller, Kathleen Raine.[1] You will have seen the work of these in "Poetry London" if it gets to the USA. I could obtain the addresses of these or others at need, except that Frazer,° I believe is in the Middle East.

Of older people I suppose you have the addresses of Read and Eliot and of the Spender-Macneice° lot, who can in any case be contacted through "Horizon". E. M. Forster has seen and likes PR, and would I should think do you something if you wanted. His address is West Hackhurst, Abinger Hammer, Nr. Dorking, Surrey. William Empson who does still occasionally write something can be found care of the BBC. I don't know whether you know Mark Benney, some of whose stuff is quite good. I haven't his address but could find it out (you could send it care of me if you wanted to write to him). Ditto with Jack Common whose stuff you have possibly seen. You *might* get something very interesting out of Hugh Slater (address 106 George Street, Nr. Baker Street, London NW 1). If you are interested in Indian writers, I think the best is Ahmed Ali, whose address is care of BBC, New Delhi. He might do you something very good about present-day conditions in India especially among the younger intelligentsia. I know he is very overworked but he has recently published a book so he must have some spare time. Roy Campbell, who as you know was previously a Fascist and fought for Franco (ie. for the Carlists) in Spain, but has latterly changed all his views, has been silent for some time but may be about due to begin writing again and I could get his address at need. I am sorry I cannot suggest more names but this place is a literary desert at present.

I am leaving the BBC at the end of the next month and unless anything intervenes am going to take over the literary editorship of the "Tribune". This *may* leave me some time to do a little of my own work as well, which the BBC doesn't. You may be interested to hear that I have contacted several American soldiers via PR. A chap called Julius Horowitz brought a message from Clement Greenberg whom he had met in the army somewhere, and a boy named John Schloss who had read my letters in PR rang me up at the office and we met for a few drinks. Another fellow named Harry Milton who was with my lot in Spain and whom I think you may possibly know is also here. I wonder whether a Canadian airman named David Martin, who went across recently to finish his training, has shown up at your office. He said he would do so if in New York, and he has a message from me.

I hope all goes well.

Yours
Geo. Orwell

P.S. How about the extra copies of PR? Is it now possible to send them? If so there is no doubt we could whack up the British circulation a bit. The last I heard was it was being done in some devious way through Horizon, but they were not getting enough copies to supply all those who wanted to subscribe. The people who *are* getting it are most enthusiastic about it.

1. Most of those listed by Orwell were in correspondence with him whilst he was at the BBC. Biographical notes for some have been given earlier, but, for convenience, short identifications and cross-references follow:

Alun Lewis (1915–1944), poet and short-story writer; *Raiders' Dawn and Other Poems* (1942); see *856, n. 3.* William Robert Rodgers (1900–1969), poet; *Awake! and Other Poems* (1941; as *Awake! and Other Wartime Poems,* New York 1942). Kathleen Raine (1908–), poet and critic; *Stone and Flower: Poems 1933–43* (1943); see *1526, n. 3.* Mark Benney (1910–) became well known in 1936 for his *Low Company: Describing the Evolution of a Burglar,* written in prison; see *1936, n. 1.* Jack Common (1903–1968), writer and editor whom Orwell met through their association with *Adelphi;* see *95; 295, n. 1; 1086, n. 1.* Hugh (Humphrey) Slater (1906–1958), painter, author; fought in Spain as a Communist and became Chief of Operations of the International Brigade; with Tom Wintringham founded a Home Guard training centre in 1940; edited *Polemic,* 1945–47, to which Orwell contributed; see *731, n. 1.* Ahmed Ali (1906–), writer, academic, and BBC Listener Research Officer in India; see *1103, n. 3.* Roy Campbell (1901–1957), South African poet; *Flowering Rifle: A Poem from the Battlefield of Spain* (1939), *Collected Poems,* 3 vols. (1949–60; Chicago, 1959–60).

Rook's first name should be spelt 'Alan'; Fraser is spelt with an 's,' see *2184, n. 3.*

2315. To C. W. Valentine

14 October 1943   07/ES/EB

Dear Professor Valentine,

Thank you for your letter of the 11th October. I'm delighted to hear that you can do this broadcast.[1] The actual date of the broadcast is Thursday, 28th October, from 11.15 to 11.30 a.m. our clock-time.

We can record your talk in advance practically at any time to suit your convenience. If, as you suggest, you let us have your script by the 21st October, it will have to be typed and censored before the Recording takes place, and I therefore suggest that we record your talk on Monday, 25th October; this recording, with rehearsal beforehand, can take place from Birmingham—and your talk can be recorded by Line from Birmingham to London. This would save you coming to London. We have been in touch with Mr. Holland Bennett in Birmingham, and you will shortly be hearing from his office with regard to this recording.

Yours truly,
[Initialled] E.A.B
Eric Blair
(Talks Producer)
Indian Section.

1. Valentine had written on 11 October to say he would broadcast on the 28th in order to accommodate Dr. Isaacs's wish to delay her talk. At the foot of Valentine's letter Orwell wrote in pencil: am: Rec:. B'cast 28th Oct.

2316. English Newsletter for Indonesia, 15

15 October 1943

This was written and read by George Orwell. No script has been traced.

2317. To J. C. Flugel

15 October 1943

Dear Mr. Flugel,
Very many thanks for your draft script,[1] which reached here a couple of days ago. I believe you sent a copy to Mr. Laws and will settle any final minor alterations with him. Your talk is on Thursday, the 21st October, at 11.15 a.m. standard time. If you could be here (200 Oxford Street) at 10.30 a.m. that would give us time to rehearse the talk before going on the air.

Yours truly,
[Initialled] E.A.B
Eric Blair.

1. Flugel had written to Orwell on 11 October when sending the draft script to say that he had added a personal note and made particular reference to India. He explained that, before the war, there had been so many students from India at University College London he thought this a good opportunity to bring in an intimate note. However, he would willingly change his script if this was thought to be inappropriate. Orwell showed Flugel's letter and script to Bokhari, who wrote as follows to Flugel on 15 October: 'Mr. Blair has shown me your letter of the 11th October with the draft of your talk for the 21st October. I know that he has already acknowledged it, but I thought you might like to know that I, as an Indian, feel that you have handled the references to India extremely happily, and that the script is exactly what we want.'

2318. To Desmond Hawkins

16 October 1943   07/ES/EB/?[1]

Dear Hawkins,
The last "Backward Glance" programme went off very smoothly and was an extremely good programme, I thought. I liked the use of the man and woman, two voices. Could you make the same treatment in your next programme, which goes on the air on Wednesday, the 27th October, from 11 to 11.30 a.m. Douglas Cleverdon is again producing this programme, this time from London and not from Plymouth, thank goodness. We have already booked Freda Falconer and Arthur Bush to take part in it and Douglas Cleverdon is having a rehearsal on the Tuesday afternoon, the 26th October, so if you could possibly let us have the script a littler earlier than usual this time, say the Thursday or Friday in advance, it would be a great help.

Yours truly,
George Orwell.
dispatched in his absence by [no initials]

1. The secretary's initials look like MH, but although there were several secretaries on the 21.8.43 staff list with these initials—M. R. Huggett, B. M. Hobdey, M. G. Hushar—they were in other sections. The 'H' may be a slip for 'B,' the typewriter keys being diagonally adjacent. This would probably indicate Mary Blackburn. She wrote to Hawkins on Orwell's behalf about this series on 5 August 1943; see 2222.

2319. *Macbeth* by William Shakespeare, Adapted and Introduced by George Orwell

BBC Eastern Service, 17 October 1943

In a letter to Eleanor Jaques of 18 November 1932 Orwell wrote, 'I so adore Macbeth' (presumably the play rather than the character) and he arranged to go with her to the Old Vic to see the play on 26 November 1932. Orwell's talk on *Macbeth* for 'Calling All Students', which was the first in his 'Great Dramatists' series for Indian university students, is illustrated by what the script calls a fifteen-minute version of the play. This is made up of Acts I.7, V.3., V.5., V.7.1–23, and V.8, with a linking narrative. As broadcast, these excerpts ran for 16 minutes 30 seconds; Orwell's talk took 9 minutes 26 seconds, which, with the continuity announcements, would fit neatly into the half-hour allowed. Both scripts are marked 'as broadcast,' but only the version of the play has been so marked by Orwell himself. The censor was Bokhari. Orwell evidently recorded his talk; its disc number (DOX 22346) is written on the script.

Orwell's talk indicates that the dramatised excerpts were presented in two parts. He starts his talk by saying, 'Those lines you have just heard come from "Macbeth", by William Shakespeare'; later he says, 'The witches have made another prophecy which seems to promise Macbeth immunity. How that prophecy is fulfilled . . . you will hear in the acted extract from the play.' The script does not show how the play was divided, but it is almost certain that the section from I.7 started the broadcast; Orwell's talk followed; and the programme ended with the excerpts from Act V. This is the arrangement made here.

A few lines of the play are marked off between heavy square brackets and there is a bold 'T' in the margin. (Only the brackets are reproduced here.) It would be strange if these $6\frac{1}{2}$ lines were to be omitted—they would hardly affect the timing. The significance of this marking is not known.

No actors' names are given against the cast list, but the Programme-as-Broadcast report names Abraham Sofaer, Laidman Brown, Griselda Harvey, Frank Cockran (Cochrane, presumably, a well-known actor), Richard Williams, Carl Bernard, Alan Blair, and Arthur Ridley, all of the BBC Repertory Company. This was a distinguished cast. The music was 'Abercairney Highlanders' (1' 30") played on the bagpipes by Pipe-Major Mackinnon (Regal Zonophone T 5806).

The version given here has been reproduced from the typescripts used for the broadcast (arranged as indicated above). The talk script looks like Orwell's typing. There are a couple of amendments in his hand. Near the end of the script, Orwell calls Edmund of *King Lear*, Edgar. This has been corrected and footnoted. A number of typing slips have been corrected silently; the most significant is the spelling of Antony with an 'h' in the reference to *Antony and Cleopatra*. The typescript omits some directions, especially from V.3. Essential entries and exits have been added in square brackets.

Almost a month later, on 10 November 1943, PasB gives details of a half-hour programme, 'Backward Glance No 8' which evidently included a replay of Orwell's version of *Macbeth*. The programme is described as a 'Return visit into some of our programmes for India' and was transmitted on the Purple Network to India, Burma, and Indonesia. Part of the half-hour was made up of 'Live programmes with commercial discs—script compiled by Desmond Hawkins.' Four commercial discs were used and five BBC recordings. The disc number for

Macbeth was given as DOX 22346. It is possible that the whole broadcast was recorded and that the number for that recording was DOX 23496. The programme was produced by Douglas Cleverdon and taking part were Arthur Bush and Freda Falconer.

Cast: Macbeth   Young Siward
Macduff   Servant[1]
Lady Macbeth Messenger
Doctor   Narrator
Seyton

NARRATOR: We are starting with the great scene early in the play when Lady Macbeth persuades her only half-willing husband to murder Duncan. Duncan, King of Scotland, is a guest at Macbeth's castle. In an earlier scene three witches have foretold to Macbeth that he himself will one day be King of Scotland, and the idea of killing Duncan and seizing the throne has already crossed his mind. Indeed, he has spoken of it with his wife. But he still shrinks from the deed; and he is musing alone, half tempted and half horrified, when Lady Macbeth enters and with a few skilful speeches nerves him for the murder.

MACBETH: If it were done, when 'tis done, then 'twere well
It were done quickly ....
.... He's here in double trust;
First, as I am his kinsman, and his subject,
Strong both against the deed; then, as his host,
Who should against his murderer shut the door,
Not bear the knife myself. Besides, this Duncan
Hath borne his faculties so meek, hath been
So clear in his great office, that his virtues
Will plead like angels, trumpet-tongu'd against
The deep damnation of his taking-off;
And pity, like a naked new-born babe,
Striding the blast, or heaven's cherubin, hors'd
Upon the sightless couriers of the air,
Shall blow the horrid deed in every eye,
That tears shall drown the wind. I have no spur
To prick the sides of my intent, but only
Vaulting ambition, which o'erleaps itself,
And falls on the other. How now? what news?
               [Enter Lady Macbeth]

LADY M: He has almost supp'd: why have you left the chamber?
MACBETH: Hath he ask'd for me?
LADY M: Know you not he has?
MACBETH: We will proceed no further in this business:
He hath honour'd me of late, and I have bought

Golden opinions from all sorts of people,
Which would be worn now in their newest gloss,
Not cast aside so soon.

LADY M: Was the hope drunk,
Wherein you dress'd yourself? hath it slept since?
And wakes it now to look so green, and pale,
At what it did so freely? From this time,
Such I account thy love. Art thou afeard
To be the same in thine own act and valour
As thou art in desire? Wouldst thou have that
Which thou esteem'st the ornament of life,
And live a coward in thine own esteem?
Letting 'I dare not' wait upon 'I would',
Like the poor cat i' the adage?

MACBETH: Prithee peace;
I dare do all that may become a man,
Who dares no more, is none.

LADY M: What beast was't then
That made you break this enterprize to me?
When you durst do it, then you were a man;
And, to be more than what you were, you would
Be so much more the man. Nor time, nor place,
Did then adhere, and yet you would make both:
They have made themselves, and that their fitness now
Does unmake you. I have given suck, and know
How tender 'tis to love the babe that milks me:
I would, while it was smiling in my face,
Have pluck'd my nipple from his boneless gums,
And dash'd the brains out, had I so sworn
As you have done to this.

MACBETH: If we should fail?
LADY M: We fail?
But screw your courage to the sticking-place,
And we'll not fail: when Duncan is asleep,
(Whereto the rather shall his day's hard journey
Soundly invite him) his two chamberlains
Will I with wine and wassail so convince,
That memory, the warder of the brain,
Shall be a fume, and the receipt of reason
A limbec only: when in swinish sleep
Their drenched natures lie as in a death,
What cannot you and I perform upon
The unguarded Duncan? what not put upon
His spongy officers, who shall bear the guilt
Of our great quell?

MACBETH: Bring forth men-children only;
For thy undaunted mettle should compose

> Nothing but males. Will it not be receiv'd,
> When we have mark'd with blood those sleepy two
> Of his own chamber, and us'd their very daggers,
> That they have don't?

LADY M: Who dares receive it other,
> As we shall make our griefs and clamour roar
> Upon his death?

MACBETH: I am settled, and bend up
> Each corporal agent to this terrible feat.
> Away, and mock the time with fairest show:
> False face must hide what the false heart doth know.

Those lines you have just heard come from "Macbeth", by William Shakespeare. He wrote it towards the end of his life, in his last great period,[2] about the beginning of the seventeenth century.

"Macbeth" is probably the most perfect of Shakespeare's plays. I mean by that that in my opinion Shakespeare's qualities as a poet and as a dramatist are combined in it more successfully than in any other. Especially towards the end it is full of poetry of the very highest order, but it is also a perfectly constructed play—indeed it would still be a good play if it were quite clumsily translated into some foreign language. I don't want here to say anything about the verse in "Macbeth". You will hear some of the best passages from it acted in a few minutes' time. I am concerned simply with "Macbeth" as a tragedy, and I had better give a short outline of the plot.

Macbeth is a Scottish Nobleman of the early Middle Ages. One day he is returning from a battle in which he has particularly distinguished himself and won the King's favour, when he meets three witches who prophecy to him that he will become king himself. Two other prophecies which the witches have made[3] are fulfilled almost immediately, and it is inevitable that Macbeth should find himself wondering how the third is to be fulfilled, since the King, Duncan, is still alive and has two sons. It is clear that almost from the moment of hearing the prophecy he has contemplated murdering Duncan, and though at first he shrinks from doing it, his wife, whose will appears to be stronger than his own, talks him over. Macbeth murders Duncan, contriving that suspicion shall fall on Duncan's two sons. They fly the country, and as Macbeth is the next heir he becomes king. But this first crime leads inexorably to a chain of others, ending in Macbeth's ruin and death. The witches have told him that though he himself will become king, no child of his will succeed to the throne, which will fall to the descendants of his friend Banquo. Macbeth has Banquo murdered, but Banquo's son escapes. They have also warned him to beware of Macduff, the Thane of Fife, and half-consciously Macbeth knows that it is Macduff who will finally destroy him. He tries to have Macduff murdered, but once again, Macduff escapes, though his wife and family are murdered in a peculiarly atrocious way. By an inevitable chain of circumstances Macbeth, who has started out as a brave and by no means bad man, ends up as the typical figure of the terror-haunted tyrant, hated and feared by everyone, surrounded by spies, murderers and sycophants, and living in constant dread of treachery and rebellion. He is in fact a sort of primitive medieval version of the modern Fascist dictator. His situation forces him to become more cruel as time goes on. Whereas at the beginning it is Macbeth who shrinks from murder and Lady Macbeth who jeers at him for his squeamishness, in the end it is Macbeth who massacres women and children without a qualm and Lady Macbeth who loses her nerve and dies partially insane. And yet—and this is the greatest psychological achievement of the play—Macbeth is quite recognizably the same man throughout and speaks the same kind of language; he is pushed on from crime to crime not by native wickedness but by what seems to him inescapable necessity. In the end rebellion breaks out and Macduff and Duncan's son Malcolm invade Scotland at the head of an English army. The witches have made another prophecy which seems to promise Macbeth immunity. How that prophecy is fulfilled, and how, without being falsified, it ends in Macbeth's death, you will hear in the acted extract from the play. In the end he is killed by Macduff, as he has known all along that he would be. When the full meaning of the prophecy becomes clear to him he gives up hope and dies fighting from the mere instinct of a warrior to die on his feet and never surrender.

In all of Shakespeare's major tragedies the theme has some recognizable connection with everyday life. In "Antony and Cleopatra", for instance, the theme is the power which a worthless woman can establish over a brave and gifted man. In "Hamlet" it is the divorce between intelligence and practical ability. In "King Lear" it is a rather subtler theme—the difficulty of distinguishing between generosity and weakness. This reappears in a cruder form in "Timon of Athens". In "Macbeth" the theme is simply ambition. And though all of Shakespeare's tragedies can be translated into terms of ordinary contemporary life, the story of Macbeth seems to me the nearest of all to normal experience. In a small and relatively harmless way, everyone has at some time done something rather like Macbeth, and with comparable consequences. If you like, "Macbeth" is the story of Hitler or Napoleon. But it is also the story of any bank clerk who forges a cheque, any official who takes a bribe, any human being in fact who grabs at some mean advantage which will make him feel a little bigger and get a little ahead of his fellows. It centres on the illusory human belief that an action can be isolated—that you can say to yourself, "I will commit just this one crime which will get me where I want to be, and after that I will turn respectable." But in practice, as Macbeth discovers, one crime grows out of another, even without any increase of wickedness in yourself. His first murder is committed for self-advancement; the even worse ones which follow from it are committed in self-defence. Unlike most of Shakespeare's tragedies, "Macbeth" resembles the Greek tragedies in that its end can be foreseen. From the beginning one knows in general terms what is going to happen. This makes the last act all the more moving, but I still think the essential commonplace-ness of the story is its chief appeal. "Hamlet" is the tragedy of a man who does not know how to commit a murder; "Macbeth" is the tragedy of a man who does. And though most of us do not actually commit murders, Macbeth's predicament is nearer to everyday life.

It is worth noticing that the introduction of magic and witchcraft does not give the play any air of unreality. Actually—although the climax of the last act depends on the exact working-out of the prophecy—the witches are not absolutely necessary to the play. They could be cut out without altering the essential story. Probably they were put in to attract the attention of King James I, who had just come to the throne and who was a firm believer in witchcraft. There is one scene which was quite certainly put in with the idea of flattering the King—this scene, or part of a scene,[4] is the only flaw in the play and should be cut out of any acting version. But the witches, even as they stand, do not offend one's sense of probability. They do not alter anything or upset the course of nature, they merely foretell the future, a future which the spectator can in any case partly foresee. One has the feeling that in one sense Macbeth foresees it too. The witches are there, in fact, simply to increase the sense of doom. A modern writer telling this story, instead of talking about witchcraft, would probably talk about Macbeth's subconscious mind. What is essential is the gradually unfolding consequences of that first crime, and Macbeth's half-knowledge, even as he does it, that it *must* lead to disaster. "Macbeth" is the only one of Shakespeare's plays in which the villain and the hero are the same character. Nearly always, in Shakespeare, you have the spectacle of a good man like Othello or King Lear, suffering misfortune; or of a bad man, like Edmund or[5] Iago, doing evil out of sheer malice. In "Macbeth" the crime and the misfortune are one; a man whom one cannot feel to be wholly evil is doing evil things. It is very difficult not to be moved by this spectacle. And since the play is so well put together that even the most incompetent production can hardly spoil it on the stage, and since it also contains some of the best verse that Shakespeare ever wrote, I think I am justified in giving it the description I gave it at the beginning—that is, Shakespeare's most perfect play.

NARRATOR: After the death of Duncan, Macbeth becomes king, even as the witches had prophecied. Duncan's son Malcolm is at first suspected of the murder of his father and has fled to England. Macbeth's first crime brings many others in its train. By an inexorable logic he is led from murder to murder, and he rules over Scotland with an atrocious tyranny against which rebellion soon begins to gather. Lady Macbeth, who at the beginning had seemed more ruthless than her husband, begins to lose her reason. On top of this comes the news that Macduff, whose wife and children Macbeth has murdered, and Malcolm, the rightful heir to the throne, are invading Scotland at the head of an English army. Macbeth's power is crumbling; many of his followers have already deserted him. The witches, however, have made two prophecies which seem to show that he is in no danger. One is that no evil can befall him till Birnam Forest shall come to Dunsinane. The other, that no man born of woman will ever be able to harm him. He reassures himself with the thought of these prophecies as he waits in his castle at Dunsinane for the approach of the English army.

MACBETH:	Bring me no more reports, let them fly all:
	Till Birnam wood remove to Dunsinane,
	I cannot taint with fear. What's the boy Malcolm?
	Was he not born of woman? The spirits that know
	All mortal consequences have pronounc'd me thus:
	'Fear not, Macbeth, no man that's born of woman
	Shall e'er have power upon thee.' Then fly, false thanes,
	And mingle with the English epicures:
	The mind I sway by, and the heart I bear,
	Shall never sag with doubt, nor shake with fear.
	The devil damn thee black, thou cream-fac'd loon!
	Where got'st thou that goose look?

[Enter a Servant]

SERVANT:	There is ten thousand—
MACBETH:	Geese, villain?
SERVANT:	Soldiers, sir.
MACBETH:	Go prick thy face, and over-red thy fear,
	Thou lily-liver'd boy. What soldiers, patch?
	Death of thy soul! those linen cheeks of thine
	Are counsellors to fear. What soldiers, whey-face?
SERVANT:	The English force, so please you.
MACBETH:	Take thy face hence. [Exit Servant] Seyton! — I am sick at heart,
	When I behold — Seyton, I say! — This push
	Will cheer me ever, or disseat me now.
	I have liv'd long enough: my way of life
	Is fall'n into the sear, the yellow leaf,
	And that which should accompany old age,
	As honour, love, obedience, troops of friends,
	I must not look to have; but, in their stead,
	Curses, not loud but deep, mouth-honour, breath,
	Which the poor heart would fain deny, and dare not.
	Seyton!

[Enter Seyton]

SEYTON:	What's your gracious pleasure?
MACBETH:	What news more?
SEYTON:	All is confirm'd, my lord, which was reported.
MACBETH:	I'll fight, till from my bones my flesh be hack'd.
	Give me my armour.
SEYTON:	'Tis not needed yet.
MACBETH:	I'll put it on.
	Send out moe horses, skirr the country round,
	Hang those that talk of fear. Give me mine armour.
	How does your patient, doctor?
DOCTOR:	Not so sick, my lord,
	As she is troubled with thick-coming fancies
	That keep her from her rest.

MACBETH:
　　　　　　　　　　　　　Cure of that.
Canst thou not minister to a mind diseas'd,
Pluck from the memory a rooted sorrow,
Raze out the written troubles of the brain,
And with some sweet oblivious antidote
Cleanse the stuff'd bosom of that perilous stuff
Which weighs upon the heart?

DOCTOR:
　　　　　　　　　　　　　　Therein the patient
Must minister to himself.

MACBETH: Throw physic to the dogs, I'll none of it.
Come, put mine armour on; give me my staff.
Seyton, send out. Doctor, the thanes fly from me.
Come, sir, dispatch. If thou couldst, doctor, cast
The water of my land, find her disease,
And purge it to a sound and pristine health,
I would applaud thee to the very echo,
That should applaud again. Pull't off, I say.
What rhubarb, senna, or what purgative drug,
Would scour these English hence? Hear'st thou of them?

DOCTOR: Ay, my good lord; your royal preparation
Makes us hear something.

MACBETH:
　　　　　　　　　　　Bring it after me.
I will not be afraid of death and bane,
Till Birnam forest come to Dunsinane.
　　　　　　　　　[Exit Macbeth and Seyton]

DOCTOR: Were I from Dunsinane away, and clear,
Profit again should hardly draw me here.

NARRATOR: As the English army approaches Dunsinane it halts in
Birnam wood. Malcolm gives orders that every soldier is to
cut a bough from a tree and carry it in front of him, in order
to deceive the enemy as to the numbers of the army. The
soldiers march out of the wood carrying their boughs, and
giving in the distance the appearance of a forest moving.

(Trumpet call)

MACBETH: Hang out our banners on the outward walls;
The cry is still 'They come:' our castle's strength
Will laugh a siege to scorn: here let them lie
Till famine and the ague eat them up;
Were they not forc'd with those that should be ours,
We might have met them dareful, beard to beard,
And beat them backward home.
　　　　　　(A cry within of women)
　　　　　　　　　　　　　What is that noise?

SEYTON: It is the cry of women, my good lord. 　　　　(Exit)
MACBETH: I have almost forgot the taste of fears:

The time has been, my senses would have cool'd
To hear a night-shriek, and my fell of hair
Would at a dismal treatise rouse, and stir
As life were in't: I have supp'd full with horrors,
Direness, familiar to my slaughterous thoughts,
Cannot once start me.
     (Re-enter Seyton)
        Wherefore was that cry?

SEYTON: The queen, my lord, is dead.

MACBETH: She should have died hereafter;
There would have been a time for such a word.
To-morrow, and to-morrow, and to-morrow,
Creeps in this petty pace from day to day,
To the last syllable of recorded time;
And all our yesterdays, have lighted fools
The way to dusty death. Out, out, brief candle,
Life's but a walking shadow, a poor player
That struts and frets his hour upon the stage,
And then is heard no more. It is a tale
Told by an idiot, full of sound and fury,
Signifying nothing.
     (Enter a Messenger)
Thou com'st to use thy tongue; thy story quickly.

MESSENGER: Gracious my lord,
I should report that which I say I saw,
But know not how to do it.

MACBETH: Well, say, sir.

MESSENGER: As I did stand my watch upon the hill,
I look'd toward Birnam, and anon methought
The wood began to move.

MACBETH: Liar, and slave!

MESSENGER: Let me endure your wrath, if't be not so:
Within this three mile may you see it coming;
I say, a moving grove.

MACBETH: If thou speak'st false,
Upon the next tree shalt thou hang alive
Till famine cling thee: if thy speech be sooth,
I care not if thou dost for me as much.
I pull in resolution, and begin
To doubt the equivocation of the fiend,
That lies like truth: 'Fear not, till Birnam wood
Do come to Dunsinane;' and now a wood
Comes toward Dunsinane. [Arm, arm, and out!
If this which he avouches does appear,
There is nor[6] flying hence nor tarrying here.
I 'gin to be a-weary of the sun,
And wish the estate o' the world were now undone.

Ring the alarum-bell! Blow, wind, come, wrack,
At least we'll die with harness on our back.]   (Exeunt)
                    (Trumpet call)
                    (Enter Macbeth)
MACBETH: They have tied me to a stake, I cannot fly,
              But bear-like I[7] must fight the course. What's he
              That was not born of woman? Such a one
              Am I to fear, or none.
                        (Enter young Siward)
Y. SIWARD: What is thy name?
MACBETH: Thou'lt be afraid to hear it.
Y. SIWARD: No; though thou call'st thyself a hotter name
              Than any is in hell.
MACBETH: My name's Macbeth.
Y. SIWARD: The devil himself could not pronounce a title
              More hateful to mine ear.
MACBETH: No, nor more fearful.
Y. SIWARD: Thou liest, abhorred tyrant; with my sword
              I'll prove the lie thou speak'st.
                  (They fight, and young Siward is slain)
MACBETH: Thou wast born of woman;
              But swords I smile at, weapons laugh to scorn,
              Brandish'd by man that's of a woman born.   (Exit)
                          (Alarums)
                        (Enter Macduff)
MACDUFF: That way the noise is. Tyrant, show thy face!
              If thou be'st slain and with no stroke of mine,
              My wife and children's ghosts will haunt me still.
              I cannot strike at wretched kerns, whose arms
              Are hir'd to bear their staves: either thou, Macbeth,
              Or else my sword with an unbatter'd edge
              I sheathe again undeeded. There thou shouldst be;
              By this great clatter, one of greatest note
              Seems bruited: let me find him, fortune,
              And more I beg not.   (Exit)
                          (Alarums)
                        [Enter Macbeth]
MACBETH: Why should I play the Roman fool, and die
              On mine own sword? whiles I see lives, the gashes
              Do better upon them.
                        (Enter Macduff)
MACDUFF: Turn, hell-hound, turn!
MACBETH: Of all men else I have avoided thee:
              But get thee back, my soul is too much charg'd
              With blood of thine already.
MACDUFF: I have no words,

My voice is in my sword, thou bloodier villain
Than terms can give thee out!   (They fight)

MACBETH: Thou losest labour;
As easy mayst thou the intrenchant air
With thy keen sword impress, as make me bleed:
Let fall thy blade on vulnerable crests,
I bear a charmed life, which must not yield
To one of woman born.

MACDUFF: Despair thy charm,
And let the angel whom thou still hast serv'd
Tell thee, Macduff was from his mother's womb
Untimely ripp'd.

MACBETH: Accursed be that tongue that tells me so;
For it hath cow'd my better part of man!
And be these juggling fiends no more believ'd,
That palter with us in a double sense,
That keep the word of promise to our ear.
And break it to our hope. I'll not fight with thee.

MACDUFF: Then yield thee coward,
And live to be the show and gaze o' the time:
We'll have thee, as our rarer monsters are,
Painted upon a pole, and underwrit,
'Here may you see the tyrant.'

MACBETH: I will not yield
To kiss the ground before young Malcolm's feet,
And to be baited with the rabble's curse.
Though Birnam wood be come to Dunsinane,
And thou oppos'd, being of no woman born,
Yet I will try the last: before my body
I throw my warlike shield: lay on, Macduff;
And damn'd be him that first cries 'Hold, enough!'
                    (Exeunt, fighting.
                    Alarums)

1. Servant] Sewart *in typescript; presumably confused with* Siward *above*
2. period,] period, which also produced "Hamlet" and "King Lear" *in typescript, but crossed through*
3. Two other . . . have made] *handwritten alteration of typescript's* The first two prophecies
4. Orwell presumably refers to IV.3, especially 146–59, where reference is made to the King of England's ability to cure scrofula, 'The King's Evil', and possibly 97–100, which may refer to James VI and I's desire to make a universal peace.
5. Edmund or] Edgar of *in typescript*
6. nor] not *in typescript*
7. *omitted from typescript*

2320. To Frederick Laws

18 October 1943

Dear Laws,

I rang up Harding[1] who expressed himself willing to do a talk. He seemed slightly uncertain as to whether intelligence tests would be the best subject for him, but I have no doubt he can be persuaded. I said that you would write to him and would let him know about the series and who are the other speakers. His address is: 6th Floor, Centre Block, Bush House.

As for Number 7, I don't think it is worth bothering with Burt,[2] so do you think you could approach Professor Wolters?[3]

Yours sincerely,
[Initialled] E.A.B
Eric Blair

1. Denys Wyatt Harding (1906–), Assistant Lecturer and Lecturer in Social Psychology, London School of Economics, 1933–38; Senior Lecturer in Psychology, University of Liverpool, 1938–45; war service, 1941–44; Professor of Psychology, University of London, 1945–68, was a member of the editorial board of *Scrutiny*, 1933–47, and editor of the *British Journal of Psychology* (General Section), 1948–54. His publications include *The Impulse to Dominate* (1941), *Social Psychology and Individual Values* (1953), *Experience into Words: Essays on Poetry* (1963), *Words into Rhythm* (1976).
2. Sir Cyril Lodowic Burt (1883–1971), Psychologist to the London County Council Education Department, 1913–32; Professor of Education, University of London, 1924–31; Professor of Psychology, University College London, 1931–50, served on the Advisory Committee set up by the War Office on Personnel Selection. His many publications included *The Distribution of Mental Abilities* (1917), *Mental and Scholastic Tests* (1921), *The Young Delinquent* (1925), *The Measurement of Mental Capacities* (1927), *The Subnormal Mind* (1935), *A Psychological Treatment of Typography* (1959). Eileen Blair and Lydia Jackson studied in his department in the 1930s. Burt's work in psychometrics (the measurement of intelligence) was inspired by the biologist Sir Francis Galton, who investigated heredity, and Charles Spearman, with whom he worked on the statistical analysis of intelligence measurement. Burt was an advocate of 11-plus testing, assessing children to determine what form of education was appropriate for them. This approach was adopted towards the end of the war, but after a couple of decades began to fall into disfavour, especially with the Labour Party. After its virtual abandonment in the 1970s, Burt's own work was challenged, and shown, at least in part, to be fabricated.
3. Albert William Phillips Wolters (1883–19??), author of *The Evidence of the Senses* (1933).

2321. To George Bernard Shaw

18 October 1943   GO/MEI[1]

Dear Mr. Shaw,

I believe the B.B.C. Copyright Department wrote to you a few days ago asking whether we could broadcast an extract from "The Doctor's Dilemma". I hope you will consent to this as these fragments from British dramatists, which we broadcast, have been popular with the Indian student audience and they would always listen with particular attention to anything of yours. You allowed us to broadcast a fragment from "Arms and the Man" on a previous occasion and it went over very successfully. I would, of course, follow your wishes as to which part of the "The Doctor's Dilemma" we broadcast, but I would like to choose a bit near the beginning where the four doctors are talking among themselves. The other plays which are being broadcast in this series are "Macbeth", "An Enemy of the People", "The Cherry Orchard", "R.U.R.", and "Lady Windermere's Fan". The accompanying talk on "The Doctor's Dilemma" would be given by Desmond MacCarthy.

Yours truly,
[Initialled] E. A. B
George Orwell.

1. Unidentified.

2322. To Norman Collins

19 October 1943   Handwritten

Following Orwell's request to the General Overseas Service Manager, Norman Collins, on 4 October 1943 (see *2293*) that Sir Richard Acland and Aneurin Bevan be used in the series 'The Debate Continues,' Collins sent Orwell the following memorandum on 10 October:

'Before you approach either could I please have a note of the brief you are proposing to give these two speakers. It would be undesirable, for instance, for Acland to talk about the Commonwealth as such, if he is being introduced in the series on the basis of his being an M.P.—I will clear up about *both* speakers as soon as I get your note.

Could you please let me have a list of the M.P's who have already spoken in these series?'

Perhaps the typist, rather than Collins, has confused the British Commonwealth with Acland's Common Wealth Party—completely different entities—though Collins might have been expected to note that when signing his memorandum. Common Wealth was still typed as a single word on 20th October (below).

On 19 October, Orwell sent a handwritten response to Collins on the back of the latter's memorandum:

i. We have not fixed dates for these two speakers (Bevan & Acland) yet but wished to know whether we could add them to our repertory. It is difficult to fix subjects long in advance because these arise out of the week's debate, eg. if there is a coal bill we might get some one to talk about the mining industry, etc. There would of course be no question of getting Acland to talk about Common Wealth (I should think he might talk on agriculture for instance). I know both these people & could handle them.

ii. MPs who have spoken are Winterton, Quintin Hogg, Hugh Molson, Hinchingbrooke, Brian Brooke, Sorensen, Gallacher, Ellen Wilkinson, Edith Summerskill, King-Hall, V. Bartlett, Butler (Education), Strauss, Laws, & one or two others.[1]

Eric Blair 19.10.43

289

On 20 October, Collins sent this memorandum to J. B. Clark, Controller, Overseas Service: 'You will remember that Blair asked if these could be approached for THE DEBATE CONTINUES. I asked for particulars of the brief which it was proposed to give to each speaker and said at the time that though I thought Acland would be suitable for a general subject, but definitely unsuitable on Commonwealth, I thought that Aneurin Bevan would be better left alone. The attached is Blair's reply. Could you please confirm that it is O.K. to go ahead on Acland?'

Collins sent Orwell the following adjudication on 21 October:

'It really isn't possible simply to add an M.P. to the repertory as you suggest. In due course, if E.S.D. agrees speaker *and subject*, there is no reason to suppose that Acland will not be O.K.—but please check with me again to see what other commitments (if any) have been entered into by the B.B.C. as a whole so far as this speaker is concerned.

Bevan is less certain—but please similarly refer:

(a) speaker *and subject* to E.S.D. and

(b) to me for general clearance.

The (b) part of this procedure once (a) is complete should not take more than a few hours.'

1. There are at least two ironies in this list which Collins must surely have noted. Ellen Wilkinson (see *422, n. 3; 1471, n. 2*) had once been a Communist. She entered Parliament in 1921 and was long associated with Jarrow, as M.P. and as a leader of the Hunger March from that distressed town to London. She became Minister of Education in the Labour government of 1945. Willie Gallacher (see *560, 27.7.39, n. 2*) joined the Communist Party in 1921 and remained in it. He entered Parliament as a Communist M.P. in 1935. These two might have been expected to raise the hackles of a BBC vetting committee, official or unofficial, even though, as Orwell put it in his London Letter to *Partisan Review* for Spring 1944, dated 15 January 1944, Gallacher was on the road to becoming the pet of the House of Commons, corrupted by that institution's familiarity; see *2405*.

2323. To André Van Gyseghem

20 October 1943   07/ES/EB

Dear Mr. Van Gysegham,[01]

I rather think that Narayana Menon has already asked you whether you could do a talk for us on The Cherry Orchard. What we want is a ten minutes' talk to precede an acted extract from the play and tell the audience, which is an audience of Indian probably° students, a certain amount about Chekov's work in general as well as this particular play. The date is November 7th at 4.15 p.m. As this is a Sunday you could record before hand if you wish, but I would like to have the script not later than the end of October. Could you please confirm whether you would like to do this. I can give you any further particulars you wish.

Yours truly,
[Initialled] E.A.B
(Eric Blair)

1. André Van Gyseghem (1906–), actor and producer, took a special interest in Russian theatre

and published *Theatre in Soviet Russia* (1943). Orwell (or his secretary) misspells Van Gyseghem's name.

2324. BBC Talks Booking Form, 20.10.43

Dr. Susan Isaacs: 'Calling All Students,' Psychology; fifth talk in the series; recorded 8.11.43; broadcast 11.11.43; fee £10.10s + 12s.0d fare. Signed: Z. A. Bokhari.

2325. BBC Talks Booking Form, 20.10.43

Professor C. W. Valentine: 'Calling All Students,' Psychology; third talk in the series; recorded 25.10.43 (in Birmingham); broadcast 28.10.43; fee £10.10s. Signed: Z. A. Bokhari.

2326. Newsletter in Tamil, 27

21 October 1943

The English version was written by Eric Blair. No script has been traced.

2327. Review of *The Adventures of the Young Soldier in Search of the Better World* by C. E. M. Joad

The Listener, 21 October 1943

A man's body, so we are told, is composed of a few bucketfuls of water, a few pounds of lime and carbon, and a few pinches of phosphorus, all exactly measurable. But you cannot make a man simply by adding those ingredients together, and the same rule seems to apply to a book, even a political or sociological book. Professor Joad knows all the questions that will beset the post-war world; he also knows all the answers. But something, some vital spark, perhaps simply the power to believe definitely in any one theory of life, is missing, with the result that what was intended to be a parable degenerates into a chronicle, or even a catalogue.

The book is modelled, not altogether wisely, on *Alice in Wonderland.* A young soldier loses his way in the forest and meets with a series of monsters typifying current trends of thought. There is a Red-tape Worm who signifies bureaucracy, an Ultra-red Robot signifying Marxism, a Mr. Transportouse who is ready to solve all problems by common sense, a Mr. Heardhux who is merely a disembodied voice preaching detachment from worldly things, and various others. The story ends with the soldier meeting a Philosopher (incidentally Mr. Peake's drawing of Professor Joad is the nicest thing in the book), who advises him to cheer up, disbelieve what the others have told him, keep a nice balance between Faith and Works and hope for the best. Not all of the various monsters are regarded as being on the same level of folly. Professor Joad has a certain weakness for Mr. Transportouse, the Beveridge-minded town-planner, but curiously enough the fallacy that he finds it the most difficult to expose is that of the mystical Mr. Heardhux. Having been told that science and politics are folly and that the duty of man is to cultivate his spirit by means of meditation, fasting and breathing exercises, the young soldier can only murmur that it 'sounds a bit arid and lonely'. It does not occur to him to point out the really damaging weakness in the position of the latter-day yogis—the fact that while they are fasting and meditating others have got to work to keep them alive, and that their 'spirituality' is simply the by-product of money and military security. He does not even pause to wonder why the cult of 'detachment' always has to be practised in a warm climate.

But the central weakness of the book is that Professor Joad's own creed, however sensible it may be, lacks the intensity that belongs to even the stupidest of his adversaries. Seemingly it is not enough to be moderate and kind. It is not enough to point out that society must have plans to deal with unemployment and inequality, but not too much planning lest initiative be destroyed, and that men must believe in something or other, but not believe too blindly lest they give themselves over to bigotry and persecution. Intelligent hedonism is a poor guide in a world where millions of people are ready to shed their own or anybody else's blood in the name of half-a-dozen kinds of folly. No doubt it is *not* the truth that the middle way is always wrong, but that is the conclusion that one carries away from Professor Joad's book, and it is the exact opposite of what he is trying to convey. Perhaps a touch of bigotry is the condition of literary vitality; at any rate, this is a notably lifeless book, and it is not helped by the—for the most part—rather silly illustrations by Mervyn Peake.

[Fee: £2.2s; 31.8.43]

2328. Who Are the War Criminals? Review of *The Trial of Mussolini* by 'Cassius'[1]

Tribune, 22 October 1943

On the face of it, Mussolini's collapse was a story straight out of Victorian melodrama. At long last Righteousness had triumphed, the wicked man was discomfited, the mills of God were doing their stuff. On second thoughts, however, this moral tale is less simple and less edifying. To begin with, what crime, if any, has Mussolini committed? In power politics there are no crimes, because there are no laws. And, on the other hand, is there any feature in Mussolini's *internal* régime that could be seriously objected to by any body of people likely to sit in judgment on him? For, as the author of this book abundantly shows—and this in fact is the main purpose of the book—there is not one scoundrelism committed by Mussolini between 1922 and 1940 that has not been lauded to the skies by the very people who are now promising to bring him to trial.

For the purposes of his allegory "Cassius" imagines Mussolini indicted before a British court, with the Attorney-General as prosecutor. The list of charges is an impressive one, and the main facts—from the murder of Matteoti° to the invasion of Greece, and from the destruction of the peasants' co-operatives to the bombing of Addis Ababa—are not denied. Concentration camps, broken treaties, rubber truncheons, castor oil—everything is admitted. The only troublesome question is: How can something that was praiseworthy at the time when you did it—ten years ago, say—suddenly become reprehensible now? Mussolini is allowed to call witnesses, both living and dead, and to show by their own printed words that from the very first the responsible leaders of British opinion have encouraged him in everything that he did. For instance, here is Lord Rothermere in 1928:

> "In his own country [Mussolini] was the antidote to a deadly poison. For the rest of Europe he has been a tonic which has done to all incalculable good. I can claim with sincere satisfaction to have been the first man in a position of public influence to put Mussolini's splendid achievement in its right light. . . . He is the greatest figure of our age."

Here is Winston Churchill in 1927:

> "If I had been an Italian I am sure I should have been wholeheartedly with you in your triumphant struggle against the bestial appetites and passions of Leninism. . . . [Italy] has provided the necessary antidote to the Russian poison. Hereafter no great nation will be unprovided with an ultimate means of protection against the cancerous growth of Bolshevism."

Here is Lord Mottistone in 1935:

> "I did not oppose [the Italian action in Abyssinia.] I wanted to dispel the ridiculous illusion that it was a nice thing to sympathise with the underdog. . . . I said it was a wicked thing to send arms or connive to send arms to these cruel, brutal Abyssinians and still to deny them to others who are playing an honourable part."

Here is Mr. Duff Cooper in 1938:

> "Concerning the Abyssinian episode, the less said now the better. When old friends are reconciled after a quarrel, it is always dangerous for them to discuss its original causes."

Here is Mr. Ward Price, of the *Daily Mail*, in 1932:

> "Ignorant and prejudiced people talk of Italian affairs as if that nation were subject to some tyranny which it would willingly throw off. With that rather morbid commiseration for fanatical minorities which is the rule

with certain imperfectly informed sections of British public opinion, this country long shut its eyes to the magnificent work that the Fascist régime was doing. I have several times heard Mussolini himself express his gratitude to the *Daily Mail* as having been the first British newspaper to put his aims fairly before the world."

And so on, and so on, and so on. Hoare, Simon, Halifax, Neville Chamberlain, Austen Chamberlain, Hore-Belisha, Amery, Lord Lloyd and various others enter the witness-box, all of them ready to testify that, whether Mussolini was crushing the Italian trade unions, non-intervening in Spain, pouring mustard gas on the Abyssinians, throwing Arabs out of aeroplanes or building up a navy for use against Britain, the British Government and its official spokesmen supported him through thick and thin. We are shown Lady (Austen) Chamberlain shaking hands with Mussolini in 1924, Chamberlain and Halifax banqueting with him and toasting "the Emperor of Abyssinia" in 1939, Lord Lloyd buttering up the Fascist régime in an official pamphlet as late as 1940. The net impression left by this part of the trial is quite simply that Mussolini is not guilty. Only later, when an Abyssinian, a Spaniard and an Italian anti-Fascist give their evidence, does the real case against him begin to appear.

Now, the book is a fanciful one, but this conclusion is realistic. It is immensely unlikely that the British Tories will ever put Mussolini on trial. There is nothing that they could accuse him of except his declaration of war in 1940. If the "trial of war criminals" that some people enjoy dreaming about ever happens, it can only happen after revolutions in the Allied countries. But the whole notion of finding scapegoats, of blaming individuals, or parties, or nations for the calamities that have happened to us, raises other trains of thought, some of them rather disconcerting.

The history of British relations with Mussolini illustrates the structural weakness of a capitalist state. Granting that power politics are not moral, to attempt to buy Italy out of the Axis—and clearly this idea underlay British policy from 1934 onwards—was a natural strategic move. But it was not a move which Baldwin, Chamberlain and the rest of them were capable of carrying out. It could only have been done by being so strong that Mussolini would not dare to side with Hitler. This was impossible, because an economy ruled by the profit motive is simply not equal to re-arming on a modern scale.

Britain only began to arm when the Germans were in Calais. Before that, fairly large sums had, indeed, been voted for armaments, but they slid peaceably into the pockets of the shareholders and the weapons did not appear. Since they had no real intention of curtailing their own privileges, it was inevitable that the British ruling class should carry out every policy half-heartedly and blind themselves to the coming danger. But the moral collapse which this entailed was something new in British politics. In the nineteenth and early twentieth centuries, British politicians might be hypocritical, but hypocrisy implies a moral code. It was something new when Tory M.P.s cheered the news that British ships had been bombed by Italian aeroplanes, or when members of the House of Lords lent themselves to organised libel campaigns against the Basque children who had been brought here as refugees.

When one thinks of the lies and betrayals of those years, the cynical abandonment of one ally after another, the imbecile optimism of the Tory press, the flat refusal to believe that the Dictators meant war, even when they shouted it from the housetops, the inability of the moneyed class to see anything wrong whatever in concentration camps, ghettoes, massacres and undeclared wars, one is driven to feel that moral decadence played its part as well as mere stupidity. By 1937 or thereabouts it was not possible to be in doubt about the nature of the Fascist régimes. But the lords of property had decided that Fascism was on their side and they were willing to swallow the most stinking evils so long as their property remained secure. In their clumsy way they were playing the game of Macchiavelli, of "political realism," of "anything is right which advances the cause of the Party"—the Party in this case, of course, being the Conservative Party.

All this "Cassius" brings out, but he does shirk its corollary. Throughout his book it is implied that only Tories are immoral. "Yet there was still another England," he says. "This other England detested Fascism from the day of its birth. . . . This was the England of the Left, the England of Labour." True, but only part of the truth. The actual behaviour of the Left has been more honourable than its theories. It has fought against Fascism, but its representative thinkers have entered just as deeply as their opponents into the evil world of "realism" and power politics.

"Realism" (it used to be called dishonesty) is part of the general political atmosphere of our time. It is a sign of the weakness of "Cassius's" position that one could compile a quite similar book entitled The Trial of Winston Churchill, or The Trial of Chiang Kai-Shek, or even The Trial of Ramsay MacDonald. In each case you would find the leaders of the Left contradicting themselves almost as grossly as the Tory leaders quoted by "Cassius." For the Left has also been willing to shut its eyes to a great deal and to accept some very doubtful allies. We laugh now to hear the Tories abusing Mussolini when they were flattering him five years ago, but who would have foretold in 1927 that the Left would one day take Chiang Kai-Shek to its bosom? Who would have foretold just after the General Strike that ten years later Winston Churchill would be the darling of the Daily Worker? In the years 1935–39, when almost any ally against Fascism seemed acceptable, Left-wingers found themselves praising Mustapha Kemal and then developing a tenderness for Carol of Rumania.

Although it was in every way more pardonable, the attitude of the Left towards the Russian régime has been distinctly similar to the attitude of the Tories towards Fascism. There has been the same tendency to excuse almost anything "because they're on our side." It is all very well to talk about Lady Chamberlain photographed shaking hands with Mussolini; the photograph of Stalin shaking hands with Ribbentrop is much more recent. On the whole, the intellectuals of the Left defended the Russo-German pact. It was "realistic," like Chamberlain's appeasement policy, and with similar consequences. If there is a way out of the moral pig-sty we are living in, the first step towards it is probably to grasp that "realism" does *not* pay, and that to sell out your friends and sit rubbing your hands while they are destroyed is *not* the last word in political wisdom.

This fact is demonstrable in any city between Cardiff and Stalingrad, but not many people can see it. Meanwhile it is a pamphleteer's duty to attack the Right, but not to flatter the Left. It is partly because the Left have been too easily satisfied with themselves that they are where they are now.

Mussolini, in "Cassius's" book, after calling his witnesses, enters the box himself. He sticks to his Macchiavellian creed: Might is Right, *væ victis!*[2] He is guilty of the only crime that matters, the crime of failure, and he admits that his adversaries have a right to kill him—but not, he insists, a right to blame him. Their conduct has been similar to his own, and their moral condemnations are all hypocrisy. But thereafter come the other three witnesses, the Abyssinian, the Spaniard and the Italian, who are morally upon a different plane, since they have never temporised with Fascism nor had a chance to play at power politics; and all three of them demand the death penalty.

Would they demand it in real life? Will any such thing ever happen? It is not very likely, even if the people who have a real right to try Mussolini should somehow get him into their hands. The Tories, of course, though they would shrink from a real inquest into the origins of the war, are not sorry to have the chance of pushing the whole blame on to a few notorious individuals like Mussolini and Hitler. In this way the Darlan-Badoglio manœuvre is made easier. Mussolini is a good scapegoat while he is at large, though he would be an awkward one in captivity. But how about the common people? Would they kill their tyrants, in cold blood and with the forms of law, if they had the chance?

It is a fact that there have been very few such executions in history. At the end of the last war an election was won partly on the slogan "Hang the Kaiser," and yet if any such thing had been attempted the conscience of the nation would probably have revolted. When tyrants are put to death, it should be by their own subjects; those who are punished by a foreign authority, like Napoleon, are simply made into martyrs and legends.

What is important is not that these political gangsters should be made to suffer, but that they should be made to discredit themselves. Fortunately they do do so in many cases, for to a surprising extent the war-lords in shining armour, the apostles of the martial virtues, tend not to die fighting when the time comes. History is full of ignominious getaways by the great and famous. Napoleon surrendered to the English in order to get protection from the Prussians, the Empress Eugenie fled in a hansom cab with an American dentist, Ludendorff resorted to blue spectacles, one of the more unprintable[3] Roman emperors tried to escape assassination by locking himself in the lavatory, and during the early days of the Spanish civil war one leading Fascist made his escape from Barcelona, with exquisite fitness, through a sewer.

It is some such exit that one would wish for Mussolini, and if he is left to himself perhaps he will achieve it. Possibly Hitler also. It used to be said of Hitler that when his time came he would never fly or surrender, but would perish in some operatic manner, by suicide at the very least. But that was when Hitler was successful; during the last year, since things began to go wrong, it is difficult to feel that he has behaved with dignity or courage. "Cassius" ends his book with the judge's summing-up, and leaves the verdict open, seeming to invite a decision from his readers. Well, if it were left to me, my verdict on both Hitler and Mussolini would be: not death, unless it is inflicted in some hurried unspectacular way. If the Germans and Italians feel like giving them a summary court-martial and then a firing-squad, let them do it. Or better still, let the pair of them escape with a suitcase-full of bearer securities and settle down as the accredited bores of some Swiss pension. But no martyrising, no St. Helena business. And, above all, no solemn hypocritical "trial of war criminals," with all the slow cruel pageantry of the law, which after a lapse of time has so strange a way of focusing a romantic light on the accused and turning a scoundrel into a hero.

[Fee: £5.5s; 18.10.43]

> Two weeks later, *Tribune* published letters from Gordon Bartlett, P. C. King, S. Rach, and Dr. Max Bindermann. Two of these referred to Orwell's 'refreshingly sane article' and his 'timely article,' and went on to take matters further: P. C. King argued that because both Left and Right could stand accused there was justification for the Common Wealth Party; Dr. Bindermann looked forward to what was to happen:
>
> > I am referring to Mr. G. Orwell's interesting article in your issue of October 22nd. I think that the whole problem is a little obscured by calling the Fascist and Nazi gangsters war criminals. This term is reminiscent of political criminals whom we are accustomed to look on in quite a different manner. But the robbers, torturers and slaughterers of millions of innocent and helpless people are ordinary criminals, mass murderers.
> >
> > To let them "escape with a suitcase-full of bearer securities and settle down as the accredited bores of some Swiss pension" is bare escapism and would and could not be understood by their innumerable victims, as far as they are still alive. The criminals themselves would not understand such a forgiving attitude. This is Jewish-Christian unmanliness in their dehumanised eyes. They understand only physical force, which must be meted out to them in full. Besides, to leave them at large would mean to court disaster as these gangsters will not content themselves to be only "accredited bores" but will try to stir [up] troubles. *Ecrasez l'infame!*

1. Michael Foot; see *1241, n. 2*.
2. *væ victis!*: 'woe to the vanquished!', Livy, *History*, V, xlviii, 9.
3. Possibly 'unprincipled' was intended.

2329. English Newsletter for Indonesia, 16

22 October 1943

This was written and read by George Orwell. No script has been traced.

2330. To Susan Isaacs

22 October 1943   07/ES/EB/JEL

Dear Dr. Isaacs,

I have arranged a recording for your talk on Monday, November 8th at 10.45 a.m. Could you be at 200 Oxford Street (opposite Studio One Cinema) at 10.15 a.m. to run through and time the talk?[1]

Yours truly,
[Initialled] E.A.B
(Eric Blair)

1. Dr. Isaacs replied on 26 October to say that she might be a little late. She told Orwell that her book *The Nursery Years*—a particularly influential work—had just been translated into Marathi and reference to that might be 'a useful passport to listeners in India.' Orwell wrote on this letter, in pencil, 'Noted E.A.B'. She sent her script on 31 October with a covering note saying she had read it aloud several times and each time it ran for fourteen minutes. Orwell wrote on this letter, in pencil, 'Please ack. E.A.B'. On 3 November, she wrote to ask for a studio pass for use when the recording was made. This letter is annotated by Orwell, in pencil, 'Please send p.c. E.A.B'.

2331. To Blanche Patch, Secretary to George Bernard Shaw

22 October 1943   Top and carbon copies   07/ES/EB

On 21 October, Blanche Patch, on Shaw's behalf, had replied to Orwell's letter of 18 October (see *2321*) to say that Shaw could not imagine any bits of *The Doctor's Dilemma* being interesting or intelligible detached from the play as a whole. However, he was prepared to consider a specific proposal. Orwell marked her letter, 'Ansd. 22.10'; this is that reply:

Dear Madam,

On looking carefully through The Doctor's Dilemma I think the best passage would be in Act I, starting (page 107 in Constable's edition) Ridgeon: I tell you for the fiftieth time I won't see anybody, down to (page 113) Ridgeon: I will. Good bye. We could perhaps put in the remaining few lines of the scene but a remark in them refers back to something else. This passage would, I should say, take ten or twelve minutes. There would also be a commentary by a narrator explaining clearly the plot of the play. I should be glad of a decision quickly because if this is to be done at all, the script will have to be got ready early next week.[1]

Yours faithfully,
[Signed] Geo. Orwell[2]
(George Orwell)

1. At the foot of the top copy of the letter, Shaw wrote: 'Quite impossible. Cut it out. The scene would be uninteresting and only half intelligible by itself. I veto it ruthlessly. G. Bernard Shaw 26/10/1943.' Shaw's strong reaction might be read in the light of Orwell's comment in his review of Thomas Mann's *Order of the Day* in *Tribune*, 10 September 1943 (see *2271*): 'One

has only to compare [Mann's] remarks on Hitler and Mussolini with, say, those of Bernard
Shaw to see that respect for common decency is not a bad guide, even in international politics.'
2. The top copy of this letter (in the Orwell Archive) is signed 'Geo. Orwell'; the carbon copy (in
the BBC Archives) is initialled 'E.A.B'.

2332. BBC Talks Booking Form, 22.10.43

Oliver Bell: 'Films of the Month' (monthly film talk); broadcast 17.11.43; fee
£10.10s. Signed: Z. A. Bokhari.

2333. To André Van Gyseghem
22 October 1943   07/ES/EB/JEL

Dear Mr. Van Gyseghem,
Many thanks for your letter of the 21st. The talk should take ten minutes,
which probably means not much over 1200 words. I cannot say with
certainty what fee you will get for doing it, but I should say ten guineas. The
date is the 7th November and I would like to have the script a week earlier,
that is to say October 31st.

Yours truly,
[Initialled] E.A.B
(Eric Blair)

2334. BBC Talks Booking Form, 22.10.43

W. J. Turner: 'Great Dramatists,' 'R.U.R. by Karel Capek'°; '10 mins talk
approx. in the form of a discussion with Noel Iliffe (staff)'; broadcast 14.11.43;
fee £8.8s. Signed: Z. A. Bokhari.

2335. BBC Talks Booking Form, 22.10.43

André Van Gyseghem: 'Great Dramatists,' 4, 'The Cherry Orchard by Anton
Chekov'; broadcast 7.11.43; fee £8.8s. Signed: Z. A. Bokhari.

2336. BBC Talks Booking Form, 22.10.43

D. W. Harding: 'Calling All Students,' 4, Psychology, Mental Tests[1];
broadcast 4.11.43; fee £10.10s. Signed: Z. A. Bokhari.

1. Harding sent his script to Orwell on 31 October. In his covering letter he said he had changed

the title to 'Intelligence Tests' because 'Mental Tests' included so much that May Smith would probably be dealing with. He had not gone into detailed use of the tests to avoid overlapping with what Valentine, Isaacs and Smith were discussing. May Smith (1879–1968) was Senior Investigator to the Industrial Health Board, 1920–44, and Lecturer in Applied Psychology, Birkbeck College, University of London, 1944–55. Her publications included *An Introduction to Industrial Psychology* (1943).

2337. Orwell's Sick Leave

The BBC Staff Record shows that Orwell had one day's sick leave from Monday, 25 October, to Tuesday, 26 October 1943. Presumably he was away on the Monday.

2338. On Orwell's behalf to Desmond Hawkins

27 October 1943   07/ES/EB

Dear Mr. Hawkins,
I enclose scripts for the next Backward Glance programme. The transmission is on Wednesday, 10th November. Could you let us know in advance of sending the script what copyright material you are going to use. This will give our Copyright Department slightly longer to cover the copyright.

Yours sincerely,
[Initialled] JEL
for George Orwell

2339. Extracts from Minutes of Eastern Service Meeting

27 October 1943

<u>Talks on Set Books in English Literature for Arts Degree Examinations at leading Indian Universities</u>   As in previous years, it is hoped to include a series of such talks early in the new schedule. Information from India showed that January and February were the most suitable months for putting out this series. Mr. Brander to obtain urgently from India particulars of the syllabus.
<u>Mr. Blair</u>   Mr. Lawson-Reece reported with regret that Mr. Blair had resigned from the Corporation. The meeting expressed its appreciation of Mr. Blair's work in handling the English programmes to India during the past eighteen months. No successor had yet been appointed,[1] but from now until the end of the year the English programmes will be under the direct supervision of Mr. Bokhari.

1. Orwell was replaced by Miss Sunday Wilshin, with the title Assistant, English Programmes

for India (see *2600*, *n. 1*). She contributes an engaging memoir of Orwell to *Remembering Orwell*, edited by Stephen Wadhams (1984), 125–26. About 1 January 1944, Charlotte Haldane (wife of J. B. S. Haldane until their divorce in 1945) started work as a talks producer in the Indian Section, see *2369*, *n. 2*. She had organised the dependants' aid committee set up to help the families of British volunteers in Spain and worked within this Communist organisation in Paris. See her *Truth Will Out* (1949) and *374A* for a reference to it (*n. 27*). Her son by her first marriage, J. B. S. Haldane's stepson, Ronald, was killed in Spain fighting against Franco's forces.

2340. Newsletter in Tamil, 28

28 October 1943

The English version was written by Eric Blair. No script has been traced.

2341. To D. W. Harding

28 or 29 October 1943[1]

Dear Mr. Harding,
I am just writing to remind you about your talk for Thursday November 4th. Could I have the script by Monday 1st at the very latest. I think I asked you when I spoke to you over the 'phone if you would be kind enough to send a copy to Mr. Laws at the same time. The time of the broadcast is 11.15 a.m., so if you arrive here (200 Oxford Street) at 10.30 that will give us time for a run through before hand.

Yours sincerely,
[Initialled] E.A.B
(Eric Blair)

1. The carbon copy shows that the '8' and '9' have both been struck, the incorrect figure not having been erased on the copy.

2342. BBC Talks Booking Form, 28.10.43

L. A. G. Strong: 'Great Dramatists,' 'The Taming of the Shrew'; 'talk of approx. 9 mins.'; recorded 30.10.43; broadcast 31.10.43; fee £8.8s. Signed: Z. A. Bokhari.

2343. English Newsletter for Indonesia, 17

29 October 1943

This was written and read by George Orwell. No script has been traced.

2344. Newsletter in Tamil, 29

4 November 1943

The English version was written by Eric Blair.[1] No script has been traced.

1. Exceptionally, this newsletter was not translated and read by J. D. S Paul, but by G. J. C. Francis. The Reverend Gordon Matthews continued as switch censor.

2345. English Newsletter for Indonesia, 18

5 November 1943

This was written and read by George Orwell. No script has been traced.

2346. To Reginald Reynolds

5 November 1943   07/ES/EB

Dear Reg,

With reference to our conversation the other day. I have put you down for a 15 minutes talk on Kropotkin,[1] on November 25th. This means that I would want the script a good week before hand, that is to say not later[2] than November 18th at the latest. The length should be as before, that is 15 or 16 hundred words. The time of broadcast is 4.15 p.m., which means your coming here at about 3.45. Please let me know *at once* if you can't undertake this.

Yours,
[Initialled] E.A.B
(Eric Blair)

P.S. [in shorthand] What would [   ] to a short account re SGAT? If so I can come over tomorrow morning.[3]

1. Peter Kropotkin (1842–1921), a Russian prince, trained as a scientist, renounced his title, espoused populism, socialism and then anarchism, and supported the interest of the peasants. Imprisoned in Russia in 1874, he escaped to England in 1876, before moving to Switzerland and France, where he was imprisoned for three years, and then settled in England, 1886–1917. He wrote much, including *The Great French Revolution, 1789–1793* (1909) and the book regarded as his best work, *Mutual Aid* (1902), in which he argued that co-operation, not conflict, was the most significant element in the evolution of the species. He returned to Russia after the Revolution but was bitterly disappointed by the truimph of Bolshevism because its methods were authoritarian rather than liberatarian. Ironically, he supported the First World War against Germany.
2. 'less' was typed but altered in a hand other than Orwell's to 'later.'
3. The second sentence is faily certain and the initials of the first look clear; there is probably one word after 'would'; but 'short' and the whole first sentence are uncertain. This postscript has been written (by Miss Light?) on the carbon copy of the letter to Reynolds. It may have been typed on the top copy, but it may not have been intended for Reynolds.

2347. Review of *Lest We Regret* by Douglas Reed; *I Sit and I Think and I Wonder* by Sidney Dark

The Observer, 7 November 1943

It seems strange to look back five years and remember Mr. Douglas Reed as a Cassandra figure warning a heedless world that the Nazis were dangerous. And it is even stranger to think of the enthusiasm with which "Insanity Fair" was greeted in the Left-wing Press. "Anti-Fascist" was the term generally applied to it—for in those days anyone who opposed Chamberlain's policy was held to be anti-Fascist. The ancient truth that "he who fights too long against dragons becomes a dragon himself" had been forgotten for the time being.

Readers of an earlier book will remember Mr. Reed's admiration for Otto Strasser, the "black" Nazi, Hitler's Trotsky.[1] Strasser's programme, set forth by Mr. Reed without much sign of disapproval, was simply a modification of Hitler's. Nazism was to be more or less retained, the Jews were to be persecuted, but a little less viciously, and Britain and Germany were to gang up for an attack on the U.S.S.R. In his present book Mr. Reed does not mention Strasser, but spends his time in maundering about Britain's post-war policy, the dominant notes being: back to the land, more emigration, down with the Reds, and—above all—down with the Jews.

Much of what Mr. Reed says about the evils of private property in land, and the monstrous crime committed against the English people by the enclosure of the commons, would be impressive if it did not remind one all the time of the articles that used to appear in Mosley's *British Union*; and also if it were accompanied by any comprehensive economic programme, or even any intelligible agricultural policy. But though an enemy of landlords Mr. Reed does not seem to be an enemy of private property. His chief quarrel with the Enclosures is apparently that they have made things difficult for hikers; and he opposes the electrification of the Highlands on the ground that it would spoil the scenery. Mixed up with this are complaints about the victimisation of the middle classes (even the tyres of their laid-up motor-cars are taken away from them!)[2] and tirades against bureaucrats and "alliens."°

Mr. Reed objects equally strongly to "aliens" being given jobs and to Fascist sympathisers being interned under 18B. And, above all, he objects to the notion that the German Jews somehow merit our sympathy. For the Jews, it appears, have never been persecuted in Germany, or not to speak of. Everybody else has been persecuted, but not the Jews; all the stories about pogroms, and so forth are just "propaganda."

Now, the general pattern of Mr. Reed's thought is a familiar one. The ex-officers who formed an important part of Mosley's following believed just the same things about Jews, reds, aliens, bureaucrats, agriculture, and the need for more emigration. On top of this, however, Mr. Reed is notable for a very marked dislike of his own country. The climate, the manners, the social customs, the politics of England all repel him. He has lived long in Central Europe, and where it is possible to compare the British and the German way of doing things he makes no disguise of preferring the German way.

Nevertheless, Mr. Reed is as certain as ever that Britain must defeat Germany, and in alliance with the U.S.S.R. must dominate the Continent. The desire to see Britain beat Germany is the one thing in which he has never wavered. Even when he backed Otto Strasser he made the reservation that he himself did not wish to see Germany again become a great military Power.

It is here that the psychological puzzle comes in. For one is obliged to ask, if Britain is the Jew-haunted plutocracy that Mr. Reed believes, what is it that makes him wish to see Britain victorious?[3] This question is not answered by the familiar pacifist claim that war induces a Fascist mentality. But it is worth thinking over, for Mr. Reed is a persuasive writer, with an easy journalistic style, and capable of doing a lot of harm among the large public for which he caters.

Mr. Sidney Dark, the vehement pamphleteer and (till recently) editor of the *Church Times*,[4] is a change from Mr. Reed. His politics are almost exactly those of the Popular Front, and he is worth the attention of left-wingers who have failed to notice the political tendencies of the Anglo–Catholic movement and lightheartedly assumed that every religious believer is a reactionary. In a way, in spite of his allegiance to the Church, he is almost too ready to bow to left–wing orthodoxy and to accept over-simple solutions to difficult questions—the Palestine question, for instance. Also it is a pity that Mr. Dark deals in literary judgments as well as political ones. It will distress some of his colleagues of the *Church Times* to see him walloping his co-religionist Mr. T. S. Eliot, with great violence but with no apparent understanding of what Mr. Eliot is after. But there is no rancour in Mr. Dark: he can like people even when he disagrees with them; and at his most Marxist moments he never loses touch with the fundamental Christian belief that every human being is an individual and capable of salvation.

[Fee £5.5s; 5.11.43]

1. Otto Strasser (1897–1974) and his brother, Gregor (1892–1934), were leading figures in the development of the Nazi Party in the early 1920s. Otto became disillusioned because the Party was insufficiently orientated towards the working class; he left the Party in 1930 to found the Black Front. Gregor remained loyal to Hitler but was shot during the Röhm Purge. Otto escaped and settled for a time in Canada. His *Hitler and I* was published in 1940. The brothers were instrumental in introducing Goebbels into journalism on behalf of the Nazis.
2. Private motoring was banned for much of the war to save petrol and motorists were encouraged to hand in car tyres for recycling.
3. In *The Weekly Review* for 9 December 1943, A. K. Chesterton (nephew of G. K. Chesterton), discussed Orwell's, demand to know why Reed should want a plutocratic Britain to win (as he put it). In a column headed 'Patriot's Duty,' he maintained that 'My country—right or wrong' was a maxim 'which apparently has no place in Mr Orwell's philosophy.' Was Orwell's support of Britain, he asked, only because he could discover no blemish in her—and if he did 'he would throw her to the lions—or the Germans'? The answer to Orwell was: 'We want Britain to win because she belongs to us and we belong to her; our lives derive from her soil and our spiritual roots lie deep in her tradition.' But in winning the war, Britain must not again lose the peace, for 'that would be mortal.' Peace could be lost by false doctrines—pacifism, meaningless slogans such as 'collective security,' and insidious daily doses of propaganda. The battle for the peace, he concluded, would be 'a fight to the death between the soul of Britain and cosmopolitan finance, which is determined that the fruits of victory shall be nothing less than the nations of the world in pawn to international usury and control.' For Orwell's riposte to A. K. Chesterton, see 'As I Please,' 4, 24 December 1943, *2396*.

4. Sidney Dark (1874–1947) edited the *Church Times* from 1924 to 1941. He published a number of biographies—among them works on Thackeray (1912), Dickens (1919), Cardinal Newman (1934), Cardinal Manning (1936)—and many religious books. Orwell was required to tone down a reference to the *Church Times* in *A Clergyman's Daughter*: the description of its 'chosen sport of baiting Modernists and atheists' was altered to its being 'in the forefront of every assault upon Modernists and atheists'; see *CW*, III, 66, line 22 and note; also Orwell's letter to his publishers, 10 January 1935, *223*. Orwell included Dark in his list of Crypto-Communists and Fellow-Travellers (see *3732*), but later crossed out this entry.

2348. Newsletter in Tamil, 30

11 November 1943

The English version was written by Eric Blair. No script has been traced.

2349. To Ivor Brown

11 November 1943   07/ES/EB

Dear Ivor Brown,

I think you wanted some particulars of the talk we should like you to do on Thunder Rock[1] for December 19th. These are half hour programmes and consist of an acted extract from the play with a talk on the play and sometimes on the author's work in general by some qualified person. The programme starts off with a short trailer from the play itself then the speaker follows (so that your talk should start "Those lines you have just heard come from Thunder Rock," or words to that effect) and after that comes the extract from the play. The length would be about ten minutes or twelve hundred words. I would like to have the script a week before the date of transmission. As these programmes go out on Sunday you will probably prefer to record your talk beforehand, and we can arrange a recording anytime convenient to you.

Yours sincerely,
[Initialled] E.A.B
(George Orwell)

1. By Robert Ardrey (1908–1980). Orwell reviewed the play in *Time and Tide*, 29 June 1940; see *645*. Shortly afterwards it was made into a powerful film by the Boulting brothers.

2350. To Harold Laski

11 November 1943   07/ES/EB

Dear Professor Laski,

Would you like to do a ten minutes talk for the Indian Section of the BBC on Galsworthy's play "Strife"? I should think that from a socialist point of view it is by now a rather interesting period piece. The date of the talk would be the 5th December. If you are interested I will send fuller particulars.

Yours sincerely,
George Orwell
Dictated by George Orwell
and dispatched in his
absence by: [Initialled] JEL

2351. English Newsletter for Indonesia, 19

12 November 1943

This was written by George Orwell.[1] No script has been traced.

1. PasB has 'English Newsletter in Indonesia written by George Orwell,' with no 'read' included.

2352. To Reginald Reynolds

12 November 1943   07/ES/EB

Dear Reg,

I am sorry but the Kropotkin talk is off. I have been told that we ought not to give publicity on the air to a notorious anarchist. I am very sorry about this and hope you have not already been let in for a lot of work.

Yours,
[Initialled] E.A.B
(Eric Blair)

2353. BBC Talks Booking Form, 15.11.43

Professor H. J. Laski: 'Great Dramatists,' 8, "Strife"; broadcast 5.12.43; fee £8.8s. Signed: Z. A. Bokhari

2354. To Edmund Blunden

16 November 1943   07/ES/EB/—

Dear Blunden,

I wonder if you could be kind enough to approach Professor Nicol-Smith and get him to do another talk for us. I am writing to you because we approached him through you before. We want a talk on Thackeray for December 23rd, which would mean that we would want the script by about December 15th.

What we want is a fifteen minute talk (that is about 1600 words) giving a general account of Thackeray's work, and explaining why he is an important writer, aimed at the Indian student audience. I hope Professor Nicol-Smith will undertake this. His last talk was very successful and I think he enjoyed doing it. I wonder if you could be kind enough to let us know about this. I am sorry to give you this trouble.[1]

Yours sincerely,
[Initialled] E.A.B
(George Orwell)

1. Blunden replied on 28 November, saying Nicol-Smith had declined; he had 'some work on hand' which made it impossible for him to do the necessary reading in time. He suggested George Sampson and William Plomer. In the event, as the PasB shows, Blunden gave the talk.

2355. To H. J. Laski

16 November 1943   07/ES/EB

Dear Professor Laski,
I am so glad to hear that you are willing to do the talk on "Strife". I had better explain just what is wanted. These are half hour programmes, each consisting of an acted extract from a play and a ten minutes talk on the play by some qualified person. We aim as far as possible at giving some idea of the dramatist's work in general, besides the particular play that[1] is being acted. I am sending herewith a specimen copy of a talk from an earlier programme. I don't think you will find that the censorship will impose much limitation on what you say. I should think the principle° point would be the altered atmosphere in the Labour Movement, and in the degree of knowledge a middle class writer would have of it. If you make your talk 1200 words that would be about right. The date of transmission is Sunday December 5th, which means that we would like to have the script by the end of this month. As the 5th is a Sunday you will no doubt like to record before hand and we can arrange a date.

Yours sincerely,
[Initialled] E.A.B

1. From the erasure marks on the carbon copy, it looks as if the typist first typed 'which' and then substituted 'that.' The erroneous spelling of 'principal' passed unnoticed.

2356. To S. Moos

16 November 1943   Typewritten[1]

10a Mortimer Crescent   London   NW 6

Dear Mr. Moos,

I hope you will forgive my long delay in commenting on and returning the enclosed manuscript, but I have been in poor health in recent weeks, and I am also very busy, as you can perhaps imagine.

I find what you say very interesting, but I have two criticisms of a general nature to make. The first is that I think you are concerned with 'what' a little too much to the exclusion of 'how'. It is comparatively easy to see the evils of modern industrialised society, and it is only one more step beyond that to see the inadequacy of the solutions put forward by Socialists etc. The real trouble begins when one wants to communicate these ideas to a large enough number of people to make some actual change in the trend of society. We certainly have to decide what kind of world we want, but I suggest that the greatest problem before intellectuals now is the conquest of power. You speak of forming a 'new elite' (which I think there probably must be, though I am inclined to shrink from the idea). But how to start forming that elite, how one can do such things *inside* the powerful modern state which is controlled by people whose interest is to prevent any such thing—that is another question. If you have seen anything of the innumerable attempts during the past 20 years to start new political parties, you will know what I mean.

Secondly, I think you overestimate the danger of a 'Brave New World'— i.e. a completely materialistic vulgar civilisation based on hedonism. I would say that the danger of that kind of thing is past, and that we are in danger of quite a different kind of world, the centralised slave state, ruled over by a small clique who are in effect a new ruling class, though they might be adoptive rather than hereditary. Such a state would not be hedonistic, on the contrary its dynamic would come from some kind of rabid nationalism and leader-worship kept going by literally continuous war, and its average standard of living would probably be low. I don't expect to see mass unemployment again, except through temporarly° maladjustments; I believe that we are in much greater danger of forced labour and actual slavery. And at present I see no safeguard against this except (a) the war-weariness and distaste for authoritarianism which may follow the present war, and (b) the survival of democratic values among the intelligentsia.

I don't know whether these cursory comments are much use to you. They might be worth thinking over. I should say that Faber's or somebody like that might publish your MS as a pamphlet—at any rate it would be worth trying. But I would brush up the English a bit (rather involved and foreign-sounding in places) and get the MS retyped before submitting it.

Once again, please forgive the delay.

Yours sincerely,
Geo. Orwell

1. This is reproduced from a typewritten original in the possession of the recipient (who wrote to Orwell as a reader of *Tribune*). The error 'temporarly' is in the original. The original is signed by Orwell as above.

2357. 'The Detective Story' [Grandeur et décadence du roman policier anglais]

17 November 1943

Orwell's essay 'The Detective Story' (the title Orwell gives it in his 'Notes for My Literary Executor,' 1949) was published in French in *Fontaine*, Nos. 37–40, 1944, as 'Grandeur et décadence du roman policier anglais.' This cumulative issue of some 500 pages was devoted to English literature, 1918 to 1940, and, though dated 1944, was published in Algiers in the spring of 1945. Because the delay in publication was so great, it is reproduced here under the date of its completion, given in Orwell's Payments Book; an English translation, not made by Orwell, follows. The Payments Book has, against the date 17 November, 'Fontaine Article (2000) H': the figure is the number of words; 'H' probably means 'Held over.' There are only dashes where payment should be recorded. The essay exists only in the translation made for *Fontaine* by Fernand Auberjonois, so an exact word count of the English version is not possible, but 2,000 is clearly an underestimate; inaccurate estimates are quite common in the Payments Book.

Another version of *Fontaine*, 37–40, was published as a book under the title *Aspects de la Littérature Anglaise (1918–1945)*. This was brought to the editor's attention by Ian Willison. From the colophon this seems to have been registered in 1947 ('Dépôt légal 1er trimestre 1947') but to have been printed a year earlier ('Achevé d'imprimer en février 1946'). The edition claims to have corrected the first, 1944, edition; it omits Wyndham Lewis and Charles Morgan and three translations, but adds William Empson, Dorothy Richardson, and Sacheverell Sitwell and five translations. Copies were advertised as being available in 'England [and the] British Empire' from *Horizon* at 15 shillings. There are very slight variations in the text of Orwell's article in 1947 as compared with 1944. In 1947, initial capitals are slightly reduced; there is an increase in punctuation, chiefly in marking off dependent clauses, but one or two commas are omitted; in the main, words in 1944 between *flèches* are set in italic; there are one or two corrections of accent. One verbal change is in paragraph 5: 'surtout durant les épisodes' becomes, in 1947, 'surtout au cours des épisodes'; in the only other such change, the second note is omitted and 'Jack the Ripper,' to which it refers, becomes 'Jack l'Eventreur.'

There is a very curious advertisement on the front flap of the dust-jacket. In a list of books due to appear is 'George Orwell LA FILLE DE L'AIR.' This seems a slightly unusual title for *Coming Up for Air*. 'Jouer la fille de l'air' means 's'enfuir,' to take flight, perhaps referring directly to George Bowling's 'getting away from it all,' rather than to the sea-turtles 'coming up for air' (see *CW*, VII, 177).

The book was to have been produced by Éditions de la Revue Fontaine in the series La Malle de la Manche, directed by J. B. Brunius and M. P. Fouchet. On 3 September 1945, Brunius wrote to Orwell, who had not received copies of *Fontaine*, to say one had been sent in May and another in June. He was now sending a third. He took the opportunity of asking Orwell whether *Animal Farm*, or perhaps one of Orwell's earlier books, might be included in a series of English books to be published by Éditions Fontaine. The first, to be published in October 1945, was to be Rex Warner's *The Aerodrome*. None of Orwell's books was published in this series, and *Coming Up for Air* was eventually published in French by Amiot Dumont in 1952 as *Journal d'un Anglais moyen*, and later, in 1983, by Éditions Champ Libre, as *Un peu d'air frais* (which carries echoes of *Coming Up for Air* and 'La fille de l'air'). Brunius also asked Orwell if he would 'write a talk for my series of broadcasts on English literature for the French programme of the B.B.C.' Orwell does not seem to have done so.

Before the issue of *Fontaine* was published, it was attacked as Roman Catholic literary propaganda by 'Francophil' in *Tribune*; see correspondence following 'As I Please,' 46, 27 October 1944, *2568*. The London correspondent of *Fontaine*, J. B. Brunius, then took up the criticism in *Tribune*, 1 December 1944. He said he had not expected criticism before *Fontaine* was published but 'was waiting for the fun to begin afterwards.' He rejected strongly the suggestion that he was 'implicated in a Catholic anthology,' deduced by Francophil because the issue had been edited by Kathleen Raine and Antonia White, 'both Catholics,' and because they had included no fewer than 'ten people who could have indeed qualified for a religious anthology.' Brunius, in addition to dispelling what he took to be 'a most libellous suspicion' that he was involved in producing a Catholic anthology, listed the steps he had taken for this 'concours':

'1. To make sure that the Introduction by E. M. Forster should be well translated.

'2. To insist on the inclusion in the number of David Garnett, Richard Hughes, Richard Hillary, George Orwell, Herbert Read, G. B. Shaw, H. G. Wells, Rex Warner.

'3. To propose that some of those who had been prominent in English surrealism should be represented, and to send to *Fontaine* poems by Humphrey Jennings, translated by myself, and a poem by Roland Penrose translated by [E. L. T.] Mesens.

'4. To protest that the younger generation of poets was insufficiently represented, and that writers like Alex Comfort should be included; to send a certain number of little reviews to *Fontaine* to choose from, among them *Now*, *Wales*, *Poetry London*, *Poetry Scotland*, *Poetry Quarterly*, *Dint*,[1] etc. . . . '

The translation reproduced here is based on those made by Dr. Shirley E. Jones and Janet Percival, modified in the light of comments made by Professor Patrick Parrinder, Ian Willison, and the editor. For a comment on this essay, see Patrick Parrinder, 'George Orwell and the Detective Story,' *Journal of Popular Culture*, 6 (1972–73), reprinted in *Dimensions of Detective Fiction*, edited by L. N. Landrum and P. and R. B. Browne (Bowling Green, Ohio, 1976).

Orwell's Payments Book records against 28 December 1945 the sum of £3.3s in payment for 'Second Rights' for this essay, paid by the Ministry of Information. The use to which the MOI put the article has not been traced, but Orwell, in his 1949 notes for his literary executor, mentions a Russian translation of this essay; the second rights may have been for that translation. No Russian translation has been found.

C'est de 1920 à 1940 que fut lu et écrit le plus grand nombre de romans policiers et c'est précisément durant cette période que le roman policier en tant que genre littéraire devint décadent. Au cours de ces années inquiètes et futiles, les «crime stories» comme on les appelait (en désignant ainsi le roman détective proprement dit aussi bien que le «thriller» où l'auteur utilise la formule grand-guignolesque) constituaient en Angleterre un palliatif universel au même titre que le thé, l'aspirine, les cigarettes et la radio. Ces ouvrages parurent en quantité industrielle et l'on ne peut qu'être surpris de compter parmi leurs auteurs des professeurs d'économie politique et des prêtres tant catholiques qu'anglicans. L'amateur que jamais l'idée d'écrire un roman n'avait effleuré se sentait de taille à taquiner le roman policier que n'exige que de très vagues connaissances de toxicologie et un alibi plausible derrière lequel dissimuler le coupable. Bientôt pourtant le roman policier tendait à se compliquer; il demandait à l'auteur plus d'ingéniosité car il fallait satisfaire chez le lecteur un appétit de violence et une soif de sang toujours croissants. Les crimes devinrent plus sensationnels et plus difficiles à déceler. Mais il n'en reste pas moins que dans cette multitude d'ouvrages l'on n'en trouve point ou presque qui vaille la peine d'êtres relus.

Il n'en fut pas toujours ainsi. La littérature distrayante n'est pas forcément de la mauvaise littérature. Entre 1880 et 1920 nous avons eu, en Angleterre, trois spécialistes du roman détective qui firent preuve de qualités artistiques indéniables. Conan Doyle appartenait bien entendu à cette trinité et, avec lui, deux écrivains qui ne le valent pas mais que l'on ne doit pas mépriser: Ernest Bramah et R. Austin Freeman. Les «Mémoires» et les «Aventures de Sherlock Holmes», «Max Carrados» et les «Yeux de Max Carrados» de Bramah, «L'Œil d'Osiris» et «L'Os qui chante» de Freeman sont, avec les deux ou trois nouvelles d'Edgar Allan Poe dont ils s'inspirent, les classiques de la littérature détective anglaise. L'on retrouve dans chacun de ces ouvrages des qualités de style, et mieux encore une *atmosphère* auxquelles les auteurs contemporains ne nous ont guère habitués (Dorothy Sayers, par exemple, ou Agatha Christie ou Freeman Wills Croft). Il vaut la peine d'en rechercher les raisons.

Aujourd'hui encore, plus d'un demi-siècle après son entrée en scène, Sherlock Holmes reste l'un des personnages les plus populaires du roman anglais. Son physique mince et athlétique, son nez en bec d'oiseau, sa robe de chambre fripée, les pièces encombrées de son appartement de Baker Street avec leurs recoins et leurs éprouvettes, le violon, le tabac dans la pantoufle hindoue, les traces de balles sur les murs, tout cela fait partie du mobilier intellectuel de l'Anglais qui connaît ses auteurs. D'autre part, les exploits de Sherlock Holmes ont été traduits en une vingtaine de langues, du Norvégien au Japonais. Les deux autres écrivains dont j'ai parlé, Ernest Bramah et R. Austin Freeman, n'atteignirent jamais un aussi vaste public, mais tous deux ont su créer des types inoubliables. Le Docteur Thorndyke de Freeman est le détective de laboratoire, l'expert médico-légal qui résout l'énigme à coups de microscope et d'appareil photographique. Quant au Max Carrados d'Ernest Bramah, il est aveugle. La cécité ayant hypertrophié ses autres sens, il n'en devient que plus fort. Si nous cherchons à déterminer les raisons pour lesquelles ces trois auteurs nous attirent, nous sommes amenés à faire une première constatation d'ordre purement technique, qui met en relief les faiblesses du roman policier contemporain et de toutes les nouvelles anglaises de ces vingt dernières années.

L'on découvre que la «détective story» de la bonne époque (de Poe à Freeman) est infiniment plus *fournie* que le roman moderne. Le dialogue est plus étoffé, les digressions sont plus fréquentes. Si les contes de Conan Doyle ou de Poe avaient été écrits hier, l'on doute fort qu'un éditeur en eût voulu. Ils sont trop longs pour les revues ramassées d'aujourd'hui et leurs interminables entrées en matière vont à l'encontre de la marotte actuelle de l' «économie».

C'est cependant d'une accumulation de détails à première vue superflus que Conan Doyle, comme Dickens avant lui, tire ses effets les plus frappants. Si l'on se livre à un examen des ouvrages de la série Sherlock Holmes, l'on s'aperçoit que les excentricités et la perspicacité de ce personnage se manifestent surtout durant les épisodes qui ne rentrent pas intégralement dans la trame du roman. Holmes brille surtout par sa méthode de «raisonnement par déduction» qui stupéfie le bon docteur Watson et dont nous trouvons un exemple au début du «Blue Carbuncle». Il suffit à Holmes d'examiner un chapeau melon trouvé dans la rue pour qu'il donne une description minutieuse—et, comme la suite le prouve, exacte—de son propriétaire. L'incident du chapeau n'a pourtant que des rapports très vagues avec l'événement principal; plusieurs épisodes sont précédés de conversations qui remplissent jusqu'à six ou sept pages et ne prétendent pas être autre chose que de la digression pure et simple. C'est surtout par le truchement de ces conversations que sont démontrés le génie de Holmes et la naïveté de Watson.

Ernest Bramah et R. Austin Freeman travaillent eux aussi avec ce même mépris de l'économie. Si leurs récits sont des œuvres littéraires et non de simples «puzzles» c'est beaucoup grâce aux digressions que l'on y trouve.

Le roman policier des bonnes années n'est pas nécessairement échafaudé sur un mystère et il se laisse lire même s'il ne se termine pas par une surprise ou une révélation sensationnelles. Ce qui nous agace le plus chez l'écrivain de «détective stories» modernes c'est l'effort constant, douloureux presque, auquel il se livre pour cacher l'identité du coupable—formule d'autant plus agaçante que le lecteur, en se blasant, finit par trouver les procédés de dissimulation grotesques. Au contraire, dans bon nombre de nouvelles de Conan Doyle et dans le célèbre conte de Poe, «The Purloined Letter», l'auteur du crime est connu dès le début. Comment le coupable manœuvre-t-il, comment sera-t-il enfin livré à la justice? Toute la question est là. Austin Freeman pousse parfois l'audace jusqu'à décrire d'abord le crime par le menu détail, puis se borne à expliquer la manière dont l'énigme a été résolue. Dans les romans de la première heure, le crime n'est donc pas forcément sensationnel ou ingénieusement conçu. Dans le roman policier moderne l'incident-clef est presque toujours un assassinat (la formule ne varie guère: un cadavre, une douzaine de suspects, ayant chacun leur alibi étanche); mais chez les précurseurs il est souvent question d'humbles méfaits, le coupable n'est peut-être qu'un filou de troisième zone. Peut-être découvre-t-on même qu'il n'y a ni coupable ni crime. Nombreux sont les mystères sondés par Holmes qui placés en pleine lumière ne sont que des trompe-l'œil. Bramah écrivit dix ou vingt contes, dont deux ou trois seulement ont trait à un assassinat. Les auteurs peuvent se payer ce luxe car le succès de leur ouvrage ne dépend pas de la découverte du criminel mais bien de l'intérêt que présente pour le lecteur un exposé des méthodes de détection chères à Holmes, Thorndyke ou Carrados. Ces personnages exaltent l'imagination et le lecteur, s'il réagit comme on entend le faire réagir, fait d'eux des géants intellectuels.

Il nous est possible maintenant d'établir une distinction fondamentale entre les deux écoles du roman policier—l'ancienne et l'actuelle.

Les précurseurs croyaient en leurs propres personnages. Ils faisaient de leurs détectives des êtres exceptionnellement doués, des demi-dieux pour lesquels ils éprouvaient une admiration sans bornes. De nos jours, dans notre décor de guerres mondiales, de chômage universel, de famines, d'épidémies et de totalitarisme, le crime a beaucoup perdu de sa saveur; nous sommes par trop conscients de ses causes sociales et économiques pour faire du simple policier un bienfaiteur de l'humanité. Il ne nous est pas facile non plus de considérer comme un but en soi la gymnastique de l'esprit que nous impose ce genre d'ouvrage. Assis dans l'obscurité qui l'accompagne partout, le Dupin de Poe exerce ses facultés mentales sans songer un instant à l'action; de ce fait, il ne provoque pas chez nous toute l'admiration que lui voue Poe. «Le mystère de Marie Roget», exemple typique de pure acrobatie de l'esprit, exigeant du lecteur l'agilité d'un démêleur de mots croisés, ne pouvait voir le jour qu'à une époque de loisirs. Dans les histoires de Sherlock Holmes l'on surprend l'auteur tirant un évident plaisir de ces jongleries qui paraissent se détacher complètement de la trame. Il en est de même pour «Silver Blaze», «Le Rite de Musgrave», «The Dancing Men» ou cet épisode qui permet à Holmes de déduire l'histoire d'un passant de son apparence extérieure ou d'ébahir Watson en devinant ses pensées du moment. Pourtant, l'œuvre que ces détectives s'efforçaient d'accomplir revêtait aux yeux de leurs créateurs une importance évidente. Durant les paisibles années de la dernière fin de siècle, la Société pouvait passer pour composée essentiellement de bonnes gens dont le criminel seul troublait la quiétude. Aux yeux de ses contemporains, le docteur Moriarty était un personnage aussi démoniaque qu'Hitler de nos jours. Le vainqueur de Moriarty devenait un chevalier errant ou un héros national. Et Conan Doyle, lorsqu'il fait passer Holmes de vie à trépas, à la fin des «Mémoires»,★ inspire à Watson les mots d'adieu de Platon à Socrate, ceci sans nulle crainte du ridicule.

Parmi les modernes, il en est deux seulement qui nous paraissent croire à leurs détectives: ce sont G. K. Chesterton et Edgar Wallace. Leurs motifs n'étaient pourtant pas aussi désintéressés que ceux de Doyle ou de Freeman. Wallace, écrivain extraordinairement prolifique et doué, dans le genre morbide, était inspiré par une forme de sadisme particulière que nous n'avons

★ 1. Doyle avait eu l'intention de terminer, avec les «Mémoires» sa série Sherlock Holmes; pourtant ses lecteurs protestèrent avec une telle vigueur qu'il se sentit obligé de poursuivre. De toutes les parties du monde les lettres affluèrent et, dit-on, certains de leurs auteurs menaçaient Doyle de lui faire un mauvais parti s'il ne reprenait pas les aventures de Holmes. Ainsi les «Mémoires» furent-ils suivis de plusieurs volumes. Les premiers restent pourtant les meilleurs.

pas le temps d'analyser ici. Le héros de Chesterton, le Père Brown, est un prêtre catholique dont Chesterton se sert comme d'un instrument de propagande religieuse. Dans les autres romans policiers, du moins dans tous ceux que j'ai lus, je constate soit un côté burlesque, soit un effort peu convaincant de la part de l'auteur de créer une atmosphère de terreur autour de crimes qu'il a lui- même de la peine à trouver horribles. Et puis, pour arriver à leurs fins, les détectives du roman contemporain comptent avant tout sur la chance et sur l'intuition. Ils sont moins intellectuels que les héros de Poe, Doyle, Freeman ou Bramah. Il est clair que Holmes, Thorndyke, et d'autres encore, sont chacun dans l'esprit des précurseurs, le prototype de l'homme de science, mieux, de l'omniscient, qui doit tout à la logique et rien au hasard. Le père Brown de Chesterton possède, à peu de choses près, les pouvoirs du magicien. Holmes est un rationaliste du XIXme siècle. En créant ce personnage Conan Doyle ne faisait que reproduire fidèlement l'image que ses contemporains se faisaient du savant.

Le détective du siècle passé est invariablement célibataire. Il faut voir là une preuve de plus de sa supériorité. Le détective moderne a, lui aussi, un goût marqué pour le célibat (il est vrai que dans un roman policier une épouse complique beaucoup les choses); pourtant le célibat de Holmes et de Thorndyke a ceci de particulier qu'il est monastique. Il est dit carrément de ces deux individus qu'ils ne portent aucun intérêt au sexe opposé. Le sage, estime-t-on, ne doit pas être marié; tout comme le Saint doit pratiquer le célibat. Le sage doit avoir à portée de la main un personnage complémentaire: le sot. Par contraste, le sot rehausse les qualités du sage. Tel est le rôle réservé au préfet de police dont Dupin résout les problèmes dans «The Purloined Letter». Jarvis, le sot qui seconde le Docteur Thorndyke manque d'ampleur, mais M. Carlyle, l'ami de Max Carrados, est un type bien campé. Quant à Watson dont l'imbécilité est presque chronique, il est un personnage plus vivant encore que Holmes lui-même. C'est à dessein et non par accident que les premiers détectives sont des amateurs et non des fonctionnaires de la police. C'est Edgar Wallace qui devait lancer la mode du policier professionnel de Scotland Yard. Le respect de l'amateur est un trait caractéristiquement britannique. L'on trouve chez Sherlock Holmes une certaine ressemblance avec un de ces contemporains: Raffles, le voleur-gentilhomme, équivalent anglais d'Arsène Lupin. Pourtant le rôle officieux que joue le limier de la première heure sert encore une fois à faire ressortir ses dons supérieurs. Dans les premiers Sherlock Holmes et dans certaines aventures du Dr. Thorndyke, la police se montre nettement hostile à l'égard des enquêteurs du dehors. Les professionnels se trompent régulièrement et n'hésitent pas à accuser les innocents. Le génie analytique de Holmes, les connaissances encyclopédiques de Thorndyke n'en brillent que d'un éclat plus vif, comparés à la plate routine des organisations officielles.

Dans cette brève étude je n'ai pu parler un peu longuement que d'un seul groupe d'écrivains et j'ai dû passer sous silence les auteurs étrangers, les romanciers américains à l'exception de Poe. Depuis 1920, la production de romans policiers a été énorme et la guerre ne l'a pas ralentie; cependant, pour des raisons que je me suis efforcé de souligner, la baguette du magicien d'autrefois a perdu ses pouvoirs. L'on trouve dans le roman moderne une plus grande ingéniosité, mais l'auteur semble incapable de créer une «atmosphère». Parmi les modernes, il faut sans doute placer en tête de liste le sombre Edgar Wallace, plus enclin à terroriser son lecteur qu'à le guider dans le maquis des problèmes complexes. Il faut mentionner aussi Agatha Christie qui manie élégamment le dialogue et trace avec art les fausses pistes. Les nouvelles tant vantées de Dorothy Sayers n'auraient probablement guère attiré l'attention si l'auteur n'avait eu l'astuce de faire de son détective le fils d'un Duc. Quant à l'œuvre des autres contemporains, de Freeman Wills Croft, de G.D.H. et Margaret Cole, de Ngaio Marsh ou de Philip Macdonald, elle n'a guère plus de rapports avec la littérature que le mot croisé.

L'on imagine aisément que le roman conçu comme pur exercice intellectuel—«Le Scarabée d'Or», par exemple—puisse renaître un jour. Mais il est peu probable qu'il reparaisse sous la forme d'un roman policier. J'ai déjà signalé, et le fait me paraît significatif, que les meilleurs auteurs de romans policiers ont pu tirer parti de méfaits sans envergure. Comment croire que le jeu des Gendarmes et des Voleurs puisse inspirer encore des écrivains du calibre de Conan Doyle, sans parler de Poe. Le roman policier tel que nous l'avons connu appartient au XIXme siècle, et surtout à la fin du XIXme siècle. Il appartient au Londres de 1880 et de 1890, au Londres triste et mystérieux où, dans la lumière tremblotante des reverbères à gaz glissaient des chapeaux melons à la calotte surélevée, où les grelots des *hansom cabs* tintaient dans d'éternels brouillards; il appartient à cette époque où l'opinion anglaise était plus profondément remuée par les exploits de Jack The° Ripper* que par les problèmes de la «Home Rule» d'Irlande ou par la bataille de Majuba.

Translation

It was between 1920 and 1940 that the majority of detective stories were written and read, but this is precisely the period that marks the decline of the detective story as a literary genre. Throughout these troubled and frivolous years, 'crime stories' as they were called (this title includes the detective story proper as well as the 'thriller' where the author follows the conventions of Grand Guignol), were in England a universal palliative equal to tea, aspirins, cigarettes and the wireless. These works were mass-produced, and it is not without some surprise that we find that their authors include professors of political economy and Roman Catholics as well as Anglican priests. Any amateur who had never dreamed of writing a novel felt capable of tackling a detective story, which requires only the haziest knowledge of toxicology and a plausible alibi to conceal the culprit. Yet soon the detective story started to get more complicated; it demanded more ingenuity if its author were to satisfy the reader's constantly growing appetite for violence and thirst for bloodshed. The crimes became more sensational and more difficult to

* Equivalent londonien de Landru, qui sévit à l'époque dans la capitale anglaise et sema l'épouvante dans le pays tout entier.

unravel. It is nevertheless a fact that in this multitude of later works there is hardly anything worth re-reading.

Things were not always like this. Entertaining books are not necessarily bad books. Between 1880 and 1920 we had in England three specialists in the detective novel who showed undeniably artistic qualities. Conan Doyle of course belonged to this trio, together with two writers who are not his equal, but who should not be despised: Ernest Bramah and R. Austin Freeman. The *Memoirs* and the *Adventures of Sherlock Holmes*, *Max Carrados* and *The Eyes of Max Carrados* by Bramah, *The Eye of Osiris* and *The Singing Bone* by Freeman are, together with the two or three short stories of Edgar Allan Poe which inspired them, the classics of English detective fiction. We can find in each of these works a quality of style, and even better an *atmosphere*, which we do not usually find in contemporary authors (Dorothy Sayers, for example, or Agatha Christie or Freeman Wills Croft). The reasons for this are worth examining.

Even today, more than half a century after his first appearance, Sherlock Holmes remains one of the most popular characters in the English novel. His slim, athletic build, his beaky nose, his crumpled dressing gown, the cluttered rooms of his Baker Street flat with their alcoves and test tubes, the violin, the tobacco in the Indian slipper, the bullet marks on the walls, all this is part of the intellectual furniture of the Englishman who knows his authors. Moreover the exploits of Sherlock Holmes have been translated into some twenty languages, from Norwegian to Japanese. The other two authors I mentioned, Ernest Bramah and R. Austin Freeman, never reached such a wide public, but both of them created unforgettable characters. Freeman's Dr Thorndyke is the laboratory detective, the forensic scientist who solves the mystery with his microscope and camera. As for Ernest Bramah's Max Carrados, he is blind, but his blindness only serves to sharpen his other senses, and he is all the better because of it. If we seek to determine why we are drawn to these three authors, we are led to a preliminary observation of a purely technical nature, one which emphasises the weakness of the modern detective story and of all English short stories of the past twenty years.

We can see that the vintage detective story (from Poe to Freeman) is much more *dense* than the modern novel. The dialogue is richer, the digressions more frequent. If the stories of Conan Doyle or Poe had been written yesterday, it is doubtful whether any editor would have accepted them. They are too long for the compact magazines of today, and their interminable opening scenes run counter to the current fad for economy.

Yet it is by accumulating details which at first seem superfluous that Conan Doyle, like Dickens before him, gains his most striking effects. If you set out to examine the Sherlock Holmes stories, you find that the eccentricities and the perspicacity of a character are principally revealed in episodes which do not form an integral part of the plot. Holmes is especially distinguished by his method of 'reasoning by deduction' which amazes the good Doctor Watson. We can see an example at the beginning of *The Blue Carbuncle*. Holmes only has to examine a bowler hat found in the street to give a detailed—and, as subsequent events prove, exact—description of its owner. Yet the hat incident has only the vaguest connection with the main events; several episodes are preceded by six or seven pages of conversation which do not claim to be anything but digressions pure and simple. These conversations act as a vehicle to demonstrate Holmes's genius and Watson's naivety.

Ernest Bramah and R. Austin Freeman also write with the same contempt for conciseness. It is largely thanks to their digressions that their stories are literary works and not mere 'puzzles'.

The vintage detective story is not necessarily founded on a mystery, and it is worth reading even if it does not end with a surprise or a sensational revelation. The most annoying thing about the writers of modern detective stories is their constant, almost painful effort to hide the culprit's identity— and this convention is doubly annoying because it soon palls on a reader, who eventually finds the intricacies of concealment grotesque. On the other hand, in several of Conan Doyle's stories and in Poe's famous story *The Purloined Letter*, the perpetrator of the crime is known at the outset. How will he react? How, in the end, will he be brought to justice? That is what is so intriguing. Austin Freeman sometimes has the audacity to describe the crime first in minute detail, then merely explains how the mystery was solved. In the earlier stories, the crime is not necessarily sensational or ingeniously contrived. In the modern detective story the key incident is almost always a murder (the formula hardly changes: a corpse, a dozen suspects, each with a watertight alibi); but the earlier stories often deal with petty crimes, perhaps the culprit is no more than a third-rate thief. There may even turn out to be neither culprit nor crime. Many of the mysteries investigated by Holmes fade away in the broad light of day. Bramah wrote ten or twenty stories, of which only two or three deal with a murder. The authors can indulge themselves like this because the success of their work depends, not on the unmasking of the criminal, but in the interest the reader finds in an account of the methods of detection so dear to Holmes, Thorndyke or Carrados. These characters appeal to the imagination, and the reader, if he reacts as he is meant to, transforms them into intellectual giants.

It is now possible for us to make a fundamental distinction between the two schools of detective story—the old and the new.

The earlier writers believed in their own characters. They made their detectives into exceptionally gifted individuals, demi-gods for whom they felt a boundless admiration. Against our present-day background of world wars, mass unemployment, famines, plague and totalitarianism, crime has lost much of its savour; we know far too much about its social and economic causes to look upon the ordinary detective as a benefactor of mankind. Nor is it easy for us to consider as an end in itself the mental gymnastics demanded of us by this kind of work. Sitting in the darkness that accompanies him everywhere, Poe's Dupin uses his mental faculties without ever thinking of action; because of this, he does not arouse in us quite the admiration which Poe feels for him. *The Mystery of Marie Roget*, a typical example of pure mental acrobatics, demanding from its reader the agility of a crossword-puzzle addict, could only have appeared in a more leisured age. In the Sherlock Holmes stories you catch the author taking evident pleasure in this display of virtuosity, which seems totally detached from the plot. It is the same with *Silver Blaze, The Musgrave Ritual, The Dancing Men,* or the sort of episode that allows Holmes to deduce the life-history of a passer-by from his appearance, or to astound Watson by guessing what he is thinking at that very moment. And yet the work which these detectives were striving to accomplish was obviously important for their creators. During the peaceful years at the close of the last century, Society seemed mainly composed of law-abiding people, whose security was disturbed only by the criminal. In his contemporaries' eyes, Dr Moriarty was as demoniac a figure as Hitler is today. The man who defeated Moriarty became a knight errant or a national hero. And when Conan Doyle, sending Holmes to his death at the end of *The Memoirs,** allows Watson to echo the words of Plato's farewell to Socrates, there is no fear of his seeming ridiculous.[2]

Among modern writers, there are only two who seem to us to believe in their detectives: G. K. Chesterton and Edgar Wallace. Yet their motives are not as disinterested as those of Doyle or Freeman. Wallace, an extraordinarily prolific and gifted writer in a morbid genre, was inspired by his own private form of sadism which there is no time to analyse here. Chesterton's hero, Father Brown, is a Catholic priest used by Chesterton as an instrument of religious propaganda. In the other detective stories, at least in those I have read, I can see either a comic side, or a rather unconvincing effort on the author's part to create an atmosphere of horror around crimes which he himself has great difficulty in finding horrific. And then, to achieve their aims, the detectives in contemporary novels rely first and foremost on luck and intuition. They are less intellectual than the heroes of Poe, Doyle, Freeman or Bramah. It is clear that for the earlier writers, Holmes, Thorndyke and many others are all the prototype of the man of science, or, rather, of omniscience, who owes everything to logic and nothing to chance. Chesterton's Father Brown possesses almost magical powers. Holmes is a nineteenth-century rationalist. In creating this character Conan Doyle faithfully reproduced his contemporaries' idea of a scientist.

In the last century the detective was always a bachelor. That must be taken as further proof of his superiority. The modern detective also has a marked taste for celibacy (a wife does rather complicate matters in a detective story), but the celibacy of Holmes and Thorndyke is of a particularly monkish kind. It is stated categorically that neither of them is interested in the opposite sex. It is felt that the wise man should not be married, just as the Saint must practise celibacy. The wise man should have a complementary character beside him—the fool. The contrast accentuates the wise man's good qualities. This role is reserved for the police chief whose problems are solved by Dupin in *The Purloined Letter.* Jarvis, the fool who seconds Dr Thorndyke, lacks depth, but Mr Carlyle, Max Carrados's friend, is a well-rounded character.

---

* Doyle had intended to finish his Sherlock Holmes series with *The Memoirs*, but his readers protested so vehemently that he felt obliged to carry on. Letters poured in from all over the world, and some were said to threaten Doyle with violence if he did not carry on with Holmes's adventures. So *The Memoirs* was followed by several more volumes. Yet the earlier ones are the best [Orwell's footnote].

As for Watson, whose imbecility is almost chronic, he is a more lifelike character than Holmes himself. It is by design, and not accidental, that the early detectives are amateurs rather than police officers. It fell to Edgar Wallace to set the fashion for the professional Scotland Yard officer. This respect for the amateur is characteristically British. We can see in Sherlock Holmes a certain resemblance to one of his contemporaries, Raffles, the gentleman thief, the English counterpart of Arsène Lupin. Yet the unofficial role of the early sleuth serves once again to reveal superior gifts. In the early Sherlock Holmes stories and in some Dr Thorndyke adventures, the police are clearly hostile to outside investigators. The professionals constantly make mistakes and do not hesitate to accuse innocent people. Holmes's analytical genius and Thorndyke's encyclopaedic knowledge only shine more brightly against the background of humdrum official routine.

In this brief study I have only been able to write at length about one group of writers and I have not discussed foreign writers or American novelists apart from Poe. Since 1920 the output of detective stories has been enormous and the war has not slowed it down, yet, for the reasons I have tried to stress, the magic wand of yesteryear has lost its power. There is more ingenuity in the modern novel, but the authors seem incapable of creating an atmosphere. First place among modern writers should probably go to the brooding Edgar Wallace, more likely to terrorize his reader than to guide him through a jungle of complex problems. Mention must be made of Agatha Christie, who handles dialogue elegantly and shows artistry in laying false trails. The much vaunted short stories of Dorothy Sayers would probably have attracted little attention if the author had not had the bright idea of making her detective the son of a Duke. As for the works of the other contemporary writers, Freeman Wills Croft, G. D. H. and Margaret Cole, Ngaio Marsh and Philip Macdonald, they have scarcely more relevance to literature than a crossword puzzle.

It is not difficult to imagine that a novel conceived as a pure intellectual exercise, like *The Gold Bug*, might appear again one day. But it is unlikely to reappear as a detective story. I have already said, and this seems to me a significant fact, that the best detective story writers could exploit small-scale crimes. It is hard to believe that the game of cops and robbers could still inspire writers of the stature of Conan Doyle, let alone Poe. The detective story as we know it belonged to the nineteenth century, above all to the end of the nineteenth century. It belonged to the London of the eighties and nineties, to that gloomy and mysterious London where men in high-domed bowler hats slipped out into the flickering light of the gaslamps, where the bells of hansom cabs jingled through perpetual fogs; it belonged to the period when English public opinion was more deeply stirred by the exploits of Jack the Ripper* than by the problems of Irish Home Rule or the Battle of Majuba.[3]

---

* The London counterpart of Landru who was loose in the English capital at the time, and who struck terror into the whole nation [Orwell's foonote].

1. *Dint* was a literary magazine edited by Feyyaz Fergar and Sadi Cherkeshi. The first number came out in 1944, probably in the early summer (for it is referred to by Robert Herring in *Life and Letters*, August 1944). A second number was published probably in January 1945; W. P. Rilla reviewed it in *Tribune*, 12 January 1945. (*Tribune* tended to review journals promptly.) Among those who contributed to *Dint* whom Orwell would have known were Henry Treece, Nicholas Moore, and John Atkin. Feyyaz Kayacan Fergar (1919–1993) was born in Istanbul but was of Armenian descent. He wrote poetry in French, Turkish, and English, short stories (his 'Shelter'—on life in wartime London—was awarded the Turkish Language Academy Prize), and translated English into Turkish (notably T. S. Eliot's *Four Quartets*) and Turkish into English (recently, *Modern Turkish Poetry*, 1992). He came to study in England in 1940 at King's College, Newcastle upon Tyne, where he founded *Dint* and *Fulcrum* (titles suggested by his friend James Kirkup). Alex Comfort arranged for a volume of Fergar's surrealist poems, *Gestes à la mer*, to be published in 1943. His surrealist poetry was defended by E. L. T. Mesens and Jacques Brunius. He wrote much under the pseudonym Feyyaz Kayacan, especially whilst working for the BBC, where he worked for more than thirty years in the Turkish Section, becoming its head, 1974–79.
2. In the last paragraph of 'The Final Problem,' at the end of *The Memoirs of Sherlock Holmes*, Watson, who is looking for Holmes, finds a 'small square of paper' held down by Holmes's cigarette case at 'the fall of Reichenback.' The note asks Watson to 'tell Inspector Patterson that the papers which he needs to convict the gang are in a pigeon-hole, done up in a blue envelope and inscribed "Moriarty".' Holmes continues: 'I have made every disposition of my property before leaving England, and handed it to my brother Mycroft' and asks Watson to give his greetings to Mrs Watson. Holmes says that these few lines have been written 'through the courtesy of Mr. Moriarty' before they engaged in their final struggle which, in this story, seems to end with both their deaths in the chasm below. Dr Watson's final words describing Holmes as 'him whom I shall ever regard as the best and the wisest man whom I have ever known' echo Plato's in the *Phaedo* on Socrates, 'Such was the end, Echecrates, of our friend, whom I may truly call the wisest, and justest, and best of all men whom I have ever known' (L. J. Hunt to the editor, quoting Jowett's translation). Orwell similarly links the classical and contemporary in *Burmese Days*. Flory's complaint that the British 'build a prison and call it progress' alludes to the *Agricola* by Tacitus. The British leader at the battle of Mons Graupius declares that those who created the Roman Empire, 'when they make a desert, call it peace,' an allusion Flory fears Dr Veraswami 'would not recognise' (CW, II, 41).
3. At the Battle of Majuba, 1881, General Pietrus Jacobus Joubert (1831–1900) routed the British forces in the First Boer War.

2358. BBC Talks Booking Form, 17.11.43

Oliver Bell: Monthly Film Talk; broadcast 15.12.43; fee £10.10s. Signed: Z. A. Bokhari.

2359. *Talking to India: A Selection of English Language Broadcasts to India*

Published 18 November 1943

Orwell edited and contributed to *Talking to India*, which was published by George Allen & Unwin. The talks were split into General and Political. The former, in addition to Orwell's talk, included, in the order of printing (for Forster and Dover, of their first talk): E. M. Forster, 'Edward Gibbon' and 'Tolstoy's Birthday' (the former first published in *London Calling*, 30 July 1942, and both included, with alterations, in *Two Cheers for Democracy*, 1951, as 'Gibbon and his Autobiography' and 'Three Stories by Tolstoy'); Cedric Dover, 'Paul Robeson,' 'Freedom and Cultural Expression,' and 'Nationalism and Beyond'; Ritchie Calder, 'Microfilms'; Hsiao Ch'ien, 'China's Literary Revolution'; Wilfrid David, 'Karl Peters: A Forerunner of Hitler'; K. K. Ardaschir, 'The Marriage of the Seas'; Professor Gordon Childe, 'Science and Magic'; J. G. Crowther, 'Science in the USSR'; Reginald Reynolds, 'Prison Literature'; Wickham Steed, Hamilton Fyfe, and A. L. Bakaya, 'The Press and its Freedom'; J. M. Tambimuttu, 'T. S. Eliot'; C. H. Waddington, 'Science and Modern Poetry'; Venu Chitale, 'The Children's Exhibition'; Cyril Connolly, 'Literature in the Nineteen-Thirties.' The Political talks were: Mulk Raj Anand, 'Open Letter to a Chinese Guerrilla'; I. B. Sarin, 'What to Do in an Air Raid'; R. R. Desai, 'Open Letter to a Nazi'; Subhas Chandra Bose's talk and Orwell's 'Five Specimens of Propaganda.' Talks written and broadcast 'by Indians and Asiatics' were marked with an asterisk—11 (which should have been 12) of 22 speakers. Orwell's work as editor is mentioned from time to time in earlier correspondence. He made at least three contributions: the Introduction (see *2360*); 'The Re-discovery of Europe,' broadcast 10 March 1942 and printed in *The Listener*, 19 March 1942 (see *1014*); and 'Five Specimens of Propaganda,' sections of BBC Newsletters broadcast in November 1941, February 1942, two in April 1942, and one in July 1942; see *893, 970, 1081, 1105, 1324*. He probably also provided the notes on the contributors. These suggest what he found interesting about each of those whose talks were chosen for this volume. These notes here follow his introduction.

An interesting inclusion, on which Orwell comments in his Introduction, is a talk by Subhas Chandra Bose broadcast from Berlin in May 1942; for Bose, see *1080, n. 1* and *1119, n 5*. The BBC paid a copyright fee of one guinea to the Custodian of Enemy Property for reproducing this talk, according to the *Evening Standard*, 16 August 1943, 2. The talk was evidently taken from a BBC or All-India Radio transcript. Several passages have had to be clarified and one sentence was unintelligible, presumably a result of poor reception. In the talk, Bose in part defenced his own position: 'Britain's paid propagandists have been calling me an enemy agent. I nned no credentials when I speak to my own people. My whole life is one long persistent, uncompromising struggle against British Imperialism, and is the best guarantee of my *bona fides*.' He was concerned to argue that 'in spite of all that British propaganda,' the true enemy of India was not the Axis but British imperialism, 'the enemy who sucks the life-blood of Mother India,' and he endeavoured to dissuade members of the Indian National Congress from advocating a policy of co-operation with Britain following Sir Stafford Cripps's mission to India, and despite its failure. He also argued that the British, 'under the plea of fighting Japanese aggression, have opened the door to American aggression. . . . The British have been ousted from their position by Wall Street and the White House.' West: *Broadcasts* prints three interesting documents in Appendix C on 'The principles of Axis & Allied propaganda,' 289–93.

George Allen & Unwin published 2,017 copies of *Talking to India*. The edition was sold out by 1945; 1,018 copies were sold in the United Kingdom and 897 overseas; 102 copies were given away.

2360. *Talking to India*: Introduction

The B.B.C. broadcasts in forty-seven languages, including twelve Asiatic languages. Five of these belong to the mainland of India, but Hindustani is the only (Indian) language in which transmissions are made every day. The Hindustani broadcasts, including news bulletins, occupy eight and a quarter hours a week. There is also an English language programme intended primarily for the European population and the British troops.

But in addition to these programmes, three quarters of an hour every day is set aside for English broadcasts aimed at the Indian and not the British population. It is from this period that the talks in this book have been selected. The main reason for keeping this service going is that English, although spoken by comparatively few people, is the only true lingua franca of India. About five million Indians are literate in English (including some hundreds of thousands of Eurasians, Parsis and Jews) and several millions more can speak it. The total number of English speakers cannot be more than 3 per cent of the Indian population, but they are distributed all over the sub-continent, and also in Burma and Malaya, whereas Hindustani, spoken by 250 millions, has hardly any currency outside Northern and Central India. In addition, the people who speak English are also the people likeliest to have access to short-wave radio sets.

The work of organising and presenting the English language programmes from London has been done mainly by Indians, in particular by Mr. Z. A. Bokhari. A fairly large proportion of the speakers have also been Indians or other Orientals. Much that is broadcast (for instance, plays, features and music) is not suitable for reproduction in print, but otherwise the talks included in this book are a representative selection. It will be seen that they are predominantly "cultural" talks, with a literary bias. Frequent or regular speakers in this service have been E. M. Forster, T. S. Eliot, Herbert Read, J. F. Horrabin, William Empson, Desmond Hawkins, Stephen Spender, Edmund Blunden, Clemence Dane, Bonamy Dobrée, Cyril Connolly, Rebecca West, and other writers have also broadcast from time to time. At least one half-hour programme every month has been devoted to broadcasting contemporary English poetry. Obviously the listening public for such programmes must be a small one, but it is also a public well worth reaching, since it is likely to be composed largely of University students. Some hundreds of thousands of Indians possess degrees in English literature, and scores of thousands more are studying for such degrees at this moment. There is also a large English-language Indian Press with affiliations in this country, and a respectable number of Indian novelists and essayists (Ahmed Ali, Mulk Raj Anand, Cedric Dover and Narayana Menon, to name only four) who prefer to write in English. It is these people, or rather the class they represent, that our literary broadcasts have been aimed at.

In order to give a true balance, some talks of a more definitely political type have been printed as an appendix, including five passages from weekly news commentaries. These are not consecutive, as they have been specially chosen from weeks when the war situation was being discussed, and Axis propaganda answered, in general terms. For the purpose of comparison we also include a verbatim transcript of a broadcast from Berlin by the Bengali leader, Subhas Chandra Bose. This has been chosen because it represents, as it were, the high-water mark of Axis propaganda. The general run of Axis propaganda to India is poor stuff, but Bose, who is potentially as important a quisling as Laval[1] or Wang Ching Wei,[2] is in a different category, and his speech is worth examining in detail.

It will be seen that for propaganda purposes Bose is reduced to pretending that the Axis powers have no imperialist aims, and that "the enemy" consists solely of Britain and the U.S.A. Actually, this speech is remarkable for containing a reference to the war in China. So far as I know this is the only occasion on which Bose has mentioned the Sino-Japanese war, and even then he is obliged to claim that in some mysterious way it has changed its character during the past year or two. (Only a few years back Bose was prominent on various "aid China" committees.) But there is one thing for which you would search in vain through Bose's many broadcasts, and that is any admission that Germany is at war with Russia. This fact does not fit in with his general propaganda line, and so it has to be simply ignored. Nor does he on any occasion make any reference to the fact that both Italy and Japan possess subject Empires, or that the Germans are forcibly holding down some 150 million human beings in Europe. In other words, he is obliged to avoid mention of the major issues of the war, and of somewhere near half the human race.

There is a difference between honest and dishonest propaganda, and Bose's speech, with its enormous suppressions, obviously comes under the latter heading. We are not afraid to let these samples of our own and Axis broadcasts stand side by side.

George Orwell.[3]

A Note on Contributors

[Fuller details of these contributors are given in the footnotes in this edition]

E. M. FORSTER. Author of *Howards End* and *A Passage to India*, etc.

CEDRIC DOVER. Young Eurasian writer, author of *Half Caste*, and *Hell in the Sunshine*, etc. Now serving in the R.A.O.C.[4]

RITCHIE CALDER. Author of *The Birth of the Future*, *The Lesson of London*, etc. The only lay member of the British Association for the Advancement of Science. Special correspondent of the *Daily Herald* during the London blitz.

HSAIO CH'IEN. Young Chinese student, author of *Etching of a Tormented Age* (a booklet on modern Chinese literature) and *China but not Cathay*.

J. M. TAMBIMUTTU. Young Ceylonese Tamil poet, editor of *Poetry*, the only existing English magazine devoted solely to poetry.

GEORGE ORWELL. Author of *The Road to Wigan Pier*, *Burmese Days*, etc.

PROFESSOR GORDON CHILDE. Professor of Prehistoric Archæology at Edinburgh University. Born and educated in Australia. (For publications see *Who's Who*.)

J. G. CROWTHER. (British Association. See *Who's Who*.)

REGINALD REYNOLDS. Young English writer. While in India closely associated with the Congress Movement. Author of *The White Sahibs in India, Cleanliness and Godliness*, etc.

WICKHAM STEED. (Many years editor of *The Times*. See *Who's Who*.)

HAMILTON FYFE. (See *Who's Who*. Best known by his book on Lord Northcliffe.)

C. H. WADDINGTON. Biologist. Author of *The Scientific Attitude*.

CYRIL CONNOLLY. Novelist and critic. Editor of *Horizon* and literary editor of *The Observer*. Author of *Enemies of Promise*, etc.

MULK RAJ ANAND. Well-known Indian novelist, born and educated in the Punjab. Author of *Untouchable, Two Leaves and a Bud*, and many other novels.

1. Pierre Laval (1883–1945), French politician, first a socialist, later transferring his allegiance to the right, was Premier, 1931–32 and 1935–36; advocated Franco-German co-operation, and served as Foreign Minister after the fall of France, under Marshal Pétain, until dismissed by him. He returned to power in 1942 and acted, in effect, as an agent for the German occupying power. He was executed for treason following a much-criticised trial. See also *644, n. 2*.

2. Wang Ching-wei (1883–1944), Chinese politician and early hero of the Republican Revolution following an attempt to assassinate the regent to the Imperial Chinese throne in 1910, was for a number of years personal assistant to the Nationalist leader, Sun Yat-sen, and a trusted official of the Kuomintang (Nationalist) Party. He opposed Chiang Kai-shek, but after a period of reconciliation he threw in his lot with the Japanese and in 1940 became head of a Japanese puppet government in Nanking, which ruled the Japanese-occupied areas of China. He died in Japan.

3. *Talking to India* was reviewed in *Tribune*, 26 May 1944, by Narayana Menon, who had broadcast frequently for Orwell. Menon appreciated that the best broadcast talks were not necessarily those that read best and that, conversely, a good essay might prove to be a bad broadcasting script. 'Few of our serious writers recognise this, with the result that a good many straight talks—particularly the more serious ones—sound pedantic, hidebound and dull, though they *read* very well in *The Listener* a week later. No one seems to realise this more than E. M. Forster, whose two contributions to this volume are not only models of broadcast scripts but at the same time witty and penetrating essays in criticism.' He described Orwell's 'The Rediscovery of Europe' as 'very salty, biting, pungent in the best Orwell manner. He pulls his listener's legs, talks with his tongue in his cheek. He loves to shock people, debunk accepted platitudes, mock mischievously,' and he quotes Orwell's explanation that the basis of Bernard Shaw's attacks on Shakespeare is that 'Shakespeare wasn't an enlightened member of the Fabian Society.' Besides Forster's essays, Menon thought highly of Orwell's essay and Connolly's 'Literature in the Nineteen-Thirties': 'two of the best essays on contemporary literature that I have seen for some time.' He thought Mulk Raj Anand's 'Open Letter to a Chinese Guerrilla' 'a touching document whose genuineness and sincerity would drive its point home far more effectively than any of the usual propaganda stunts.'

4. Royal Army Ordnance Corps.

2361. *The Emperor's New Clothes* by Hans Andersen, Adapted by George Orwell

BBC Eastern Service, 18 November 1943

The text for this dramatization, produced by Douglas Cleverdon, is printed from a fair-copy typescript probably made professionally at the BBC. It has no markings of any kind within the text, and the names of the actors have not been added. The PasB is lost, so the actors' names cannot be recovered from that source. The typescript is annotated at the top of the first page, 'Please return to Play Library, 5118 B[roadcasting] H[ouse] for WARE' and 'ONLY COPY.' It could have been made as a fair copy for file purposes after the broadcast, but the inclusion of rehearsal details (not found in the script for *Crainquebille*) suggests it was one of the copies made for those taking part in the broadcast. Three rehearsals, amounting to 4½ hours, were arranged.

There are rather a large number of instances in an otherwise well-typed script in which an additional space appears between two letters of a word—as in 'w as'; this may indicate haste in the production of the typescript or a defective space-bar. With one exception—a sound effect—directions are not underlined within dialogue; those typed outside dialogue are underlined (and printed in italic here), with the exception of the first, printed in small capitals. Apart from closing up spaces, the silent correction of a very few typing mistakes, and the provision in square brackets of two missing words, the text follows the typescript (including its stylisation).

One minute of a recording of the programme was later included in Desmond Hawkins's 'Backward Glance, 10' on 8 December 1943, according to the PasB (record no. DN 18021). No details of the cast are given.

Orwell believed this programme was broadcast on other services. Writing to Geoffrey Earle, a programme assistant in the Educational Unit, 8 August 1945 (*2715*), Orwell said he thought the best of all his dramatised stories was this fairy story, which 'went out on other services besides the Indian.' No other broadcasts have been traced.

On 25 January 1947, Orwell wrote to Rayner Heppenstall to say that he wished the BBC would rebroadcast 'The Emperor's New Clothes': 'I expect the discs would have been scrapped, however. I had them illicitly re-recorded at a commercial studio, but that lot of discs got lost'; see *3163*.

REHEARSALS:	NOVEMBER 18th	10.00 — 11.00 a.m.	Grams OS4
		11.30 — 1.00 p.m.	Cast OS4
		2.00 — 4.00 p.m.	,,
TRANSMISSION:	NOVEMBER 18th	4.15 — 4.30 p.m.	OS4

EASTERN SERVICE, PURPLE NETWORK

CAST:	The Emperor	A weaver
	The Lord Chancellor	A man
	A Courtier	A woman
	First Court Lady	A child
	Second Court Lady	Narrator

(TRUMPET FANFARE)

NARRATOR: The Emperor of Bithynia cared for nothing except his clothes. He spent so much time in adorning himself that just as in other countries people will say, "The King is in the Council Chamber", in Bithynia they used to say, "The Emperor is in his dressing-room". More than half of the public revenues was spent on the Emperor's clothes. But the people did not mind. They were rather proud of being ruled over by the best-dressed monarch in Christendom; and they were always ready to leave their work in order to watch the Emperor march through the streets in velvet and cloth-of-gold, with his jewels flashing, and a dozen courtiers following him to hold up his train.

One day two weavers from a foreign country arrived in the capital. These men claimed to be able to make a kind of cloth more beautiful than any in existence—and a cloth, moreover, that had some mysterious or magical quality, though nobody quite knew what. I need hardly say that the Emperor was one of the first to hear of their arrival; and the very next day, in obedience to his command, they presented themselves at the palace. The Chancellor was rather perturbed to hear of their arrival.

CHANCELLOR: Your Majesty, those two foreigners who arrived here yesterday—

EMPEROR: Oh, the weavers. Yes, I sent for them. Are they here?

CHANCELLOR: They are, your majesty. But—

EMPEROR: Well?

CHANCELLOR: Common swindlers, I have no doubt, your majesty.

EMPEROR: Ah, well, we shall see about that. I understand that they are able to make a very remarkable kind of cloth. I feel that I have been dressing myself too plainly lately. I should like something a little more magnificent for a change.

CHANCELLOR: If I might make so bold, your majesty—the peasants have been rather slow with their taxes this year. It might be better to avoid extravagance.

EMPEROR: I am never extravagant. If you want money, make a cut in the Civil Service estimates. Bring these men before me.

CHANCELLOR: Yes, your majesty . . . Bring in the two weavers!

MAJOR-DOMO: (distant) Bring in the two weavers! . . . (Door opens) The two weavers!

CHANCELLOR: Your majesty, here are the two weavers.

WEAVER: Your majesty . . .

EMPEROR: Ha! Now what is this wonderful cloth of yours that I have heard about? I should like to see a sample of it.

WEAVER: The most beautiful cloth in the world, your majesty. Nothing like it has ever been seen. But we shall have to weave it before you can see it. And we are tailors as well, your majesty. After weaving the cloth we will cut it and fit it for you. But we make no charge for that—only for the cloth itself. The price—to *you*, your majesty—is a hundred crowns a yard.

CHANCELLOR: (coughs)

EMPEROR: A hundred crowns a yard. Let me see, suppose we said fifty yards—oh, yes, I think we can manage that.

WEAVER:	And we shall be requiring raw silk as well, your majesty, and also ten pounds of gold leaf. We use it in the embroidery, you see.
EMPEROR:	Ten pounds of gold leaf? Very well, my Chancellor will give you anything you need.
CHANCELLOR:	(coughs) Your majesty! In the present state of the Treasury—
EMPEROR:	Nonsense! Give them whatever they ask for. Now, the sooner you two men get to work, the better.
WEAVER:	There is just one other point, your majesty. Naturally we are very anxious that your majesty shall not be disappointed. Your majesty's royal neighbour, the King of Pontus—
EMPEROR:	That wretched impostor!
WEAVER:	He suffered a disappointment, your majesty. At his command we made seventy-five yards of cloth, but when it was made he was unable to see it.
EMPEROR:	Couldn't see it!
WEAVER:	Our cloth is no ordinary cloth, your majesty. To those who can see it, it is the most magnificent cloth in the world. But not everyone can see it. Its peculiar quality is that it can only be seen by the good and the wise. To any foolish man, or to any man who is unfitted for the position he holds, this cloth is quite invisible. If you hold up a piece of this cloth, a wise man can see it as clearly as I see your majesty; while to a fool or an impostor there appears to be nothing there.
EMPEROR:	Invisible to fools, eh! Ha, ha! No wonder poor old Pontus couldn't see it. Just what I should have expected. And invisible, you say, to anyone who is unfitted for his position? I shall be able to try it on some of my ministers. (sycophantic laughter of courtiers) How much did you say the King of Pontus ordered?
WEAVER:	Seventy-five yards, your majesty.
EMPEROR:	Make me eighty yards. (cough from Lord Chancellor) You shall start work today.
NARRATOR:	A large room in the palace was set aside for the two weavers, and nothing was seen of them for three days. Servants who peeped through the keyhole reported only that the weavers had set up a great loom at the far end of the room and seemed to [be] very busy upon it. The Emperor could hardly contain his curiosity. On the fourth day he sent the Lord Chancellor with orders to visit the two workmen and find out what this wonderful cloth was like. The Lord Chancellor came back with a solemn and rather curious expression on his face.
EMPEROR:	Have you seen it? You *could* see the cloth, of course?
CHANCELLOR:	Oh, yes, your majesty! I could see it clearly.

EMPEROR: Good! I should be sorry to have to change my Chancellor. And what is it like?

CHANCELLOR: Well, your majesty, I should say—an *unusual* cloth; that would be my description of it. Like—er, like velvet, and yet, on the other hand, *not* like velvet, if your majesty understands me.

EMPEROR: And the colour?

CHANCELLOR: I should describe it as green, your majesty. Or perhaps it was nearer to blue, or even to red. It was decidely an *unusual* colour.

EMPEROR: I must see it at once. I can't wait any longer. Warn them that I am coming.

NARRATOR: The Emperor made his way to the room where the two weavers were working. He entered. Sure enough, there at the other end was the great loom and the weavers busily at work upon it, moving the shuttles up and down, reaching out for fresh threads and calling out instructions to one another.

(sound of hand-loom)

NARRATOR: But a terrible shock awaited the Emperor.

EMPEROR: (whispering) I can't see the cloth! There's nothing there!

WEAVER: It is a magnificent cloth, is it not, your majesty? Does your majesty observe the pattern we are weaving into it?

EMPEROR: What? Yes, of course, of course. (whispering) This is terrible. To my eye there appears to be nothing on that loom whatever. And even that old fool of a Chancellor could see it. This will never do. I shall have to— (aloud) Excellent! Excellent! The finest cloth I have ever had. Well worth the money. When do you expect that it will be ready?

WEAVER: Only a few days now, your majesty.

EMPEROR: Good, If you want any more gold leaf, apply to the Lord Chancellor.

NARRATOR: Three days later the weavers announced that the cloth was finished. They were bidden to bring it to the audience room, and all the court assembled to see it. No one had any doubts that he would be able to see the cloth, since no one had any doubts about his own wisdom. The weavers entered, staggering under a vast wicker-work basket which they set down and opened in front of the throne. Then they made the motions of taking out a bale of cloth, unrolling it, and holding it up for the Emperor's inspection. The whole court burst out into cries of admiration.
(loud ah-ah-ah)

EMPEROR: Very fine. Very fine indeed.

1st LADY: Isn't it *lovely*!

COURTIER: That gold leaf is magnificent.

1st LADY: And the colour!

2nd LADY:	Can *you* see it, my dear?
1st LADY:	Of course I can see it!
2nd LADY:	How funny! Because you're looking in the wrong direction.
CHANCELLOR:	A very superior cloth. A little expensive, perhaps.
EMPEROR:	Make the train twenty yards long. A soon as my new clothes are ready I shall make a royal progress through the capital. My people will enjoy seeing me, I am sure. I will wear my small crown—the one with the pearls.
NARRATOR:	Now that the cloth was woven the next thing was to make the clothes. The two weavers were busy for a whole day taking measurements and cutting out the cloth. They snipped their scissors through the empty air, ran their tape-measures round the Emperor's chest, and with their mouths full of pins made the movements of fitting the pieces of cloth about his body. Then they sat up all night, sewing—so they said; at least they had needles in their hands and went through the motions of sewing. The clothes were to be ready in the morning. It had already been proclaimed that the Emperor intended to make a progress through the Capital in his new clothes. Everyone was full of curiosity; no one doubted his ability to see the clothes. In the morning the weavers entered the Emperor's chamber, appearing to carry something over their arms. The Emperor took off the clothes he was wearing, and the weavers helped him on with the new ones.
WEAVER:	Permit me, your majesty. The girdle should be a little tighter. Now the cloak—just so. You will notice that we have made this a little full in the shoulders. It suits your majesty's style. Now the shoes—there. The great thing about this cloth of ours, your majesty, is that it is so light. It is like a spider's web. Your majesty might almost think you had nothing on. Yes . . . Quite, quite perfect!
EMPEROR:	Good . . . Major-Domo!
MAJOR-DOMO:	Your majesty!
EMPEROR:	You may admit the members of the court.
MAJOR-DOMO:	Yes, your majesty . . . (Door opens: chorus of exclamation).
1st LADY:	Oh, what *lovely* clothes!
COURTIER:	They fit your majesty like a glove.
2nd LADY:	What it must have cost! It will take twelve men at least to hold up that train.
EMPEROR:	The procession will start in half an hour. Chancellor, warn the heralds to be ready. I do not intend to distribute any largess today. I think the people will be quite satisfied with the spectacle of my (modest cough) new clothes.
NARRATOR:	In fact, the people had been lining the streets since early morning. At last the procession came into sight, with the heralds riding ahead of it on their white chargers.

(Fade up distant trumpeters: cheering)

1st MAN:	Look, here they come!
1st WOMAN:	There they are!
2nd MAN:	That's the Emperor—him under the umbrella. Hurray!
3rd MAN:	Long live the Emperor! Three cheers for the Emperor!

(Trumpeters and cheering nearer)

2nd WOMAN:	Don't he look fine?
1st MAN:	Glorious! It's worth paying taxes for, that is!
CHILD:	Mummy!
1st WOMAN:	Drat the child! Long live the Emperor!
CHILD:	Mummy! The Emperor's got no clothes on!
3rd MAN:	What did the child say?
CHILD:	He's got no clothes on! Look at him! He's got nothing on 'cept his crown!
3rd MAN:	Why, so he hasn't! The child's right!
1st WOMAN:	Nothing on! Well, now!

(cheering dies down)

1st MAN:	Got no clothes on.
2nd WOMAN:	Disgraceful I call it.
2nd MAN:	No business to come out like that.
1st WOMAN:	Wouldn't have noticed it if it hadn't been for the child.
3rd MAN:	He'll catch his death of cold, too.
2nd WOMAN:	Disgraceful.
1st MAN:	Go home!
2nd WOMAN:	Ought to be ashamed of yourself! At your age, too!
VOICES:	Boo! Down with the Emperor! Boo!

(Fade up booing above trumpeters: fade out)

NARRATOR:	At last the Emperor realised what had happened. But it did not seem to him that he could do anything about it now. There was nothing for it but to walk majestically onward, pretending not to notice that there was anything wrong.

(Trumpeters: booing in background)

EMPEROR:	(whispering) This [is] terrible! And I made sure they could all see the clothes except me. No matter, I must put a good face on it. After all, I *am* the Emperor. (aloud) Chancellor!
CHANCELLOR:	Sire?
EMPEROR:	Tell those courtiers to hold my train up more carefully. They're letting it trail in the mud.
NARRATOR:	So the procession moved stiffly onwards, with the heralds blowing their trumpets, and the twelve courtiers pretending to hold up a train which was not there, and all the people booing.

(Fade up booing above trumpeters: fade out)

NARRATOR:	As soon as they got back to the palace the Emperor put his clothes on, real ones this time, and then—
EMPEROR:	Chancellor!
CHANCELLOR:	Sir?

EMPEROR:	Those two abominable scoundrels—those two men who called themselves weavers—
CHANCELLOR:	Yes, your majesty?
EMPEROR:	Cast them into the lowest dungeons immediately.
CHANCELLOR:	Certainly, your majesty.
EMPEROR:	And tell the executioner to sharpen his sword up.
CHANCELLOR:	With pleasure, your majesty.
NARRATOR:	But as it turned out, it was too late. The two weavers were sought for, but they were never found. Indeed the servants reported that they had left the palace as soon as the procession started out. And after that—taking with them the eight thousand crowns for the cloth, as well as the silk and the ten pounds of gold leaf—they had vanished for a distant country; and they were never seen again.

2362. [Newsletter in Tamil, 31]

[18 November 1943]

The English version was written by Eric Blair. No script has been traced, and the PasB has not survived, so it can only be presumed that this broadcast was made.

2363. English Newsletter for Indonesia, 20

19 November 1943

This was written and read by George Orwell. No script has been traced.

2364. To V. S. Pritchett

19 November 1943   07/ES/EB

Dear Pritchett,

I wonder whether you would like to do a featurised short story for the Indian Section on the 29th of December. We have once a month a half hour programme consisting of a suitable short story featurised (not too many effects) with a narrator and about half a dozen other voices. I[1] send you a script of one of the others as a specimen. The story we want to do this time is Merimee's° "Carmen". It is not very easy because "Carmen" as it stands is[2] much too long so one would have to select as well as adapt. Would you please let me know as soon as possible whether you can do this. We should want to [ha]ve the script by December 19th at latest.[3]

Yours sincerely,
[Initialled] E.A.B
(George Orwell)

1. 'I will send' was originally typed, but the carbon shows that x's were typed over 'will' indicating, presumably, that a script was enclosed.
2. it] *typed as* is
3. Pritchett wrote accepting this commission.

2365. Review of *Subject India* by Henry Noel Brailsford[1]

The Nation, 20 November 1943

If there is one point in the Indian problem that cannot be disputed—or, at any rate, is not disputed, outside the ranks of the British Conservative Party—it is that Britain ought to stop ruling India as early as possible. But this is a smaller basis of agreement than it sounds, and the answers to literally every other question are always coloured by subjective feelings. Mr. Brailsford is better equipped than the majority of writers on India in that he is not only aware of his own prejudices but possesses enough background knowledge to be unafraid of the "experts." Probably he has not been very long in India, perhaps he does not even speak any Indian language, but he differs from the vast majority of English left-wingers in having bothered to visit India at all, and in being more interested in the peasants than in the politicians.

As he rightly says, the great, central fact about India is its poverty. From birth to death, generation after generation, the peasant lives his life in the grip of the landlord or the money-lender—they are frequently the same person— tilling his tiny patch of soil with the tools and methods of the Bronze Age. Over great areas the children barely taste milk after they are weaned, and the average physique is so wretched that ninety-eight pounds is a normal weight for a full-grown man. The last detailed survey to be taken showed that the average Indian income was Rs.62 (about £4 13s. od.) per annum: in the same period the average British income was £94. In spite of the drift to the towns that is occurring in India as elsewhere, the condition of the industrial workers is hardly better than that of the peasants. Brailsford describes them in the slums of Bombay, sleeping eight to a tiny room, with three water taps among four hundred people, and working a twelve-hour day, three hundred and sixty five days a year, for wages of around seven and sixpence a week. These conditions will not be cured simply by the removal of British rule, but neither can they be seriously improved while the British remain, because British policy, largely unconscious, is to hamper industrialization and preserve the status quo. The worst barbarities from which Indians suffer are inflicted on them not by Europeans but by other Indians—the landlords and money-lenders, the bribe-taking minor officials, and the Indian capitalists who exploit their working people with a ruthlessness quite impossible in the West since the rise of trade unionism. But although the business community, at any rate, tends to be anti-British and is involved in the Nationalist movement, the privileged classes really depend on British arms. Only when the British have gone will what Brailsford calls the latent class war be able to develop.

Brailsford is attempting exposition rather than moral judgment, and he gives no very definite answer to the difficult question of whether, in balance, the British have done India more good than harm. As he points out, they have made possible an increase of population without making it possible for that population to be properly fed. They have saved India from war, internal and external, at the expense of destroying political liberty. Probably their greatest gift to India has been the railway. If one studies a railway map of Asia, India looks like a piece of fishing-net in the middle of a white tablecloth. And this network of communications has not only made it possible to check famines by bringing food to the afflicted areas—the famine now raging in India would hardly have been a famine at all by the standards of a hundred years ago—but to administer India as a unit, with a common system of law, internal free trade and freedom of movement, and even, for the educated minority, a lingua franca in the English language. India is potentially a nation, as Europe, with its smaller population and great racial homogeneity, is not. But since 1910 or thereabouts the British power has acted as a dead hand. Often loosely denounced as "fascist," the British régime in India is almost the exact opposite of fascism, since it has never developed the notion of positive government at all. It has remained an old fashioned despotism, keeping the peace, collecting its taxes, and for the rest letting things slide, with hardly the faintest interest in how its subjects lived or what they thought, so long as they were outwardly obedient. As a result—to pick just one fact out of the thousands one could choose—the whole subcontinent, in this year of 1943, is incapable of manufacturing an automobile engine. In spite of all that can be said on the other side, this fact alone would justify Brailsford in his final conclusion: "Our day in India is over; we have no creative part to play."

Brailsford is justifiably bleak about the future. He sees that the handing over of power is a complicated process which cannot be achieved quickly, especially in the middle of a war, and that it will solve nothing in itself. There is still the problem of India's poverty and ignorance to be solved, and the struggle between the landlords, big business, and the labour movement to be fought out. And there is also the question of how, if at all, a backward agricultural country like India is to remain independent in a world of power politics. Brailsford gives a good account of the current political situation, in which he struggles very hard not to be engulfed by the prevailing left-wing orthodoxy. He writes judiciously about the tortuous character of Gandhi; comes nearer to being fair to Cripps than most English commentators have been—Cripps, indeed, has been the whipping-boy of the left, both British and Indian—and rightly emphasises the importance of the Indian princes, who are often forgotten and who present a much more serious difficulty than the faked-up quarrel between Hindus and Moslems. At this moment India is such a painful subject that it is hardly possible to write a really good book about it. English books are either dishonest or irresponsible; American books are ignorant and self-righteous; Indian books are coloured by spite and an inferiority complex. Well aware of the gaps in his knowledge and the injustices he is bound to commit, Brailsford has produced not only a transparently honest but—what is much rarer in this context—a good-tempered book. Nearly all books written about the British Empire in these days have the air of being written *at* somebody—either a Blimp, or a Communist, or an American, as the case may be. Brailsford is writing primarily for the ordinary British public, the people who before all others have the power and the duty to do something about India, and whose conscience it is first necessary to move. But it is a book that the American public might find useful too. Perhaps it is worth uttering the warning that— owing to war-time conditions—there are many misprints, and as some of them have crept into the statistics these are apt to be misleading.

[Fee £4.00; 27.10.43]

1. For Brailsford, see *2168, n. 1.*

2366. Talk on *Lady Windermere's Fan* by Oscar Wilde

BBC Eastern Service, 21 November 1943

The text of this talk for 'Calling All Students,' Great Dramatists Series, 6, is reproduced from the original typescript prepared for the broadcast. It looks as if it had been typed by Orwell, and the script was read by him. It carries Bokhari's signatures as censor for Policy and for Security dated 17 November 1943, but does not bear Orwell's familiar 'As b'cast,' with the timing. There is one handwritten alteration: the typescript had 'revenged' in the final paragraph but 're' has been changed (in Orwell's hand?) to 'a'—'avenged.' Orwell's common misspelling, 'Ernest,' in the title of *The Importance of Being Earnest*, has been silently corrected here, as have one or two minor typing slips. In the penultimate paragraph a missing 'as' has been added in square brackets.

No cast list is given of those who performed the extract from the play. The names of the actors are included in the PasB sheet. They were drawn from the BBC Repertory Company and were: Charles Mansell, Norman Claridge, Harold Scott, Franklin Bellamy, William Trent, Joan Carrol, Lydia Sherwood, and Duncan MacIntyre. The incidental music was *The Good-Humoured Ladies* by Domenico Scarlatti, played by the London Philharmonic Orchestra conducted by Eugene Goossens (HMV C2846, the first of the two-record set).

According to the PasB for 22 December 1943, 'Backward Glance,' a 'mosaic of words and music compiled by Desmond Hawkins and produced by Douglas Cleverdon,' included an extract from this broadcast. The BBC disc played (one of nine with another nine commercial records) was DLO 46801.

The Wilde programme included a long section of the third act of his play, from Mrs Erlynne's, 'Lady Windermere! Thank heaven I am in time. You must go back to your husband's house immediately,' to her admission, 'I am afraid I took your wife's fan in mistake for my own, when I was leaving your house to-night. I am sorry.' This amounts to about twenty per cent of the whole play, so there must have been a fair amount of cutting to avoid over-running.

Those lines you have just heard come from "Lady Windermere's Fan", by Oscar Wilde. This play was first acted in 1892, more than half a century ago. It has been seen on the stage less often than "The Importance of Being

Earnest", but it has worn well, and by and large it is probably Wilde's most successful play.

Wilde is a difficult writer to judge, because it is very hard to disentangle his artistic achievement from the events of his life; also because he himself was never fully certain of what he wanted to say. Like many others of his time, Wilde professed to be a devotee of "Art for Art's sake"—that is, of the idea that Art has nothing to do with religion, morals or politics. He set it down as one of the tenets of his creed that "Every work of Art is completely useless". But in practice he contradicts this by making nearly everything that he writes turn upon some point of morals. And there is a further contradiction in the fact that he is never certain whether he is attacking current morality or defending it. The dialogue of his plays and stories consists almost entirely of elegant witticisms in which the notions of right and wrong which ruled Victorian society are torn to pieces; but their central theme, curiously enough, often points some quite old-fashioned moral. His novel "Dorian Grey", for instance, is a deeply moral book. Although it was denounced as cynical, frivolous and so forth at the time when it was published, it is in essence a religious parable. Quite a lot of the time Wilde is uttering the maxims of the copybook in the language of light comedy; he wants at all costs to be clever, without being quite certain what he is to be clever *about*, and at the same time he is never fully able to escape from the effects of a mid-Victorian upbringing. The thing that saves him from the results of this intellectual chaos is that he is, after all, a genuinely gifted dramatist: he can construct a play neatly, and he has the light touch that Irish writers more often possess than English ones—for Wilde, like most of the best British dramatists, was an Irishman. These faults and these qualities are well displayed in "Lady Windermere's Fan". But to get a full understanding of the play one ought to see it against the background of its time.

When "Lady Windermere's Fan" was first acted, what is now called "British hypocrisy" was still immensely powerful. To defy accepted beliefs, particularly religious or moral beliefs, needed more courage than it does now. Notions of right and wrong do not change so suddenly or completely as some people like to think, but it is a fact that certain things which seemed immensely important in the 'nineties now seem comparatively trivial. One of the subjects about which this play turns is divorce. Now, nobody thinks that divorce is desirable in itself or that it is not an immensely painful event in anyone's life: but still it is not the case in our own time that a divorced woman is ruined for life. When "Lady Windermere's Fan" was written it was an accepted fact that a divorced woman must become almost an outcast; she was practically debarred from decent society for the rest of her life. This should be kept in mind, because it gives point both to certain episodes in the play, and to Wilde's incidental attacks upon current morality.

The plot of the play, as briefly as I can outline it, is this. Lady Windermere, an affectionate but rather puritanical young woman, believes that her husband is unfaithful to her with a woman of very doubtful antecedents called Mrs Erlynne. In reality she is quite mistaken. Her husband has indeed been associated with Mrs Erlynne, but not for the reason that she imagines.

Mrs Erlynne is Lady Windermere's own mother. But she is also a divorced woman, and the knowledge—as it would then have seemed, the almost unbearable knowledge—that she is the daughter of a divorced woman has been kept from Lady Windermere, who imagines her mother to be dead. Mrs Erlynne has been blackmailing Lord Windermere, holding over him the threat that she will reveal her identity to her daughter. What she wants from him is partly money, but still more, a re-introduction into fashionable society. Lady Windermere has an admirer, Lord Darlington, who is trying to persuade her to leave her husband and elope with him. (Parenthetically I must point out that the very great prevalence of lords, dukes and what-not in Wilde's plays is a period touch. The British public of those days liked to see titled people on the stage, and the majority of dramatists were quite ready to humour them). In normal circumstances Lady Windermere would be very unlikely to listen to Lord Darlington, but finally her jealousy brings her to the point of deciding to leave her husband. She goes to Lord Darlington's rooms, intending to leave England with him. Mrs Erlynne finds out what is happening, and when she sees her daughter, as she thinks, going the same road as she has gone herself, her maternal instincts revive. She follows her to Lord Darlington's rooms, intending to dissuade her. It is this scene that you will hear acted in a few minutes' time, and I won't describe in detail what happens. The point is that Mrs Erlynne, still acting the repentant mother, saves her daughter from ruin by taking all the blame upon herself. Lady Windermere goes back to her husband, and—since this is a comedy and has to end happily all round—Mrs Erlynne also manages to find her way back into respectable society by marrying a foolish but good-natured old man.

You can see that this play, as I have outlined it, is a harmless and even edifying story by the standards current at the time. The situation in which somebody is the child of somebody else, the parent being aware of it and the child not, was a favourite on the Victorian stage. The mother sacrificing herself for her child was another favourite. And the unjustly suspected person who has to suffer in silence rather than reveal some deadly secret—the part played here by Lord Windermere—was yet another. Mrs Erlynne's behaviour involves one of those sudden and drastic changes of character which were a regular occurrence in Victorian fiction though they are unknown in real life. She is shown first of all as taking no interest in her daughter for twenty years and as having no aim in life except to get back into so-called "good" society, and as being willing to make use of blackmail in the most cynical way in order to achieve this. Then, in the moment of crisis, she is shown throwing away the very thing she has been scheming for, and all for the sake of a daughter whom she has hitherto used simply as a pawn in her game. Psychologically this is an absurdity, though by skilful writing Wilde is able to make it seem credible. In its plot and its main action the play is a sentimental romance with a touch of melodrama. Yet that is not the impression it gives when one reads it or sees it acted, and we may guess that that was even less the impression it gave at the time. So far from seeming sentimental and edifying, the play appears frivolous and what used to be called "daring". Why? Because in addition to the central characters there is a kind of chorus of worldly "sophisticated" people who keep up a ceaseless running attack upon all the beliefs current in Wilde's day—and in our own day, to a great extent. In the contradiction between the action of the play and its language one can see Wilde's own uncertainty as to what he is after.

Wilde's greatest gift was his power of producing those rather cheap witticisms which used to be called epigrams. These are stuck all over his writings as arbitrarily as the decorations on top of a cake. Nearly always they take the form of a debunking of something that his contemporaries believed in, such [as] religion, patriotism, honour, morality, family loyalty, public spirit, and so on and so forth. Remarks like, "I can resist anything except temptation", or "Men become old, but they never become good", or "When her third husband died her hair turned quite gold from grief", occur on almost every page that Wilde ever wrote. The essence of this kind of witticism is to disagree with the majority at all costs. Clearly, this kind of thing is more effective when there is a really strong and vocal majority opinion to be reckoned with. Remarks like, "There's nothing in the world like the devotion of a married woman. That's a thing no married man knows anything about", are less likely to shock anyone in 1943 than in 1892, and to that extent they are less amusing. But Wilde does this kind of thing so well, so naturally one might even say, that his dialogue is still charming even when it has ceased to seem wicked or iconoclastic. So long as no serious emotion enters he has also a fairly good grasp of character and situation. But his great charm is his neat rapid dialogue, which is freer from padding, and conceals its machinery more successfully, than anything that has since been seen on the English stage.

Wilde lived at the moment when the literate public was just becoming emancipated enough to enjoy seeing the Victorian conventions attacked. It was therefore natural for him to make a name by laughing at the society he lived in; though that society avenged itself in the end, when Wilde was sent to prison for a sexual offence. If he had lived earlier the sentimental and melodramatic strain in him, which is clear in all his work except for "The Importance of Being Earnest" and a few short stories, would probably have predominated. It is quite possible to imagine him as a sensational novelist, for instance. If he had lived in our own day, when debunking no longer seems worth while as an end in itself, it is harder to say what he would have done. It is uncertain whether he had anything in him except his native wit and his intense desire to be famous. Coming just when he did, he won an easy fame by pushing over an idol that was toppling already. In its fall the idol killed him, for Wilde never recovered from the shock of his trial and imprisonment, and died soon after he was released. He left behind as his essential contribution to literature, a large repertoire of jokes which survive because of their sheer neatness, and because of a certain intriguing uncertainty—which extends to Wilde himself—as to whether they really mean anything.

2367. To Production Department, Penguin Books

21 November 1943

10a Mortimer Crescent
London NW 6
21.11.43

Dear Sir,

I am returning herewith the proofs of the Penguin edition of "Burmese Days". I have corrected them carefully. There were very few misprints, and most of these I think carried forward from the original edition, but I have also made a few minor alterations. I draw attention to these as it is important that they should not be missed. Throughout, whenever it occurs in the *text*, ie. not in the dialogue, I have altered "Chinaman" to "Chinese". I have also in most cases substituted "Burmese" or "Oriental" for "native", or have put "native" in quotes. In the dialogue, of course, I have left these words just as they stand. When the book was written a dozen years ago "native" and "Chinaman" were not considered offensive, but nearly all Orientals now object to these terms, and one does not want to hurt anyone's feelings. If the corrections I have made are followed there will not be any trouble. I don't think they cause any overrunning to speak of.[1]

Yours faithfully
[Signed] Geo. Orwell
(George Orwell)

1. For a further comment by Orwell on these changes, see 'As I Please,' 2, 10 December 1943, *2391* and also Textual Note to *Burmese Days, CW*, II, 309–10.

2368. To Allen & Unwin

23 November 1943   Original   BBC   letterhead

Dear Sir,

Many thanks for the cheque[1] and the twelve copies of "Talking to India". I wonder what arrangement you have made about review copies. If you have not already sent me one, I think it is worth sending a copy to The Tribune,[2] where I can arrange to get it reviewed; also will it be possible to send any copies, i.e. for sale, to India?

Yours truly,
[Signed] Geo. Orwell
(George Orwell)

1. The amount is not recorded by Orwell in his Payments Book, *2831*, so the amount for the year (£154.19s.0d) understates the actual earnings by at least the amount of this cheque. A royalty of £16 was recorded for 6 October 1945.
2. The letter has been annotated in Allen & Unwin's office, '? already sent' and crossed through.

2369. To Cecil Day Lewis

23 November 1943   07/ES/EB

Dear Mr. Day Lewis,[1]

Would you like to do a talk for the Indian Section of the BBC? We have a series called Great Dramatists, which are half-hour programmes, each consisting of an extract from a play, taking about quarter of an hour, and a talk on the play—if possible also giving some idea of the author's works as a whole—by some qualified person. The one we would like you to undertake is Clifford Odets's play "Till the Day I Die". The date of the programme is Sunday, December 26th, which would mean we would like the talk by December 20th. 1200 words would be roughly the right length. Could you let us know whether you would like to undertake this?[2]

Yours sincerely,\
[Initialled] E.A.B\
(George Orwell)

1. Cecil Day Lewis (1904–1972), poet, critic, writer of fiction (his detective fiction published under the name Nicholas Blake). He signed himself 'C. Day Lewis' (no hyphen). He was appointed Professor of Poetry at the University of Oxford in 1951 and succeeded John Masefield as Poet Laureate in 1968. His *Collected Poems* was published in 1954. When Orwell wrote to him, his *Poems in Wartime* (1940) had been reprinted in *Word Over All* (1943). After World War II he hyphenated his name.
2. This letter appears to be the last Orwell wrote when in the British Broadcasting Corporation's service. Day Lewis replied on 25 November that he did not know enough about Odets to prepare a talk by 20 December, but hoped he would be offered other work. On 4 January 1944, Charlotte Haldane, as talks producer for the Indian Section (see *2339, n. 1*), asked Orwell to prepare a script on Hardy for the series 'Prescribed Poetry' to be broadcast on 17 January 1944, and one on Tennyson for the series 'Unwillingly to School' to be broadcast on 17 February 1944. Orwell accepted neither commission. She then asked Day Lewis to speak on Hardy's poetry, apologising for the short notice as she had just taken over as talks producer in the Indian Section (on 1 January?), and on 12 January she asked him to speak on two poems by Tennyson set for Indian university students. He agreed and talks booking forms were issued. She also arranged for him to broadcast to India in May and June 1944.

2370. Extract from Minutes of Eastern Service Meeting

24 November 1943

"Talking to India"   Mr. Blair reported that he had written to Allen & Unwin, asking whether copies of *Talking to India* were being sent to India. He asked whether, if [the] reply should be in the negative, some arrangement could be made to get copies of the book to India. Miss Booker replied that, if difficulties were encountered, reference could be made to the India Office who might be able to help.

This meeting was held on Orwell's last day of service with the BBC.

2371. Newsletter in Tamil, 32

25 November 1943

The English version was written by Eric Blair and transmitted the day after he had left the BBC's service. No script has been traced.

2372. Roy Walker to Orwell

25 November 1943   Typewritten

Roy Walker, of the Peace Pledge Union, had written to Orwell on 28 September (see *2259*) and Orwell had written 'several long replies' following that letter; these have not been traced. In a letter to Ian Angus, 13 January 1964, Walker recalled the nature of the correspondence:

I had written a biography of Gandhi[1] and was an advocate of non-violence, and I think Orwell had published an article or essay critical of Gandhi [his review of Lionel Fielden's *Beggar My Neighbour*, *Horizon*, September 1943; see *2257*]. I wrote to him and I think there were two letters on each side. Orwell was an extreme critic of Gandhi in his letters. To him Gandhi's voluntary poverty was suspect because he was surrounded by and (Orwell thought) influenced by wealthy men. Also Gandhi's celibacy was compromised by his acceptance of (and Orwell thought, his pleasure from) feminine disciples, notably the former Miss Slade. This led up to what seemed to me the most Orwellian thought that admiration of the Gandhian example as exalted asceticism was misplaced. It did not compare, he thought, with the privations, sacrifices and unpublicised endurance and courage and wisdom of ordinary working-class people. I hope this thought still survives somewhere in Orwell's own words.

Walker's letter of 25 November 1943 may have influenced Orwell's 'Reflections on Gandhi,' which appeared in *Partisan Review* in January 1949; see *3516*. See also 'As I Please', 37, 11 August 1944, *2530*.

Dear George Orwell,
It was my turn to be ill, with nothing more eventful than flu; but however late, I'm bound to write you once more if only to reply to your last paragraph.
I do not, I assure you, hate you like the devil. I do not hate you at all. On the contrary I have considerable respect for you as a writer, as an older and more widely experienced man, and—what is much rarer, at least in the sense in which I am talking about it—an honest man. I therefore think it worth while to write to you to say quite candidly and bluntly that I think what you wrote about Gandhi in "Horizon" was unfair and that the arguments you produce in defence are unconvincing. May I not hate—if

that is the word—the sin (as I see it) without in the least feeling evilly-disposed towards the sinner? And I think it is a little unkind when I send you a copy of my book to reply that I obviously hate you like the devil. Even putting my defence of Gandhi at its lowest, surely you don't think that the missionary hates the heathen who gives him his raison d'etre?

No, I don't think pacifists are good haters—except among themselves. I find we are pretty bitter about one another, but embarrassingly affectionate to all who differ from us. Consider for example the Duke of Bedford who really does—I can assure you it is so—understand Hitler, knows he has a good heart, and wants to bring out the best in him—by talking to him in a nice friendly way.[2]

I hope I did not say that you could not form an opinion of Gandhi unless you claimed to be a better man. I do suggest that it is as well not to state one's opinion in terms of moral judgment unless one's own position is pretty firm. There is no reason why the British Government should not form an opinion about the evils of French Imperialism in the Lebanon, but if they get morally indignant about it everyone will remind them that their record in India and elsewhere is not quite blameless.

For instance, the only "phoney" thing you can think of about Gandhi's fasts is that in the last one he took lime juice and glucose. (I know the reports said 'sweetened lime juice'—do you happen to know the source for saying definitely that it was glucose and how much glucose; I would really like to know.) What you do not reckon with is that Gandhi announced the fast as to capacity and *not* to death, and said beforehand that he would take lime juice, "fruit juices" because otherwise his system will not now take water. So there is nothing particularly "phoney" about that. But if you think that this means his life was never in danger during the 21 days I suggest you have another look at the doctors' bulletins, remembering that some of those doctors were nominated by the Government of India.

Have you read Gandhi's own reasons for his spinning-wheel programme? 700,000 villages, men, women and children mostly illiterate, idleness° for several months of the years°; those were the terms of the problem. What can you do as an immediate measure to help those villagers to increase their purchasing power? Gandhi's answer was the charka.[3] Industrialism simply isn't relevant, particularly until independence is achieved. Isn't it a case of the charka or nothing?

Last night I read Louis Fischer's short book just published—"A Week with Gandhi"—you may have seen it by now.[4] It has some bearing on what we've been discussing. Gandhi makes no secret about the extent of the financial support from "big business" but doesn't modify his programme a jot because of it; he admits that the standard of living at the Ashram is higher than it could be; he quite cheerfully amends his view about the presence of British troops in India as Fischer talks to him. Fischer, another honest man I should think, puts all this down fairly and makes his own comment at the end, with some of which I don't—of course—agree. But I should not dream of writing to him if he were in England as I've been writing to you.

What I have been writing to you about is simply this. I thought that if you had been to see Gandhi as Fischer has, or had mugged up Gandhi's own writings, as I have, you would have been fairer to him. By that I don't mean that you should not have formed opinions, or passed judgments, but that you would not have made that sort of sneer about his "financial background"[,] you would not have said his fasts were "phoney" or that the man himself was a "bit of a charlatan." This has nothing to do with your agreeing with me about Gandhi, or about your agreeing with Fischer.

It would mean, if I may preach your sermon back at you, that you would always make it clear in writing about him that he is greatly good although in your opinion greatly mistaken.

You seem to me not to understand that Gandhi is both peacemaker and rebel. His efforts at conciliation and compromise are genuine and often call forth a measure of genuine good will in response, as when the judge expressed his view of Gandhi's way of life in sentencing him. You seem to feel that if the peacemaking is sincere the rebellion must be phoney. If the rebellion is real then it must take violent form when the crisis comes and peacemaking would then for a time be as suspect as the appeasement policy of 1938.

I believe that the Gandhian position shows us the way to a synthesis of all that is best in the Christian ethic and all that is essential in the Socialist recognition of the inevitability of mortal struggle against selfishness, greed and pride. But I can't expect to persuade you to see it so . . .[5]

May I end where I began? There is no ill-will I assure you on my side, and I have sensed none in your letters to me. I'm grateful to you for finding time to write several long replies to what you seem to have found very exasperating admonitions. Henceforth you will be able to pursue your literary career without the embarrassment of my dubious good advice. I feel a little like apologising for my impertinence in saying as much as I have in these letters. Do, please, put me down as at any rate well-meaning.

1. Walker's biography of Gandhi, *Sword of Gold*, was not published until 1945. He has probably confused this with his selection, *The Wisdom of Gandhi in His Own Words* (1943). For Walker's publications, see Orwell's 'Gandhi in Mayfair,' September 1943, *2259, n. 1*.
2. This paragraph has two heavy lines against it in the margin, probably drawn by Orwell, for he roughly quotes this passage in 'As I Please,' 37, 11 August 1944, *2530*. For Orwell's comments on the Duke of Bedford and a note about Bedford, see Orwell's London Letter, *Partisan Review*, 1 January 1942, *913, ns. 6* and 7.
3. *charka*, properly *charkha*, is the Hindustani word for a spinning wheel. Gandhi advocated its use in village communities, and as part of his daily regime he spent some time working at his spinning wheel. This was particularly remarked upon in the British press when he attended the Round Table Conference in 1931 as the representative of the Indian National Congress. He stayed in the East End of London and devoted part of each day to working at his *charkha*. Walker's reference to the *charkha* thus had considerable emotive force for Gandhi's followers and, rather differently, for many British people.
4. Louis Fischer also wrote *The Life of Mahatma Gandhi* (1950).
5. Ellipsis as in the original; nothing has been omitted.

2373. English Newsletter for Indonesia, 21

26 November 1943

This was written by George Orwell before he left the BBC's service. It was read by John Morris.[1] No script has been traced.

1. Morris succeeded L. F. Rushbrook Williams as Eastern Service Director in 1943 and held that post until 1952; he was then, until 1958, Controller of the BBC Third Programme. Whilst a talks producer, he had the office next to Orwell's; see *1965, n. 1.*

APPENDIX 1

2374. Laurence Brander's Report on Indian Programmes

11 January 1943

Laurence Brander, the BBC's Eastern Service Intelligence Officer, produced this detailed report for those directing the Eastern Service to India; see *1815.* It is not known whether Orwell read it, but there can be no doubt that he learned of its contents from conversations with Brander. The report graphically explains the difficulties faced by the Eastern Service, as well as noting its shortcomings; it therefore provides important background for understanding the context in which Orwell and his colleagues operated. See also earlier reports, *1145* and *2277.*

There are 121,000 receiver sets owned by Indians in British India. That is a very small number among three hundred million people, even if we suppose every set capable of short-wave reception. But even with that small number at their disposal, the enemy has succeeded in doing a great deal of damage. The work of the Counter-Propaganda Department of the Government of India is lively and is very largely concerned with countering enemy wireless. I went to Simla and worked in their office at their invitation. I learned (to give a few typical examples) how Bombay had been partially evacuated largely thanks to Japanese wireless propaganda: how great efforts were made by the Japanese to close down the biggest armament factories in India: how many Indians owning small businesses had sold out at great loss because of enemy wireless threats: how, when the troubles came, sabotage was inspired by Saigon radio, just as it is inspired by us in Europe.

The BBC has not been equipped to fight in this battle. But very soon it will be, with an office in Delhi and with the opportunity of recruiting first-class Indians with recent knowledge of conditions in their own country. The Director of Counter-Propaganda (Francis Watson) is eager for all possible liaison, and the visit of Puckle[1] suggests an opportunity for organising it (Watson works to Puckle). But to help them effectively we must, as the Americans say, 'get ourselves organised'.

THE BROADCASTING WAR

On the one hand we have All India Radio and the BBC. No other United Nation signal reaches India except the Russian, which is now very weak.

AIR is a good engineering job. Its news bulletins are satisfactory. It does very little propaganda and takes no clear propaganda line. It does very little to counter or contradict enemy radio propaganda. Its programmes are of very poor quality.

Nearly all sets in India are good short-wave sets. With very poor medium-wave programmes, much short-wave listening is done. There the competition begins.

On the other side are Germany, Italy and Japan with her captured satellite stations, notably Saigon, Singapore and Batavia.

The competition is in:
(1) News in English.
(2) Western entertainment (mostly music) and propaganda.
(3) Indian language news.
(4) Indian entertainment and propaganda.

Present form is:
(1) The BBC wins. The All-India hook-up of the 1500 GMT News is accepted as the most truthful and complete account of the day's news.
(2) Germany and Japan (especially through Batavia) win. The BBC gave a strong challenge last year, and once the signal becomes good again there is no reason to doubt further success.
(3) Germany and Japan win.
(4) Germany and Japan win.

This report tries to show why we have not won (3) and (4), and how we can put that right.

BBC PROGRAMMES TO INDIANS

It is necessary to point out first of all how entirely our Indian programmes have been built on speculation. Practically no factual evidence has been available. The best information available has been from those who have served with All India Radio. All India Radio has no machinery for Listener Research. In all its history it has attempted only two small investigations: a questionnaire issued in Bombay by Fielden and Lakshmanan which gave useful information, and a small survey by a professor in the Calcutta University which was unprofitable.

Until I was able to tell them, AIR did not know in what proportions receiver sets were owned by Hindus, Moslems, Europeans and others. The other means by which opinions on wireless programmes are usually expressed are little used in India. AIR stations have fanmails averaging less than one letter a day; I have never heard of any telephoning of opinion. The Press ignores radio (a few papers print the programmes; and one Madras paper, "The Hindu", has a weekly article). It is clear that the best opinions available to us were based on speculation rather than on scientific investigation.

Our speculations have not been fortunate, and we have failed to attract the Indian audience. Some of the causes of our failure are set out here, and that will be followed by suggestions. This report is itself based on very insufficient factual evidence. With so much discussion of expanded schedules going on, however, it seems desirable to make a preliminary report which can be checked and amended very soon; for a useful amount of good evidence is now being collected in Delhi and will be available within a few weeks.

The basis of this report is my tour, together with the weekly reports from Delhi which have been based on a considerable vernacular correspondence, a few questionnaires and the daily contacts of the Delhi staff.

Reasons for our failure in Indian Programmes

A. Hindustani News:
  (1) We began late, so the stigma 'propaganda' was at once attached to the bulletins.
  (2) At first the language was coarse, even including 'galli' (disgusting swear-words). This revolts the Indian audience, and is the reason why the Italian Hindustani bulletins have no audience. (On our first Hindustani bulletins, see the Wali Mohammad Report).
  (3) Under new direction, we swung over to the very chaste Urdu which can only be fully understood by the small Muslim audience in Delhi and the U.P.
  (4) It is still generally regarded as 'propaganda', which means that we are still looking for the secret of attracting an audience and then convincing it.
  (5) Microphone 'personality' is not used.

B. Other Indian Languages:
  (1) We broadcast once weekly. It is difficult to get an audience to remember and to tune in to a single weekly broadcast of 15 minutes. Against our weekly 15 minutes in Bengali and Tamil the enemy totals are approximately 500 and 600 minutes respectively. When we expand to 15 minutes daily we shall have to reorganise drastically, for,
  (2) The scripts are unsatisfactory. True, until recently the choice was often between a rehash of bad news or a commentary on bad news. Every script has been written by an Englishman who has not been in India, because the speakers employed are incapable of script-writing. His acknowledged brilliance as a writer apparently has not overcome this difficulty. It is impossible for one man to pretend that he is a Bengali, a Madrasi, a Mahratha and a Gujerati° once a week and every week.
  (3) The translations have been poor. All India Radio reports suggest that they may be compared to the cheapest type of Latin crib. This has been due partly to hurried translation, partly to the difficulty of supervision. In any case, few Indians have a thorough knowledge of their own vernaculars when they have enjoyed a Western education.

345

(4) The voices and pronunciation in every language have been adversely criticised. Few Indians know their own vernaculars well enough to broadcast in them. There is little evidence of effort to train them in elocution and microphone technique.

C. Other Hindustani Programmes:
  (1) There is no evidence of any success for translations of English commentators and newspaper articles.
  (2) Of all the Hindustani programmes, the only reactions have been to the Features, the Children's Programmes and the Women's Programmes.
  Features: Until July, the reactions to features were sporadic and adverse—'they are vulgar'. Since then, the volume of praise has continued to grow.
  Children's Programmes have had an extraordinary success.
  Women's Programmes were received expectantly, and letters came to Delhi before they came on the air, hailing the idea. The idea was certainly excellent—radio has given the first opportunity in history of addressing purdah women, who wield great social power. The programmes have not been successful. The compere apparently knows very little of purdah life and does not speak Hindustani.
  (3) The Army in India was not aware that Greetings Programmes from Indian troops in Britain were on the air. Apparently this information was given to All India Radio, which did nothing about it. (That is now organised).
  (4) There was no publicity whatsoever for Hindustani programmes which indeed were not planned far enough ahead for publicity to be possible. Planning was arranged and the usual publicity channels through the Government of India were used. Nothing was done. (Very recently, the Delhi Office was able to take that over, and for the first time radio programmes have appeared in the vernacular press of India).

D. English Programmes to Indians:
  This has been our most damaging failure. It was a daring decision to attempt to catch the young Indian intellectual. Unfortunately, it was believed that in order to do so it was necessary to put over programmes which could not attract the rest of our audience. Even without competition, few listeners could stand up to these extraordinary programmes. There has always been a proportion—sometimes a high proportion—of good radio in the programmes, but all the evidence available from the audience condemns them. Since September experiment has been possible—for example, Indian announcers have been dropped and Lady Grigg has been able to put over musical programmes; but even so, the latest report (17.12.42) from Delhi speaks of 'that damned 45 minutes'. Investigation among Indian university teachers and students in July and August showed:—
  (1) Indians do not want to hear Indians from London speaking on

intellectual subjects. An Indian professor said: "If we want to hear Indians, we can hear far better ones on AIR".

(2) Indians do not expect to hear Indian music from London in English transmissions. They do not like tinkering with Eastern-Western music, and discussion of the two is regarded as meaningless, if not charlatan. They show no pleasure in having our music 'interpreted' for them; like the rest of our audience in India, they prefer it unadorned.

(3) Indians have no use for the English man or woman who has had a career in India. (It should be reserved° that no attempt has been made to bring experts to the microphone).

(4) If intellectual programmes are attempted for Indians, let them be intellectual. Indians may drivel away themselves a good deal, but they are quick to discriminate between the intellectually honest and the amateurish. It meanwhile drives the eavesdropping Englishman to simple fury that such stuff should be presented as the 'intellectual' life of his country.

(5) Radio is entertainment, especially in short-wave competitive conditions in hot countries. Honest intellectualism can be perfectly good entertainment for a minority audience—the talks of E. M. Forster were a perfect delight to us in the Delhi office—but it must be on that level.

How we can put these things right
We now have the machinery in India for checking our experiments. Davenport[2] expresses satisfaction with it, and it is being regularly used. The audience is showing signs of co-operating, and questionnaires in Urdu have already brought returns numerically useful. Planned experiment can now be undertaken under conditions the Empire Service has never enjoyed before. With such a great expansion being planned more things than programme content have to be thought of, and it may be useful to touch on them all here.

A. Hindustani News
(1) Language: In the projected programmes our Hindustani audience will range from Malaya to the East Coast of Africa. Malaya apparently requires a very simplified Hindustani. But surely most of our Indian audience does too. Nearly half the sets in India are in Bombay and Bengal, which cannot understand our present Hindustani. We can increase our audience many times over if we use a more common, though still correct, accent and vocabulary.

(2) Content: Before I went to India, I.E. briefed me to find out what the content of our Hindustani News Bulletins should be, and I have found it difficult to give an answer. My own enquiries led me to suggest what is now backed by the two latest reports from India: the same news range should be covered as in the English bulletins. This may mean sacrificing geographical and other explanations. (The Ministry of Information may be going to print maps for distribution

347

to our audience. This would make geographical explanations unnecessary). I suggested interpretation, for example explaining the implications of a victory. It may be argued that this contradicts the statement on the range of news which should be covered; but, with our European News in English in mind, I suggest that this may be a matter of composition.

(3) <u>Composition</u>: With allowance for exceptional really important 'breaks', I feel a bulletin should be completely composed for microphone presentation; the design being in the spirit of attack employed in our English European bulletins. 'Spicy' presentation was the word used by English journalists of long experience in India. The only skilled propagandists I met in India (Colonel Wheeler and Palmer, both Near Eastern experts) said the same.

The temptation to add things at the microphone to fill up at the end should be resisted as they sometimes give an effect of bathos at the end of a good bulletin. The King Emperor's 'double' has become the stock example of this mistake.

(4) <u>Personality</u>: News no doubt should be anonymous. Commentaries should be by microphone personalities. Avowed translations are relatively without appeal. I imagine Sarin (alas, that we are losing Ashraf, the golden voice of Hindustani radio),[3] with expert handling and scripts provided, would do well. The scripts would have to come from Delhi.

(5) <u>Countering</u>: Some countering of enemy extravagances seems desirable, if only because of the great demand for it. This is discussed later.

B. <u>Other Indian Language News</u> (with the expanded schedule in mind)

(1) Script writers and readers must be recruited in India. "Pre-war knowledge of India might as well be pre-Flood knowledge" (Puckle). That has been our trouble all along—no contact with the war moods and thoughts of our audience. If they come from India now, there is reasonable prospect that the Delhi office can keep them in touch.

(2) Daily close supervision by an Englishman expert in studio work. Without this there will be no organisation and a rapid deterioration in efficiency.

(3) They will all require speech training and microphone training even though they come from AIR. They should arrive weeks before their work begins, so that they can go to school and still have adequate time for departmental training in script-writing and speaking.

(4) I like to think that bringing in men from Bengal, Madras and Bombay will add immensely to the intellectual weight of the Indian Department. Almost inevitably, recruiting has been in the Punjab (apart from the News Department); and, fine fellows as they usually are, Punjabis are intellectually despised by the more cultivated peoples of India. I hope, therefore, that from each place—Bengal,

Madras and Bombay—we shall be able to recruit at least one man of middle age and intellectual standing and responsibility, so that we Englishmen on the staff will have colleagues whose opinions will be of real assistance when the time comes for propaganda work.

(5) With 15 minutes only at their disposal, every minute should be devoted to news which will be prepared in the same way as the Hindustani news. As padding is disliked by all listeners, when there is insufficient news commentaries can be used; or little features can be recorded and used as opportunity offers.

C. Other Hindustani Programmes

(1) Children's Programmes:

I.E. has suggested that when we come to look back at all our work we may well decide that Ashraf's children's programmes have been our greatest propaganda success. So far, they have been our only success, with the likelihood of our Hindustani Features becoming a useful second. I have suggested that we have two or three of these children's programmes weekly in the expanded schedule; but unless we find a successor to Ashraf, or give him time to record many before he leaves us, we had better not try. We shall be lucky to find anyone who combines his creative fancy and microphone personality. His successor must be a native Urdu speaker and not a Punjabi, who would only be laughed at. We might try a Punjabi programme for children, but that would mean a new children's audience.

(2) Women's Programmes:

The unprecedented opportunity that radio offers to influence the purdah women of India should be exploited to the full and kept entirely free from reactionary influence. To be successful, the programmes should be:

(a) Prepared and written by an Indian woman who really knows about purdah life.

(b) Spoken by an Indian woman who can speak good Hindustani fluently, and has the quality to become a microphone personality.

(c) Made up of talks, stories and features (in which males may quite properly appear.)

(d) If it must instruct, let it instruct by pleasing. Five talks on looking after babies nearly killed this programme.

(3) Other programmes (evening)

The most popular programmes on AIR are:

(a) Poetry, chanted by the author.

(b) Music.

Poetry: As the Delhi office is run by a distinguished Urdu writer,[4] on terms of personal friendship with many Urdu poets, we can get recordings made. The difficulty is expense. We can and should afford the money, but I judged it wise in the early days not to suggest

349

any competition with AIR. It pays rates so low that they could not be offered to good poets, nor would they be accepted by them. With our expanded schedule it does not seem possible any longer to allow AIR's disabilities to interfere with our programme standards. If we can arrange to acquire recordings by the best poets it will give us a long lead over any radio competitors.

Music: We urgently require a large library of recordings to sustain our great programme expansion. There is a classical, popular, folk and film music corresponding to every Indian language we broadcast, and we should be fully equipped in all kinds. The only doubt is on film music. AIR uses these commercial records extensively as soon as they are published, and by the time we can get them (even if we organise so as to avoid Customs delays) they have outlived their popularity. The other kinds of music do not enjoy so ephemeral a popularity, and we are likely to be weak in them all except Hindustani and Punjabi. We are particularly weak in classical music, and we shall require a great deal of that, especially in the ragas appropriate for morning use. These will have to be recorded by musicians from Jaipur, Lucknow and Baroda.

Features: Favourable reaction was first reported in July and August, and has grown in volume since. The only recent adverse criticism has been of the 'Punjabi' Urdu; if our recruits are native Urdu speakers that difficulty will disappear. The efforts of Bakaya[5] and Sahni in this kind deserve every praise. It is a kind which has practically no competition from AIR which cannot afford it; and none that I know of from the enemy, except the religious plays in Tamil from Japan. The kind is obviously worth developing. The scripts and productions still show some signs of hurry and lack of finish. I would suggest when staff is available that special training be offered to one Indian producer, who would afterwards set about recording features to help us in overcoming the prevailing scurry in Hindustani programme production.

Plays and dramatised stories: In the same way we could prepare and record translations of English plays. There is a great range in Arabic, Persian, Sanskrit and modern Indian language literatures (perhaps more in story than in drama), which has never been touched by broadcasters. A recent suggestion from Delhi was that some of the untranslated 'Arabian Nights Entertainments' could be used in this way. If, as I have suggested, we get some literary people on our staff, we can get a wonderful amount out of books.

(4) Hindustani Programmes (morning).

The Indian poet and musician is very sensitive to times of day, and so are all our Indian listeners. The decision to run a full hour programme in Hindustani every morning therefore requires thorough planning. The Delhi office is going to find out the potential audience. It will probably consist of men. The best lead-in will be a News Bulletin after a tuning signal of morning music. AIR programmes give little guidance; although they may be suitable they can provide no absolute criterion, because they have done little experiment and no research.

I have already suggested that readings from the Koran and Gita, even of the Nikayas (with an eye on Burma) might be suitable. Possible disadvantages are obvious, but these are being examined in Delhi. The Gita and Nikayas would have to be recorded in India. Religious plays and features (in *pure* Urdu and Hindi) can be prepared for festivals. Classical music will certainly be required—in the three ragas (scales) which can be used in the morning.

I feel strongly that our approach to a considerable programme of this kind should be Oriental. If we can catch the Oriental morning mood of Delhi, Lucknow and Benares it will have a goodwill value; and at that time of day we shall have a good signal and little competition. To get that outlook, we are arranging through Delhi to 'test' reactions to programme suggestions. Delhi will make positive suggestions as well, and these are awaited with interest.

D. <u>General Statement on News in Indian Languages</u>

The United Nations are now passing over to the attack, and we should develop a spirit of attack in our broadcasting to India. We can attack enemy broadcasting in two ways:—

(1) By pointing out how wrong he is.

(2) By having something to say on our own account.

(1) <u>Countering:</u> Enemy lies go unchallenged. They are often repeated and eventually believed. We can counter them by direct exposure and contradiction, and in more indirect ways. The German output can be collected here; but the Japanese has to be collected in India. That will be a big job, for it means persuading the Government of India to monitor at least part of the great Japanese output in Hindustani, Bengali and Tamil. It would have to be cabled here quickly and regularly. If we achieved this, it would save India a great deal of distress. I was very often asked in India: "Why don't you expose their lies?" I suggest in all seriousness that we cannot defeat this broadcasting attack on India—probably the heaviest in this war—by ignoring it.

(2) <u>Policy:</u> Until we can present a policy operating through all our news bulletins, our news broadcasting is ultimately meaningless. Until we have a policy we cannot plan propaganda. Is there any reason why we should not approach the Government for a policy? Puckle's visit is an opportunity. The crazy state of things is that we now have the Indian audience because we have the victories. They are listening to our bulletins; but these victory bulletins bring many of them no joy, for they see no hopeful future for India in our victories.

The enemy attack on India is vigorous and clever. To fight back we must have something to offer, and go on offering it. It has been suggested that AIR has this responsibility. But German and Japanese propaganda is directed against *us*, not against AIR and Indians. I doubt whether AIR wants to accept the responsibility; it certainly has not organised to accept it.

E. <u>English Programmes to Indians</u>

The failure of these programmes need not discourage us. The causes of failure are clear, and the conditions of success easy to outline. We should certainly continue to try to attract the Indian intellectual; for when all is said and done, the ties of the Indian to this country are intellectual ties. The programmes must be organised by someone in touch with intellectual life here, and supervised by someone in touch with intellectual life in India. Since Indian intellectuals expect the best English material available, it is natural to suggest that the programmes be organised by an Englishman; and this is in any case inevitable, as no intellectual Indian is available. He can be advised by those on the staff who have worked in Indian universities, and are still in contact with Indian intellectual life.

If he puts on programmes which pass intelligent Englishmen as good radio—sensible, cultivated, gracious and interesting withal—he need have no fears about pleasing intelligent Indian listeners. At the same time, he will entertain a large cross-section of our Forces and Exile audiences. For the programmes will be at a peak listening hour among English people, who are all denied immediate cultural contacts with their homeland.

The programme content may be:

(1) <u>Classical music:</u> (Not a special desideratum of Indian students, but a steady success with a proportion of every part of our audience, and especially acceptable at the new timing).

This need not be specially 'presented'. While we have been 'presenting', our potential listeners have been listening to the stream of music from Germany and Italy and Batavia.

(2) <u>Plays:</u> A great success with the Indian audience. There are no regular theatres left in India: the talkies have killed the few there were. AIR has not the funds to do plays regularly, but when Lucknow put on 'Romeo and Juliet' last year it had a record fanmail.

The best plays to put over are those used as texts by students; and after that, plays which have been seen by Indian students while in this country. These will also appeal to a proportion of every part of our audience.

(3) <u>Features:</u> These are immensely popular among all Indian listeners. Half-hour features from the Home Programmes, especially those which describe actual fighting. "Take us to the battlefield", said the bellicose student to me again and again. They should be the very best all-English products.

(It is possible that these three kinds are going to appear in the Red Network). There is still a place for them in these special programmes, which would also include:—

(4) <u>Talks:</u> On literature, economics and academic politics. These will commonly be designed in series, and can now be prepared for printing in pamphlet form in India. They will have to be timed, both on the air and in printed form, to catch the Indian student. The two forms will react favourably on one another. When pamphlets are read, talks will begin to have a greater audience; while good talks will be looked forward to in print. With long-term planning, it might even be a good thing to record a series, issue it in printed form and then put it on the air—as this would be of great assistance to Indian students in learning to speak English. (Many Indian teachers of English have never heard an English voice).

Talks by English experts on Indian thought, and on Indian archeology, architecture, sculpture and painting, would have great value as goodwill propaganda. They should be subsequently well printed and properly illustrated. The ignorance of Indians about their own country is notorious.

Such publications would have an importance out of all proportion to their peacetime value; for India is starved for good reading, with communications as they are at present. The Government of India attempts nothing in this way. The only effort is made by the Oxford University Press in India, and they are suffering from the dearth of good writers. The field is open to us. There is every prospect that the Ministry of Information will finance us.

Some day the British Council may take over this work, but that is looking a long way ahead.

(5) <u>Discussions:</u> The projected Round Table Talks should be a great advance on anything radio has hitherto been able to contemplate in the way of active intellectual contact with India. They should give us for the first time a good press; and they will also, it is presumed, be published.

As pure radio, they are expected to bring direct audience reaction, which expects an answer on the air. That will be a most important development. Questions and comments will be invited, forwarded by the Delhi office, and dealt with in later discussions. It is just that sort of audience contact which has been lacking.

CONCLUSION

In earlier reports I recommended expansion in Delhi. This report is really a corollary to those earlier ones. For if we are going to play our part in the radio war in India, we must have a staff and organisation capable of carrying out recommendations from Delhi.

VS.[6]

11.1.1943.

APPENDICES TO REPORT ON INDIAN PROGRAMMES

1. HINDUSTANI AND PUNJABI

(This note is by Ahmed Ali, a wellknown Urdu writer of the Delhi School):

As you know perhaps, Punjabis speak Urdu with the most awful accent and their pronunciation is simply dreadful. For instance, *qaaf* becomes *kaaf*, *ghain* becomes *gain*, and so on. Urdu or Hindustani as spoken by them is therefore most laughable. People often laugh at the BBC Punjabi announcers. I have even seen them switch off because of the badly spoken Hindustani. Urdu as spoken by Punjabis sounds to us very much as English spoken by Indians sounds to you. The fact that all our BBC Hindustani announcers, except Ashraf, Maqbool and Haider, are Punjabis stands in the way of our popularity. Urdu is not the mother-tongue of Punjabis. It is only their second language, though they speak it and read it from childhood. Their everyday social and even official business is carried on in Punjabi. Punjabi is a harsh and rugged language, quite different from Urdu or Hindustani. Urdu writers and journalists speak strongly about this. Molana Abdul Wahid of Badaun, a wellknown figure in Urdu journalism and religious society, is definite on the point. Kwaja Hasan Nizami (a Pir and newspaper proprietor) who came to see me the other day said that London should broadcast good Hindustani. He was pleased with the general standard of announcing from London, but said there were some Punjabis who were not good announcers, and hoped that we shall not lower the standard of Urdu by mutilating its grammar and pronunciation.

2. REPORTS ON NEWSLETTERS

Barns, Chief News Editor of AIR, had the following reports prepared for our Delhi office:

Gujerati° Newsletter broadcast from London at 8.15 p.m. on 7th December 1942

GENERAL IMPRESSSION:	Far better than the Newsletter on 30th November.
ANNOUNCING:	Comments in report on Newsletter of 30th Nov. still hold good. Lacking in fluency; there was a general clumsiness, particularly in the way in which the items were brought to an abrupt end.
LANGUAGE:	Commendably simple. There were one or two jarring notes; for example the use of 'Vayuma' instead of 'Havama', and 'Balako No Pedash' instead of 'Janma-praman'. These were possibly due to a too literal translation of an English script.
CONTENTS:	These covered a wider field than on 30th November, and the comments on events were interesting. The explanation of the Beveridge scheme was particularly good—simple, lucid. Russia was the only subject not dealt with adequately or given sufficient prominence.

Marathi Newsletter broadcast from London on 3rd December 1942

GENERAL

IMPRESSSION: Dull

ANNOUNCING: Unimpressive; weak.

LANGUAGE: Good but not simple enough—still bookish. Many of the sentences were long and unsuited to the spoken word. Also there was an impression throughout that the person preparing the newsletter was thinking in terms of the English original. "Tank" could more easily have been translated as 'Ranagada', which is the word most commonly used.

Tamil Newsletter broadcast from London on 3rd December 1942

GENERAL

IMPRESSSION: Satisfactory.

ANNOUNCING: Not sufficiently intimate and lacking in modulation.

LANGUAGE: Much better than in the Newsletter on 26th Nov.

CONTENTS: Most of the time was given to the Pacific, Burma and China, which was not inappropriate. It was noticed in referring to H.M.I.S. 'BENGAL' the newsletter spoke of the crew as consisting of men from the Punjab to Bengal—thus omitting any reference to South Indian members of the crew, which included Malayees. This was unfortunate in a Tamil newsletter.

3. TYPICAL QUOTATION ON OUR BENGALI NEWS BEING WEEKLY, AND OUR LACK OF THEIR MUSIC (quoted verbatim):

It is a pity that you announce Bengali news once a week for 60 million or more Bengali speaking listeners and there are only 130 million Hindustani speaking listeners and rest is Gujrat, Tamil, Telegu, Punjabi, Maharatti, Onya, Assamese, whereas the foreign countries give Bengali news every day with Bengali gramophone records. On Saturday 21st your announcer told in reply to Miss Anema Mukherji (Bihar) that it was difficult for him to broadcast Bengali records—curiously, Bengali news was followed by a Hindustani record instead of Bengali. I think you need to play Bengali records daily—in Bihar, U.P., Assam and Orissa there are at least one third to half a million Bengali speaking men. This omission brings in people to listen to foreign Bengali news which is full of filth and abuses. Reasonable mentioned° not to listen to it. This is very demoralising but people cant° help as they want direct news.

4. NUMBER OF RECEIVER SETS IN BRITISH INDIA

In July, when Posts & Telegraphs gave me the breakdown, the totals were:—

Indian-owned	121,294	
European-owned	34,614	(This is an inflated figure, as it was not possible to distinguish between European, Anglo-Indian & Indian Christian. The great majority are owned by Europeans.)

This gives a round
total of   155,908

AIR recently published a figure giving a round total of 162,000.

5. **POSTAL INTERCEPT SHOWING THAT THE ENEMY THINKS IT WORTH WHILE TO TRY TO GET RECEIVER SETS INTO BRITISH INDIA:**
Letter intercepted:

From: H. Ritschard & Cie, Geneva   (Transport Agents, acting as forwarding agents for German and Czech firms)

To: Netherlands Trading Society, Bombay.

Enclosures:
1 Invoice from E. Paillard & Cie, Switzerland, dated 2.7.1942, pertaining to 9 cases of radios to Bombay via Lourenco Marques.
2 Invoices from Ritschard (4 cases & 5 cases respectively).
In each invoice, one of the items included is for Italian Customs formalities.

1. Probably Sir Frederick Hale Puckle (1889–1966) who se. ved the Government of India from 1937–43 and previously the Government of the Punjab, 1919–37.
2. Not identified; see *1145, n. 1* and *1645, n.1*
3. I.B. Sarin was a Programme Assistant, and one of Orwell's colleagues, in the Indian section of the Eastern Service. A. M. Ashraf was described as 'Announcer-translater, Indian Unit, Empire Department' in the list of those taking the induction course attended by Orwell, 18–30 August 1941.
4. For Ahmed Ali, see *1103, n. 3*.
5. A. L. Bakaya was a Hindustani translator in the BBC's Indian section.
6. Probably Miss V. B. Silk, a secretary in the Intelligence Unit.

APPENDIX 2

2375. Orwell's Notes: For "The Quick & the Dead" and For "The Last Man in Europe"

Dating the compilation of the notebook containing Orwell's notes described as *For* 'The Quick and the Dead' and *For* 'The Last Man in Europe' (the 'For,' not underlined, may be important) is difficult but, because of its association with

Nineteen Eighty-Four, important. Professor Bernard Crick, who reproduced part of the notebook in *George Orwell: A Life* (as Appendix A), suggested that 'the notebook is certainly no later than January 1944 when [Orwell] mentioned in *Tribune* a list of "childhood fallacies" which he had in a notebook.'[1] Crick also draws attention to a horse called Boxer being whipped, which associates 'The Quick and the Dead' with *Animal Farm*, and he refers to Orwell's letter to Fredric Warburg of 22 October 1948 in which he said that he had first thought of *Nineteen Eighty-Four* in 1943; see *3477*. However, in a letter written to Roger Senhouse on 26 December 1948 he said he had thought of the novel in 1944 'as a result of the Teheran Conference' (end of November 1943) which divided the world into 'Zones of influence,' as Orwell put it, a characteristic of *Nineteen Eighty-Four*; see *3513*. W. J. West suggests that the outline of *Ninety Eighty-Four* is closely linked with Orwell's time at the BBC, 'having been written either while he was working through his last two months at the BBC or a few weeks later' (West: *Broadcasts*, 60, n. 122). It is possible, however, that these notes were first put down earlier— even much earlier—and only re-ordered into the form that we now have them in this notebook at the time Orwell conceived of the idea for *Nineteen Eighty-Four*. There are few certainties here, and first consideration should be given to the physical characteristics of the notebook.

The notebook measures approximately $9 \times 6\frac{3}{4}$ inches. Although not written on a single occasion, nor even over a short period of time, it is clearly a very well-ordered set of notes. Notes of this kind are often jotted down in a disordered manner, at different times, lack formal organisation, and include a variety of 'jottings,' false starts, crossings-out, and even entries at odd angles (as are Orwell's arithmetical calculations, which eventually found their way into print in *The Road to Wigan Pier*). Although there are some differences in writing materials and a few crossings-out, these notes look much more like a fair copy of earlier notes than notes written down for the first time.

The notes are in three sections. The first two have identically-styled headings in the form of individual title-pages, each title being within double quotes and underlined, with the word 'For' not so distinguished. The first section, 'The Quick and the Dead,' has notes written on 19 rectos in blue-black ink, pencil, and, on the last three folios, a few lines in red ink amidst the blue-black. The use of red ink does not seem to be significant. The final line on folio 11, 'Golden opportunity' is in blue-black Biro. There are then fourteen blank folios followed by the title-page for 'The Last Man in Europe.' This is followed by four recto folios of notes in blue-black ink with a few pencil-markings (X and O) on the third folio. There is then a blank folio, followed by six recto folios and two versos (the last) intermittently interspersed with blanks, set out for lists, all written in blue-black Biro. As the transcript shows, these lists are not very full and two headings have no entries. The overall impression is of careful arrangement and clean execution. The writing in Biro cannot have been entered before early 1946. Orwell used the pen invented by László Biró (1899–1985). Although not listed in the *Trade Marks Journal* until 29 October 1947 (660/2), Orwell ordered a Biro from David Low (Booksellers) of 17 Cecil Court, Charing Cross Road, London WC2 in February 1946. They replied on the 19th saying they had none in stock but would supply one when they had. Orwell refers to using a Biro in a letter to Julian Symons, 26 December 1947, when seeking a refill; see *3318*.[2]

The notebook contains two kinds of material: notes which have, presumably, been re-ordered from one or more earlier notebooks; and additions to this material made between mid-1946 and early 1948, probably at Barnhill or when

Orwell lay ill in Hairmyres Hospital. (He found a Biro particularly useful for writing when he was in bed.) The date when the notes *not* written in Biro were compiled can only be guessed at. There are several possibilities:

1. Orwell took a fortnight's holiday from his BBC duties 4–20 September 1943. He probably then finally made up his mind to leave the BBC and he resigned shortly after his return in a letter dated 24 September 1943. While on holiday he might not only have decided on his future but also reorganised his notes as a prelude to starting on a new book. This date makes psychological sense.

2. Orwell told Heppenstall on 24 August 1943 that he was 'definitely' leaving the BBC 'probably' in about three months' time (2247). He might have written out earlier notes when working his two months' notice at the BBC. This is not so likely. He was nothing if not conscientious, and he complained in normal times of the enervating burden of administrative work that hindered his creative writing. He clearly ensured a smooth changeover of duties, organising talks for at least two series to be given after he left and writing Newsletters to the very last moment, two of which were transmitted after he had gone, that for Indonesia being read by John Morris on his behalf. He was also not particularly well, taking a few days' sick leave.[3]

3. The notes could have been written up immediately after Orwell left the BBC at the end of November 1943. There would be an urge to do that, but he was at once thrust into writing reviews, starting 'As I Please,' and organising his work as literary editor of *Tribune*. If he did any creative work at this time, it must surely have been on *Animal Farm*, which he completed within three months of leaving the BBC.

4. Possibly the notebooks were reorganised concurrently with *Animal Farm*, a possibility strengthened by the quotations in *Tribune*, 28 January 1944, mentioned by Crick, which give six of Orwell's 'Fallacies.' However, these quotations were, presumably, available in the earlier notebooks, which were reorganised in the form we now have them. It is noticeable that the 'Fallacies' in *Tribune* are not in the order they are in the surviving notebook: five of them come from folios 1 and 2, one is from folio 17; and, though the phrasing is identical for four of the six, two show differences: that relating to dogs and sulphur is summarised in the notebook, and the notebook's 'That bulls are enraged at the sight of red' is, in *Tribune*, 'That bulls become infuriated at the sight of blood.' The evidence is slight but sufficient, perhaps, to suggest that this notebook was not reorganised concurrently with 'As I Please' for 28 January 1944, and hence not with *Animal Farm*.

5. A final suggestion (and other times are not inconceivable) is either after the completion of *Animal Farm*, mid-February 1944, or after the completion of *The English People*, mid-May 1944. By mid-February, Orwell had written and had published some 45,000 words of reviews and articles since mid-1943; by mid-May that figure had risen to 75,000 words (including 'As I Please'), *in addition to* the 30,000 words of *Animal Farm* and 15,000 words for *Britain in Pictures* and all his BBC work. There was, in truth, not much breathing space after he handed in *The English People* on 22 May 1944, but his weekly rate dropped from something like 2,750 words a week (plus books and BBC material) for the preceding forty-four weeks to about 1,900 words a week for the five weeks after handing in *Britain in Pictures* to his being bombed out of his Mortimer Crescent flat on 28 June 1944. In that five-week period, he adopted a baby, Richard, which meant preoccupations other than writing, but also, perhaps, an incentive to thinking what kind of a world Richard would live in. Thus, *the copying* of earlier notes into this notebook may have been done as early as his summer vacation in September

1943 or as late as the time Richard was adopted in mid-1944. It is this uncertainty as to dating that has led to this material being arranged here outside the chronological ordering, as an Appendix.

To hazard a guess, an earlier rather than a later time in this period seems likely. Whilst he was on holiday (4–20 September 1943), there can be little doubt that Orwell gave thought to his future, especially in the light of his feeling that he was wasting his days at the BBC. That would be likely to prompt him to sort through his ideas for books he wished to write, to reorganise those ideas, and, perhaps, prepare a fair copy from his earlier jottings. His marking these For 'The Quick and the Dead' and For 'The Last Man in Europe' (and these two titles were conceivably written into the notebook at the same time) looks as if this notebook formed part of a plan of campaign on these lines: he would leave the BBC; take on the Literary Editorship of *Tribune*; write *Animal Farm*; and then write his two novels, 'The Quick and the Dead' and 'The Last Man in Europe.' It would be rational, if this hypothesis is correct, for him to have organised his thoughts on these two novels, written them up neatly, and marked them 'for the two novels,' as if to ensure that his ideas were not lost or confused whilst he was getting on with the other parts of his programme. I would, therefore, date this notebook late September 1943, conscious of how tentative such a dating must be.

What of the section in Biro, which must have been written in later? This seems to be associated with 'The Principles of Newspeak,' the Appendix to *Nineteen Eighty-Four*, and possibly the glossary Orwell prepared but which has not survived (see *Facsimile*, xi, n. 6). The plan for 'The Last Man in Europe,' though showing similarities to *Nineteen Eighty-Four*, is different from even the earliest surviving draft of the novel (which has, for example, three, not two parts).

If the notebook does represent a reorganisation of earlier notes, it becomes even more difficult to date its elements, since they surely were changed and smoothed in the course of re-ordering. Thus, the word 'egregious,' listed under the heading 'Adjectives' on f. 40, well illustrates the problem of dating. It is written in Biro, so cannot have entered the notebook until 1946 at the earliest. However, 'egregious' is given marked attention by Orwell in his review of Lancelot Hogben's *Interglossa* in the *Manchester Evening News*, 23 December 1943, three years earlier; see *2395*. It can be demonstrated from *Burmese Days* that a single word could, as it were, float in Orwell's subconscious for an even longer period (see *CW*, II, 310, for his wish to substitute 'knelt' for 'sit'). And that review seems to lie behind a phrase or two of the 'Principles of Newspeak,' which has: 'Its vocabulary was so constructed to give exact and often very subtle expression to every meaning that a Party member could properly wish to express, while excluding all other meanings and also the possibility of arriving at them by indirect methods' (*CW*, IX, 312–13). Writing of international languages in his review of *Interglossa* in 1943 (and doubtless having in mind his association with the Esperantists, Eugène Adam and the Westropes), Orwell wrote: 'They must be capable of expressing fairly subtle meanings with the maximum of clarity, but in that case they must be devised by someone who really cares about clarity and would, for instance, bother to find out the meaning of the word "egregious". In the next paragraph he writes: 'anything which draws attention to the urgent need for some universal medium of communication, and to the sinister way in which several living languages are being used for imperialist purposes, is to be welcomed.' Orwell was able to reach back into the past, into the recesses of his memory, to find words and ideas to suit his needs. Whether 'egregious' was listed in 1943 in some now lost notebook is impossible to tell; it might have been pinned down in writing only after a gap of three years, together with the ideas associated with it in the review of *Interglossa*: Newspeak was the imperialist language *par excellence*.

Although precise dating is impossible, there might be another clue to the origins of what survives in this notebook. The references to the years 1974, 1976, and 1978 on ff. 37 and 38 call to mind Orwell's shifting of the year of his novel from 1980 to 1982, and then to 1984 (see *Facsimile*, 23) and his adjusting the presumed year of Winston Smith's birth (1942/44 and 1943/45) to keep his age at thirty-nine (*Facsimile*, 25). (Orwell, incidentally, was thirty-nine in 1942.) If, when drafting his novel between 1946 and 1948, Orwell had in mind some time thirty-five years ahead, for the years 1974, 1976, and 1978 it would be necessary to go back to 1939, 1941, and 1943. These years can be linked with the statement made to Warburg that he first thought of the novel in 1943, and his statement in his Autobiographical Note of 17 April 1940 that he was 'projecting a long novel in three parts to be called either The Lion and the Unicorn or The Quick and the Dead'; see *613*.

There is yet one more faint clue. It has been suggested by Daphne Patai that Orwell may have been inspired by Katharine Burdekin's *Swastika Night*, first published in 1937 but reissued by the Left Book Club in 1940 (under the name Murray Constantine; see *Facsimile*, x and n. 4). Orwell never mentions this book. Conspiracy theorists suggest Orwell wished to hide an indebtedness to Burdekin, but because he did not conceal books that might have prompted his ideas, it is more likely that he missed the book, or thought it so poor as not to be worth reviewing with, say, Jack London's *The Iron Heel* and H. G. Wells's *The Sleeper Awakes* in *Tribune* under the heading 'Prophecies of Fascism,' 12 July 1940; see *655* and *Orwell: A Literary Life* (1995), 160–62.

It is a reasonable guess that Orwell drafted the originals of the notes in the surviving notebook when time lay heavy on his hands at Wallington in the early months of the war. He may have been prompted by various things, but not least by thoughts of his experience in Spain in 1937 and, in particular, the thought that a German victory might lead to his name being on a list like that in Spain and then to the activities of the secret police, house searches, and the need, but impossibility, of escaping across a border to a friendly country. Whereas Orwell was able to slip out of Spain—in a first-class restaurant car, indeed—he, and others, would have been trapped in Britain. Moreover, the time was un-propitious for creative writing. As he wrote to Rayner Heppenstall on 16 April 1940, the day before he composed his Autobiographical Note, 'I keep reviewing and not getting on with my own book. God knows whether it will ever get written; see *612*.'

The manuscript is reproduced without changes. A few matters of interest are noted. It has not proved possible to explain the significance of I, II, X and O marked in pencil in the manuscript. They may be indications for a later re-ordering. Folio breaks, as given by Orwell, are in square brackets.

1. 'As I Please,' 9, 28 January 1944; see *2412*.
2. The Oxford English Dictionary Supplement gives a letter by Orwell of 2 January 1948 as its first recorded use of 'Biro.' As late as Christmas 1947 it was still an expensive novelty, costing some £3.
3. Although less correspondence has been traced for the period 1–24 November, Orwell wrote for the BBC in this period (according to what has been traced), 10 letters, 4 Newsletters in English for Indonesia, and 4 English-language versions of Newsletters for translation into Tamil. *The Emperor's New Clothes* and *Lady Windermere's Fan* were produced and Orwell probably wrote these programmes in this period. He also wrote to Penguin Books, prepared

two reviews, and his long essay on the detective novel was, according to his Payments Book, completed on 17 November. He was thus not particularly inactive in the eighteen and a half working days of this period.

2376. [unfoliated] For "The Quick & the Dead"

[f1]
I[1] "Corf, corf, corf! We shall 'ave to send you to Corfe Castle, my boy."

I Er — bide with me fast — falls the yeventide,
Ther — darkness deeperns — Lord with me erbide,
Whe — nother helpers — fail ern comforts flee,
Hel — pov the helpless soh er — bide with me!

I Their beliefs:
That you will be struck dead if you go into a church with your hat on.
That you can be had up for putting a stamp on a letter upside down.
That if you make a face & the wind changes you will be struck like that.
That if you wash your hands in the water that eggs have been boiled in you will get warts.
That there is a reward of £50 for spending a [f2] night in the Chamber of Horrors at Madame Tussaud's.
That bats get into women's hair, after which the women's heads have to be shaved.
That if you cut yourself between the thumb & forefinger you get lockjaw.
That powdered glass is poisonous.
That bulls are enraged at the sight of red.
That a swan can break your leg with a blow of its wing.

II One thing that was notable about them was the way in which their interests had narrowed down until their whole life-work consisted in keeping house. Although they were not strictly speaking poor, & certainly were not overworked or pressed for time — for after all, they had nothing to do *except* to keep house — they had no outside interests whatever.
Looking backwards a quarter of a century, H. dimly remembered that at that time they had gone to church [f3] fairly regularly, had belonged to the Navy League & other patriotic organisations, had helped to organise fêtes & tableaux for the local Conservative Party, & on the other hand had dabbled in Women's Suffrage, the R.S.P.C.A., spiritualism & Christian Science. All this had disappeared utterly. Life was lived from meal to meal & from chore to chore — the only long-term activity was the occasional buying of clothes, linen & crockery — & yet without any intense interest even in these things, because the guiding principle was always to save trouble. The work was not scamped, the house was always

tidy, meals were always punctual, but everything was "such a nuisance", "too much fag", "makes such a lot of work," "too expensive." Recurrent remarks:

"Don't dirty a clean plate. I'll use this one."

"I hope nobody wants a second helping."

"You don't want any water, do you? It means washing up the glasses."

"Don't take all the hot water".

"I vote we don't have a Christmas dinner this year. It makes such a lot of work."

"Come on, let's get this beastly meal over."

[f4] All life centred round cooking & sewing, & yet none of them enjoyed their food — indeed, none of them ever seemed to be hungry — & all their clothes were dowdy. All outside interests were rejected on the ground that they cost money & interfered with home life. Religion was rejected partly because "it isn't true" but in the main because the clergy are "only after your money".

So also with politics; in any case they were unable to conceive how anyone could feel any interest in politics. Voluntary public activity of any kind seemed to them incomprehensible, or even wicked. They had ceased to feel the sentiment of patriotism. Charities of all kinds were, once again, "just trying to get money out of you", & beggars were always² turned from the door because "I don't believe he's genuine". They showed undeviating firmness in refusing to buy from pedlars, gypsies or hire-purchase touts, or to subscribe to the Salvation Army or take tickets for the Church social. Of pleasure and work they knew nothing. They assessed all jobs or professions simply by the amount of money that could be earned at them, & were unable to imagine that anyone could have a different motive. [f5] Of sexual love they knew chiefly by hearsay. It was a thing that happened to other people, & had perhaps happened to themselves long ago — but never again, to themselves or anyone of their blood. Marriage was merely a disaster. For the man it meant adding a woman to his household expenses, to the woman it meant extra housework & the danger of children. Children were always spoken of as "such a worry" & "such an expense", because "the school-fees are so terrible nowadays."

As H. contemplated them it struck him that they were not living, which implies growth, but simply existing, with the minimum of activity in any direction whatever. There had perhaps never been people quite like them in any civilization the world had seen. At all times there had been people & classes who lived on the labour of others, consuming without producing, & also without breeding, but there had never perhaps been people who did this without any colour, pleasure, intensity or sense of purpose in their [f6] own lives. There had never been people who, consuming without producing, also made it an object to consume as little as possible, & while lacking any sense of purpose or vocation, also did nothing for pleasure & shunned every luxury or amusement as an extravagance. He could hardly imagine that in any other age any body of people had contrived in the same way to be stationary, negative & meaningless, & to remain so for decades at a stretch.

I Their rhymes:
>Oxford upstairs, eating all the cakes,
>Cambridge downstairs, washing up the plates.

>High up the mountain
>Green grows the grass;
>Down came an elephant
>Sliding on his arse.

[f7]
I Misquotations:
>Lead on, MacDuff.
>Peace on earth & goodwill to all men (even done in pokerwork).
>A little knowledge is a dangerous thing.
>Stuff a cold & starve a fever (taken as meaning that we should stuff a cold).

I Their sexual beliefs:
Very early in life that° they believed that the doctor brought the baby with him in his black bag, but by 8 or 9 (or perhaps somewhat later) they had learned that it had something to do with the man's & the woman's sexual organs. They nevertheless had to rediscover this knowledge after having more or less possessed it & then passed through a period of ignorance. Thus at the age of 6 B. had played with the plumber's children up the road, until his mother found out & stopped him, & their [f8] play was largely sexual. They played at "doctors", & also at "mothers & fathers" (coming from a more crowded home the plumber's children were more precocius° in this) & both boys & girls inspected each other's sexual organs with great interest. Yet by about 9 years of age B. seemed to have forgotten all about this & had to have it explained to him by a schoolfellow of the same age. The schoolfellow's explanation was: "You know those two balls you have — well, you know. Well, somehow or other one of them gets up into the woman's body, & then it grows into a baby." This remained the sum of B.'s knowledge for several years. The whole subject made him feel so sick that he disliked thinking about it. In order to be a daredevil & impress younger boys he used the words bugger & fuck, but attached no concrete meaning to them. By about 13 he thought more frequently about sexual intercourse, chiefly because of the constant references to it in classical literature & [f9] the Bible, but it still disgusted him. As his practical knowledge of the subject was derived from rabbits, he believed up to the age of fifteen, or nearly sixteen, that human beings do it in the same attitude as animals. At fifteen he suddenly discovered that sex was attractive after all, & began masturbating, but he had no lifelike mental picture of sexual intercourse for a year or more after this. Till the age of 16 he continued to believe that babies are born through

363

the navel, & he only learned of menstruation at the age of 18. For several years after beginning to masturbate he believed that this would lead to insanity, but this did nothing towards curing him of the habit.

I   Rhymes:

>Good King Wenceslas looked out
>On the feast of Steven;
>Someone hit him in the snout
>And made it all uneven.

[f10]

>Old King Cole was a merry old soul,
>And a merry old soul was he,
>He called for a light in the middle of the night
>To go to the W.C.

>The moon was shining on the old barn door,
>The candle had a fit,
>And old King Cole fell down the hole
>And that was the end of it.

I   Treat him with the contempt he deserves
Punishment he so richly deserved
But he was swiftly undeceived
But it was not to be
Sickening trend
The doom that lay in store for him
Might have been observed
He little knew

[f11]

>"No, not with Kate — never. She's not that kind of girl at all."
>"Oh, I'm *that kind of girl*, am I? *Thank* you!"
>"I only meant she isn't interested in men."
>"Oh, I'm *interested in men*, am I? That *is* nice. *Thank* you!"

I   Infra dig
In the circs.
How much do they rush you?
The gathering of the clans
Steady the Buffs (eg. "Steady the Buffs with the butter")
The psychological moment
Golden opportunity[3]

[f12]

I–II   The soldiers marching down the road, at ease, & singing. It is a pleasant summer evening, the men are a little dusty, very sunburnt, & their tunics are open at the neck. They are marching in beautiful rhythm, singing tunefully & not very loud, & have the air of regarding the war as a joke they can take in their stride. The officer is not singing, but he is smiling with the men & sometimes swinging his cane in time.

"No, lady, No, lady,
"No shine to-dye!
"They was all shined yester–dye!
"So we laid down the bucket
"And we all says "Fuck it!
"We'll clean no windows to-dye!"

Then the photograph of a column of soldiers marching, twenty years afterwards. It has the blurry & grotesque look of old photographs. What chiefly strikes H. is the raggedness of the men's moustaches. They look like walruses & moreover they are small & their uniforms are ill-fitting. H. [f13] has the feeling that something somewhere has shrunken & undergone a radical transformation. He is unable to understand how he could once have regarded such men as demi-gods.

I   Mr Chapman, the retired butler who lived up the road & with whom B. used to go & talk. The conservatory where he grew his tomatoes. B. greatly impressed by the warmth of the conservatory. Mr. Chapman's alpaca coat, slippers, rather plump face & watery eyes. His talk chiefly about his (dead) wife who used to be a stewardess & how she used to sing & dance to entertain the passengers during stormy weather. He seldom speaks of her without tears coming into his eyes. "My dear wife". Seemingly rather glad to have a confidant aged 6 & talking to B. as an equal (a rare thing in B.'s experience). But one day when syringing his tomatoes thinking it rather funny to squirt water (not in very large quantities) over B. B. at first entering into the spirit of it, but finally [f14] angered by a feeling of impotence against the big grown-up man with a syringe in his hand, & suddenly siezing° a can of water & drenching Mr Chapman. B. feels a sense of guilt even as he does it, because, though Mr Chapman is not very badly wetted, there is distinctly more water on him than has been squirted onto B. with the syringe. Mr Chapman very angry. A long time afterwards, during the next holidays, B. goes to see Mr Chapman again to some extent the quarrel is made up, but things are never the same again.

I   The dying horse (presumably in the retreat in 1918). It is old Boxer, who either used to work on the farm or else pulled a coal cart. The boy hitting him to make him get up, but not very hard. Then the officer arriving. "What, won't get up, won't he? I'll get him up". The officer is a short powerfully-built man with a white face which at the moment needs shaving. He takes the whip & lashes terrible blows on to the horse, [f15] not losing his temper but calculatingly & with terrible force. The whip screams as it flies through the air, enough to frighten the boy. At last with a scream the dying horse struggles to its feet & the gun (or whatever it is) moves slowly onwards. All this against a background of debris & distant gunfire.

I–II   The scene in Charing Cross Station (1918).
General impression — the station densely packed with people, the

365

train crowded with khaki-clad men & their equipments, the platform mostly thronged with women, but many wounded men in their bright blue uniforms & red ties. Much laughing, shouting, singing, but a general feeling of hysteria. The station not only seems crowded, but very hot. As the train draws out the men in it break into song. (q. what song?) A great wave of hysteria seems to pass over the people left behind & the platform is thronged by women all in tears. General [f16] picture — the train slowly drawing out, window after window full of brown khaki-framed faces, weeping women, crowds, heat, hysteria & the tune of (?).

H. has wandered into this on his way to somewhere or other. For a year or more he has lived in a world in which there might as well be no war going on, except for the food shortage. The war is something disgusting which you do not talk about, & which at any rate cannot conceivably bring any benefit to yourself. His mind is full of (what?) The scene on the platform half brings the war into his consciousness.[4] Then suddenly, outside, coming on his cousin, Arthur Barker,[5] being carried out on a stretcher. Blankets, elegant officer's cap laid on the body (body very flat under the blankets), & a waxy white face with nose strangely sharp. Suddenly H. knows that the war is going on, that people older & more responsible than he are fighting it & think it supremely important to win it. He has a sudden terrible vision of the life of the trenches going on & on while he & his kind are [f17] safe in the background & forget that the war is happening. His death in Spain in 1937 is the direct result of this vision.

Fallacies (contd.)[6]

That if you tell a lie you get a spot on your tongue.
That people who have a touch of the tarbrush can be detected by their fingernails.
Sulphur in a dog's drinking water (as a "tonic").
That orientals are not subject to sunstroke.
That dogs are good judges of character.
That all toadstools are poisonous.
That pigs cannot swim because if they do so they cut cut° their throats with their trotters.[7]
The wisdom of the elephant —
Longevity of the elephant —
Sudden reversion in the case of people who have dark blood.
That snakes sting.
[f18]
I didn't half give him what-for[8]
Something chronic
Now isn't that aggravating
Not if it was ever so
Laugh? I thought I should have died
Not if I live till I draw my last breath
That's just where it is

She didn't half take on
It's a good thing that was put a stop to
Now you've been & gone & done it
That's me all over
Did you ever? No, I never
Well, I never!
You could have knocked me down with a feather
Carrying on (with)
Creating
[f19]
    & anachronistic[9]
Dead metaphors:
New wine in old bottles
Ring the changes
No stone unturned
Pave the way
A bitter pill
[ff. 20–33 blank]

1. The roman numerals, I and II, were added to the manuscript in pencil.
2. There is a diagonal line in ink on either side of 'always'; perhaps Orwell intended to add something interlinearly.
3. 'Golden opportunity' is written in blue-black Biro; it must, therefore, have been added in or after 1946.
4. consciousness] *Orwell originally wrote* confidence
5. Barker could possibly be 'Barber.'
6. This line and the next three are in red ink.
7. trotters] *Orwell originally wrote* fore-paws
8. This line and the next four are in red ink.
9. All the entries on this page are crossed through. The first three lines are in red ink.

2377. [f34] For "The Last Man in Europe"

[f35] <u>To be brought in</u>

Newspeak (one leading article from the "Times")[1]
Comparison of weights, measures etc.
Statistics.
Window boxes.
Rectification.
Position of R.Cs.
Pacifists.
Interrelation between the Party & the Trusts.
Position of the proles.
Sexual code.
Names of B.M. etc.

Films.
The party lowdown.
Dual standard of thought.
Bakerism[2] & ingsoc
The party slogans (War is peace. Ignorance is strength. Freedom is slavery).
World geography.
The Two Minutes Hate.

[f36]

<u>The general lay-out as follows.</u>

Part I   Build-up of —
     a.[3] The system of organised lying on which society is founded.
     b.   The way in which this is done (falsification of records etc.).
     c.   The nightmare feeling caused by the disappearance of objective truth.
     d.   Leader-worship etc.
     e.   The swindle of Bakerism & Ingsoc.
     f.   Loneliness of the writer. His feeling of being *the last man*.
     g.   Equivocal position of the proles, the Christians & others.
     h.   Antisemitism (& terrible cruelty of war etc.)
     i.   The writer's approaches to X & Y.
     j.   The brief interlude of the love affair with Y.
Part II.   *a.* Declaration of war against Eastasia.
     b. The arrest & torture.

[f37]   *c.* Continuation of the diary, this time not written down.
     d. The final consciousness of failure.

All in *long* chapters, & therefore the layout more accurately might be thus:

     Part I divided into about 6 parts, comprising:
     i. Lies, hatred, cruelty, loneliness. X[4]
     ii. Pictures of London, the swindle of Bakerism. X
twice ‖ *iii.* Fantasmagoric effect, rectification, shifting of dates etc. doubts of own sanity. X
     iv. Position of the proles etc.
     v. Successful approach to X & Y.

30,000
words *vi.* Love affair with Y. Conversations with X.

     Part II to be divided into 3 main parts comprising:
15,000
words *i.* The torture & confession. X
10,000
words *ii.* Continuation of the diary, mentally. X
5000
words *iii.* Recognition of own insanity. O
   ?

The fantasmagoric effect produced by:
Were we at war with Eastasia in 1974? Were we [f38] at war with
Eurasia in 1978? Were A, B & C present at the secret conference in
1976? Impossibility of detecting similar memories in anyone else.
Non-memory of the proles. Equivocal answers.
Effect of lies & hatred produced by:
Films. Extract of anti-Jew propaganda. B'casts.
The Two Minutes Hate. Enemy propaganda & writer's response to
it.

[f39 blank]

[From hereon the text is written in Biro.]

[f40]

Adjectives.

Unforgettable
Veritable
Egregious

[f41]

Adjectives & nouns

[f42 blank]

[f43]

Metaphors.

[ff 44 and 45 blank]

[f46]

Metaphorical words & phrases

Bone of contention
Spearhead
Yardstick
Melting pot
Bitter pill
Cornerstone
Keystone

[f47]

Redundancies

For all the world
Naturally
Literally (inaccurate)
For the simple reason that

[f48]

Stale slang & jargon phrases

In short supply
In short order
In due course (filler?)

[ff49–54 blank with about seven folios torn out between ff 52 and 53]

[f54 verso]
ship
J.B.

[f55 verso]

People's Democracy	One party dictatorship
Economic sanctions	Food politics
Annexation of the Sudan	Unity of the Nile Valley
Acceptance in principle	Refusal
Great power unity	the veto

1. Page 26 of the quarto typescript of the draft of *Nineteen Eighty-Four*, probably prepared in the summer of 1946, refers to a kind of feat 'that would always earn an approving leading article in the *Times*'; see *Facsimile*, 197.
2. Bakerism has not been identified and what follows is speculative. The name might have been suggested by that of John R. Baker (1900–84). Baker wrote a 'counterblast to Bernalism,' attacking Bernal's *The Social Future of Science*, in *The New Statesman*, 29 July 1939. He was a founder-member of the Society for Freedom in Science in spring 1941. Gary Werskey described him as a 'conservative, rectionary eugenist' with 'no faith in the democratic process,' who believed that High Science should be used against claims by the masses for egalitarianism (*The Visible College* (1978), 282–84). When he wrote these notes, Orwell had not read any book by Baker and he may have had a mistaken understanding of what Baker stood for. When in the spring of 1946 he read one of Baker's books, he was keen to associate him with a projected organisation to defend the interests of the individual. In the event, he did not use the term 'Bakerism.' See *2836, n. 1, 2837*, and *2955*. Orwell mentions Baker favourably in his review of *Freedom of Expression*, 12 October 1945 (*2764*).
3. Letters and small numerals marking sections are double underlined in the manuscript—one of Orwell's idiosyncracies. This usually indicates that the material should be set in small caps. To preserve the lower-case letters and numerals, they are here printed in italic.
4. The markings X and O are in pencil.

INDEX
Volume XV

This is an index of names of people, places, and institutions, and of titles of books, periodicals, broadcasts, and articles; it is not (with a very few exceptions) a topical index. It indexes all titles of books and articles in the text, headnotes and afternotes; incidental references to people and places are unindexed. In order to avoid cluttering the index (and wasting the reader's time), names and places that appear very frequently are only listed when a specific point is being made and Orwell's tentative suggestions for talks and his speculations as to the way the war might develop, are only lightly indexed. Numbered footnotes are indexed more selectively; for example, books listed by an author who is the subject of a footnote are not themselves indexed unless significant to Orwell. Unless there is a significant comment or information, the BBC is not itself indexed. At the BBC Orwell was usually referred to as Blair; such references are indexed under Orwell. Titles of broadcasts are entered under their author's name and, if they form a coherent group (such as "How it Works") under the title of the series; miscellaneous broadcasts given in such series as "We Speak to India" and "Through Eastern Eyes" are indexed individually. All broadcasts are denoted as such by '(B)' and are listed chronologically. Talks Booking Forms (TBFs) and Programmes as Broadcast (PasBs) are not themselves indexed (though the programmes and people to which they refer are). Orwell's news commentaries are given various descriptions (Newsletter, News Review, News Commentary, etc.: see XIII 82–92), but they are all indexed under News Review; the description used is given at the page referred to.

Orwell's book titles are printed in CAPITALS; his poems, essays, articles, broadcasts, etc., are printed in upper and lower case roman within single quotation marks. Book titles by authors other than Orwell are in italic; if Orwell reviewed the book (in this volume), this is noted by 'Rev:' followed by the pagination and a semi-colon; other references follow. Both books and authors are individually listed unless a reference is insignificant. If Orwell does not give an author's name, when known this is added in parentheses after the title. Articles and broadcasts by authors other than Orwell are placed within double quotation marks. Page references are in roman except for those to numbered footnotes, which are in italic. The order of roman and italic is related to the order of references on the page. Editorial notes are printed in roman upper and lower without quotation marks. If an editorial note follows a title it is abbreviated to 'ed. note:' and the pagination follows. First and last page numbers are given of articles and these are placed before general references and followed by a semi-colon; specific pages are given for each book reviewed in a group. The initial page number is given for letters. Punctuation is placed outside quotation marks to help separate information.

Letters by Orwell, and those written on his behalf (for example, when he was ill) are given under the addressee's name and the first letter is preceded by 'L:', which stands for letters, memoranda, letter-cards, and postcards; telegrams are distinguished by 'T:' to draw attention to their urgency. If secretaries sign letters on Orwell's behalf, they are not indexed. However, the convention, 'L:' is *not* used in association with the organisation of broadcasts unless the letter contains other information. Against each title of a broadcast, relevant letters and Talks Booking Form references are listed by page number without distinguishing the nature of the source. Letters from someone to Orwell follow the name of the sender and are indicated by 'L. to O:'. References to letters are given before other references, which are marked off by a semi-colon. Letters or notes printed in response to Orwell's articles and reviews which are printed or summarised in afternotes and footnotes are indicated by (L) after the respondent's name and/or the page number. Letters to and from correspondents other than Orwell are double-entered under sender and recipient. References to Orwell in letters or articles of others are listed under 'Orwell, refs to:'.

Items are listed alphabetically by the word or words up to the first comma or bracket, except that Mc and M' are regarded as Mac and precede words starting with 'M'. St and Sainte are regarded as Saint.

Three cautions. First, some names are known only by a surname and it cannot be certain that surnames with the same initials, refer to the same person. If there is doubt, both names are indexed. Secondly, the use of quotation marks in the index differs from that in the text in order to make Orwell's work listed here readily apparent. Thirdly, a few titles and names have been corrected silently and dates of those who have died in 1997 (after the page-proofs of the text were completed) are noted in the index.

The loose ends and the incompleteness of the information uncovered for the three BBC volumes is particularly apparent in this volume. Thus, some names in the last paragraph of p. 289, the details available for the series of broadcasts on psychology (see pp. 225 and 254), and some of the speakers and broadcasts printed in *Talking to India* (see p. 321), are obvious indications of gaps in our information.

P.D.; S.D.

Index

Index